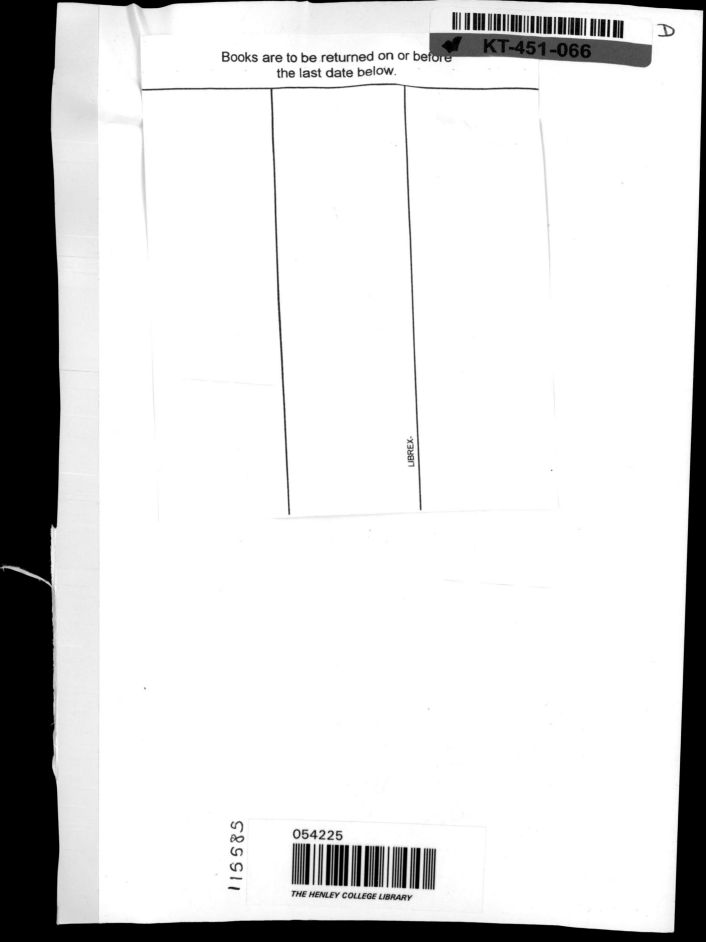

Books are to be returned on or before
the last date below.

LIBREX-

STAGECOACH TO TOMBSTONE

The Filmgoers' Guide
to the Great Westerns

HOWARD HUGHES

I.B. TAURIS

LONDON · NEW YORK

Published in 2008 by I.B. Tauris & Co Ltd
6 Salem Road, London W2 4BU
175 Fifth Avenue, New York NY 10010
www.ibtauris.com

In the United States and Canada distributed by Palgrave Macmillan,
a division of St. Martin's Press, 175 Fifth Avenue, New York NY 10010

ISBN 978 1 84511 498 5 (Hb)
     978 1 84511 571 5 (Pb)

A full CIP record for this book is available from the British Library
A full CIP record for this book is available from the Library of Congress
Library of Congress catalog card: available

Typeset in Ehrhardt by Dexter Haven Associates Ltd, London
Printed and bound in the United States by Maple Vale.

CONTENTS

PREFACE: COLT MOVIES

Legendary tales of gunfighters and outlaws and 'cowboys and Indians' have given cinema some of its most popular films. From John Ford's *Stagecoach* to the revisionary *Tombstone* I've chosen 27 key movies for this book in order to reveal their place in western film history. They include the best, from giants John Ford, with *My Darling Clementine*, *She Wore a Yellow Ribbon* and *The Searchers*, and Howard Hawks, with *Red River* and *Rio Bravo* – both of whom moulded the screen image of western icon John Wayne. This book also looks at the enduring classics: Gary Cooper waiting for *High Noon*, Alan Ladd as *Shane*, James Stewart as *The Man from Laramie*, and the still-hugely popular *The Magnificent Seven* and *Butch Cassidy and the Sundance Kid*.

From well-known blockbusters to B-movie oaters, *Stagecoach to Tombstone* makes many stops along the way, discussing films as diverse as *Hell's Hinges*, *The Big Trail*, *Randy Rides Alone*, *Duel in the Sun*, *The Tall T*, *3:10 to Yuma*, *Warlock*, *Duel at Diablo*, *El Dorado*, *Blazing Saddles*, *Pat Garrett & Billy the Kid*, *Pale Rider*, *Open Range* and *Dead Man*. Key chapters focus on the best comedy westerns with *Support Your Local Sheriff!*, lively adventures 'south of the border' in *Vera Cruz*, big-budget action westerns like *Gunfight at the O.K. Corral*, and the varied depiction of Native Americans on screen, from *Broken Arrow* to *Dances With Wolves*, via *Ulzana's Raid*. I also chart the genre's timely renovation in the sixties by Sam Peckinpah with *Ride the High Country* and *The Wild Bunch*, Sergio Leone's *Once Upon a Time in the West* and Clint Eastwood's revisionary masterpieces *The Outlaw Josey Wales* and *Unforgiven*. There are critical appraisals of Budd Boetticher's *Ride Lonesome* and Samuel Fuller's *Forty Guns* and interesting genre one-offs: Nicholas Ray's extravagant *Johnny Guitar*, Marlon Brando's moody *One-Eyed Jacks* and Robert Altman's muddy *McCabe & Mrs Miller*.

I have enjoyed watching westerns for as long as I can remember, first viewing John Wayne matinees on TV in the seventies with my father and then on to the late-night violence, grit and style of Leone, Eastwood and Peckinpah. As I get older, I find I still enjoy these films, but the best of them offer something new, aspects I perhaps failed to see when I was younger. Examples include the father-son relationship between Josey and Jamie in *The Outlaw Josey Wales*, which grows deeper and more affecting with the passing years, John Wayne's final walk into uncertainty at the end of *The Searchers*, or the dialogue between Shane and Joey about being unable to change, of breaking the mould, in the film *Shane*. While writing this book I have watched some actors' entire western careers spool by in an instant. Many are no longer with us, and it is strange how moving it has been, as so many westerns are concerned with changing times, with ageing and the vigour and misunderstanding of youth. To see John Wayne as a young man, working on Monogram Studios' cheapies in the thirties, or Clint Eastwood in the fifties TV series *Rawhide*, and then follow them both through to old age – it just seems to have gone by so fast.

The continued popularity of these films has ensured that just about every western, of the thousands made, is available somewhere, with the Internet and collectors facilitating the location of curiosities and cult items, previously long forgotten. TV schedules are still filled with westerns and through video and DVD, the genre lives on – even if the production of new westerns has slowed from a seemingly never-ending stampede to an occasional stray. *Stagecoach to Tombstone* is the story of the west on screen, through its shooting stars and the directors who shot them.

ACKNOWLEDGEMENTS

I would like to thank Philippa Brewster, my editor at I.B.Tauris, for commissioning *Stagecoach to Tombstone* and for her support, comments and great ideas throughout its writing. Thanks also to Elizabeth Galloway, Paul Davighi and Stuart Weir at I.B.Tauris, cover designer Chris Bromley and Gretchen Ladish at Dexter Haven Associates for their hard work on the project.

Thank you to Sir Christopher Frayling, Alex Cox, Andrew Collins, Philip French, Kim Newman, Paul Duncan, Edward Buscombe and Tom Betts for their western top tens. Their lists prove that as well as the expected popularity of actors John Wayne and Clint Eastwood, and directors John Ford, Sam Peckinpah, Sergio Leone and Howard Hawks, there is still considerable interest in the work of Anthony Mann, Delmer Daves, Robert Aldrich, John Sturges and especially Budd Boetticher.

Thanks again to Paul Duncan for providing several key silent source materials, including early works by Ford and William S. Hart. Thanks also to Tom Betts and Mike Coppack, both of whom helped with further research, either loaning me source materials, proofing material or offering insights on westerns and the west itself. Tom was particularly helpful on modern westerns, some of which haven't yet made it to the UK.

I must also thank Andy Hanratty who has done a splendid job with the stills, posters, artwork and pressbooks reproduced here, in addition to tracking down many rare resources.

Many of the posters have been kindly provided by Ian Caunce from his private collection. The still from *The Wild Bunch* is from Kevin Wilkinson's archive. Thanks to both of them for allowing me to reprint them here. The photographs of Monument Valley as it appears today were taken by Victoria Millington and Mark Chester during their trip to Utah in August 2006. They have succeeded in capturing the beauty and grandeur of this unique location. Thank you both for permitting me to reprint your work, as a reminder of one of cinema's most iconic settings. The remainder of the illustrative material is from my own collection.

Thanks too, to the following people who have contributed to the writing, research and production of *Stagecoach to Tombstone*, whether they realise it or not: Belinda and Chris Skinner, Alex and Isabel Coe, Gareth Jones, Ann Jackson, Don Bruce, David Weaver, Clive Ingram, Dave Lewis, William Connolly, Dave Worrell, Nick Rennisson, Rene Hogguer and Lionel Woodman.

Thanks to my parents, Carol (who has again helped proofing the manuscripts) and John. And finally thanks to Clara, who has seen more than enough of John Wayne and Clint Eastwood over the last few months. As always, without her help, support and encouragement, this book would never have been written.

OUT OF THE WEST: AN INTRODUCTION TO WESTERNS

SILENT GUNS

By the time American filmmakers began making movies about the folk heroes and villains of their wild west at the beginning of the twentieth century, the 'wild' west was a fading memory. Famed lawman Pat Garrett was murdered near Las Cruces, New Mexico on 29 February 1908. That same year Butch Cassidy and the Sundance Kid were killed by Bolivian soldiers in San Vicente, Bolivia in the spring. The wild west died with them. The heyday of the gunfighter lasted only twenty years, beginning in the post-Civil War 1865 period, with the most aggressive year according to statistics being 1878, when 36 gunfights were recorded. But the settling of the west, the battles with its Native American inhabitants and subsequent feuds between settlers, spanned most of the nineteenth century. Its brutality, casual violence and bloodshed gave birth to romanticised dime novel myths and historical whitewash, predominantly invented 'back east'.

The reality was rather more complicated and much bloodier. Following the shooting in 1853 of Mexican renegade Joaquin Murieta, famed for killing miners in the California gold fields, a poster advertised a forthcoming exhibition double-bill of 'The Head of Renowned Bandit Joaquin' (though no one really knew what Murieta looked like) and 'The Hand of Three Fingered Jack' (presumably this was easily identifiable). Murieta's head was pickled in a bottle for the enjoyment of the paying public. His story, later much romanticised, rechristened him 'The Robin Hood of El Dorado', a folk hero to those in distress. Judge Roy Bean's skewed version of law and order 'west of the Pecos' in 1880s Vinegaroon, Texas, has become the stuff of legend. When acting as coroner for a man who had plummeted from a viaduct, Bean thought he should have more than his $5 fee and claimed he was also justice of the peace. Bean searched the body and discovered a pistol and $40, so he found the corpse guilty of carrying a concealed weapon: 'And I fine it $40.'

When Hollywood began making westerns in the early twentieth century, there was an overlap between the real west and the west on screen. Experienced wranglers and cowboys came to work in the movies, and actual outlaws and lawmen acted as 'technical advisors'. Outlaw Emmett Dalton, for example, moved to Los Angeles in the twenties and even wrote movie scenarios, while both Wyatt Earp and Pinkerton agent Charles Siringo were photographed watching the action on movie sets. The first American narrative film telling an engaging story, not simply a series of filmed events, was a western: Edwin S. Porter's 12-minute *The Great Train Robbery* (1903). Here, four outlaws tie up a telegrapher and board a train, cleaning out the safe. The outlaws halt the engine and line up the passengers, arms aloft; one makes a break for it and an outlaw shoots him in the back. The sheriff is interrupted at a hoedown with the news and gives chase with his posse. The outlaws flee, but one outlaw is killed by the posse during their pursuit through an autumnal forest. The three remaining badmen split the cash deep in the woods, but with their horses tethered nearby they are trapped by the law. Their pistols are no match for the posse's rifles and the outlaws are cut down.

Produced by Thomas Alva Edison's studio and reputedly based on the exploits of Butch Cassidy's Wild Bunch, *The Great Train Robbery* has the ring of authenticity (in July 1903, the Bunch carried out their last train robbery) despite the fact that it was filmed in New Jersey, mainly on the Delaware and Lackawanna Railroad, near Dover. The film is well made, with some convincing gunplay, despite some overly theatrical death throes, and in one scene an outlaw manhandles the body of the train's fireman (actually a stunt dummy) off a bridge. The film's most famous shot is of a moustached outlaw (George Barnes) shooting directly at the camera. When the film was distributed, a note decreed that the shot could be placed at the beginning or the end of the film. Most prints have it as a shock ending, but occasionally it precedes the title card. *The Great Train Robbery*, an iconic piece of cinema history and the beginning of the genre, has since been referenced in many westerns, including *Butch Cassidy and the Sundance Kid* (1969), *Big Jake* (1971) and *Tombstone* (1993).

The first cowboy hero in the cinema was 'Broncho Billy' Anderson, an extra on *The Great Train Robbery*. His real name was Max Aronson, which he changed to Gilbert Max Aronson, though he signed his films 'G. M. Aronson'. 'Broncho Billy' (sometimes spelt 'Bronco') was his alter ego in many of his 400 silent 'shorts' and in 1915 he moved into features, which were less successful. Anderson retired in 1920 before the coming of sound, though he did return for a cameo in *The Bounty Hunter* (1965).

Another early cowboy star was Tom Mix, with his horse Tony. Mix also rose to fame in a series of western shorts, but his ambition was greater and when he teamed up with Fox Studios in 1917, he began to make features, which proved even more popular. Mix retired a wealthy man in 1929, but he came back with his first sound westerns, Universal's *Destry Rides Again* (1932) and *My Pal, the King* (1932 – set in Ruritania). An expert rider and rodeo champion, Mix rarely used stunt doubles and later toured with his Wild West Show. He was a man of action, having served in the US Army in the Spanish–American War, the Philippines, the Boxer Rebellion in China, the Mexican Revolution and as a bronco buster in the Boer War. He was also a Texas Ranger and a sheriff, before he became a western star. His 'dude' cowboy outfits were stylised and unrealistic, with outsized chaps and spurs, fancy embroidered shirts, fringed gauntlets, massive hats and tooled boots. Mix didn't like talkies and his last contribution to the genre was *The Miracle Rider* (1935), a 15-part serial, which made a fortune in the US – costing only $80,000, it took $1 million. Mix was killed in a car crash on 12 October 1940. A statue of a riderless horse was erected at the site in memory of 'The hero of a million boys'.

The finest actor of these early cowboy stars was William Surrey Hart. With his long, chiselled face, he'd played a couple of villains before his first lead role as Jim Stokes in the short, *The Bargain* (1914). He continued with such films as *The Sheriff's Streak of Yellow* (1915) and as 'Silent' Texas Smith in *On the Night Stage* (1915), and was often saddled with ridiculous western stage names – Bad Buck Peters,

Frosty Blake, Dakota Dan and Keno Bates (in the straightforward *Keno Bates, Liar* [1915]), and the title roles in *Mr 'Silent' Haskins* (1915), *Selfish Yates, Shark Monroe* (both 1918) and *Square Deal Sanderson* (1919). He played Draw Egan in *The Return of Draw Egan* (1916) and Jefferson 'On the Level' Leigh in *The Cold Deck* (1917). Among his best-known films were *The Toll Gate* (1920 – with Hart as Black Deering) and *Travelin' On* (1922); here Hart played J.B. 'The Stranger', opposite James Farley as Dandy Dan McGee.

In *Hell's Hinges* (1916), Hart starred as the appropriately named Blaze Tracey, a badman in the town of Placer Centre, known as Hell's Hinges, 'a good place to ride wide of – a gun-fighting, man-killing devil's den of iniquity that scorched even the sun-parched soil on which it stood'. Blaze works for Silk Miller (Alfred Hollingsworth), the saloon owner, and is hired to scare off the recently arrived parson Robert Henley (Jack Standing), who has been dispatched from the city to their country parish. In the course of the film, these two men take divergent moral journeys. Blaze falls for Henley's primly righteous sister Faith (turning him against Silk), while the parson descends into hell, drinking whisky and smoking, bewitched by gypsy seductress Dolly, who wears hooped earrings, headscarf and an off-the-shoulder number. Drunk and 'past the point of sane thought', the parson torches

Blaze Tracey (William S. Hart) faces his former boss, saloon owner Silk Miller (Alfred Hollingsworth), prior to torching the town in the silent classic, *Hell's Hinges* (1916).

the newly built church with the help of the hedonistic rabble, while Blaze has gone to fetch a doctor to help him. On his return, and with the parson now dead, Blaze exacts revenge on the town, burning it to the ground, before leaving with Faith, restored. Shot from September to October 1916, *Hell's Hinges* is a great early western, which tells its complicated morality tale slickly, with some pithy intertitles. Silk Miller mingles 'the oily craftiness of a Mexican, with the deadly treachery of a rattler'. When Blaze, 'a man killer' whose credo is 'shoot first and do your disputin' afterwards', sees Faith he surmises, 'When I look at you, I feel I've been ridin' the wrong trail.' As Blaze hits the vengeance trail, the locals warn, 'Look out! Blaze is comin', killin' mad, and with a gun in each hand' and the gunman himself is in no mood for mercy, as he sets fire to their saloon, 'I'm shootin' straight tonight and I'm plum willin' to kill.' The sight of the burning church, with its flaming cross atop the steeple, is a powerful moment (tinted red for added hellish effect), while the story evocatively depicts the deep well of corruption in the town – the contrast between the righteous 'Petticoat Brigade' and the godless locals, and between the church and 'Silk Miller's Palace of Joy Saloon and Dance Hall'.

Hart's approach to the west made his films very popular worldwide; in France he was called 'Rio Jim'. He retired in 1923, but returned two years later to make probably the most famous silent western, *Tumbleweeds*, based around the celebrated 'Cherokee Strip' Oklahoma Land Rush of 1889. Hart poured $100,000 of his own money into the project (the budget was $312,000), producing and co-directing with King Baggott. Hart starred as drover Don Carver ('Just another tumbleweed') and the film delineates, through song lyric intertitles, the contrast between settlers ('the punkins') who stay on their own patch, and the tumbleweed: 'it jumps the fence and heads for other parts'. For the Cherokee Land Rush scene – 'The Maddest Stampede in America History' – scores of wagons, riders, buckboards, hacks and carriages were lined up. At 12 noon, a cannon signalled the commencement and the wagons hurtled off. Carver, wrongly imprisoned in a bullpen stockade as a jumping-the-gun 'sooner', wants to reach the Box K ranch before evil land-grabber Bill Freel (Richard R. Neill) and claim it for himself; the Box K controls the waterways for the local ranches. Carver whittles a pole from the stockade fence, vaults out of the corral and jumps on his horse, Fritz. Like a bullet from a gun, Carver overtakes the rush and reaches the homestead first, exposing Freel into the bargain: Freel's horse is covered in soapsuds, rather than sweat, revealing that he is the 'sooner'. Hart's distinctive, ramrod straight-backed riding style is seen to great effect in this sequence – even more impressive, as Hart was by now 60. Genre clichés, such as riding through a windblown tumbleweeded landscape, began here with Hart's romanticised approach.

Although *Tumbleweeds* was very successful, Hart was tired with the film industry (though he once said that making westerns was, 'As the breath of life to me') and retired to live on his ranch 'Hills of the Wind' and write western fiction. So popular was his last film that it was re-released in 1939 by Astor Pictures, with a moving, sentimental, eight-minute spoken introduction by Hart, then aged 74. It was filmed at the Horseshoe Ranch, Newhall, and new sound effects (such as crowd hubbub, hooves and rolling wagons) were dubbed onto the movie. 'Adios amigos,' says Hart at the monologue's close, 'God bless you each and every one.' By Hart's retirement, the genre had further progressed and produced its first epic: Paramount's pioneer spectacular *The Covered Wagon* (1923), directed by James Cruze, which grossed $5 million.

The most important director of the early western genre was John Ford. Born on 1 February 1894 in Cape Elizabeth, Maine, Ford claimed his name was Sean Aloysius O'Feeney or O'Fearna, but it has since been revealed that it was John Martin Feeney. Ford directed his first film, *The Tornado* (1917), aged 22, as 'Jack Ford'. He soon developed a fruitful partnership with actor Harry Carey, directing him in two- and three-reelers, before making their first feature, *Straight Shooting* (1917), a five-reeler (a reel of film is roughly ten minutes of screen time). Carey played wanted outlaw Cheyenne Harry, 'The Prairie Kid', who is hired in a water rights dispute by rancher Thunder Flint (Duke Lee) to run farmers like Sweet Water Sims off the range. But Harry is consumed by self-doubt when he sees his targets, especially Sims's daughter, Joan (Molly Malone), and sides against the ranchers. The finale has Flint's gang attack Sims's, with Harry riding to the rescue leading Black-Eye Pete's outlaw gang. Offered the chance to stay on at the ranch, the film had two different endings: one where Harry leaves, in a shot which anticipates the famous final doorway scene of *The Searchers* (1956) and one where he settles down. Carey was a great silent actor, unaffected and spontaneous. His first appearance in the film sees him popping his head out of a hollow tree, moments after his own $1,000 reward poster has been nailed to it. Ford's pace is slower and the plot more sentimental than other action westerns, like those of Mix and Hart, while the arresting visual imagery, signatures and compositions of his future films are already present, albeit in rough–

hewn form. For instance, the squally storm in which Cheyenne Harry and other cowboys wear long, rain-slicked duster coats is an effect later repeated in *My Darling Clementine* (1946) and there is a memorable scene where Harry faces villainous rancher Placer Fremont (Vester Pegg) in a Winchester shootout on the streets of Smithfield, which Ford repeated in *Stagecoach* (1939).

After seven years making two-reelers and features, many of which have since been lost, Ford directed his first epic, the

'A shining path from sea to sea': The rails are laid for the transcontinental railroad in John Ford's 1924 epic *The Iron Horse*, one of the most influential westerns of all time.

133-minute *The Iron Horse* (1924), for William Fox Studios (though it is often abridged to 119 minutes on US TV). Instead of using a wagon train as the focus for the action, Ford concentrated on the building of the transcontinental railroad ('a shining path from sea to sea') by the Union Pacific, heading west, and the Central Pacific, moving east. Ford filmed on location in Nevada and deployed several authentic props, including the actual 'Jupiter' Central Pacific and '#116' Union Pacific locomotives when the rail lines meet at Promontory Point, Utah on 10 May 1869. Beginning in 1862, the story mainly follows the Union Pacific as it crawls through the wilderness, hauling locomotives overland on sledges, chipping through mountains and repulsing Indian attacks. Ford's depiction of the first coast-to-coast rail link is authentically presented, with great attention to detail. The tinted British Film Institute print of the film, complete with 'Intermission' and an enlightening score by John Lanchbery (conducting the City of Prague Philharmonic) looks remarkably crisp and fresh even today. The footage of Abraham Lincoln (lookalike Charles Edward Bull) appears to be a Mathew Brady portrait, eerily brought to life. The disparate railroad crews are represented by a prominent Irish immigrant contingent, augmented with Italians, who are presented as mutinous and cowardly in the face of danger, and Chinese – the actual construction imported 15,000 workers from China. The boomtowns of North Platte and Cheyenne were constructed for the film, populated by such characters as Jedge Haller. 'Souperier Jedge by Speshal Aptyntment' reads the sign in his 'likker bar' courthouse. Ford deftly crosscuts between the great adventures of the American west and the lives of his protagonists, including surveyor and Pony Express rider Davy Brandon (George O'Brien) and his nemesis, Cheyenne renegade Bauman (Fred Kohler). Guilty of murdering Davy's father, Bauman is a particularly wily, underhand villain, who also incites the Cheyenne to attack the railroad to his own ends. His identifying mark – a right hand with only two fingers remaining – is concealed in his pocket throughout the story, only to be revealed at the film's climax.

Ford followed *Iron Horse*, which took $2 million in the US, with another epic, *3 Bad Men* (1926), also with O'Brien in the lead, and Frank Campeau, J. Farrell MacDonald and Tom Santschi as the badmen: gambler 'Spade' Allen, Mike Costigan and 'Bull' Stanley, who are introduced via their $2,000 reward posters. The outlaws help two pioneers, Irishman Dan O'Malley (O'Brien) and Lee Carleton (Olive Barden), against crooked sheriff Layne Hunter (Lou Tellegen), whose ghoulish make-up makes him resemble a vampire; his dramatic demise even recalls the death of Count Orlok in F. W. Murnau's *Nosferatu* (1921). Ford's work was often cited as a key influence on Japanese director Akira Kurosawa and the original title of Kurosawa's *The Hidden Fortress* (1958) – *Kakushi-Toride No San-Akunin* – translates as 'Three Bad Men in a Hidden Fortress'. *3 Bad Men* again staged a land rush scene, this time in June 1877 in the Black Hills of Dakota, but the film was a financial failure, prompting Ford to abandon the genre with which he was most associated, for 13 years.

BIG TRAILS

With the coming of sound in 1927, squeaky voices, stutters and lisps put paid to many an actor's career. *In Old Arizona* (1929) was the first 'talkie' to take microphones out onto location and Warner Baxter starred as the Cisco Kid, for which he won Best Actor at the Academy Awards. *Cimarron* (1931), an epic western production starring Richard Dix and Irene Dunne, proved very popular and also won the Best Film Oscar. The film staged the Cherokee Strip Land Rush yet again. Dix had previously appeared in the acclaimed *The Vanishing American* (1925) which detailed the exploitation of Native American Navajos, shot in Monument Valley. In addition to these award-winning offerings, there were all sorts of genre variations, such as Hoot Gibson send-ups *Spurs* and *The Concentratin' Kid* (both 1930), westerns with black casts to appeal to black audiences, like *Harlem on the Prairie* (1937) and *Harlem Rides the Range* (1939), and even an all-midget western: the infamous *The Terror of Tiny Town* (1938). Regular western stars included Ken Maynard and his horse Tarzan, Maynard's younger brother Kermit, Buck Jones and Tex Ritter with his horse White Flash. There was also Johnny Mack Brown who starred as *Billy the Kid* (1930) and used one of Billy's real pistols, loaned to him for the film by William S. Hart.

In 1930, Raoul Walsh was preparing his wagon train epic, *The Big Trail*. In the lead role of scout Breck Coleman, Walsh cast 23-year-old unknown prop man and bit-part player, Duke Morrison, after Tom Mix and Gary Cooper had turned it down (Cooper starred as scout Clint Belmet in Paramount's almost identical *Fighting Caravans* the following year). *The Big Trail* tells the story of a wagon train of pioneers who trekked from the banks of 'The Big River' – the Mississippi – to the Promised Land of Oregon, 2,500 miles away, and details their surmounting of hazards en route. Scout Breck is also looking to exact 'frontier justice' on the killers of his best friend – the train's bullwhacker Red Flack and his sidekick Lopez are the culprits. Flack is a memorable characterisation by Tyrone Power Snr, a snaggle-toothed, bullwhipping monster with a face like a bear trap.

The making of *The Big Trail* was chaotic, with filming taking place across Arizona, California, Utah, Wyoming and Montana. For part of the shoot, Morrison had dysentery; Marguerite Churchill, his beautiful leading lady, remained only intermittently beautiful between bouts of chronic acne; and most of the cast got drunk. The logistics for such an epic $2 million production involved co-ordinating hundreds of extras and props, including dozens of heavy, ox-drawn Conestoga 'prairie schooners' (so-called because of their boat-shaped hulls). In one scene, the wagons descended sheer cliffs on primitive pulleys (filmed at Hurricane Bluffs, Zion National Park); in another, they ford a swollen, muddy, storm-lashed river. The film was shot in two different formats – 35mm and 70mm widescreen 'Grandeur'. Before subtitling and dubbing, Hollywood films were often lensed simultaneously in other languages, with different stars. *The Big Trail* was also shot in German (released as *Der Große Treck* or *Die Große Fahrt*) and Spanish (as *Horizontes Huevos*). The German version starred Theo Shall, Marrion Lessing and El Brendel. The main action of all the different versions was the same, with substitute actors in the close-ups. In the

English-language central role, Duke Morrison was full of beans, but his inexperience with dialogue, even after coaching from celebrated Shakespearean actor Lumsden Hare, showed through.

Before shooting began, William Fox Studios decided they weren't very happy with Duke's name. His real name was Marion Mitchell Morrison (some sources misquote his middle name as Michael, a myth started by the actor himself), which was equally unsuitable for an action hero. So Morrison was renamed 'John Wayne' for the publicity. The 70mm print of *The Big Trail* was exhibited at 158 minutes in only two cinemas in Hollywood and New York, while everywhere else showed the 125-minute version in 35mm. Its intertitle cards recalled silent epics, but *The Big Trail* was a big flop. Wayne was soon dropped by Fox and the action from the film was sold to Republic, where many a B-movie hero subsequently fell under stock footage Indian attack. Viewed today, with its impressive sweep and scope, *The Big Trail* remains one of the great early westerns. The 79-minute German print was very successful in Europe, while UK versions run a scant 104 minutes, though this does improve the film's pace – when the wagons are stationary, the story also grinds to a halt.

SERIAL KILLERS, COWBOY SINGERS AND MATINEE FILLERS

Among the early western's biggest successes were serials – adventure stories told in multiple 'chapters', with each week's instalment ending on a nail-biting, potentially fatal moment of jeopardy for the hero. The first successful serial was the 20-chapter *The Perils of Pauline* (screened April to December 1914) starring Pearl White as the heroine surviving weekly cliffhangers; in one she is pushed downhill off a mountain by a group of Indians, and has to try to outrun a giant boulder. As the rock is about to flatten her, 'Continued Next Week' flashes on the screen and at the commencement of the next episode, she is lassoed to safety. Western serials include Ken Maynard's *Mystery Mountain* (1934), Buck Jones's *The Red Rider* (1934), Tom Mix's *The Miracle Rider* (1935) and *The Great Adventures of Wild Bill Hickok* (1938), plus entries from the Lone Ranger and Zorro, including the classic *Zorro's Fighting Legion* (1939).

Perhaps the greatest, and certainly the most engaging serial is Mascot's 12-chapter *The Phantom Empire* (1935), starring Gene Autry, its singing cowboy hero, and 'Featuring the Futuristic City of Murania', thousands of miles underground. It manages to incorporate detective stories, Boy's Own adventure, war movies, musicals, espionage, mad scientists, epics, westerns, science fiction and comedy – you name the genre, it's in there somewhere. Rancher Gene broadcasts his country and western show from 'Radio Ranch', but begins to experience interference, both from the subterranean Muranian radio transmitters and a band of crooked scientists, who believe there is a lucrative radium mine on the site. But the mine entrance in Thunder Valley is the portal to the underground kingdom of Murania, ruled by Queen Tika and jealous Argo, her Lord High Chancellor. Gene, with his two kiddie companions Frankie and Betsy Baxter, plus comedy sidekicks Pete (William Moore) and Oscar (played by Lester 'Smiley' Burnette, who spends much of the adventure in drag) end up in this futuristic subterranea, while the chancellor foments a rebellion against the queen. The cavernous metropolis, straight out of *Flash Gordon*, offers a chilling vision of the future, a world ruled by robots armed with giant cricket bats, Lithium ray guns shaped like marrows, flame-throwers, ground-to-air missiles, and death by 'Lightning Chamber' and the 'Disintegrator Atom-smashing Machine'. The cliffhangers are integrated well into the scenario, as the villains try to ensure Gene's 'lips are forever sealed', while the hero has to keep popping back to his ranch to helm his radio show, performing such numbers as 'Silver-Haired Daddy of Mine' (his first million seller) and 'Uncle Noah's Ark' (complete with animal impersonations). *Phantom Empire* has a busy, fast-moving plot, but from the moment the Muranian 'Thunder Riders' hurtle across the screen wearing gas masks, helmets and capes, entertainment is assured. 'Wait Boys and Girls', flashed across the screen after episode one, 'You've seen nothing yet!'; for once, they were right.

Like most serials, *Phantom Empire* was later condensed to feature length, entitled *Radio Ranch* (1935) or *Men with Steel Faces* (1940). Autry followed this with his first proper film, *Tumbling Tumbleweeds* (1935), although he was already an established country star on Columbia Records (*Phantom Empire* billed him as 'Radio's Singing Cowboy'). He nearly always played himself, a cowboy named 'Gene' in a white hat who takes on various 'man-sized jobs', protecting the innocent and the oppressed. Until 1941 he was often teamed with sidekick Burnette, as cowardly sidekick Frog Milhouse. In all his adventures he rode Champion and most outings included a tie-in record for fans. Later Autry westerns saw the hero backed by the Cass County Boys, a vocal harmony trio. Autry's west was a modern world, a strange hybrid of old-style western settings and contemporary technology, with telephones, motor vehicles and sheriffs armed with tear gas. In *Twilight on the Rio Grande* (1948) Autry (or rather Autry's stuntman) escapes from the jewel-smuggling baddies by jumping Champion onto a moving truck.

Exemplifying these outings was *Riders of the Whistling Pines* (1949). Here forester Gene and the Cass County Boys find themselves battling a moth infestation munching its way through the 'Whistling Pines'. The setting is a lumber mill, with lorries, bulldozers, planes and caterpillar-tracked heavy plant. The heroes kill off the moths by aerial spraying the woods with DDT ('What's gonna happen to the fish?' asks an ecologically-minded local); Autry here really is a 'high planes drifter'. Periodically the action halts for another musical interlude, by Gene, accompanied by the Cass County Boys, who have an octave-spanning vocal range (including a bald member with a disconcertingly high voice) or the Three Pinafores (who serve up the less-than-catchy 'Tooly-Ooly-Dooly-Oo'). Autry was not a great actor, but he could certainly hold a tune and the action scenes benefit from superior stunt work and staging. He had a ten-point code of conduct, the so-called 'Cowboy Commandments', outlining western chivalry and general decent behaviour for non-smoking, non-drinking cowboys, including 'never go back on your word', 'always tell the truth', 'be gentle with children, elderly people and animals', 'don't possess racially or religiously intolerant ideas', 'always help people in distress' and 'be a patriot'.

Autry was tremendously popular, and was voted by *Motion Picture Herald* the most bankable western star from 1937 to 1942, when he began his war service in the US Air Transport Command. On his return, Autry continued making westerns, until *Last of the Pony Riders* (1953). By then, he had already moved into television, with *The Gene Autry Show* (also titled *Melody Ranch*) running from 1950–1955. Even Champion got his own show: 26 episodes of *The Adventures of Champion* (1955–1956), shown on UK TV as *Champion the Wonder Horse*. Autry's films, and those of other series western stars, have been endlessly reissued and repackaged with little attention to detail. A DVD of *Riders of the Whistling Pines*, for example, has a portrait of fifties western star Audie Murphy on the cover, captioned 'Gene Autry'.

The actor who knocked Autry off poll position as the biggest moneymaking western star in 1943 and remained there until 1954 (when the *Herald* ceased to compile the list), was another crooning cowboy, Roy Rogers. Republic's *Under Western Skies* (1938) gave Rogers his first starring role, with Carol Hughes as the love interest and horse Trigger as the animal interest. Smiley Burnette, cast as Rogers's sidekick, had defected from Autry, though the union was short-lived and George 'Gabby' Hayes became Rogers's regular henchman. Typical of their output was Republic's *Bad Man of Deadwood* (1941), with Rogers as William J. Brady, alias 'Brett Starr', a shootist with a travelling medicine show run by Professor Mortimer Blackstone (Hayes). They arrive in Deadwood to find trouble afoot – a crooked civil league of businessmen are behind a series of robberies carried out by outlaw Ripper (Hal Taliaferro, alias Wally Wales). One heist involves the 'unrobbable' treasure coach, an ironclad stagecoach resembling *The War Wagon* – but the plot is interrupted at regular intervals for Rogers to burst into song. One such highlight depicts the professor's daughter Sally, impersonating a Kickapoo Indian princess, strumming a guitar and duetting on a song with Rogers, while the hero simultaneously shoots down balls being juggled by the professor. In the colour feature, *Bells of San Angelo* (1947), Rogers introduced bloodier action into his scenarios, for which he was criticised. But through such adventures, Rogers became 'King of the Cowboys' and a huge star, first at the cinema, and later on TV with *The Roy Rogers Show* (1951–1957) and *The Roy Rogers and Dale Evans Show* (1962); Evans was his wife from 1947. The best film of the Rogers-Evans-Trigger-Hayes team was *My Pal Trigger* (1946), an equine love story, which was also Rogers's personal favourite. It charted the birth of Palomino Trigger (hence 'my pal') and included such tongue-twisting lyrics as, 'All the cowhands want to marry Harriet, Harriet's handy with a lariat'.

Another crowd puller was the series western: a succession of films with familiar characters, often from the world of literature or comic books, and regular cast members. A good example of this is the 'Hopalong Cassidy' series. William Boyd, a silent actor for De Mille, starred in some early westerns, including *The Painted Desert* (1931 – as 'Bill Boyd'), before his appearance as *Hop-a-Long Cassidy* (1935), a $100,000 production based on the books of Clarence E. Mulford. Boyd was initially approached to play ranch foreman Buck Peters, but wanted the limping title role. A big success, the hero had lost his limp and hyphens by the time of *Hopalong Cassidy Returns* (1936). Boyd, with his horse Topper, starred in 41 Cassidy films for

Paramount, until he was dropped in 1943, whereupon he made a further 25 for United Artists until 1948 – producing 12 of them himself. The best of these was *Hoppy Serves a Writ* (1943), which featured an early performance by Robert Mitchum. The 'Hoppy' movies grossed on average $200,000. Astutely, Boyd owned the rights to all his movies and through their television broadcasts, became a star all over again in the early fifties.

Another series was the adventures of the 'Three Mesquiteers'. Ray 'Crash' Corrigan (so-called, not because of his inept driving, but for his stunt work) appeared as Tucson Smith, with Robert 'Bob' Livingstone as Stony Brooke and Syd Saylor as Lullaby Joslin in *The Three Mesquiteers* (1936). In subsequent adventures, Saylor was replaced by comic Max Terhune, a ventriloquist, and his dummy, Elmer (who count as one mesquiteer). Elmer is conveniently transported in a carpetbag. Probably their finest outing was the mysterious *Riders of the Whistling Skull* (1937), produced by Nat Levine (the brains behind *The Phantom Empire*). The Mesquiteers accompany a party of archaeology professors, their Indian guide Otah (Yakima Canutt) and Betty Marsh (Mary Russell), to the lost city of Luka-tuka; Betty is also looking for her missing father. Forever guided by the eerie 'Whistling Skull' (a weird rock formation atop a mesa through which the wind howls) and shadowed by ghostly figures, the party travel into the sierras, where they start to drop like flies. The lost city, hidden in the mesa and littered with skeletons, cobwebs and mummies, is home to a cave-dwelling, fanatical Indian cult ('The Sons of Anatasia'), who capture Betty. Guide Otah turns out to be a member of the cult. The Mesquiteers charge to Betty's rescue. Stony is about to be sacrificed when a rockslide started by Lullaby and the arrival of Tucson with a posse save the day.

After four years of successful Mesquiteering, Corrigan left to play 'Crash Corrigan' in 24 'Range Busters' adventures for Monogram, beginning with *The Range Busters* (1940). Max Terhune joined him to play 'Alibi' Terhune (still with Elmer in tow), with John King (as 'Dusty King') and later Dennis Moore (as Denny Moore) completing the trio. Meanwhile Livingstone continued to Mesquiteer, with a succession of replacements. He also played the Lone Ranger in a 15-chapter serial *The Lone Ranger Rides Again* (1939) and appeared in another series western as 'The Lone Rider', where he was teamed with sidekick Al 'Fuzzy' St John in such films as *Death Rides the Plains* (1943). But by the late forties, series westerns had lost their appeal, with every formula mined and every canyon explored.

After the failure of *The Big Trail* in 1930, John Wayne became a B-western star, firstly at Warners, then with 16 films at Monogram Pictures, the so-called Lone Star westerns. The 'Lone Star' logo was sometimes incorporated into the rowel design on Wayne's spurs, while saloons plied 'Lone Star Whiskies – the Best in the West'. Wayne was much more at home in these films, where he played a freelance do-gooder, often a secret agent or lawman, with an uncanny knack for being in the right place at the right time. Beginning with *Riders of Destiny* (1933) and including *Randy Rides Alone, The Star Packer, The Lucky Texan, Blue Steel, 'Neath the Arizona Skies, West of the Divide, Lawless Frontier* (all 1934) and *The Dawn Rider* (1935), the series ended with *Paradise Canyon* (1935), which saw Wayne hiding out with a travelling medicine show (plying 'Dr Carter's Indian Remedy') to break up a counterfeiting ring. Each instalment was filmed in ten to 15 days on familiar Californian valley locations around Chatsworth and the Simi Valley and Thousand Oaks areas, near Monogram Studios (including the western town set at Kernville), for between $10,000 and $15,000. Robert N. Bradbury directed most of them and the casts were also reused from film to film, with George 'Gabby' Hayes, cadaverous Earl Dwire and ace stuntman Yakima Canutt as regular contributors. Only Wayne's leading ladies changed for each outing. For one such adventure, Wayne had to stand at a well and have a ladle shot from his hand – a stunt that was actually performed, with no stand-in for Wayne and a sharpshooter taking the shot. Many of these Lone Star six-reelers (running about 55 minutes) now stored in the UCLA Archives, have new synthesised scores by William Barber, though the original versions have also been exhibited. Some prints have been colourised for TV showings and others even re-voiced by a Wayne impersonator.

In *Riders of Destiny*, Wayne memorably played Singin' Sandy Saunders, a warbling gunfighter. In a famous scene, Sandy croons a gloomy ballad, 'Tonight you'll be drinking your drink with the dead', as he faces Slippery Swift Morgan, a hired gun (played by Dwire), whom Sandy shoots through both wrists in the main street of Starbuck. Sandy is later revealed to be a secret service agent. He is sheltered by rancher Faye Denton (Cecilia Parker) and her dad (Hayes) during his investigations. In a musical interlude out at the ranch, Sandy plays them a tune – Faye is enraptured while pappy puffs on his pipe, grinning. 'I could listen to that all night,' he says without irony. The plot has Forrest Taylor stalking around town as water claim jumper Kincaid; at one point he threatens *Godfather*-like retribution, 'I've made Denton an offer he can't refuse.' The epitome of these low-budget westerns, *Riders of Destiny* included a lot of fancy ridin', wooden acting, large hats, fisticuffs, great stunts, unsynchronised sound-effects, hold-ups, claim jumps and shootouts. The musical score telegraphs every plot development and emotional swell (with bad news greeted with an emphatic 'dun-dun-dar!'), the supposed comic relief offers tiresome slapstick, while audiences wondered how everyone's massive hats stayed on in the frantic horseback chase scenes.

In *The Lucky Texan*, one of the liveliest entries, Wayne chased a bank robber by water-skiing down a sluice-way, Hayes appeared in drag as Charlie's Aunt and the high-speed, Mack Sennett-style final chase deployed a horseman pursuing a jalopy and a motorised railcar. *Blue Steel* found Wayne facing outlaw Dandy, alias 'The Polkie-dot Bandit' (played by Canutt), in a tussle over gold fields in 'Homestead Valley' (filmed in Lone Pine, California). In *West of the Divide*, Wayne impersonated outlaw Gat Ganns to infiltrate a gang led by his father's murderer, whom he recognises from his sadistic laugh. Wayne sang again, dubbed by Smith Ballew, in *The Man from Utah*, the tale of a rigged rodeo, which bizarrely features Ganns's wanted poster outside a sheriff's office.

A cult favourite, if only for its hokey title, *Randy Rides Alone* starred Wayne as undercover agent Randy Bowers, who arrives in the 'Half Way House' saloon. Although he can hear a piano playing, all the patrons are dead (the music is from a pianola) and a mysterious pair of eyes watch his every move through eyeholes in a photograph. Hayes plays Matt the Mute, a hunchback who writes down all his dialogue, then holds up the notepad, which fills out the running time. Removing his false hump and moustache, and miraculously regaining the power of speech, Matt is really outlaw Marvin Black. Canutt was cast as Spike, Marvin's lieutenant, wearing a ten-gallon hat that looks like it could hold 20, while Dwire is the sheriff, searching for the outlaws' waterfall hideout. Black is finally blown to pieces when he accidentally detonates a strongbox that is rigged with dynamite.

In *The Star Packer*, Wayne is teamed with Yak, his Indian sidekick (Canutt, in an Apache wig, headband and feather), who arrives by canoe. Sheriffs are being picked off in Little Rock, plugged by a mysteriously sniper. 'More trouble, more fun,' laughs Yak. Hayes was cast as Matt Matlock, a respectable citizen whose alter ego is outlaw 'The Shadow', while Earl Dwire played a mean-looking outlaw. Weird, distorted faces appear at a homestead window to scare the heroine (Verna Hillie), and telephones, flashlights and a machine gun enhance the surreal atmosphere. Little Rock's main street has a secret tunnel, enabling the sniper to murder the sheriffs while disguised as a tree stump. You can never accuse Lone Star westerns of being dull, though Wayne must have wondered what had happened to the script when he had to deliver lines like, 'I got the stump covered'.

In 1935, Monogram was absorbed by the merger of Liberty, Majestic, Mascot and Monogram that resulted in Republic Pictures, with Wayne starring as the leader of 'The Singing Riders' in *Westward Ho!* (1935). Wayne continued working for Republic in westerns such as *Lawless Range* (1935), which again cast him as a singing undercover agent. Supported by Canutt and Dwire, it was an upmarket version of his Lone Star movies – instead of two riders chasing one covered wagon, 20 riders pursued five wagons through magnificent Lone Pine locations. Wayne then moved to Universal for some non-westerns, returning to Republic in June 1938, where he now found himself cast as Stony Brooke in eight 'Three Mesquiteers' adventures, beginning with *Pals of the Saddle*. It was four films into this series, in November 1938, that Wayne was saved from B-movie obscurity by a call from his old friend John Ford, with a ticket to ride on a stagecoach to Lordsburg…

TEN TOP TENS

ALEX COX

Alex Cox is a director of features and documentaries, and a writer and broadcaster. He also presented the Moviedrome television series for many years on BBC2 in the UK, introducing such cult westerns as *The Hired Hand*, *Johnny Guitar*, *The Good, the Bad and the Ugly*, *The Big Silence*, *The Long Riders*, *One-Eyed Jacks* and *Ulzana's Raid*.

Stagecoach (1939)
The Wild Bunch (1969)
For a Few Dollars More (1965)
The Big Silence (1967)
McCabe & Mrs Miller (1971)
Ride the High Country (1962)
Yellow Sky (1948)
The Man Who Shot Liberty Valance (1962)
A Bullet for the General (1966)
The Big Gundown (1967)

ANDREW COLLINS

Film critic Andrew Collins is a presenter, novelist and broadcaster, and film editor at the *Radio Times*. He has also contributed to the *Radio Times Guide to Film 2007* and presented *Back Row* and *Collins & Maconie's Movie Club*.

Red River (1948)
High Noon (1952)
The Good, the Bad and the Ugly (1966)
Rio Bravo (1959)
The Big Country (1958)
The Searchers (1956)
Brokeback Mountain (2005)
Blazing Saddles (1974)
Dead Man (1995)
Rio Grande (1950)

Just outside his top ten are *The Wild Bunch* (1969), *Bad Day at Black Rock* (1955), *Unforgiven* (1992) and *Stagecoach* (1939).

CHRISTOPHER FRAYLING

Sir Christopher Frayling is the Rector of the Royal College of Art, London, and a writer, critic and historian. He has written and broadcast widely on the work of Sergio Leone, including *Sergio Leone: Once Upon a Time in Italy*, *Sergio Leone: Something to Do With Death*, his definitive Leone biography, and *Spaghetti Westerns: Cowboys and Europeans from Karl May to Sergio Leone*. His list, actually a top 12, is chronological:

My Darling Clementine (1946)
Shane (1953)
Johnny Guitar (1954)
Vera Cruz (1954)
The Tall T (1957)
Man of the West (1958)
Warlock (1959)
The Magnificent Seven (1960)
Lonely are the Brave (1962)
Ride the High Country (1962)
Once Upon a Time in the West (1968)
The Outlaw Josey Wales (1976)

EDWARD BUSCOMBE

Edward Buscombe is an authority on westerns and is the author of several books on the genre. He was editor of the *BFI Companion to the Western* and *Back in the Saddle Again*, and has published three volumes in the BFI Film Classics series: *Stagecoach*, *The Searchers* and *Unforgiven*. He has recently written *100 Westerns* and *Injuns! Native Americans in the Movies*, in addition to *Cinema Today*, his look at the film industry worldwide since 1970. His top ten westerns (not in order of merit) are:

The Searchers (1956)
Man of the West (1958)
Ride Lonesome (1959)
Rio Bravo (1959)
Unforgiven (1992)
Ride the High Country (1962)
One-Eyed Jacks (1961)
Ulzana's Raid (1972)
Heller in Pink Tights (1960)
The Hanging Tree (1959)

KIM NEWMAN

Kim Newman is a film critic for *Empire*, and a novelist and broadcaster, who has written extensively on the western genre. He is the author of many books, including *Wild West Movies: How the West was Found, Won, Lost, Lied About, Filmed and Forgotten*, and is the co-author of *Horror: The Complete Guide to the Cinema of Fear*. He has contributed to the Aurum Film Encyclopedia series and the *BFI Companion to the Western*.

McCabe & Mrs Miller (1971)
The Naked Spur (1953)
Once Upon a Time in the West (1968)
Pat Garrett & Billy the Kid (1973)
Red River (1948)
Ride Lonesome (1959)
The Searchers (1956)
3:10 to Yuma (1957)
Ulzana's Raid (1972)
Unforgiven (1992)

He also mentions the importance of some TV westerns (*Maverick*, *Lonesome Dove* and *Deadwood*) and has compiled a second top ten of 'overlooked, unheralded, small-scale pictures. These aren't in any way classics, but they are all smart, surprising, worthwhile little films that reward the afternoon TV viewer': *At Gunpoint* (1955), *Big Deal at Dodge City* (1966), *Curse of the Undead* (1959), *Fury at Showdown* (1957), *The Man Behind the Gun* (1953), *Posse from Hell* (1961), *Ride in the Whirlwind* (1966), *Tension at Table Rock* (1956), *Silver Lode* (1954) and *Terror in a Texas Town* (1958).

PAUL DUNCAN

Paul Duncan is editor of the Taschen Film series, including *John Ford: The Complete Films* and *Clint Eastwood: Go Ahead, Make My Day*. He is the editor of *The Third Degree: Crime Writers in Conversation* and the author of several cinema books, including *Alfred Hitchcock*, *Orson Welles* and *Film Noir: Films of Trust and Betrayal*.

3 Bad Men (1926)
The Searchers (1956)
The Good, the Bad and the Ugly (1966)
Shane (1953)
My Darling Clementine (1946)
The Wild Bunch (1969)
Last of the Mohicans (1992)

Hell's Hinges (1916)
The Beguiled (1971)
The Ballad of Little Jo (1993)

PHILIP FRENCH

Philip French, film critic at the *Observer* since 1978, has written widely on cinema and the western in particular, especially his seminal 1973 book *Westerns: Aspects of a Movie Genre*, updated in 1977 and since reprinted and expanded to include *Westerns Revisited*. He also introduced films in the UK *Film Club* television seasons on BBC2, including the restored version of Sam Peckinpah's *Pat Garrett & Billy the Kid* and Monte Hellman's little-seen *China 9, Liberty 37*. His list is chronological, one per director.

Stagecoach (1939)
High Noon (1952)
3:10 to Yuma (1957)
Man of the West (1958)
Rio Bravo (1959)
Ride Lonesome (1959)
Ride the High Country (1962)
Once Upon a Time in the West (1968)
Heaven's Gate (1980)
Unforgiven (1992)

TOM BETTS

Tom Betts is the editor of *Westerns All'Italiana!* ('Westerns, Italian-style'), a fanzine published in California since 1983, and has written extensively on European westerns.

Once Upon a Time in the West (1968)
The Good, the Bad and the Ugly (1966)
For a Few Dollars More (1965)
The Magnificent Seven (1960)
Hour of the Gun (1967)
The Professionals (1966)
3:10 to Yuma (1957)
The Forgotten Pistolero (1969)
El Dorado (1967)
The Searchers (1956)

HOWARD HUGHES

Film writer Howard Hughes is the author of *Once Upon a Time in the Italian West*, *Crime Wave: The Filmgoers' Guide to the Great Crime Movies*, *The American Indian Wars* and *Spaghetti Westerns*.

Rio Bravo (1959)
The Good the Bad and the Ugly (1966)
The Searchers (1956)
The Magnificent Seven (1960)
Shane (1953)
The Man from Laramie (1955)
Ulzana's Raid (1972)
Ride the High Country (1962)
Forty Guns (1957)
Ride Lonesome (1959)

My runners-up include *My Darling Clementine* (1946), *The Outlaw Josey Wales* (1976), *The Shooting* (1966), *The Wild Bunch* (1969), *Hell's Hinges* (1916), *McCabe & Mrs Miller* (1971), *The Ox-Bow Incident* (1943), *For a Few Dollars More* (1965) and *Django* (1966).

Compiling these top tens provides a further roll call of the genre's best, based on the frequency of their appearances on the lists:

1. *The Searchers*
2. *Ride the High Country*
3. *The Good, the Bad and the Ugly*
= *Once Upon a Time in the West*
= *Ride Lonesome*
= *Rio Bravo*
4. *The Magnificent Seven*
= *Man of the West*
= *Shane*
= *3:10 to Yuma*
= *Ulzana's Raid*
= *Unforgiven*

1

'The Tumbril Awaits'

— *Stagecoach* (1939)

Stagecoach (1939)
Credits
DIRECTOR – John Ford
EXECUTIVE PRODUCER –Walter Wanger
STORY – Ernest Haycox
SCREENPLAY – Dudley Nichols
DIRECTOR OF PHOTOGRAPHY – Bert Glennon
EDITORS – Dorothy Spence and Walter Reynolds
ART DIRECTOR – Alexander Toluboff
MUSIC DIRECTOR – Boris Morros
MUSIC ARRANGERS – Richard Hageman, W. Franke Harling,
    Louis Gruenberg, Leo Shuken and John Leipold
A Walter Wanger Production
Released by United Artists
97 minutes
Cast
    Claire Trevor (Dallas Jeffries); John Wayne (Henry, alias
    The Ringo Kid); John Caradine (Hatfield, the gambler);
    Thomas Mitchell (Dr Josiah Boone); Andy Devine (Buck
    Rickabaugh, the driver); Donald Meek (Samuel Peacock,
    whisky drummer); Louise Platt (Lucy Mallory); Tim Holt
    (Lt Blanchard); George Bancroft (Curley Wilcox, Sheriff of
    Tonto); Berton Churchill (Henry Gatewood, the banker);
    Tom Tyler (Luke Plummer); Chris-Pin Martin (Chris, at
    Apache Wells); Elvira Martin (Yakima, Chris's wife); Francis
    Ford (Sgt Billy Pickett, at Dry Fork); Marga Daighton
    (Mrs Pickett); Kent Odell (Billy Pickett Jnr); Yakima Canutt
    (Cavalry scout); Chief John Big Tree (Cheyenne army scout);
    Jack Pennick (Jerry, barman); Many Mules (Geronimo);

Cornelius Keefe (Captain Whitney); Florence Lake
(Mrs Nancy Whitney); Louis Mason (Sheriff); Duke Lee
(Sheriff of Lordsburg); Brenda Fowler (Mrs Gatewood);
Walter McGrail (Captain Sickel); Joseph Rickson (Hank
Plummer); Vester Pegg (Ike Plummer); Nora Cecil (Doc
Boone's landlady); Mary Kathleen Walker (Lucy's baby);
Iron Eyes Cody (Apache archer)

*   *   *

Stagecoach, John Ford's first sound western, a desert-set tale of Apache attacks and human endurance, had its unlikely origins in European literature. 'Stage to Lordsburg', a story written by Ernest Haycox, was published in *Collier's* magazine in April 1937. Haycox's story was partially inspired by 'Boule de Suif' ('Ball of Fat') by Guy de Maupassant, the story of a group of Dieppe-bound coach passengers during the Franco-Prussian War. At an inn, Elizabeth Rousset, a prostitute passenger (whose unflattering nickname gives the story its title) sleeps with a Prussian officer to ensure their safe passage, thus saving the lives of her fellow travellers ('The need justifies the means'). But thereafter, they ostracise her, refusing to share their food, even though previously she has shared hers with them, revealing their hypocrisy.

In 'Stage to Lordsburg', eight passengers travel the dangerous road from Tonto, Arizona, through Apache country, to Lordsburg, New Mexico. They travel via stops at Gap Station and Al Schrieber's ranch. After Schrieber's, which they discover is a burnt-out ruin, the Apaches attack, but the group manage to struggle through. During the journey, prostitute Henriette falls for drifter Malpais Bill, who is travelling to Lordsburg to 'collect a debt': mysterious revenge on two men, Plummer and Shanley. In Haycox's story, the disparate passengers are mostly nameless: a woman on her way to marry an infantry officer, a gambler, a whisky drummer from St Louis, a cattleman en route to New Mexico, an Englishman with a sporting rifle, Henriette (who runs a brothel in Lordsburg), Malpais Bill, driver Happy Stuart and shotgun rider John Strang.

Director Ford liked the story and bought the rights for $7,500. In Dudley Nichols's reworked screenplay, retitled *Stagecoach*, the driver is named Buck, his shotgun rider is Sheriff Curley Wilcox, while the passengers are Lucy Mallory (the pregnant wife of a cavalry officer), Hatfield (a gambler), Doc Boone (a drunken quack), Samuel Peacock (a whisky drummer), Henry Gatewood (an embezzling banker), Dallas Jeffries (a prostitute who has been run out of Tonto) and wanted outlaw the Ringo Kid, who is travelling to Lordsburg to take revenge on Luke Plummer, the murderer of his father and brother. The stagecoach leaves Tonto, escorted by the cavalry led by Lieutenant Blanchard. Geronimo is on the warpath, having jumped the reservation. Outside town, escaped convict Ringo joins the party, hoping to travel to Lordsburg, but is arrested by Sheriff Wilcox, riding shotgun. They pass through the swing station at Dry Fork, separating from their escort, and continue to Apache Wells, where drunken Doc has to sober up to deliver Mrs Mallory's baby girl. The party press on to Lee's

Ferry, but discover the Apaches have beaten them to it: burning the buildings, massacring the inhabitants and demolishing the ferry. The stagecoach manages to ford the river, but the Apaches attack. Hatfield is killed, and Buck and Peacock are wounded. Ringo's heroics save the day, but the defenders are out of ammunition when the 7th Cavalry arrive in the nick of time, routing the raiders. In Lordsburg, the travelling companions go their separate ways and Gatewood is arrested. The sheriff releases Ringo long enough for him to take revenge on the Plummer boys and then allows Ringo and Dallas to ride away together.

Both Gary Cooper and Joel McCrea were suggested for Ringo, but Ford wanted John Wayne. Then languishing in B-westerns at Republic, Wayne cut an imposing figure at six-feet-four-inches tall, plus his hat. Ford had known Wayne since Wayne was a prop man. He had given Wayne bit parts in the Irish-set *Hangman's House* (1928 – with Wayne overenthusiastically cheering a cross-county steeplechase won by 'The Bard') and the naval dramas *Salute* (1929) and *Men Without Women* (1930). The actor then had a brief brush with stardom on *The Big Trail*. Marlene Dietrich was a prospective Dallas, but Ford thought her too old and cast Claire Trevor, who received top billing and the highest fee: $15,000. Other roles were taken by reliable character actors: Thomas Mitchell, a stage actor, was cast as Josiah Boone, M.D. Cadaverous John

The timeless panorama of Monument Valley: The East and West Mitten and Merrick Butte, which John Ford first featured in *Stagecoach* (1939). The stage route can still be seen winding through the valley. (Photograph courtesy of Victoria Millington and Mark Chester.)

Carradine, a future horror regular, played cad Hatfield, complete with cane and cape, who resembled villainous Bill Freel from *Tumbleweeds*. Glasgow-born Donald Meek was nervous drummer Peacock. Andy Devine (real name Jeremiah Schwartz) with his honking voice, became synonymous with westerns following his casting as stage driver Buck. He was cast because first choice Ward Bond 'couldn't drive a six-up' rig. Series western hero Tom Tyler was cast against type as Luke Plummer and Wayne's friend Yakima Canutt appeared as an Indian scout. Ford cast his brother Francis in a cameo as veteran Sergeant Billy Pickett at Dry Fork, with Seneca Indian, Chief John Big Tree, playing a Cheyenne scout; Big Tree was born Isaac Johnny John and it is his head that appeared on the 1912 Indian Head nickel coin.

Stagecoach* was assigned a modest $546,200 budget, of which Ford received $50,000. It was shot in 47 days, from 31 October to 23 December 1938, partly in Monument Valley, on the border between Utah and Arizona. There are three types of rock formation in Monument Valley: aiguilles (the totemic tall, thin spires), mesas (flat-topped, cliff-edged 'table land') and buttes (the cathedral-like towers most associated with the valley, with their scree slopes and sheer cliffs). The Monument Valley travelling scenes were shot first, in seven days, deploying the stagecoach, the cavalry escort, an army camp and an Apache war party, played by Navajos who lived in the valley, with a few actual Apaches for close-ups; Geronimo himself was played by an Apache named Many Mules. Various monuments appear in the film, including East and West Mitten and Merrick Butte, Castle Rock, Sentinel Mesa and El Capitan. The crew moved to Lucerne Dry Lake, in the Mojave Desert, for the Apache attack (the same location used for the land rush scene in Ford's silent *3 Bad Men*). Wayne was on location for this scene, but many close-ups of the stagecoach during the attack were process shots, with the lead actors in front of a screen projecting Lucerne footage of galloping Apaches and the stage driver waggling the reins (which were usually attached to elasticated arm stretchers). These process shots look no more convincing than the risible opening shots of a low-budget production like *The Vigilantes Return* (1947 – also starring Andy Devine).

Ford's 'Overland Stage Line' coach was an authentic maroon Concord, which had seen 85 years' service on the El Paso to San Diego line (Concords were available in a variety of colours, but are almost always maroon on screen). Also named Pitchin' Betsys, due to their rocking motion, stagecoaches were so-called because they completed the journey in stages between relay stations, where the horses were changed. The rest of *Stagecoach* was shot closer to home: Lee's Ferry was on the Kern River, near Kernville. The stations at Dry Fork and Apache Wells are the same set – note the three-log corral gateway and the distinctive rock formations in the background – at the Iverson Movie Ranch, Chatsworth. Tonto was the western street at Republic, while Lordsburg was shot at the Goldwyn Studios. The distinctive gap the stagecoach drives through as the Apaches attack is Beale's Cut, Newhall, which was also the outlaw's haven of Devil's Valley in Ford's *Straight Shooting* (1917) and the Black Hills railroad shortcut 'Brandon's Pass' in *The Iron Horse*. Ford distributes the Monument Valley footage to good effect throughout the film, as punctuation between the California-shot scenes, though in one shot the stagecoach is travelling away from the East and West Mittens and Merrick Butte, then later, supposedly further on in the trip, passes them again.

Stagecoach married the frantic action of Wayne's B-westerns to real drama. Yakima Canutt worked as both stunt double and actor on Wayne's thirties westerns – in the confusing chase footage, Canutt often chased himself. Canutt was born Enos Edward Canutt, on a ranch in Colefax, Washington. He became a horse breaker, was northwest champion bronco rider and a world champion rodeo rider (in the rodeo-set *The Man from Utah* [1934] he played champion 'bronc buster' Cheyenne Kent). His name 'Yakima' came from his rodeo billing as 'The Cowboy from Yakima'. He appeared in many silent westerns, but his stunt work brought him recognition, especially in the Lone Star westerns: he later won a special Oscar in 1966 for his services to movie stunting.

On *Stagecoach*, Canutt was billed in the press as responsible for second unit direction and stunts. He doubled for the Apache who leaps onto the stage's lead horse and is then shot by Ringo. Canutt fell beneath the horses' hooves and was dragged along, before the stage rolled over him, with Canutt positioned precisely between the wheels. The Concord stage needed six horses to pull it at speed (it weighed 2,500 pounds, with an ash frame and poplar bodywork) and Ford's crew travelled along at up to 45 miles an hour to photograph the chase. There were no camera cars and the crew used normal cars with their equipment strapped on board. For a shot of the stage horses from the driver's-eye-view, Ford positioned a camera on the driver's seat and hollered instructions through the window of the speeding coach. Canutt doubled for Wayne in the scenes where Ringo climbs out of the coach onto the roof to return fire, and also when Ringo tries to bring the rein-less runaway team under control, jumping forward from one pair of horses to the next. As Wayne remembered, 'I was satisfied to settle for the close-up.' Canutt performed many horse falls in Apache garb, as part of the pursuing war party, while Cherokee Indian Iron Eyes Cody, an expert horseman, fired arrows at the stage. These high-speed stunts weren't completely new to audiences. In *Riders of Destiny* (1934) Singin' Sandy (Canutt, doubling for Wayne) had jumped from his horse onto the team pulling a water wagon, dropped down and hung under the wagon, then climbed up into the driver's seat. William S. Hart scoffed that *Stagecoach*'s chase was ridiculous, as real Apaches would have shot the horses.

Ford's style contrasts the massive empty landscapes with the intimacy of human lives played out on this grand stage. Ford's photography, by Bert Glennon, and his eye for composition are most evident in the scenes filmed in Monument Valley, which to Ford was an ethereal world of searching, towering mountains stretching heavenwards towards spectacular skies. This beauty masks the ever-present danger of imminent attack. In *Stagecoach*'s title sequence, Indian riders already stalk a cavalry patrol, setting the scene. Haycox's original story establishes this perilous atmosphere in his first sentence, 'This was one of those years in the Territory when Apache smoke signals spiralled up from the stony mountain summits and many a ranch cabin lay as a square of blackened ashes on the ground.'

After B-movies, it was obvious to Wayne that he'd have to do some proper acting in *Stagecoach*. His performance style, even in his early films, was reacting to those around him. For *Stagecoach*, Ford had the experienced actors do the acting and kept cutting back to Wayne, keeping him the centre of attention without the actor having to do anything. In *Variety* in January 1976, Wayne said, 'Perhaps I've projected something closer to my personality than other actors have. I have very few tricks...I'll stop in the middle of a sentence so they'll keep looking at me and I don't stop at the end so they don't look away.'

The stagecoach passengers split into two groups: the 'respectable' and the 'disreputable'. The respectable are Peacock, Mrs Mallory and two more dubious characters: shifty gambler Hatfield (a 'Man of Mystery' according to the film's advertising) and the president of the 'Miners and Cattlemen's Bank', Gatewood (sometimes billed as 'Gateswood'), who has stolen a payroll. The disreputable are outlaw Ringo, prostitute Dallas and cheerful drunk Doc Boone, who befriends the whisky drummer with the words, 'Samples? Mmm...' Ford deliberately blurs the lines between these groups. It is insinuated that Southern gentleman Hatfield, who sees himself as the noble protector of Mrs Mallory, is a 'backshooter', while pontificating Gatewood is actually on the run with $50,000 in stolen funds. Mrs Mallory is a prim and proper officer's wife, who dislikes Doc's cigar smoke, the dust, the bumpy journey, the presence of Dallas and Ringo, and the Apaches – in fact just about everything seems to bother her. But when she goes into labour at Apache Wells, she is forced to rely on Doc Boone's expertise, a man who has previously been described as not being capable of doctoring a horse. Characteristically, Ford reserves his most poetic compositions for Ringo and Dallas, romanticising the 'outsiders'. In a typically elegiac Fordian shot, Dallas walks down a corridor at Apache Wells, watched by Ringo, with long shadows cast by the moonlit portal.

Dallas has suffered the narrow-minded bigotry of the ladies in the Tonto Law and Order League, an uppity Temperance Union, who run her out of town. 'There's worse things than Apaches,' says Dallas, when she boards the coach, as the 'ladies' look down their noses at her. Doc notes, 'We're the victims of a foul disease called social prejudice, my child.' Doc even compares the stage to a tumbril, the vehicle used to take those condemned to the guillotine. Later, at Dry Fork, Mrs Mallory won't even sit opposite Ringo and Dallas. 'Looks like I got the plague,' observes Ringo glumly, 'I guess you can't break out of prison and into society in the same week.' But their ordeal on the journey unifies the group as they travel through the valley of death. Dallas protects Mrs Mallory's baby during the Apache attack, while Ringo's sharpshooting holds off the hostiles. In Lordsburg, Dallas and Mrs Mallory part, if not as friends, then at least on speaking terms.

Outlaw Ringo is also ostracised by the group, an outsider to civilised society. He isn't allowed to sit on a seat for much of the journey, hunched instead on the floor against the door. Real Concords had a centre seat too, doubling as a bed, which is missing here. Ford's introduction of Ringo, as he waylays the stage, became a classic western moment. A rifle shot stops the stage horses in their tracks, while Ford zooms in on Wayne, shouting 'Hold it!', twirling his Winchester with its outsized loading lever, in a cloud of dust. We later learn that Ringo is seeking revenge on the Plummers and Ford uses the final shootout in the darkened mainstreet of Lordsburg as a fitting climax to the trek. Luke Plummer is playing cards in the saloon when he hears Ringo's in town, though he should heed the omens: Luke is holding 'Aces and Eights', Wild Bill Hickok's prophetic 'Dead Man's Hand'. Their duel, with Ringo versus the three Plummers, recalls Cheyenne Harry facing Placer Fremont in *Straight Shooting* (1917); one of the Plummers is even played by 'Fremont' – actor Vester Pegg. Once avenged, Ringo is allowed by Ford to escape 'civilisation', riding away with Dallas to his half-built cabin in the hills, their haven from the world, their 'crazy dream'. 'A man could live there,' prompts Ringo, 'and a woman.'

Stagecoach was previewed in Los Angeles in February 1939, before going on general release in March. Posters ran with the taglines: 'Danger Holds the reins as the Devil Cracks the Whip!', '2 Women on a Desperate Journey with 7 Strange Men' or 'A Powerful Story of 9 Strange People'. One poster depicted a map of their journey, detailing its incident-packed route, entitled 'A Strange Frontier Incident of 1885'. The trailer voiceover marvelled: 'What fantastic stories there were in the life of a stagecoach' and its passengers 'who found romance in danger and

understanding in strange companionship.' Posters helpfully indicated, 'Due to the tremendous suspense developed in *Stagecoach* we recommend that you get to the theatre for the start of the picture'. It quickly turned Wayne into a mainstream star; 'Wayne is so good in the role,' noted the *New York Daily News*, 'that one wonders why he had to wait all this time since *The Big Trail* for such another opportunity.' Welford Beaton simplified the film to '*Grand Hotel* on wheels', while *Variety* called it a 'sweeping and powerful drama of the American frontier'. Frank S. Nugent, writing for the *New York Times*, concluded: 'This is one stagecoach that's powered by a Ford'.

The film grossed well in the US (though it wasn't the runaway hit as presumed

Original German poster artwork depicting Dallas (Claire Trevor), Ringo (John Wayne) and the title vehicle: John Ford's *Stagecoach*. (courtesy of Ian Caunce Collection).

today) and Thomas Mitchell won the 1939 Best Supporting Actor Oscar, while it failed to win Best Picture, Best Director and Cinematography. It shared the Oscar for Best Score with *The Wizard of Oz*. The score was adapted and arranged from 13 American folk tunes of the period, including 'Shall We Gather at the River?', 'Lily Dale', 'Ten Thousand Cattle', 'Jeannie with the Light Brown Hair', 'Gentle Annie', 'Rosa Lee', 'She May have seen Better Days' and 'She's More to be Pitied than Censured'. *Stagecoach* was retitled for European releases. In Germany it was titled *Ringo* or *Höllenfahrt nach Santa Fé* ('Hell Travels from Santa Fe'); in Italy it was *Ombre Rosse* ('Red Shadows'). *Stagecoach*'s release in France as *La Chevauchée Fantastique* ('The Fantastic Ride') established Ford's reputation as a major director.

The Wayne–Trevor teaming was swiftly capitalised on by RKO, who cast them in *Allegheny Uprising* (1939 – *The First Rebel* in the UK), a *Drums Along the Mohawk* rip-off, and Republic, who made the pre-Civil War *The Dark Command* (1940). The latter was notable for another spectacular stunt by Canutt: here four men drive a two-horse flatbed wagon off a cliff into a river. *Dark Command* featured Gabby Hayes in a supporting role and with its A-movie $700,000 budget was little more than an elaborate version of the Lone Star westerns, with larger sets and an expensive cast.

Optimistically, *Stagecoach* was remade twice. In 1966 the stagecoach travelled to Cheyenne, with Alex Cord (Ringo), Bing Crosby (Doc Boone), Ann-Margret (Dallas), Van Heflin (Sheriff Curly Wilcox), Slim Pickens (driver Buck), Red Buttons (Peacock), Mike Connors (Hatfield), Stephanie Powers (Mrs Mallory) and Keenan Wynn (Luke Plummer). In 1986, a TV country music version of the film featured members of the appropriately named band The Highwaymen: Johnny Cash played Sheriff Curley, Kris Kristofferson was Ringo and Waylon Jennings was Hatfield, while Doc Boone became Doc Holliday, as portrayed by Willie Nelson. June Carter Cash and her son John also appeared. The lively country shuffle theme song, voiced by Nelson, warns: 'We gotta get to Lordsburg and we gotta be on time – but there's trouble up ahead and close behind.' Other westerns following in *Stagecoach*'s tracks include *Stagecoach to Fury* (1956), *Stagecoach to Dancers' Rock* (1962) and *Hombre* (1967), with disparate groups of passengers trapped in a variety of desperate situations.

Stagecoach changed the way audiences and critics viewed westerns, and Ford was hailed a genius, re-establishing his reputation as the foremost poet of the genre after 13 years away. When asked in 1967 who were his favourite US directors, Orson Welles replied, 'The old masters, by which I mean John Ford, John Ford and John Ford.' As for John Wayne, he'd hitched a ride on a stagecoach and his career was finally going somewhere. He completed his last four 'Three Mesquiteer' outings for Republic, fulfilling his contract, and left B-movies in a cloud of dust.

2

'Shakespeare in Tombstone'

— *My Darling Clementine* (1946)

My Darling Clementine (1946)
Credits
DIRECTOR – John Ford
PRODUCER – Samuel G. Engel
STORY – Sam Hellman
SCREENPLAY – Samuel G. Engel and Winston Miller
DIRECTOR OF PHOTOGRAPHY – Joseph P. MacDonald
EDITOR – Dorothy Spencer
ART DIRECTORS – James Basevi, Lyle Wheeler, Thomas Little and
    Fred J. Rode
MUSIC – Cyril J. Mockridge and David Buttolph
A 20th Century-Fox Production
Released by 20th Century-Fox
97 minutes
Cast
Henry Fonda (Wyatt Berry Stapp Earp); Linda Darnell
(Chihuahua); Victor Mature (John Henry 'Doc' Holliday);
Cathy Downs (Clementine Carter); Walter Brennan
(N.H. 'Old Man' Clanton); Tim Holt (Virgil Earp); Ward
Bond (Morgan Earp); Don Gardner (James Earp); Alan
Mowbray (Granville Thorndyke); John Ireland (Billy
Clanton); Grant Withers (Ike Clanton); Fred Libby (Phin
Clanton); Mickey Simpson (Sam Clanton); Roy Roberts
(Mayor of Tombstone); Jane Darwell (Kate Nelson); Russell
Simpson (Deacon John Simpson); Francis Ford (Dad); J.
Farrell MacDonald (Mac, Oriental Saloon barman); Ben Hall
(Bon Ton barber); Charles Stevens (Drunken Indian
Charlie); Arthur Walsh (Hotel clerk); Jack Pennick
(Stagecoach driver); Louis Mercier (François, the chef);

Jack Curtis (Bartender); Harry Woods (Luke, Tombstone
marshal); Robert Alder and Jack Pennick (Stage drivers);
Don Barclay (Bird Cage owner); Mae Marsh (Deacon's
sister); Arthur Walsh (Mansion House clerk)

*   *   *

When a silver lode was discovered in the Apache lands of Arizona by Ed Schiefflin in
1877, the settlement of Tombstone rose around the spot; the prospector was originally
searching the area for quartz stones and the town's name came from Schiefflin's
friend who commented: 'Reckon the only stone you're gonna find'll be your tombstone.'
Tombstone has passed into legend, linked inextricably to one man: Marshal Wyatt
Earp, hero of 1881's Gunfight at the 'Old Kinderhook' (O.K.) Corral.

The accepted historical version of Earp's exploits at the O.K. Corral was
recounted in Stuart N. Lake's highly successful biography, 'Wyatt Earp, Frontier
Marshal', published in 1931 following a serialisation in the *Saturday Evening Post*. It
is here that the town-tamer image of Earp originated, but it has since been accepted
as a whitewash. Lake even armed his hero with a Buntline Special, a Colt Peacemaker
with an extra long barrel, an embellishment for which there is no evidence. Lake's
heroic Earp and his two brothers Virgil and Morgan, plus gambling dentist Doc

East Mitten Butte looms like a tombstone in Monument Valley, where John Ford
filmed *My Darling Clementine* in 1946. (Photograph courtesy of Victoria Millington
and Mark Chester.)

Holliday, faced the Clanton-McLaury clan in the streets of Tombstone on the afternoon of 26 October 1881. Later sources noted that some of the Clanton faction were unarmed. As Earp's wife Josephine once observed, 'I can't imagine why anyone called it the gunfight at the O.K. Corral. It could more accurately be called the gunfight west of Fly's house. The O.K. Corral was several doors up the street.'

Early film versions of Lake's story were *Frontier Marshal* (1934 – with George O'Brien as fictitious 'Michael Wyatt') and Alan Dwan's *Frontier Marshal* (1939). Dwan's film, as adapted by writer Sam Hellman, opens with the town's founding on a silver lode ('a mushroom metropolis sprang up overnight'), with saloon owner John Carradine claiming, 'They ran me out of Lordsburg' (an apparent in-joke reference to his appearance in *Stagecoach*). Randolph Scott starred as Wyatt Earp, who is introduced in a scene where he apprehends drunken 'Indian Charlie'. Cesar Romero was Doc Holliday (here spelt Halliday), an obstetrician, and Ward Bond appeared as the cowardly marshal of Tombstone. Some moments are quite light-hearted (a coroner's report on the corpse of Big Nose Jackson states 'Body rich in lead – too badly punctured to hold whisky'), but according to Dwan, the lawman in *Frontier Marshal* was never meant to be the 'real Earp'.

Ford knew the real Earp and kept the lawman's rifle by his bed. In Earp's later years, he lived north of Pasadena and when his wife went away for the weekend, Earp would travel up to Universal City to watch westerns being made, in his capacity as 'technical advisor'. When Earp died in 1929, aged 80, cowboy stars Tom Mix and William S. Hart were bearers at his funeral. Ford's collaborator Harry Carey had asked Earp about the O.K. Corral and Earp even drew a sketch of the shootout. Earp said that he had not been a good shot and had to get in close. He remembered that the stagecoach was due to arrive and timed it so the dust cloud would give him cover. Ford memorised such details for future reference, but as Henry Fonda noted, 'Ford used history, he wasn't married to it.'

Ford was attracted to the Earp story and had the backing of 20th Century-Fox's Darryl F. Zanuck. The director claimed not to have seen Dwan's *Frontier Marshal* (also made by Fox), but evidence proves he screened it in October 1945, when preparing his own version, to be called *My Darling Clementine*. With Lake's fiction as a basis, Ford took screenwriter Sam Hellman's Dwan adaptation as the truth. This was turned into a screenplay by Ford and Winston Miller by March 1946.

In *My Darling Clementine*, drover Wyatt Earp and his brothers Virgil, Morgan and James, are taking their cattle to market when they arrive in Tombstone. But the herd is stolen and James is killed by rustlers; local ranchers the Clantons, led by patriarch Old Man Clanton, are the chief suspects. Wyatt, an ex-lawman, agrees to become Tombstone's marshal, with Morgan and Virgil as his deputies. Wyatt meets tubercular gambler Doc Holliday, a shady character, whose relationship with saloon girl Chihuahua causes friction: she is also seeing Billy Clanton. The arrival of Holliday's lover Clementine Carter from back east further complicates matters. Wyatt and Clementine begin a hesitant courtship, but when Billy is killed by Wyatt – after the Clanton has killed Chihuahua – and the Clantons murder Virgil, the families' rivalry intensifies. At a dawn rendezvous at the O.K. Corral, the Earps face the Clantons. In the gunfight, Doc is killed, but the Clantons are wiped out. Morgan and Wyatt move on, though Wyatt promises that he'll be back one day to see Clementine, now the town's school ma'am.

Ford obviously wasn't happy with the way the script developed, as he tried unsuccessfully to convince Zanuck to alter all the names to fictional ones. In reality, Holliday survived the final gunfight and even the year on James Earp's grave is incorrect: 1882, when it should be 1881. The film had several differences from the original script; as written, Holliday is shot before the final gunfight, Old Man Clanton survives (Morgan shoots him in the film) and Clementine and Wyatt's final goodbye was in a graveyard, not on the edge of Tombstone.

Henry Fonda had worked with Ford with great success on *Young Mr. Lincoln*, *Drums Along the Mohawk* (both 1939) and *The Grapes of Wrath* (1940). He'd also appeared in William A. Wellman's powerful western allegory *The Ox-Bow Incident* (1943 – released in the UK as *Strange Incident*). Written by Lamar Trotti, after a novel by Walter Van Tilburg Clark, Fonda and Harry Morgan starred as two drifters, Gil Carter and Art Croft, who become embroiled in a lynching near the Nevada town of Bridger's Wells, in 1885. Kincaid, a local rancher, is murdered and his cattle stolen. The lynch mob find three cowboys (Dana Andrews, Anthony Quinn and John Ford's brother, Francis) camped out at the Ox-Bow, but despite their innocent protestations, the trio are hanged. Later it becomes apparent that Kincaid isn't dead and those responsible for the rustling have been caught. Some of the posse, including Carter, had tried to intervene, and Wellman's film ends on a resonant, downbeat note. In Darby's Saloon, Carter reads aloud a letter – from one of the executed men to his wife – to the hot-headed vigilantes, now ashamed, 'There can't be any such thing as civilisation unless people have got a conscience, because if people touch God anywhere, where is it except through their conscience?' Photographed in brooding, expressionistic style by Arthur Miller, and since acclaimed as one of the greatest westerns ever made and one of the first with psychological depth, *The Ox-Bow Incident*'s wartime release was tragically mistimed; the *New York Herald Tribune* called it 'a depressing arrival in days that are depressing enough already'.

The day after Fonda finished making *Ox-Bow*, he enlisted in the navy. When demobbed, in October 1945, his first role was Wyatt Earp in *My Darling Clementine*, although Tyrone Power and Douglas Fairbanks Jnr had also been in the running. Opposite Fonda, Ford cast muscly Victor Mature, an actor not known for his subtle portrayals, as tubercular, champagne-quaffing Doc Holliday, though Power, Vincent Price and James Stewart were considered. Described in his publicity as 'a beautiful hunk of a man', critics noted that Mature was 'about as tubercular as a kodiak bear'. The son of a scissors grinder, Mature went on to become a star in 'sword and sandal' epics like *Samson and Delilah* (1949), *The Robe* (1953) and *Demetrius and the Gladiators* (1954), which better suited his image, as did his turn as *Chief Crazy Horse* (1955) in the colourful Black Hills-shot biopic. Frequent Ford collaborator Wardell 'Ward' Bond appeared as Wyatt's brother Morgan; Tim Holt (from *Stagecoach*) played Virgil. Walter Brennan made a memorable Old Man Clanton, even though he hated working with Ford and vowed never to again. Popular actress Linda Darnell, who resembled

Jane Russell, had been on contract at Fox since she was 18 and played fiery Chihuahua. Alan Mowbray was a theatre actor, ideal for travelling thespian Granville Thorndyke, a 'sterling tragedian'. Jeanne Crain, Donna Reed and Anne Baxter were prospective Clementines, until Cathy Downs secured the title role. Jane Darwell was saloon madam Kate Nelson. Darwell had been memorable as an advocate of lynch law in *The Ox-Bow Incident* and as poor Ma Joad in *The Grapes of Wrath*; her last appearance was as the bird woman in *Mary Poppins* (1964), feeding the birds for 'tuppence a bag'. Charles Stevens, the grandson of Geronimo, was cast as drunkard Indian Charlie, the same role he had played in *Frontier Marshal*.

My Darling Clementine was planned in Technicolor, but even with a large $2 million budget, it was eventually photographed in black and white by Joseph P. MacDonald, from April to June 1946. Interiors were shot on Stage B at Fox Studios. In *The American West of John Ford*, Fonda revisited the levelled Fox lot in 1971 and when confronted with the modern skyscrapers standing in its place, noted, 'It's been homesteaded!' The set for Tombstone and the O.K. Corral were constructed in the north-western corner of Monument Valley for $250,000, on the site where the Visitors' Centre now stands. The Mansion House hotel, the adobe jailhouse and the smoky, lantern-lit Oriental Saloon are the settings for much of the action. The Bird Cage Theatre and the Oriental were actual establishments in Tombstone, whose busy main thoroughfare was Allen Street, filled with pool halls, drinking dens and stores. The Clantons' ranch and a Wells Fargo way station were also in Monument Valley. A frantic chase, when Wyatt pursues Doc (who is riding shotgun on the 'Bisbee-Tombstone-Tucson' bullion stage) and heads him off at the Huachuca Pass, was also filmed there. Ford filmed the Earps' cattle drive among the towering buttes and mesas, James's grave is below Castle Rock and King-on-his-Throne, and Wyatt rides off towards the distinctive, rocket-shaped El Capitan (also called Agathla Peak) at the film's conclusion. When lensing was completed, Ford donated the Tombstone set to the local Navajos. Stunning and expansive when filmed in sunlight, Monument Valley's buttes and mesas have a tendency to loom like giant grave markers during overcast or stormy weather – an apt place for Ford to construct his 'Tombstone'.

Fonda's Earp is as noble a hero as has ever appeared in a western: incorruptible and honest, tough, yet shy and nervous around Clementine. He doesn't smoke, seldom drinks and his only vice is poker. The real Earps were involved in all sorts of iniquity (they had a 10% share in the Oriental Saloon) and were known as 'The Fighting Pimps'. Tombstone is soon a much quieter place than the 'wide awake, wide open town' the Earps arrive in. But Ford also paints charming Earp as a daydreamer, leaning back in his chair outside the Mansion House, arms outstretched, balancing his feet on the porch post, then deftly skipping from foot to foot like a high-wire walker. Fonda improvised this scene on set and reckoned he was asked more about it than any other moment in his career.

Ford liked the way Fonda moved; he especially liked Fonda's unique, stately walk. For the Sunday morning church dedication scene, Wyatt takes Clementine's arm and they walk to the half-constructed church, with its spindly tower, ladder and cross, as the bell tolls and the community sing 'Shall We Gather at the River'. Wyatt gingerly asks Clementine, 'Will you oblige me, ma'am?' as the locals clear the floor so that the marshal and 'his lady fair' can dance to the folksy hoedown 'Oh, Dem Golden Slippers'. Wyatt dances stiffly but enthusiastically, awkwardly lifting his leg in the manner of a dancer who hates to be the centre of attention.

Doc Holliday, the dark antithesis of Wyatt, resembles less-than-honourable gambler Hatfield in *Stagecoach*. Doc is of the night, dressed in black and he is an alcoholic. He periodically slips away on unexplained trips to Mexico and it would have been interesting to see what horror stalwart Vincent Price would have made of the role. In reality, Holliday had a moustache and was a dentist, but Ford makes him a clean-shaven surgeon. Doc's horrible coughing fits, triggered by the chokingly smoky Oriental, are a constant reminder of his mortality; Mature is very good in the role, though he did actually have bronchial pneumonia for part of the shoot. There's a moment in Doc's haunted past he can't return to – a time when he was happy, a part of him that is now dead. When Thorndyke recites the 'To be or not to be' speech from *Hamlet* in a dingy bar ('Look Yorick, can't you give us nothin' but them poems?' complain the Clantons), Doc is able to step in when the thespian forgets his lines, 'Thus conscience,' remembers Doc, 'does make cowards of us all.' Later, tired of living, Doc decides, 'It's time I tempted fate.'

Clementine is one of Ford's best films and many fans favour it over all his other westerns. Unlike Ford's *Stagecoach* or *The Searchers* there is no journey element driving the story, but the leisurely plot is still involving. Ford explores two very different love stories: Wyatt and Clem, and Doc and Chihuahua. Tongue-tied Wyatt admires Clementine from afar. At one point he watches her talking to Doc – obviously she's still in love with the surgeon – and muses to Irish bartender Mac, 'You ever been in love?' 'No,' comes the answer, 'I've been a bartender all my life.' Wyatt emerges from the 'Bon Ton Tonsorial Parlor' with a slick new hairstyle and a whiff of perfume, and stands beside Clementine outside the Mansion House one bright Sunday morning. 'The air's so clean and clear,' says Clem, taking a deep breath, 'The scent of the desert flower.' 'That's me,' admits Wyatt, sheepishly – 'Barber.' This prudish romance is in contrast to Doc and Chihuahua's tempestuous relationship in the town bars, where she performs songs and he drinks his lunch and gambles away his life.

The unhurried middle section of the film also allows Ford to paint a moving picture of life in a growing western town, with diversions to the theatre (for a performance of 'The Convict's Oath'), to busy saloons and to a church dance – the foundations of civilisation have been laid. Ford's realistic settings and costumes give the film a documentary feel, as the prairie schooners roll by and Tombstone becomes more refined. Joseph Patrick MacDonald's monochrome photography enhances this realism, with every gnarled fence post, warped, grainy floorboard and dimly lit corner infused with the privation and toughness of frontier life in an inhospitable land.

Wyatt only becomes marshal to revenge his brother (it was in fact Virgil who took the marshal's job) and although the film begins with James's murder, the revenge element is shunted aside for almost an hour of the film. James's silver 'cingadera' cross icon is stolen during his murder and later reappears around Chihuahua's neck. She lies that she was given it as a present by Doc, but under questioning reveals it was Billy Clanton who gave it to her, implicating the clan. The Clantons are demonic villains, particularly Old Man, the patriarch, a snarling, whip-wielding maniac, who tells his sons, 'When you pull a gun, kill a man' (he resembles bullwhacker Red Flack in *The Big Trail*). When the two groups collide, Ford's gunfight at the O.K. Corral sees Morgan, Doc and Wyatt, plus two Tombstone allies (Jess and the Deacon), versus Old Man Clanton and his three sons: Ike, Phin and Sam (Billy having been killed). In actuality, N.H. 'Old Man' Clanton was dead by the time of the gunfight (murdered by Mexican *vaqueros*) and Ike was the head of the Clanton-McLaury clan, none of whom were named Sam. The historical participants were Morgan, Doc, Virgil and Wyatt facing Ike and Billy Clanton, Tom and Frank McLaury, and Billy Claiborne. All three Earps, Doc, Ike and Claiborne survived; Tom, Frank and Billy Clanton didn't. Ford butchers the entire Clanton family and kills off Doc for dramatic effect – his completely fictitious scenario rewrote history, via Stuart Lake and Wyatt Earp.

During the making of *Clementine*, Ford had pruned Fonda and Mature's dialogue and cut some scenes (for example, a fight between Chihuahua and Clementine). Producer Samuel Engel worked on the script on location and gained a co-writer's credit. Ford prepared a preview version, screened in June 1946, but Zanuck called it 'a disappointment'; the producer wanted to take out 30 minutes and re-shoot, dub and score other scenes. This he did in July, with no further involvement from Ford. Many re-shoots, including the scene where Wyatt visits his brother's grave, were directed by Lloyd Bacon. Zanuck's deletions include Chihuahua kissing Billy outside the saloon and Wyatt complaining to Doc that champagne tastes like 'fermented vinegar'. The night-time conversation between Doc and Clementine in the street was re-shot; the arrival of the settlers for the church dedication was abridged (with the folksong 'Oh Susanna' removed); and wounded Chihuahua's operation scene was originally longer.

The aftermath of the final gunfight was also considerably cut. In Ford's version, Morgan and Wyatt look down at Doc's corpse and Wyatt says, 'I'll get his boots' (Fonda still mouths this line in the cut version), then Jess and the Deacon appear and look down at the body. Also cut is a scene where Wyatt and Morgan are given some provisions by the locals outside the Mansion House ('Here's some specialities for you, Mr Marshal') and say their farewells ('Well goodbye folks. Me and my brothers, we're obliged to you'). The biggest change was the new ending, replacing Clementine and Wyatt's handshake with a kiss on the cheek. Zanuck liked the original ending, but 2,000 people at the preview didn't, feeling 'cheated'. So the kiss was filmed in October and inserted into the footage. Zanuck also tampered with the music, re-scoring some scenes and adding cues to others, to showcase the popular standard, 'My Darling Clementine', though the lyric has nothing to do with Wyatt Earp, but rather a 'miner, forty-niner and his daughter, Clementine'. *Clementine* was the last film Ford would make for Fox, a company he had been on contract with since 1921. What is left of his original preview version has now been made available on DVD from the UCLA Archive and runs six minutes longer than Zanuck's inferior, official 93-minute release.

Posters proclaimed 'Darryl F. Zanuck Presents John Ford's *My Darling Clementine*', a film that was; 'The Roaring West At Its Restless Best!' Another tagline said: 'She was Everything the West Was – Young, Fiery, Exciting!' – a more apt description of Chihuahua than Clementine. One poster depicted a large, framed painting of Chihuahua, inferring she was the 'Clementine' of the title, and Darnell appears in more of the publicity artwork than Downs. The trailer announced that 'The director of the unforgettable *Stagecoach* now thrills the world with his newest triumph – here's mighty excitement that combines the exciting action of reckless pioneer days (with) the romantic conflicts of men and women who lead perilous lives'. It was premiered in San Francisco on 16 October 1946. Critic Bosley Crowther wrote, 'Fonda, through his quiet, yet persuasive self-confidence – his delicious intonation of short words – shows us an elemental character who is as real as the dirt on which he walks'. *Lux Radio Theatre* aired an adaptation in 1947, with Fonda in the lead and the film took $2.8 million in the US on its initial release. In the UK, it received an 'A' rating. It was called *Sfida Infernale* ('Infernal Challenge') in Italy, *La Poursuite Infernale* ('The Infernal Chase') in France and *Tombstone*, a title later used for George Cosmatos's 1993 Wyatt Earp biography, in Germany.

The other big western of 1946 was *Duel in the Sun*, but the contrast with Ford's film couldn't be greater. *Duel* was driven by producer David Oliver Selznick, the man behind *Gone With the Wind* (1939), and starred his wife, Jennifer Jones, as wildcat Pearl Chavez. Pearl is sent to live with her cousin Laura Belle (Lillian Gish), who is married to Senator McCanles (Lionel Barrymore), the head of the Spanish Bit ranch. Their two sons, tough Lewt (Gregory Peck) and lawyer Jesse (Joseph Cotton), compete for Pearl's affections under the hot Arizona sun. *Duel* cost $5.25 million (including $2 million in advertising), with a railway track and the 'Spanish Bit' being built on location near Tucson. The opening scene for the debauched revelry in the vast Presidio Palace of Chance Saloon, deploys more extras than the whole of *Clementine*. *Duel* is an overblown, hysterical western, picturesque in Technicolor, but also tasteless,

Italian poster for John Ford's *My Darling Clementine* (1946), depicting Doc (Victor Mature), Chihuahua (Linda Darnell) and Wyatt (Henry Fonda). (Photograph courtesy of Ian Caunce collection.)

self-regarding and tedious. Audiences christened it, 'Lust in the Dust' due to Jones's sultry performance (Lewt describes Pearl as 'a hot tamale') and for characters like 'The Sin Killer' (a hellfire and brimstone turn by Walter Huston), who exorcises Pearl's lusty urges – or so he thinks. Following previews the censors intervened, abridging or removing 40 scenes at a cost of $200,000, while *Tidings*, the L.A. Catholic journal warned: 'It tends to throw audiences on the side of sin'. Audiences didn't mind. Accounting for inflation, *Duel in the Sun* is the most financially successful western of all time.

Ford followed *My Darling Clementine* with the Technicolor *3 Godfathers* (1946). Desperados Bob (John Wayne), Pedro (Pedro Armendariz Jnr) and the Abilene Kid (Harry Carey Jnr) rob the bank in Welcome, Arizona, and escape into the desert where they discover an expectant mother. She gives birth to a boy and before dying makes the trio promise to look after the child. Taking advice from the Bible, they follow a guiding star. Both the Kid and Pedro die of thirst, before Bob and the baby reach New Jerusalem and safety. Ford's *Wagonmaster* (1950), one of his favourite films, shared some of *Clementine*'s atmosphere and its black and white location photography, this time in Moab, Utah. It detailed a wagon train's conflict with the Clegg clan, who resembled the Clantons. In Ford's *Cheyenne Autumn* (1964), James Stewart played Wyatt Earp and Arthur Kennedy was Doc Holliday in the Dodge City sequence, reputedly based on fact, where news of Cheyenne warriors nearby causes panic in town (though some prints omit the scenes). It was intended by Ford as a comedy interlude, to lighten the mood and stop audiences drifting off to the toilet. As Ford said to Stewart, 'You're a hell of an intermission.'

My Darling Clementine is as factually inaccurate as *Frontier Marshal*, *Gunfight at the O.K. Corral* and other renderings of the Earp legend. It seems that Ford, for his artistic talent and expert drama, is excused such licence in the name of poeticism. If it's not how it actually happened, it's how it should have. In the 1971 CBS documentary *The American West of John Ford*, Stewart says of Ford, with reference to *The Man Who Shot Liberty Valance*, 'He prints the legend...and that's a fact.' Ford certainly did in *My Darling Clementine*.

3

'Your Heart's Soft ... Too Soft'

— *Red River* (1948)

Red River (1948)
Credits
DIRECTOR – Howard Hawks
PRODUCER – Howard Hawks
STORY – Borden Chase
SCREENPLAY – Borden Chase and Charles Schnee
DIRECTOR OF PHOTOGRAPHY – Russell Harlen
EDITOR – Christian Nyby
ART DIRECTOR – John Datu Arensma
MUSIC – Dimitri Tiomkin
A Monterey Production
Released by United Artists
133 minutes
Cast

John Wayne (Tom Dunson); Montgomery Clift (Matthew
Garth); Joanne Dru (Tess Millay); Walter Brennan (Nadine
Groot); Coleen Gray (Fen, Tom's girl); John Ireland (Cherry
Valance); Noah Beery Jr (Buster McGee); Harry Carey Snr
(Mr Millville); Harry Carey Jnr (Dan Latimer); Paul Fix
(Teeler Yacey); Mickey Kuhn (Young Matthew); Chief
Yowlachie ('Two Jaw' Quo); Hank Worden (Sims Reeves);
Ivan Parry (Bunk Kanaly); Hal Taliaferro (Old Leather); Paul
Fiero (Fernandez); William 'Billy' Self (Sutter, lynch mob
escapee); Tom Tyler (Drover); Glenn Strange (Maylor,
drover); Dan White (Laredo, drover); Ray Hyke
(Walt Jergens, drover); Lane Chandler (Mr Meeker,
rancher); Shelley Winters (Girl dancing with Walt);
Lee Phelps and George Lloyd (Top-hatted gamblers)

*   *   *

In August 1851 cowboys Tom Dunson and Nadine Groot are heading towards California with a wagon train out of St Louis. On the north border of Texas, in Indian country, they strike out on their own, with Dunson leaving his fiancée Fen behind. Soon afterwards the wagon train is wiped out by Indians and a lone survivor, a boy named Matthew Garth, joins Dunson and Groot. They cross the Red River into Texas where they set up a cattle ranch, 'The Red River D'. Within ten years the ranch is thriving, but the Civil War destroys the beef trade. Matthew returns from the war in 1865 and Dunson decides to drive 9,000 head of cattle to market in Sedalia, Missouri – 1,000 miles away. The trek is tough, with the drive fording swollen rivers, swallowing clouds of dust, surviving stampedes, Indians and torrential rain. The further they travel, the more tyrannical Dunson becomes, until finally he turns the drovers against him. Matthew mutinies and diverts the drive to the nearer Abilene, leaving Dunson behind. The drive saves a wagon train of gamblers, en route to Nevada, from an Indian attack and Matthew falls in love with card player Tess Millay. Eventually the herd pushes on to Abilene, arriving 14 August 1865. But Dunson, now with hired gunmen and Tess in tow, arrives in town to settle the score.

Red River was based on a five-part serial by Borden Chase called 'The Chisholm Trail' (sometimes quoted as 'The Blazing Guns on the Chisolm Trail'), named after the famous route from Texas, across the Red River, through the Indian Nations, to Kansas. The trail Dunson initially follows to Missouri – terminating at the railheads at Kansas City, Sedalia and St Louis – was actually the Shawnee Trail, which was closed during the Civil War. The other main cattle route, opened in 1866, was the Goodnight-Loving Trail (named after its founders), which leads to Colorado and Wyoming. The Chisholm Trail was by far the most travelled; it linked Texas to the cow towns of Dodge City, Ellsworth and Abilene. To aid navigation, drover guide maps were produced; for instance by 1875 the Kansas Pacific Railroad Company produced free charts for the 'Great Texas Cattle Trail – from Red River Crossing to the Old Reliable Kansas Pacific'.

Hawks bought the rights to 'The Chisholm Trail' story, which had been serialised in the *Saturday Evening Post*, for his own Monterey Productions. This was Hawks's first western, though he had worked unsuccessfully in the genre twice before: he was fired from directing *Viva Villa!* (1934 – Jack Conway completed it) and directed *The Outlaw* in 1940, until disagreements with producer Howard Hughes removed him. Hughes directed the rest of the film, completing it in 1941, but there were censorship problems for Hughes's RKO, mainly due to Jane Russell's specially designed cantilever brassiere.

For *Red River*, Hawks wanted Gary Cooper to play Dunson, but the actor turned him down. Instead he approached John Wayne, now a big star, though none of Wayne's roles at Republic, Paramount, Universal or RKO had equalled his success as Ringo. Wayne accepted for $150,000 and was aged for Dunson, with his dark, swept-back hair streaked with white. Montgomery Clift was appearing in *You Touched Me* on Broadway – he obviously touched Hawks, who cast Clift in his film debut, as

John Wayne, then only 39 years old, was aged prematurely to play Tom Dunson, the driven cattleman driving cattle to Sedalia in Howard Hawks' *Red River* (1948).

Matthew Garth; Clift couldn't ride a horse and had to take lessons. Clift received $60,000 for the role, which launched his career and led to classic performances in *A Place in the Sun* (1951) and *From Here to Eternity* (1953). Joanne Dru (real name Joanne LaCock) was cast after original choice Margaret Sheridan became pregnant. As cardsharp Tess, Dru gives one of her most assured performances, particularly in her love scenes with Clift. Hank Worden, as wrangler Sims Reeves, went on to appear in *Angel and the Badman* (1947) with Wayne, as well as 13 other films with the star. Walter Brennan, an ex-stuntman who as an actor had won three Academy Awards, appeared as irascible cook, Nadine Groot. Brennan was a friend of Hawks and his initial three day's work was expanded to six weeks, with Groot promoted to a major character. After Cary Grant turned it down, John Ireland was cast as pistolero Cherry Valance. You'd have to be tough growing up out west with a name like Cherry, and Valance, along with Dunson and Matthew, is one of the west's fastest guns.

John Ford's 'Cheyenne Harry', actor Harry Carey Snr, played Abilene stockman, Melville; his son Harry Carey Jnr appeared as singing wrangler Dan, who is trampled to death in a stampede. Dunson's wranglers included some familiar western faces: Tom Tyler was from *Stagecoach*, while Noah Beery Jnr was a B-western sidekick. Hal Taliaferro, as the Buffalo Bill lookalike Old Leather, was actually series western star Wally Wales. Chief Yowlachie, as driver Quo, was born on the Yakima Indian reservation and had a career as a classical singer before appearing in several westerns, including *Yellow Sky* (1948) and the musical comedy *A Ticket to Tomahawk* (1950).

Red River was filmed in two months during 1946, with an initial budget of $1.5 million. Hawks said in interviews that he used John Ford's style as a template – the film certainly shares Ford's lyrical photographic style, with sunlight, mountains, clouds and dust deployed to artistic effect. This is particularly evident in Hawk's filming of Dunson and Groot's Conestoga wagon, and the snaking, rumbling cattle herd beneath an immense, dominant sky. Elgin, Arizona was used as a production base, with locations including the Whetstone Mountains, Apache Peak and an 1860s ranch house for Dunson's 'Red River D' spread. The river crossing scenes were lensed on the San Pedro river, in the Rain Valley, which had to be dammed to raise the water level. Rainstorms arrived and gave Wayne and Dru colds. Production was further suspended when Hawks was hospitalised by a centipede bite.

All the night-time camp scenes were shot on a soundstage, which cost $20,000, with sand, rocks and vegetation brought from the Arizona location; there was even a portion of the Red River included, for the Indian attack on Dunson and Groot. This interior at least dispensed with the sound problems experienced on location, with thousands of locusts and the clomping cattle hooves audible on the soundtrack. 9,000 cattle were employed on the shoot, along with 70 trained riders. A stampede was filmed on location by 15 cameras in ten days and even with such precautions as two-way radios, seven of the 35 professional wranglers were injured. The authentic stampede footage was intercut with studio shots of the stars 'riding' in front of a process screen. The final cost was way over budget, at $3 million.

Red River's score was composed by Dimitri Tiomkin. It includes the ballad 'Settle Down', soothing the 'little dogies' on the drive (dogies are actually orphaned calves, though the phrase was adapted to mean any stock), and the stirring cattle drive march that propels the herd off to Missouri, deployed throughout the film in stomping instrumental cues.

Hawks accurately depicts life on the trail. Beside the herd roll the chuck wagons and the remuda, the pool of horses used by the cowboys on the drive. The trail boss rode up front. To the left and right of the cattle head rode drovers on 'point'. Further back rode the 'swing', then the 'flank', with the 'drag' riders swallowing dust in the rearguard. Drives averaged ten miles a day, which Hawks authentically incorporated into his scenario. It took approximately 100 days for the drive to travel the 1,000 miles to Abilene.

Hawks also portrays the associated hardships and dangers of a cattle drive. On a moonlit night, Bunk, a sweet-toothed cowboy topples pots and pans as he steals some sugar from the chuck wagon, the clatter spooking the already jumpy cattle into a thunderous stampeding tide. Later the drive save a wagon party from an Indian attack and hear of bushwhacking border jumpers – one night they encounter a whispering, half-lynched fugitive who recounts the tale of his trail boss being nailed to a wagon wheel by border raiders. Following the mutiny, these hazards are multiplied, with Dunson doggedly following them, forcing the pace. The herd's final arrival at Abilene is a cause for celebration: as the drive approaches they hear the whistle of a train – to the relief of Matt, who isn't even sure if there is a railhead in town. In *High Noon*, the whistle heralds the arrival of a killer, in *Red River* it's the answer to a prayer.

Like Hawks's subsequent westerns, the central dynamic of *Red River* is between three generations of men: a youngster with a lot to learn, a seasoned westerner still in his prime and a crazy old coot whose advice is often ignored. Tom Dunson has sacrificed everything he has ever had to build the herd and is willing to risk everything he has now to keep it. He leaves his fiancée Fen behind with the wagon train, and the seven graves at the Red River ranch symbolise the occasions when Dunson has had to protect his land. He is a driven man, who despises deserters ('They'll be no quitting along the way'), but this single-mindedness alienates his crew.

One of the strongest relationships in the film is between the two young guns, Matthew and Cherry Valance, a gunman of ill repute out of Valverde. When we first meet Valance he resembles a slow-talking villain. Asked his name, Valance answers, 'Some call me one thing, some another.' 'What do they call you most?' asks Dunson. 'By my name…Cherry Valance.' His relationship with Matthew is all flash and bravado. In typical western fashion, Valance recognises Matthew from his marks-manship ('Now I'll know who you'd be'), but their conversations are also loaded with cowboy innuendo. Valance examines Matthew's Colt and notes there are only two things more beautiful than a good gun, 'A Swiss watch or a woman from anywhere…you ever had a good Swiss watch?'

The characters of Nadine Groot and Sims Reeves offer two western archetypes, which actors Walter Brennan and Hank Worden would re-enact in many later westerns. Cook Groot has a bad leg, false teeth and a grubby beard, and his endless chirpy jabber plays well against Wayne and Clift. Groot loses a half share of his 'store teeth' in a game of poker to Quo, their Indian wagon driver (beautifully underplayed by Chief Yowlachie). Groot pleads that he needs them for eating. 'Come grub, you get 'em,' answers the stony-faced Indian, now renamed 'Two Jaw' Quo. Groot is sometimes too talkative for his own good and should heed Quo's advice, 'Keep face closed.' Worden's pessimistic worrier reappeared in countless westerns. In *Red River* he is initially wary that the drive is going too well; he doesn't like things to go 'good' or 'bad', 'I like 'em in-between.' Later he comments on Dunson's habit of saying prayers over mutinous drovers he has killed, 'Plantin' and readin'...why when you've killed a man, why try to read the Lord in as a partner on the job?'

It takes Matthew and Groot to take a stand against tyrannical Dunson, to curb the cattle boss's obsessive determination. Dunson says at one point of Matthew's 'betrayal', 'Thought I had a son...I haven't.' In his tyranny, Dunson has stretched the drovers' endurance, forcing some to quit and others to try to outgun Dunson. When the mutineers leave Dunson behind, he tells Matthew, 'Every time you turn around, expect to see me, 'cos one time you'll turn around and I'll be there – I'm gonna kill you Matt.' Valance has observed of Matthew, 'Your heart's soft...too soft.' When the confrontation finally comes in Abilene, Dunson wounds Valance then faces Matthew. He goads the youngster, shooting at Matthew's feet, his hat and grazing his cheek, then punching him before Matt finally snaps and lays into Dunson. Groot roots for Matt, but it is Tess who is the arbiter, breaking up the fight and forcing a reconciliation between the two men. The 'Red River D' brand will be altered, now to include an 'M'. As Dunson notes, 'You've earned it,' a typical and recurrent Hawksian acknowledgement of achievement.

In post-production, Hawks ran into problems telling his story and John Ford helped Hawks hone the film. It was Ford's idea to have Walter Brennan (in character as Groot) narrate the action. This version of *Red River* runs 125 minutes. Hawks's preferred version, which is narrated by Groot's hand-written journal pages (his 'Early Tales from Texas') is 133 minutes. Though passed for copyright in 1947, the latter version was finally released in September 1948 (the 125-minute version sometimes appears on TV, touted as the 'director's cut'). Brennan's narration can also be heard in the hour-long radio version of *Red River*, for *Lux Radio Theatre*, sponsored by Lux Toilet Soap. It starred Brennan, Wayne and Dru, with Jeff Chandler as Matthew and differs slightly from the film (for example, Dunson adds a 'G', as in 'Garth', not an 'M', to the 'Red River D' brand). After the show Wayne shamelessly plugs forthcoming projects and Dru confesses that she's been 'a Lux soap fan for a long time'.

Hawks's biggest problem when releasing *Red River* was Howard Hughes, who claimed that *Red River*'s finale copied a duel scene in *The Outlaw*, when Doc Holliday shoots nicks out of Billy the Kid's ear. Wayne, a friend of Hughes's, eventually convinced the producer not to sue. Released through United Artists, *Red River* made $4.5 million on its first release and ended up taking $10 million worldwide. Poster portraits of Wayne dodging a flaming arrow had the taglines: 'The Greatest Spectacle Ever!...In 25 Years, Only Three! *The Covered Wagon, Cimarron* and now *Red River*'. In Spain it was *Rio Rojo*, in Italy *Fiume Rosso*. In the UK it was rated 'U', following minor cuts. *Time* noted of Hawks that, 'when a picture really interests him, he gives it enough character to blast you out of your seat. *Red River* clearly interested him a lot.' The *New York Sun* called it 'a big, smashing western with good, tough direction, good tough acting'. At the Oscars, Chase was nominated for his story and Christian Nyby for his editing, but neither won. *Red River* has since been screened on TV in a colourised version that looks great in Technicolor, much better than other 'tinted' prints.

The success of *Red River* at the US box office pushed Wayne into the top ten list of stars, as compiled by the *Motion Picture Herald*. His growing popularity encouraged the star to take control of his screen image. He acted as producer on *Angel and the Badman* (1947 – for Republic), also starring as Quirt Evans, an outlaw who is pacified by Quaker Gail Russell, and reportedly co-directing with screenwriter James Edward Grant, who later became a regular Wayne collaborator, on *Hondo* (1953), *The Alamo* and *The Comancheros*.

Since *Red River*, cattle drives have featured in several westerns, or as part of TV miniseries like James A. Michener's 20-hour, 12-episode *Centennial* (1978) and the highly rated four-episode adaptation of Larry McMurtry's Pulitzer winner, *Lonesome Dove* (1988 – followed by the lesser-known, horse-herding *Return to Lonesome Dove* in 1993). *Cattle Drive* (1951) and *Cattle Empire* (1958) both starred Joel McCrea as the trail boss, while lawman Rock Hudson and outlaw Kirk Douglas sparred as they rode with a drive travelling towards *The Last Sunset* (1961). Others include the massively successful Clark Gable vehicle *The Tall Men* (1955 – which took $5 million) and *Cowboy* (1958), with Jack Lemmon as a greenhorn Chicago hotel clerk and Glenn Ford as his trail boss. In Albert Band's Italian production *The Tramplers* (1966), Gordon Scott and Franco Nero drive a herd of stock footage cattle to Abilene. Utilising film lensed on the Argentine pampas, Band splices it with his Italian-shot footage, where the steers are different colours. *Will Penny* (1968) was the tale of migrant, wintering cowboys, with Charlton Heston as Penny, an inarticulate, illiterate cowhand, 'too soon old and too late smart'. The similarly realistic *The Culpepper Cattle Company* (1972) included a cowboy uttering the classic line, in reference to his horse, 'Son, you don't give a name to something you may have to eat.' In John Wayne's unusual *The Cowboys* (1971), he hires a crew of young trail hands (literally cowboys aged between nine and 15) and ends up being shot dead by an easy riding counterculture gunman called Long Hair (Bruce Dern). In 1988, *Red River* was remade for TV, with James Arness, Bruce Boxleitner and Ray Walston as Dunson, Matt and Groot.

Perhaps the most famous cattle drive was the one from San Antonio to Sedalia, on TV every week for 217 weeks, in *Rawhide* (1959–1966). Created by Charles Marquis Warren (the director of *Cattle Empire*) and produced by CBS, it starred Eric Fleming as trail boss Gil Favor, Clint Eastwood as ramrod Rowdy Yates and Paul Brinegar as Wishbone the cook – roughly the equivalents of Wayne, Clift and Brennan. Brinegar had played the cook in *Cattle Empire*. Opening with its famous theme song by Frankie Laine ('Rollin', rollin', rollin', keep them dogies rollin''), its plots were often repetitive. One critic noted the cows either went from left to right, or right to left. But some of the episode 'Incidents' were excellent TV drama: 'Incident of the Day of the Dead', '…of the Running Man', '…of the Reluctant Bridegroom' and

'... of the Prophesy' benefited from guest stars like Dan Duryea, Robert Wilke and Warren Oates. Other guests to appear included: James Coburn, Charles Bronson, Peter Lorre, Troy Donahue, Vera Miles, Mickey Rooney, Frankie Avalon, Lee Van Cleef, Burgess Meredith, Mercedes McCambridge, Woody Strode and Cesar Romero. In the final season, when Fleming left the series, *Red River*'s John Ireland appeared as deputy trail boss, Jed Colby.

In *The Western: From Silents to Cinerama*, later reprinted as *From Silents to the Seventies*, the authors note that 'a small number of ambitious productions, such as *Red River*, *The Big Sky* and *Rio Bravo*, widely hailed as successors to *Stagecoach*, have subsequently been all but forgotten'. But Hawks is now among the most revered western directors. In 1975, Wayne presented Hawks with an honorary Oscar for his lifetime's work. In 1988, British Film Institute members voted *Red River* the fifth best western of all time – after *High Noon*, *The Searchers*, *Stagecoach* and *Shane* – and the film is routinely referred to now as an American classic. Hawks once said, 'A good movie is three good scenes and no bad scenes'; *Red River* has so much more than that.

4

'Tomorrow's All I Need'

— *She Wore a Yellow Ribbon* (1949)

She Wore a Yellow Ribbon (1949)
Credits
DIRECTOR – John Ford
PRODUCERS – John Ford and Merian C. Cooper
STORY – James Warner Bellah
SCREENPLAY – Frank S. Nugent and Laurence Stallings
DIRECTOR OF PHOTOGRAPHY – Winton C. Hoch
EDITOR – Jack Murray
ART DIRECTOR – James Basevi
MUSIC – Richard Hageman
Technicolor
An Argosy Pictures Production
Released by RKO Radio Pictures
103 minutes
Cast
    John Wayne (Captain Nathan Cutting Brittles); Joanne
Dru (Olivia Dandridge); John Agar (Lieutenant Flintridge
'Flint' Cohill); Ben Johnson (Sergeant Travis Tyree);
Harry Carey Jnr (Lieutenant Ross Parnell); Victor McLaglen
(Sergeant Timothy 'Timmy' Quincannon); Mildred Natwick
(Abby Allshard); George O'Brien (Major Mac Allshard,
commander of Fort Starke); Arthur Shields (Dr O'Laughlin);
Michael Dugan (Sergeant Hochbauer); Chief John Big
Tree (Chief Pony That Walks); Fred Graham (Sergeant
Hench); Chief Sky Eagle (Chief Sky Eagle); Tom Tyler
(Corporal Quayne); Nobel Johnson (War Chief Red Shirt);
Rudy Bowman (Trooper Smith); Francis Ford (Carty,
sutler's bartender); Fred Libby (Corporal Krumrein);
Cliff Lyons (Trooper Cliff); Mickey Simpson (Corporal

Wagner, the blacksmith); Harry Woods (Karl Rynders, the sutler)

* * *

In 1947, John Ford formed his own production company, Argosy Pictures, with Merian C. Cooper, the co-director and producer of *King Kong* (1933). They made several films together, including Ford's 'Cavalry Trilogy'. These films detailed the US 7th Cavalry ('pony soldiers' as the Indian tribes called them), made famous by General George Armstrong Custer. They depicted domestic life at *Fort Apache* (1948), Indian warfare on the plains in *She Wore a Yellow Ribbon* (1949) and a love story spanning the *Rio Grande* (1950).

Fort Apache, an Argosy production co-financed by and released through RKO Pictures, was set in the title stockade, an actual Arizona US Cavalry outpost policing disruptive Apaches, near the San Carlos Indian Agency. The arrival of martinet Lieutenant Colonel Owen Thursday (Henry Fonda) and his daughter Philadelphia (Shirley Temple) causes friction. Thursday's strict manner enrages his fellow officers,

Thursday's Last Stand: John Ford's 7th Cavalry up against the odds, but heading for glory, in *Fort Apache* (1948), shot in 'Ford Country', Rock Door Canyon in Monument Valley. Lieutenant Colonel Thursday (Henry Fonda) stands at far left.

especially Captain Kirby York (John Wayne), an Apache war veteran, and his interference in Philadelphia's love life alienates his own daughter. Thursday sees the posting as a demotion, but also as an opportunity to make the headlines as 'The man who brought Cochise back'. His inexperience and impetuousness in combating Indians leads to the massacre of his entire command, which is surrounded when Thursday foolhardily charges into a canyon swarming with Apaches. York covers up Thursday's blunder and the colonel's legend inspires the heroic painting 'Thursday's Charge'. 'Correct in every detail,' lies York, now the commander of Fort Apache.

With location scenes shot in Monument Valley, at Goosenecks on the San Juan River and at the fort at Corriganville in the Simi Valley, *Fort Apache*'s exteriors look splendid. Corriganville, the ranch site of western star Ray 'Crash' Corrigan was hired out by the actor to movie studios as a set. But the domestic scenes, shot mainly in RKO interiors, slow the film down. *Fort Apache* is saved by its action sequences: the pursuit of Diablo and his 30 warriors (who jump the reservation and join Cochise's band across the Mexican border) and the final confrontation with Cochise's force, outnumbering the cavalry four-to-one and armed with repeating rifles. Although in the wrong theatre of war (the Apache Wars rather than the Great Plains), Thursday's Last Stand closely resembles Custer's Battle of the Little Big Horn, with glory-seeking Custer a model for Thursday and cautious Major Benteen, assigned responsibility for the supply train, for York. The film was retitled *Le Massacre de Fort Apache* in France.

Fonda is excellent as the meddling, bitter Thursday, a rigid stickler for smartness and protocol. 'He must have been a great man,' a journalist says of Thursday. 'No man died more gallantly,' York replies. Temple's love interest, Lieutenant Mickey O'Rourke, was played by John Agar (Temple's real-life husband), while Wayne was cast after Ford had seen his performance in *Red River*, commenting 'I never knew the big son-of-a-bitch could act!' The supporting cast included Ward Bond (as Mickey's father, Michael) and rumbustious Victor McLaglen as big, tough Irish bruiser, Sergeant Festus Mulcahy, much given to brawling and drinking. When asked to destroy an Indian Agent's supply of whisky, he and his three cohorts drink it, landing themselves in the guardhouse. Despite mediocre reviews, *Fort Apache* (retitled *War Party* for some markets) was a great success, landing $445,000 in profit (it cost $2.1 million). The trailer called it 'A Masterpiece of the Indian Frontier, Brought Excitingly to Life'. To tie in with the film, Ford directed 30-minute radio versions of *Fort Apache* and *Stagecoach* (both with Wayne), for NBC's *Screen Director's Playhouse*.

Fort Apache was based on 'Massacre' (1947), a *Saturday Evening Post* story by James Warner Bellah who, following a stint in the Far East during the Second World War, wrote a series of cavalry stories set in Fort Starke. Ford again turned to Bellah's works, 'Command' (1946), 'Big Hunt' (1947) and 'War Party' (1948), for *She Wore a Yellow Ribbon*, named after the popular folk standard, which had already been used as an instrumental in *Fort Apache*. The practice of wearing a yellow ribbon is a signal that a woman is romancing someone in the troop, rather like the tradition of a knight courting a lady's favour.

Frank S. Nugent, who had worked on Ford's *3 Godfathers* (1948) and *Fort Apache*, adapted the screenplay with Laurence Stallings. Following the Battle of the Little Big Horn, 1876, widower Nathan Brittles, a captain at Fort Starke, has six days until his retirement on 10 July. The Indians are painted for war, with Cheyenne, Arapaho, Comanche and Kiowa uniting into a formidable army, 10,000 strong, under war chief Red Shirt. On his last routine patrol, Brittles is assigned to escort the fort commander's wife Abby Allshard and niece Olivia Dandridge to Sutros Wells to catch the stagecoach east. The escort finds the Paradise River patrol badly shot up and heads for Sutros Wells, but when they arrive they find the station and the stage burned out. Fighting a rearguard action against a mounting number of hostiles, now armed with repeating rifles sold by Fort Starke's villainous sutler Rynders, Brittles leaves a group of troopers under young Lieutenant Cohill (Olivia's beau) to protect their escape at Paradise River. Brittles effects a retreat and Cohill's party are later safely relieved. With literally hours left as an officer, and disappointed that his last mission was a failure, Brittles leads a foray against the united tribes. He talks peace with their elderly spokesman, Chief Pony That Walks, but is really using the powwow to locate the camp's horse herd. In a moonlit attack, the cavalry run off the herd. Without steeds, the tribes make their way peaceably back to the reservation and the Indian War is averted. Brittles retires with honour – for his bravery he is promoted to Lieutenant Colonel, chief-of-scouts – while Cohill, also promoted, will soon marry Olivia.

Wayne was again used by Ford in *Yellow Ribbon*, this time playing a man beyond his years; Brittles is about to retire, while Wayne was only 42 when he was cast. Joanne Dru and Harry Carey Jnr (known as 'Dobe') were also cast after Ford had seen them in *Red River*. At the time, Dru was married to actor John Ireland, while Carey Jnr was soon to be a regular Ford cast member, appearing in *Wagonmaster* (1950 – again with Dru), *Rio Grande*, *The Searchers* (1956) and *Cheyenne Autumn* (1964).

Ford filled other roles with familiar faces, building his 'Stock Company' – a family group who referred to Ford as 'Pappy'. John Agar (from *Fort Apache*) was again cast, here as Lieutenant Cohill. Ford's brother Francis had a cameo as a bartender, as he did in many of his brother's films (he died in 1953), while Ford's other brother Edward O'Fearna and brother-in-law Wingate Smith were the assistant directors. Victor McLaglen was recast as a blustering Irish sergeant, Quincannon (called Utterback in Bellah's 'Command'). McLaglen had an amazing life: born in Tunbridge Wells, England he was a boxer, a soldier in the Boer War and a captain in the Great War, before entering movies billed as the 'Beloved Brute'. Closely associated with Ford and Wayne, he won a Best Actor Oscar for Ford's *The Informer* (1935) and played Wayne's sparring partner Red Will Danaher in Ford's *The Quiet Man* (1952). He was the father of Andrew V. McLaglen, who directed several of Wayne's later movies. Tom Tyler (Luke Plummer from *Stagecoach*) was cast as wounded Corporal Quayne, the soldier who is operated on in the back of a bumpy wagon during a thunderstorm. Mildred Natwick, cast as Olivia's aunt, had played the expectant mother alone in the desert in *3 Godfathers*.

Former rodeo champion and stuntman Ben Johnson, who had worked on *Fort Apache* as Fonda's riding double and who played a posse member in *3 Godfathers*, was cast in *Yellow Ribbon* as the hard-riding point man, Sergeant Travis Tyree. Johnson's presence always guaranteed a couple of frenetic chase scenes. Wayne recalled that 'Ben liked to ride and Pappy liked to shoot him doing it.' In *Yellow Ribbon* Tyree pursues a driverless stagecoach which is owned by a US army paymaster and later is chased by Cheyenne horsemen, daringly leaping a ravine. Johnson also played scout Travis Blue, the charming lead, in *Wagonmaster* (1950), before a dispute with Ford during the making of *Rio Grande* left Johnson banished from Ford's stock company.

Budgeted at $1.6 million, *She Wore a Yellow Ribbon* was shot by Ford between November and December 1948 (Wayne had shot *3 Godfathers* in May and June, and *Wake of the Red Witch* from July to early November). For locations, Ford returned to Monument Valley. The Fort Starke frontage, a palisade and gateway, was erected in the valley beneath Ford's favourite location, the towering Mittens and Merrick Butte, with Castle Rock in the distance. Brittles's quarters were also built in the valley, protected beneath a sheer face of sandstone and still standing today. Much of the film's action was filmed in the valley itself. The misty graveyard, where Brittles visits the graves of his family (wife Mary and daughters, Elizabeth and Jane) was shot against a red sunset backdrop of Merrick Butte and the Mittens. Brittles's interior quarters and the sutler's store were recreated at Pathé Studios in Culver City. Following the shoot in December 1948, the valley was hit by terrible blizzards and Ford had food supplies airlifted into the area to sustain the Navajos.

After the black and white *Fort Apache*, Ford switched to Technicolor for *She Wore a Yellow Ribbon*, one of his most artistic films. Ford wanted two essentials from his cinematographer, Winton C. Hoch: a colour quality emulating Frederic Remington's frontier paintings, and a guarantee that one of the Indians would wear a red shirt. In the film, many of Chief Red Shirt's band wore red flannel shirts, vividly contrasting with the sandstone of Monument Valley. The valley looks splendid drenched in sunshine, yet ominous during a thunderstorm, where low clouds touch the tops of the buttes and lightning forks strobe the landscape. Remington was famous for his paintings, sketches and sculptures of cowboys, such as the paintings *The Cowboy* and the hell-for-leather *A Dash for Timber*. Charles Russell's work was also an influence on Ford. Russell often painted gunfighting scenes, for example the series of shootouts outside saloons (*Death of a Gambler*, *Smoke of a .45* and *When Guns Speak, Death Settles Disputes*), or scenes of cowboys at work (*Wild Horse Hunters* and *In Without Knocking*). Chronicling the US Cavalry, painter Charles Schreyvogel's work included *Attack at Dawn* (Custer's attack on Black Kettle's Cheyenne camp on the Washita River), *Guarding the Cañon Pass* (a panicky rearguard action), *Surprise Attack* (a trumpeter falls as an Indian dodges a cavalryman's sabre during a charge), *Defending the Stockade* (troopers try to repel an attack on a fort) and especially *On the Skirmish Line* – a beleaguered group of dismounted troopers are picked-off at distance. The three artists' work can be seen in Hoch's photography, the grand landscapes and the swirling, confused movement of battle.

Some aspects of Ford's depiction of the cavalry are overly sentimentalised and idealised, especially regarding the home life at frontier outposts, the roles of women in army routine and Ford's popular Irish rogues, epitomised by Sergeant Quincannon.

The quarters in Hollywood forts always look clean and are often furnished well, while their historical equivalents were sparser. The officers' wives and lovers seldom resembled Joanne Dru in *Yellow Ribbon*, immaculately riding side-saddle in her cavalry uniform, with tunic, forage cap and pure white gauntlets, in full make-up – even on the campaign trail. Always in Ford's cavalry westerns, there is an Irish character for whom the army is an extended family. Consistently played by Victor McLaglen as a tall, storytelling, brawling sergeant who likes a drink, these characters are charming, loveable rogues. About to take a snort of whisky when riding on patrol, Quincannon excuses himself to a young boy rescued from Sutros Wells, with, 'It's time for me to take me medicine,' then grimaces after a swig, 'It tastes horrible!'

Brittles is introduced as 'One man... fated to wield the sword of destiny'. He is hoping for an easy final patrol, but the onset of war plunges Brittles's routine into disarray. The classic scenes of Ford's 7th Cavalry riding through canyon country in column of two's towards Sutros Wells, are among the greatest scenes Ford put on film. But ultimately the mission does not succeed. They arrive at Sutros to find a huddle of troopers protecting Sutros' children, besieged by Cheyenne Dog Soldiers and Arapaho. Ma and Pa Sutros are dead. Surveying the scene, Brittles reflects, 'It's about time I did retire.' He looks at the burned-out stagecoach, 'Mission failure.

August 2006: Sightseers converge on the promontory now called 'Ford Point', where the great director often positioned his camera and ranged it across Monument Valley, as in his 7th Cavalry movies *Ford Apache* and *She Wore a Yellow Ribbon*. In the distance can be seen Merrick Butte, Big Chief and Castle Rock. (Photograph courtesy of Victoria Millington and Mark Chester.)

Well, we missed the stage, Miss Dandridge,' he addresses Olivia, who blames herself for the disaster.

Brittles uses experience and cunning, rather than tactics and force, to avert a full-scale Indian War. The cavalry's Indian opponents are based on the huge concentration of Sioux, Arapaho and Cheyenne who assembled in the summer of 1876 to crush Custer, though what tribes from the northern plains are doing in the deserts of Monument Valley is never explained. Crucially, Brittles doesn't fight, but talks peace with Pony That Walks. 'We are too old for war,' says the old chief. 'Yes … old men should stop wars,' replies Brittles. Against the clock, just prior to midnight on his last day in the army, Brittles charges his men into the Indian camp. The attack on the horse herd ends just after twelve; 'No casualties, no Indian war,' notes Brittles, in the nick of time, 'I've been a civilian for two minutes.'

There is more depth to Brittles than the usual Wayne westerner. He has moving conversations with his dead wife Elizabeth as he tends her grave, discussing what he is going to do with his retirement following his impending last mission. 'Hard to believe,' murmurs Brittles, uncomprehendingly, 'hard to believe.' Later, at his last inspection of the troop, he is presented with a solid silver watch and chain: 'To Captain Brittles from C Troop – Lest We Forget'. Brittles has to don his spectacles, which evidently embarrasses him, and he sniffs when he reads the inscription. These little details are accentuated by Ford, and Wayne's acting is highly effective – the spectacles were Wayne's idea. A lifelong soldier, Brittles knows nothing else and is not looking forward to his departure. There are moments where Wayne looks emotionally and physically drained, aptly conveying that gnawing, hollow feeling in the pit of Brittles's stomach, every time he hears the dreaded word 'retirement'. He says that as a captain he commanded men and respect, and was the focus of attention, 'Now tomorrow I'll be glad if a blacksmith asks me to shoe a horse.' But Ford provides the necessary happy ending, unlike *Fort Apache*, with Brittles appointed civilian chief-of-scouts.

If *She Wore a Yellow Ribbon* has a failing, it is the heavy emphasis on the love triangle between Olivia and her two suitors, lieutenants Flint Cohill and Ross Parnell. Much comedy is extracted from Parnell's wish to take Olivia picnicking in hostile Indian country, where the tribes are on the warpath and the medicine drums are talking. The constant bickering between the two officers on the trail does becomes tiresome, especially when contrasted with Brittles's quiet dignity and his moments of introspection.

The music is deployed to rousing effect by Richard Hageman, who had shared the Oscar for his folksong arrangements in *Stagecoach*. Ford once said that he'd 'rather hear good music than bad dialogue'. The ballad 'She Wore a Yellow Ribbon' was used as title music, sung by a lusty male chorus:

Round her neck she wore a yellow ribbon
She wore it in the winter and the merry month of May.
When I asked her why the yellow ribbon,
she said it's for my lover who is in the cavalry
Cavalry! Cavalry! She said it's for my lover in the US Cavalry.

By contrast, 'Garryowen', the fighting song of Custer's regiment (which was also deployed in Ford's 'Cavalry trilogy') was an Irish drinking ballad. Garryowen is the name of an Irish town:

> Let Bacchus' sons be not dismayed, but join with me each jovial blade
> Come booze and sing and lend your aid and help me with the chorus.
> Instead of Spa we'll drink down ale and pay the reckoning on the nail
> No man for Debt shall go to jail, from Garryowen in glory.

The former is in keeping with Ford's romantic subplots, the latter is redolent of Ford's view of the cavalry. Both compositions, as well as others used in the trilogy (including 'The Girl I left Behind Me'), reinforce the romance of the cavalry, but also its jingoistic pride, pounded home by Ford. As the final voiceover of *Yellow Ribbon* notes: 'But wherever they rode and whatever they fought for, that place became the United States.'

Posters called *Yellow Ribbon* 'John Ford's New and Finest Picture of the Fighting Cavalry!' The action-packed trailer, which implies that Indian War actually erupts, called the film 'A Lusty Romance and Adventure of the Untamed West, Brought Excitingly and Colourfully to the Screen in the John Ford Tradition of Greatness!' adding, 'Only John Wayne can give such a Rigorous Performance…Only John Ford can Stampede the Screen with such Sweep and Eloquence'. The crowds stampeded to cinemas when the film was released in October 1949 and it took $2.7 million in the US on its initial release. *Lux Radio Theatre* aired a three-part, 50-minute adaptation on 12 March 1951, with Wayne (here renamed Captain Nathan Darland), Mel Ferrer as Coghill and Mala Powers as Olivia. In Germany the film was retitled *Der Teufelschauptmann* (literally 'The Devil Captain'), in Italy *I Cavalieri del Nord Ovest* ('The Riders of the Northwest') and in France *La Charge Héroïque* ('The Heroic Charge'). In the UK it was passed certificate 'U' with minor cuts in November 1949. At the 1950 Oscars, Winton Hoch won the Academy Award for Best Cinematography, even though he reputedly filmed some of the underlit thunderstorm scenes 'under protest'.

By January 1950, Argosy had left RKO and signed a new deal with Republic Pictures. Although it is the third of the trilogy, *Rio Grande* (1950) is the second film chronologically. Wayne played Kirby York (his character from *Fort Apache*), who is a lieutenant colonel commanding Fort Starke (now relocated to Apache territory). Victor McLaglen reprised his role as Quincannon, here a sergeant major (years before his retirement under Brittles in *Yellow Ribbon*), while Ben Johnson portrays a younger Travis Tyree, a wanted man, who joins the army to hide. Harry Carey Jnr reappears, this time as rookie Daniel 'Sandy' Boone. Based on 'Mission with No Record' (1947) by Bellah, *Rio Grande* saw Yankee York in conflict with his estranged southern wife Kathleen (Maureen O'Hara) and his son Jeff (Claude Jarman Jnr), who has enlisted and been posted to his father's command. Kathleen wants Jeff out of the army. Kirby is instructed by General Sheridan to 'Hit the Apache and burn him out': three branches of the Apache (the Chiricahua [pronounced 'Chira-kowa'], the Mascalero and the White Mountain) have united and trouble is brewing. During manoeuvres, a group of children are taken hostage by the Apaches and York gives chase across the border.

Though *Rio Grande*'s landscape looks like Monument Valley, for economy it was filmed around Moab, Utah (at White's Ranch and Castle Valley), while some of the action was stock footage from *Fort Apache*. The film cost $1.2 million and was shot in 32 days, between June and July 1950. The working titles were *Rio Bravo*, then *Rio Grande Command*; the titles referred to the boundary river, called Rio Grande on the US side, the Rio Bravo on the Mexican. For one of the few times in his career Wayne wears a beard, albeit only a goatee (in the Lone Star western *Texas Terror* [1935] Wayne donned a full beard, when he went undercover as an outlaw). O'Hara and Wayne are well matched, in a dry run for *The Quiet Man*. The root of their conflict is revealed – York burned his wife's Bridesdale plantation to the ground during the Shenandoah Valley Campaign in the Civil War. Though Ford's storytelling is up to his usual standard and Victor Young's orchestral score backs it movingly, there are too many musical interludes these included the featured act: The Sons of the Pioneers (showcasing singer Ken Curtis) performing Irish standards, plus songs by Stan Jones and Dale Evans, such as Evans's lively 'Aha San Antone' (harmonised by Curtis, Johnson, Carey and Jarman). But the action, in particular the pursuit of the Apaches into Mexico and the rescue of the white captive children from an adobe church, is well handled.

Rio Grande's trailer crowed: 'The Screen Trembles with Excitement', at 'John Wayne at his Fighting Best' and 'Maureen O'Hara...Never More Appealing'. It grossed $2.25 million in the US in November 1950 and enabled Ford to make *The Quiet Man* the following year, in his treasured Ireland. Both *Fort Apache* and *Rio Grande* have since been shown in colourised versions. Ford's 'Cavalry Trilogy' is surely the most patriotic depiction of the regiment on film, yet for all their sentimentality, they still provide moments of insight into what it must actually have been like riding the trails, living rough and fighting with Indians, as '50-cent a day professionals... dog-faced soldiers in dirty-shirt blue'.

5

'What Will I Do If You Leave Me?'

— *High Noon* (1952)

High Noon (1952)

Credits

DIRECTOR – Fred Zinnemann

PRODUCERS – Carl Foreman and Stanley Kramer

STORY – John W. Cunningham

SCREENPLAY – Carl Foreman

DIRECTOR OF PHOTOGRAPHY – Floyd Crosby

EDITOR – Elmo Williams

ART DIRECTOR – Ben Hayne

MUSIC – Dimitri Tiomkin

A Stanley Kramer Production

Released by United Artists

85 minutes

Cast

Gary Cooper (Marshal Will Kane); Thomas Mitchell (Mayor
Jonas Henderson); Lloyd Bridges (Deputy Marshal Harvey
Pell); Katy Jurado (Helen Ramirez); Grace Kelly (Amy
Kane, nee Fowler); Otto Kruger (Judge Percy Mettrick);
Lon Chaney (Martin Howe); Harry Morgan (Sam Fuller);
Eve McVeagh (Mildred Fuller); Ian MacDonald (Frank
Miller); Sheb Wooley (Ben Miller); Lee Van Cleef (Jack
Colby); Robert Wilke (James Pierce); Harry Shannon
(Cooper); Morgan Farley (Dr Mahin, Priest); Jeanne
Blackford (Mrs Henderson); Larry J. Blake (Gillis, saloon
keeper); Guy Beach (Fred the coffin maker); Howland
Chamberlain (Hotel lobby clerk); Virginia Christine (Mrs
Simpson); John Doucette (Trumball); Paul Dubov (Scott);
Jack Elam (Charlie, drunk in jail); Cliff Clark (Ed Weaver);
Dick Elliot (Kibbee); Tim Graham (Sawyer); Tom Greenway

(Ezra); Virginia Farmer (Mrs Fletcher); Harry Harvey (Coy);
Chubby Johnson and Syd Saylor (Old Men on Ramirez
Hotel porch); Nolan Leary (Lewis); Tom London (Sam);
James Millican (Deputy Sheriff Herb Baker); William Newell
(Jimmy, town drunk); William Phillips (Barber); Lucien Prival
(Joe, Ramirez Hotel barman); Ralph Reed (Johnny, messenger
boy); Ted Stanhope (Hadleyville station master)

*   *   *

High Noon is a powerful allegory of its time, condemned by some as 'un-American'
and praised by *Pravda* for its depiction of 'the grandeur of the individual'. Almost
as soon as the film was released audiences questioned whether they were watching
Marshal Will Kane facing his enemies in the main street of Hadleyville, or screenplay
writer Carl Foreman, standing alone under interrogation by the House Un-American
Activities Committee (HUAC) in relation to his Communist sympathies.

In the town of Hadleyville, New Mexico, retiring Marshal Will Kane hangs up his
star and his guns on the morning of the day he marries Amy Fowler, a Quaker. News
arrives that three gunmen are waiting for Frank Miller at Hadleyville station; Kane
had put Miller in jail five years previously for murder, but Miller is paroled and will
arrive on the noon train. With the new marshal not due until the following day,
Kane wrestles with his conscience and decides to stay. Amy feels betrayed by her
new husband's disregard for her pacifist beliefs and vows to catch the noon train
for St Louis. This leaves Kane with a moral dilemma, made more difficult by the
fact that no one in town, including his deputy Harvey Pell, will help him face the
outlaws. When the train arrives, Kane ambushes the quartet, with Amy challenging
her principles and taking up arms beside her husband to defeat them.

Carl Foreman's story resembles 'The Tin Star', a two-page *Saturday Evening Post*
article written by John M. Cunningham. Even though Foreman wrote his scenario
independently, Cunningham was cited in the credits as the inspiration for it. It is
difficult to see why producer Stanley Kramer felt compelled to mention Cunningham,
as the plot resemblances are few and vague. In Cunningham's scenario, Kane is called
Doane, the Millers are the Jordans and the action takes place between 3pm and 4.10
pm. It isn't anyone's wedding day, there is no sign of Amy Fowler, there are two
deputies (named Slater and Toby) and as Doane defeats the villains he is killed. At
least the villains arrive by train.

Stanley Kramer, an independent working in Hollywood, had produced *The Men*
(1950) starring Marlon Brando. Gregory Peck was his first choice for Kane, but Peck
had recently made *The Gunfighter* (1950) and felt another overtly serious treat-ment
of the old west wouldn't be popular. Other prospective candidates included Kirk
Douglas, Henry Fonda and even Brando. Eventually the role of the pressured marshal
was offered to Gary Cooper for $60,000 plus a percentage of the profits. He took the
part even though he was suffering from a stomach ulcer, a bad hip and a hernia –
ailments that proved advantageous to his performance. Cooper had begun his film

career as a cowboy extra in 1925: 'They stuck a beard on me, thrust an old Winchester in my hand and gave me a horse – I was in the movies!' As prim Amy Fowler, Kramer cast Grace Kelly, then appearing in summer-season theatricals in Denver. Kramer remembered, 'I wanted somebody unknown opposite Gary Cooper. I couldn't afford anybody else, so I signed her.' To Zinnemann, she seemed fragile, nervous and aloof, and in her pure white gloves far too demure for their low-budget production, but ideal for the displaced Quaker in the western settlement. Zinnemann described Amy Fowler as 'sort of boring and thin-blooded, the image of virginity in a colourless sort of way'.

Chief villain Frank Miller was played by Ian MacDonald, a regular in B-movie westerns and war movies. Mexican Katy Jurado (real name Maria Cristina Jurado Garcia) was typecast as Mexican 'spitfire' Helen Ramirez, who is involved in a love triangle subplot with Miller and Kane. Jurado's inability to pronounce 'Doane' in the original script resulted in the marshal's name being altered to Kane. Kramer originally cast Lee Van Cleef (in his film debut) as Kane's deputy. Kramer had seen Van Cleef on stage in *Mister Roberts* and wanted him to have plastic surgery to alter his hawk-like nose, but the actor refused and was cast as gunman Jack Colby instead. The other two killers at the station were played by Robert Wilke and Sheb Wooley. Wooley was scout Pete Nolan in TV's *Rawhide*; he had a massive 100-million-selling single with 'Purple People Eater' (1958) and recorded the western album 'Wild and Wooley'. Lloyd Bridges was cast in the deputy role. Bridges's character refuses to help Marshal Kane, but in real life the actor was a helpful witness in the HUAC hearings.

Kramer amassed a budget of $750,000, with some of the independent finance being provided by a lettuce farmer in Salinas. Zinnemann had 28 days to shoot the movie, between September and October 1951. It was a very well planned schedule, with Zinnemann and Kramer sketching out the final gunfight on storyboards. The railway station scenes were to have been shot near Gallup in New Mexico, but the budget wouldn't stretch to such extravagance. The first scenes to be filmed were the Hadleyville church exteriors, then the town scenes (interior and exterior) and finally the railway station sequences. The church exterior was St Joseph's Catholic Church in Tuolumne City, California. The remainder of the Hadleyville town scenes were shot at Columbia Pictures, on their western town back-lot at Burbank Studios. For the location scenes, the crew flew by DC-3 to a stretch of railroad line in Sonora, California, where Zinnemann and cinematographer Floyd Crosby were nearly killed: the camera was set up on the track but the locomotive's brakes failed. The stock also survived and remains in the finished film. The opening scene, when three outlaws rendezvous in the countryside, was shot at the Iverson Movie Ranch, near Chatsworth, California. When the whirlwind shoot was completed, an exhausted Cooper commented, 'I'm all acted out.'

Kane is the central character, with Cooper on screen for the majority of the movie. He is a frightened man, who tries to hide his fears and defend a community he thinks is worth saving, but don't deserve to be. Zinnemann emphasises Kane's worsening solitude, with close-ups of the marshal's strained face or shots of him striding purposefully down the street from one potential ally to another. As his options run out, his stride becomes rather less purposeful, until finally, moments

'When the hands point straight up…the excitement starts!': Marshal Will Kane protects his wife Amy from Frank Miller. Gary Cooper and Grace Kelly pose in a publicity photo for Fred Zinnemann's *High Noon* (1952).

before noon, he slumps in his office. His last hope, a part-time deputy named Herb, has wormed his way out of responsibility. Previously Herb had been keen (claiming he'd come 'loaded for bear'), but now concedes, 'I got no stake in this.' 'Go on home to your kids, Herb,' Kane replies coldly. Alone, Kane's head falls on his desk and he sobs – an unusual and explicitly human action for a western hero.

High Noon boasts one of the most memorable opening scenes in western history in squinting Lee Van Cleef's rendezvous with unshaven Sheb Wooley and sneering Robert Wilke. The trio ride with intent, passing the church on the outskirts of town – the tolling bell setting the sleepy Sunday morning scene. They ride up the main street and a black-shawled Mexican woman wearing a hefty crucifix crosses herself as they trot by. This imagery became a cliché in establishing villainy. Throughout the film, Zinnemann returns to the gunmen at the rail depot. They are idly menacing – drinking, smoking, checking their guns, edgily squabbling – as they stare in eager anticipation at the diminishing railroad tracks which fade into the flat, ominous horizon for what seems like an eternity, until smoke from the Sierra Railroad engine appears. Given Zinnemann's build-up, the arrival of Frank Miller is something of an anticlimax, as critics of the time noted.

The real villains of *High Noon* are the Hadleyville townsfolk. Kane asks them for help, but friends he thought he could count on pretend not to be home. Judge Mettrick (played by Otto Kruger) notes that justice doesn't always favour the righteous, as he packs up his law books and flees. To him Hadleyville is 'A dirty little village in the middle of nowhere – nothing that happens here's really important'. Kane visits Martin Howe (Lon Chaney), an ex-lawman with broken knuckles. 'Ever since I was a kid I wanted to be like you,' Kane tells him, but Martin is even more disillusioned with the law than the judge, 'It's all for nothing, for a tin star.' Kane passes some children playing with wooden pistols. One shouts, 'Bang bang! You're dead, Kane!' Zinnemann shatters peaceful civilisation with the vengeful spectres of the old 'wild west', in an unsettling mix of optimism, pessimism and fear.

The Miller-supporting clientele of the Ramirez Saloon are openly hostile towards Kane. When Kane tries to recruit deputies, there are no takers in the partisan bar, except Jimmy, the town drunk with one eye and the shakes, who claims, 'I used to be good.' Down the street the coffin maker has only two caskets in stock and reasons they'll need two more, however things turn out. It is apparent which businesses were booming when Miller was around. Increasingly desperate, Kane visits the Sunday church service, but the marshal isn't a congregation regular and finds no hope there either.

High Noon unfolds in 'reel time'. The film begins at roughly 10.35 am and finishes shortly after noon; the barber's clock reads 10.37 am as three outlaws ride down the main street. Wall casement clocks with swinging pendulums, carriage clocks, grandfather clocks and pocket watches bring the noon train closer to Hadleyville. At one point Kane scrawls a note on his office door reading 'Back in 5 minutes', but arrives back in seven of screen-time. Zinnemann's one regret was that they ran out of time 'to shoot a blank clock face, without hands' to 'intensify the feeling of panic'.

Zinnemann steadily builds the tension. There is virtually no action throughout the film – a fistfight in Todd's Livery Stable between Kane and Pell, an occasional punch thrown. The action is apprehension and emotional conflict. In the finale Kane shoots Ben and Colby in a street shootout, and Amy kills Pierce. Frank uses her as a human shield, but she struggles, enabling Kane to get a clear shot at the villain. In the wordless dénouement Kane embraces Amy, and the townspeople surround them. Earlier, Kane has said of his marshal's star, 'I'm the same man, with or without this'; in the finale he disdainfully drops his badge in the dust. This particular un-American activity didn't go down very well in some patriotic quarters, but Cooper's determined face says it all, 'I did it...and I did it without you'.

The film's title song is billed in the credits as 'High Noon', though recorded versions are called 'Do Not Forsake Me Oh My Darlin'' and 'The Ballad of High Noon'. The lyrics were written by Ned Washington, with musical accompaniment by Russian composer Dimitri Tiomkin, and read in part:

> Do not forsake me oh my darlin', on this our wedding day
> The noonday train will bring Frank Miller, If I'm a man I must be brave
> And I must face that deadly killer,
> Look at that big hand move along, nearing high noon
> He made a vow while in state prison, Vowed it would be my life or his and,
> I'm not afraid of death but what will I do if you leave me?

It was Stanley Kramer's idea to have a ballad to narrate the story, though test audiences reputedly laughed at the repetitive refrain. The ballad was sung by ex-series cowboy Tex Ritter, whose gravelly voice closely resembled Cooper's. In the wake of *High Noon* the song was covered by Frankie Laine, who titled his version 'High Noon (Do Not Forsake Me)' and removed all reference to Frank Miller from the lyric.

During post-production in autumn 1951, Kramer screened a 105-minute rough-cut of the film, but audience reaction was tepid. Kelly was so unimpressed with her performance that she immediately enrolled in Sanford Meisner's acting class at the Neighbourhood Playhouse, New York. To crank up the tension, Kramer filmed more shots of Cooper's anxious face and inserted them into the footage, along with several more shots of ticking clocks and swinging pendulums. Zinnemann had already cut a subplot detailing another deputy, Toby, bringing in a prisoner and trying to attend the marshal's wedding, but getting waylaid at a Mexican stage station. Some sources note that these scenes depicted the deputy attempting to recruit help from outlying ranches, which would contradict the action outlined above. Kramer made further cuts, trimming the film by 20 minutes, resulting in the real timeframe of 85 minutes (the home video print runs at 81 minutes and 18 secs, owing to its faster frames-per-minute projection time). Expository scenes between Bridges and Jurado, Kelly and Jurado and a comedy scene with drunkard Charlie (Jack Elam) finishing off abandoned glasses of whisky in the deserted saloon were removed.

An expensive publicity campaign ensured the film enjoyed a high profile when released in the US in July 1952. Kramer's post-production tinkering had delayed release, which actually helped when the title song became a hit ahead of the film's exhibition. Posters featuring Cooper's anxious face peering through the shattered glass of the general store window were accompanied by the banners: 'There Is

Nothing Under The Sun Like The High Adventure Of *High Noon*', 'When the Hands Point Straight Up...the Excitement Starts!' and 'The Story of a Man who was Too Proud to Run'. Publicity stills depicted Cooper, gun drawn, arm protectively around Kelly's shoulder, with a wall clock pointing to noon in the background. In the UK it was passed uncut for a 'U' certificate in March 1952. Promotional material pinpointed the beginning of the action to '10.35, Hadleyville, a Sunday morning in June, 1865', though a building in Hadleyville is inscribed with the masons' date 1888. The *New York Times* called *High Noon* 'no storybook Western', rather 'a replica of actuality', while *Pravda* noted that this was a western 'in which the idea of the insignificance of the people and masses, and the grandeur of the individual found its complete incarnation'. *High Noon* took $3.4 million in the US on its first release and pushed Cooper to the top of the box-office popularity chart. It was also popular throughout Europe. It was released in Italy in 1952 as *Mezzogiorno Di Fuoco* ('Noon of Fire'); the comedy western *Blazing Saddles* (1974) was released in Italy as *Mezzogiorno e Mezzo di Fuoco* ('Noon and a Half of Fire'). Zinnemann's film was released in Germany in 1953 as *Zwölf Uhr Mittags* ('Twelve o'clock at Noon'); in France the title was *Le Train Sifflera Trois Fois* ('The Train Whistles Three Times') and in Spain it was *Solo Ante el Peligro* ('Alone in the Presence of Danger').

Oscar success followed: at the 1953 Oscars, Cooper was named Best Actor, Best Score went to Tiomkin, Best Song was shared by Tiomkin and Washington, and Elmo Williams and Harry Gerstad won the Film Editing award, but the film failed to win Best Picture, Director and Screenplay (losing out to *The Greatest Show on Earth*, John Ford for *The Quiet Man* and screenwriter Charles Schnee for *The Bad and the Beautiful*). Zinnemann did receive Best Director the following year for *From Here to Eternity*, which was also shot at Columbia Studios, with *High Noon*'s street redressed as 'Hawaii'. *High Noon* continues to be popular and in 1988 was voted the best western ever made by members of the British Film Institute.

High Noon's influence on cinema, western or otherwise, was immense. Deserted railway stations, with tracks tapering into the arid horizon, appeared in opening sequence homages by Sergio Leone (*Once Upon a Time in the West*) and Burt Kennedy (*The Train Robbers*), though in both instances it is the hero (Charles Bronson and John Wayne respectively) who steps down from the train. Titles like *A Man Alone* (1955) and *Star in the Dust* (1956) referenced the film's imagery, while variations included two Alfred Werker westerns *Three Hours to Kill* (1954) and *At Gunpoint* (1955), *The Silver Star* (1956 – co-scripted and produced by Ian MacDonald, *High Noon*'s Frank Miller) and *Fury at Gunsight Pass* (1956). Throughout the fifties, the hysteria surrounding the HUAC became a popular target for disguised criticism by filmmakers in Hollywood, outraged at the 'Reds under the bed' paranoia. An interesting western McCarthyist allegory is RKO's *Silver Lode* (1954), with duplicitous Marshal Ned McCarty (Dan Duryea) hounding respectable Dan Ballard (John Payne). Cleverly plotted, it condones the mob ethic and contains some explicitly barbed dialogue aimed at McCarthy and the HUAC. 'Are you going to take McCarty's word against his [Ballard's]?' asks a local.

Another film with thematic links to *High Noon* is Delmer Daves's *3:10 to Yuma* (1957), which sees drought-stricken Arizona farmer Dan Evans (Van Heflin) escorting wanted outlaw Ben Wade (Glenn Ford) from Bisbee to the station in Contention City, to catch the 3.10 train – to Yuma and jail. Evans is accompanied by town drunk Alex Potter (Henry Jones); the farmer needs the reward to acquire water rights to save his property, while the drunkard hopes to regain his self-esteem. Based on an Elmore Leonard story, *Yuma* is as tense as *High Noon*, especially in the scenes where the escort play cat and mouse with Wade's gang en route (filmed in Sedona) and later in Contention (lensed at Old Tucson Studios and the Columbia western street), with Evans, Potter and Wade holed-up in a hotel. Wade's oily charm shreds Evans's nerves and the outlaws' men savagely lynch Potter from a chandelier in the hotel lobby, before Evans takes the fateful walk through empty streets to catch the train. The rights to Leonard's story were originally owned by United Artists, who planned for Robert Aldrich to direct, but they instead sold them to Columbia for $30,000. A great success and still popular today, *Yuma* has a classic western theme song, belted out by Frankie Laine: 'There's a legend and there's a rumour, when you take the 3.10 to Yuma, you can see the ghosts of outlaws go riding by'.

High Noon was remade in 2000 for US Cable, with Tom Skerritt as Will Kane, based on 'a teleplay by Carl Foreman and T.S. Cook'. More damaging to the memory of Zinnemann's original is *High Noon Part II: The Return of Will Kane* (1980) starring Lee Majors (TV's *The Six Million Dollar Man*) as Will Kane, returning to Hadleyville ten years later to face a corrupt marshal. The 1981 Sean Connery sci-fi vehicle *Outland* was *High Noon* transposed to outer space, complete with digital clock countdown.

Unlike Will Kane and Handleyville, Carl Foreman lost his battle with the HUAC when he was subpoenaed halfway through *High Noon*'s shooting schedule. Though Gary Cooper was a well-known anti-Communist, he supported Foreman's stance. It didn't do Foreman any good – he was blacklisted and took exile in England. John Wayne was president of the Motion Picture Alliance for the Preservation of American Ideals, which was affiliated to the HUAC. In a private meeting he gave Foreman the opportunity to name names, but Foreman refused. Years later, Wayne recalled on the UK *Parkinson* TV show, '[*High Noon*] is the most un-American thing I've ever seen in my whole life – I'll never regret running Carl Foreman out of this country.' It seems ironic that when Wayne presented Cooper with the 1952 Best Actor Oscar he joked, 'Why can't I find me a scriptwriter to write me a part like the one that got you this?'

Foreman later co-produced the overblown *Mackenna's Gold* (1968) with composer Dimitri Tiomkin. A reference to Foreman's *High Noon* past reappeared in *Gold*; the group of 'Gentlemen' looking for the Apache 'Canyon Del'Oro' are from the town of Hadleyburg. Gary Cooper, nearing the end of his career, enjoyed a new lease of life in westerns, with *Springfield Rifle* (1952), *Garden of Evil* and *Vera Cruz* (both 1954), *Man of the West* (1958) and *The Hanging Tree* (1959) all enjoying good returns. In 1961 he received a Special Oscar for his 'many memorable screen performances'. A tearful James Stewart accepted the award for the ailing star, who died a month later of cancer. But casting a shadow over Cooper's performances is his role as the stoic, frightened marshal in *High Noon*, a man alone in the face of adversity – a triumph of the will.

6

'You Can't Break the Mould'

— *Shane* (1953)

Shane (1953)
Credits
DIRECTOR AND PRODUCER – George Stevens
ASSOCIATE PRODUCER – Ivan Moffat
STORY – Jack Schaefer
SCREENPLAY – A.B. Guthrie Jnr and Jack Sher
DIRECTOR OF PHOTOGRAPHY – Loyal Griggs
EDITORS – William Hornbeck and Tom McAdoo
ART DIRECTORS – Hal Pereira and Walter Tyler
MUSIC – Victor Young
Technicolor
A Paramount Production
Released by Paramount Pictures
118 minutes
Cast
    Alan Ladd (Shane); Van Heflin (Joe Starrett); Jean Arthur
(Marian Starrett); Brandon De Wilde (Joey Starrett); Jack
Palance (Jack Wilson); Ben Johnson (Chris Calloway); Emile
Meyer (Rufus 'Rufe' Ryker); John Dierkes (Morgan Ryker);
Edgar Buchanan (Fred Lewis); Elisha Cook Jnr (Frank
'Stonewall' Torrey); Ellen Corby (Liz Torrey); Douglas
Spencer (Axel 'Swede' Shipstead); Edith Evanson (Mrs
Shipstead); Helen Brown (Martha Lewis); Janice Carroll
(Susan Lewis); Beverly Washburn (Ruth Lewis); Leonard
Strong (Ernie Wright); Paul McVey (Sam Grafton); John
Miller (Will Atkey, Grafton's bartender); Ray Spiker (Lew
Johnson, homesteader); Martin Mason (Ed Howells,
homesteader); Nancy Kulp (Mrs Howells); Howard Negley
(Pete Potts); Charles Quirk (Clerk); Henry Wills, Ewing

Miles Brown, Steve Staines, Bill Cartledge, Jack Sterling,
Chester W. Hannan, George J. Lewis and Rex Moore
(Ryker's gang)

*   *   *

George Stevens's *Shane* has a plot as old as the Wyoming hills that serve as the backdrop to his epic western drama. The film was based on a classic 1949 novel by Jack Schaefer, rewritten for the screen by A.B. Guthrie Jnr and Jack Sher. In the summer of 1889, drifting ex-gunfighter Shane arrives in a valley at the Starrett ranch, run by Joe and Marian, with their young son Joey. The homesteaders are being pushed out by cattlemen, the Ryker brothers Rufe and Morgan, who have won a beef contract with an Indian reservation and covet the farmers' fertile grazing and water supply. During his stay, Shane works as a farm hand, and is idolised by Joey. Joe Starrett and Shane stand up to Ryker's tyranny, beating Ryker's gang in a fistfight in the Grafton Saloon in town and prompting Rufe to seek outside help from hired gun Jack Wilson. Wilson guns down 'Stonewall' Torrey, one of the homesteaders, and Joe is about to confront Wilson, but Shane intervenes. In Grafton's, Shane faces Wilson, Rufe and Morgan, and kills them, but is wounded in the fight. As Joey's imploring, 'Come back Shane!' echoes in his wake, Shane rides into the mountains, having rid the valley of guns.

All these main plot points are present in Schaefer's book, with some notable alterations for the film. In the book, black-clad gunman Shane arrives at a farm run by Joe, his wife Marian and their son, Robert MacPherson Starrett, called 'Bob', who narrates the book in the first person. Wilson is named Stark Wilson and Ryker is Fletcher. All Marian seems to do in the book is make biscuits and flapjacks, but her role is expanded in the film. In the book Torrey recounts the story of homesteader Ernie Wright, who was shot in Grafton's bar by Wilson; in the film Torrey is shot down in the street, witnessed by farmer 'Swede' Shipstead. In both cases Wilson baits his opponent into drawing, sometimes with racial taunts (he accuses Wright of being a half-breed) or ideologically (Yankee Wilson ridicules Torrey's Confederate sympathies).

The book sheds light on Shane's personality – young Bob notes, 'His past was fenced as tightly as a pasture' and a muleskinner in Grafton's calls him, 'One of these here slow-burning fuses.' 'Even his name remained mysterious,' Bob notes, 'Just Shane. Nothing else. We never knew whether that was his first name or last name or, indeed, any name that came from his family.' In the final chapter there is speculation as to Shane's identity: gossip long after Shane's departure proffers that he was a gunman and gambler from Arkansas and Texas called Shannon.

The original casting was William Holden (Joe), Katherine Hepburn (Marian) and Montgomery Clift (Shane) – Clift had just made *A Place in the Sun* with Stevens. Instead three Paramount contract players were cast: respectively Van Heflin, Jean Arthur and Alan Ladd. Paramount were unsure about casting Ladd, who was viewed as a straight action movie star, usually in westerns or *noirs*. His films never grossed more than $2.6 million and the producers worried that they were putting a low ceiling on their film as a Ladd vehicle. But Ladd also brought ambivalence to the title role, a dark side to his pin-up image, developed in his *noirs*. Ladd's previous westerns included *Branded* (1951) and the action-packed *Whispering Smith* (1948). Ex-Broadway actor Heflin stepped snugly into Starrett's work boots; it is impossible to imagine anyone else in the role of the resolute farmer. A film actress since the twenties, Jean Arthur was 47 years old when she played Marian Starrett, though she looks much younger; *Shane* was her last film. She had previously played Calamity Jane in *The Plainsman* (1936). Brandon De Wilde was nine when he played Joey; he was appearing on stage in *The Member of the Wedding* when he was chosen for the part.

Jack Palance, billed as Walter Jack Palance (his real surname was Palahnuik) was cast as Jack Wilson, the snake-faced, Cobra-quick hired killer from Cheyenne. He had never ridden a horse, nor handled a pistol and practised both while on location. For the scene where Wilson slowly mounts his horse at Starrett's, Stevens ran the

'Call me Shane': The idealised cowboy in the perfect western – Alan Ladd as the eponymous buckskinned hero, who rids the Wyoming valley of guns in George Stevens' *Shane* (1953), the most successful western of the fifties.

footage of Palance dismounting in reverse, to get the right effect. Since falling out with John Ford, Ben Johnson had played a leading role in the revenge western *Fort Defiance* (1951). Following his role as bullying Chris Calloway in *Shane*, he went back to the rodeo circuit in 1953, before returning to acting two years later. The homesteaders were played by reliable character actors, Edgar Buchanan (as Fred Lewis), Elisha Cook Jnr (as 'Stonewall' Torrey, the proud reb from Alabama), stuntman Ray Spiker (as Lew Jackson), Douglas Spencer (as Swede, Axel Shipstead), Leonard Strong (Ernie Wright), Martin Mason (Ed Howells) and Howard Negley (as harmonica-playing Yankee Pete Potts). The evil, bewhiskered Ryker brothers, Rufe and Morgan, were heavies Emile Meyer and John Dierkes. Stuntman Russell Saunders doubled for Ladd in the fight scenes. Henry Wills was the stunt co-ordinator (he also appeared as a Ryker henchman) and later worked on *The Magnificent Seven* and *One-Eyed Jacks*.

Shane was filmed in the breathtaking setting of Jackson Hole, Wyoming. The location, with its broad plain and impressive backdrop of the Grand Teton National Park mountain range had been used in westerns before, notably in Ford's *3 Bad Men* (1926) and Raoul Walsh's *The Big Trail* (1930), but Stevens gave it an added dimension. He used a telephoto lens to bring the snow-capped Tetons, wreathed in clouds (which resemble the Paramount logo), into foreboding focus. The rough settlement of shacks and tents huddled around Grafton's General Mercantile and Co, Sundries and Saloon, was constructed on Antelope Flats, on one side of the muddy street, like many nascent western towns. Cemetery Hill graveyard stood overlooking the town. Starrett's log-built homestead, plus other farms (Wright's and Lewis's) were also built in the locality. The settlers' Fourth of July dance was filmed on soundstages at Paramount – and unfortunately it looks like it. Other Starrett ranch 'exteriors' were filmed indoors, while interiors were created for Starrett's house and Grafton's saloon and store. Filming began in July and was completed in October 1951. With shooting over, the Grafton Store exterior and other buildings (the hotel and blacksmiths) were transported to the historical Rockefeller's Ferry Museum as exhibits – the town set and a cabin reappear in *Will Penny* (1968).

Ladd was only five feet six inches tall and *Shane* is notable for the ingenious ways this is disguised throughout the film. Ladd is photographed on his horse, or standing on steps, to give him stature, or else sitting down, while everyone else stands up, so there is no sense of perspective regarding Ladd's height. However, in a couple of shots, he's not much taller than Joey.

Like Schaefer's novel, *Shane* is told from the child's perspective. That was Stevens's strategy for his stylised presentation of the hero, an ideal man little Joey can look up to. Joey mimes shooting a deer as Shane approaches and is much more interested in gunplay than farming, asking his father awkward questions regarding Shane's background. When Shane walks away from a confrontation with Chris Calloway in Grafton's, Joey is unforgiving. But later, having seen Shane and Joe in action against Ryker's crew, he decides, 'I love Shane' – perhaps even more than his own father. 'Don't get to liking Shane too much,' Marian tells her son, 'He'll be moving on one day,' even though Marian herself is attracted to the stranger.

Unlike the black-clad persona in the book, Shane wears a romanticised buckskin cowboy outfit and a white hat, coupled with a fast-draw gunbelt for his Colt .45. In Stevens's west, Wilson wears black. The Starrett's initially mistake Shane for one of Ryker's hired guns. On his arrival at the farm, little Joey cocks his rifle and jumpy Shane spins around, drawing his pistol, and says, 'Sure had me snortin', son,' he tells the boy. 'Bet you can shoot,' says Joey. 'Little bit,' answers Shane. Even Ryker acknowledges of Shane, 'You don't belong on the end of a shovel.' Soft-spoken Ladd is subtly menacing, like his earlier performance as eponymous railroad agent Luke 'Whispering' Smith. As in Schaefer's book, 'Call me Shane' is his only introduction. Shane has a shadowy past – he clearly wears a wedding ring and at several points in the film, homesteaders note that Shane seems to know a lot about men like Wilson. In the end, when Shane is ready to move on, he tells Joey, 'Man has to be what he is Joey. You can't break the mould. I tried and it didn't work for me.'

The settlers are fighting for their community, their families and their future – as Joe puts it, 'All the things that will be.' Ryker's henchmen pressurise the 'sodbusters', shooting livestock, trampling crops and scaring them with threats, but nothing works. In the end, Ryker has to send for Wilson, reasoning, 'I'm through fooling…the air's gonna be filled with gun smoke.' Even after the hired gun's arrival, the burning of Lewis's house during Torrey's funeral spurs the settlers to stand together and rebuild it. Initially, Joe tells Shane, 'I want my troubles to be none of yours' and the settlers aren't gunmen – when they buy gunpowder from Grafton's it's for the fireworks on Independence Day. Cattlemen hated such 'nesters' and 'sodbusters', with these conflicts occasionally spilling over into outright hostilities, as in Wyoming's Johnson County War (the backdrop to *Heaven's Gate* [1980]). In *Shane*, the settlers' shovels are used as much for digging graves as tilling crops.

Stevens intended the film's realistic violence to put people off guns, but it doesn't work with Joey, who can't resist the lure of gunfighter lore. Shane is eventually pestered into demonstrating his prowess in Starrett's corral, with his nickel-plated Colt .45 with ivory grips. Shane advises Joey that some gunmen use shoulder holsters, some tuck it in their belt or pack two guns – 'But one's all you need if you can use it.' Shane draws and shoots a volley, an explosion of lead and dust, as his pebble target is riddled. 'Gosh almighty!' Joey whistles through his teeth, 'That is good.' Marian ushers Joey away from Shane, 'Guns aren't going to be my boy's life.' 'A gun is a tool Marian,' answers Shane, 'No better or worse than any other tool – a gun is as good or as bad as the man using it.' Marian isn't convinced, 'We'd all be better off if there wasn't a single gun left in this valley…including yours.'

The action, when it comes, is startling in its ferocity. In *Shane*'s fairytale frontier setting, the action sequences anticipate the 'mud and rags' treatment of the west over a decade later. Ryker henchman Chris tries to provoke Shane, complaining about the smell of pigs, when the stranger wanders into Grafton's bar to buy a bottle of soda pop for Joey. 'Well, what'll it be?' sneers Chris, 'Lemon, strawberry or lilac, sodbuster?' 'You speaking to me?' offers Shane, 'I don't see nobody else standing there.' Chris throws a glass of whisky down Shane's brand-new store-bought clothes ('Chris just fumigated a sodbuster,' laughs Morgan). But Shane walks away from any confrontation. Later, Shane returns to the bar to collect the deposit on Joey's empty. Ryker's gang have since christened him 'sodie-pop'. This time Shane provokes Chris, throwing whisky in his face and in a prolonged, circling fistfight, gives him a bloody nose and eventually beats him senseless. When Ryker's gang converge on Shane, Joe joins the melee, brandishing a pickaxe handle and proceeds to wallop his opponents in the violent free-for-all. The fight between Chris and Shane was carefully rehearsed by Johnson and Ladd so that Stevens could use as many close-ups as possible, while both Ladd and Heflin are doubled by stuntmen in the long shots of the subsequent brawl. These punch-ups are choreographed and edited for maximum impact. A final brawl has Shane preventing Joe from riding into a trap with Ryker. It takes place at night, outside Starrett's ranch, with neighing horses, panicky cattle and the barking dog driving Marian to hysteria. Shane can only win by breaking the code: he cold-conks Joe over the head with his pistol. To Joey this is unforgivable and he shouts, 'You hit him with your gun – I hate you.'

The niggly antagonism between Shane and Wilson, two professional gunfighters, provides the finale of *Shane* with its power. Earlier we have seen Wilson at work, when 'Stonewall' Torrey and Shipstead visit the blacksmith. The mood changes during the scene, with clouds passing overhead, altering the lighting from bright sunshine to overcast gloom, with threat added by rolling thunder. Torrey picks his way across the muddy street towards the saloon. Wilson, on the sidewalk, baits him, 'They tell me they call you Stonewall. Guess they named a lot of that southern trash after old Stonewall.' 'Who'd they name you after, or would you know?' replies Torrey. Wilson puts one black glove on his gun hand, adding, 'I'm saying that Stonewall Jackson was trash himself. Him and Lee and all the rest of them rebs … you too.'; 'You're a low-down lying Yankee,' retorts Torrey. 'Prove it,' whispers Wilson, as Torrey pulls his gun first, but Wilson kills him, blasting his body backward into the mud.

Rufe Ryker says of Starrett, 'I'll kill him if I have to,' to which Wilson replies, 'You mean I'll kill him if you have to,' and they resolve to eliminate the settler. 'Tell him I'm a reasonable man, tell him I'm beat, tell him anything – but by Jupiter get him here,' rants Rufe. Shane senses a trap and goes in Joe's place; Joey, wanting to apologise for saying he hated Shane, follows. In the empty saloon, Wilson sits at a table, Rufe waits in the corner and Morgan is hidden upstairs on the landing (in Schaefer's book, the saloon is crowded with patrons). Shane strides in and leans against the bar as Joey watches from under the saloon doors. 'You've lived too long,' Shane tells Rufe, 'Your kind of days are over.' 'My days?' blurts Rufe, 'What about yours, gunfighter?' 'The difference is I know it.' Wilson says their fight isn't with Shane. 'So you're Jack Wilson.' 'What's that mean to you Shane?' 'I've heard about you,' says Shane. 'What have you heard Shane?'; 'I've heard you're a low-down Yankee liar.' Wilson stares at him, 'Prove it.' In a flurry of shots, Shane fells Wilson and Rufe. As Shane leaves, Joey shouts a warning – Morgan hits Shane in the shoulder, but Shane kills Morgan, who crashes down from the balcony. Shane says that Joey must tell Marian, 'There aren't any more guns in the valley.' Joey, tearful that Shane isn't returning to the ranch, yells after him, his voice echoing back off the snow-capped Tetons, 'Pa's got things for you to do and mother wants you! Shane, come back!'

But the departing figure rides on, to 'One place or another…someplace I've never been'.

Shane's lilting title music, 'The Call of the Faraway Hills', was composed by Victor Young and Mack David, and Young's incidental music is equally memorable. 'The Tree Stump' is a triumphal piece that builds to a crescendo, as Shane and Joe toil to uproot a stump on Starrett's spread, 'Sometimes ain't nothin'll do but your own sweat and muscle,' says Joe of their Herculean efforts. The same music is used in the massed barroom punch-up in Grafton's – another scene where only sweat and muscle will do. 'Cemetery Hill' accompanies Torrey's funeral scene; Torrey's 'Dixie' theme and a last post on Harmonica are also woven into the score. The funeral

'Prove it': Low-down Yankee liar Jack Wilson dons one black glove before gunning down 'Stonewall' Torrey outside the Grafton Saloon in the most famous scene from *Shane*; the great Jack Palance, who sadly passed away during the writing of this book.

features Torrey's dog pawing at his master's coffin in a simple, moving moment that is enormously effective. Stevens also deploys the hymn 'Abide with Me' (at the Independence Day dance and later at the funeral) and sing-along standard 'I Ride an Old Paint, I'm A-leavin' Cheyenne', which coincides with the arrival of Wilson.

Stevens spent 16 months in post-production. He had shot miles of footage, for instance, the scene where Shane shows Joey how to shoot took two days to lens, with Stevens deploying 45 camera set-ups and 119 takes. For the fistfights and gunplay, Stevens used sound advantageously, mixing the effects loudly for maximum impact. The gunshots were recorded with howitzers firing into trashcans, mixed with whining ricochets, while the crunching, crashing fistfights were similarly intensified, with splintering furniture and shattering glass. As Stevens edited he also pruned the story – an invented subplot romance between Chris Calloway and one of Lewis's daughters was cut. In Schaefer's book Chris ended up working on Starrett's farm, replacing Shane, arriving for work carrying a soda pop for little Bob. *Shane* went so over budget that Paramount tried to sell it to Howard Hughes at RKO for its production cost, but the deal fell through. Instead Paramount hit upon an idea. In the early fifties CinemaScope rush, cinema managers wanted to project any film they had in letterboxed widescreen, regardless of its original ratio. They trimmed the frame with scant regard for the image, cutting off feet, hats, heads and landscapes to create new 'widescreen' releases. Paramount decided that *Shane* would be adapted for this new format. It was released in a widescreen 1.66:1 ratio, rather than the 1.37:1 'Academy' fullscreen ratio intended, but nobody seemed to notice the cropping.

Copyrighted in 1952, *Shane* finally made it into US cinemas in April 1953. Posters said: 'There Never Was a Man like Shane … There Never was a Picture like *Shane*'. The trailer, which includes alternate takes of Shane riding through the valley and his sharpshooting in the corral, said that Stevens's film 'enlarges the scope of the screen' with the 'stature of its moving human drama … Shane, who attracted the woman with his quiet strength … who fascinated the boy with the glint of his gun'. *Newsweek* called it 'a classic in its field'. Bosley Crowther in his April *New York Times* review, made reference to the large 'widescreen' format which 'enhances the scenic panorama', and praised the film, noting it had 'the quality of a fine album of paintings of the frontier'. Crowther picked out De Wilde for particular mention, 'with his bright face, his clear voice and his resolute boyish ways, who steals the affections of the audience'. *Variety* predicted 'strong box-office possibilities accrue to this socko drama' which had 'both class and mass appeal'. The film was nominated for Best Picture, Best Supporting Actor (Palance and De Wilde), Best Director and Best Screenplay, winning none. Having had his Teton vistas lopped, Loyal Griggs unexpectedly won the Oscar for Best Cinematography. In the UK *Shane* was passed a 'U' certificate in May 1960. Ladd and Heflin reprised their roles for a three-part, 48-minute *Hollywood Playhouse* radio presentation, recorded in front of a live studio audience and aired on 22 February 1955, with Ruth Hussey as Marian and Peter Votrian as Joey.

Shane's 'strong box-office possibilities' materialised and it took $9 million in the US initially. But it wasn't the most successful western of 1953. Nor were *The Naked*

Spur or *Hondo*. The smash hit of the year was *The Charge at Feather River*, its popularity ensured by being filmed in gimmicky 3D. Stevens's film had the last laugh and was the most financially successful western of the fifties, eventually grossing $20 million. In Italy it was *Il Cavaliere della Valle Solitaira* ('The Rider of Lonely Valley'), in Germany *Mein Großer Freund Shane* ('My Tall Friend Shane'), while in Spain it was the philosophical *Raíces Profundas* ('Deep Roots').

Shane was very influential, spawning dozens of loner westerns, with strangers who ride in and ride on. Clint Eastwood's mysterious screen persona was defined by Ladd's hero, from *A Fistful of Dollars*, through *High Plains Drifter* and *Pale Rider*, to *Unforgiven*. The supernatural *Pale Rider* is a close remake of *Shane*, with Eastwood's ghostly hero 'The Preacher' aiding a mining community against hired guns. *The New York Post* noted that it owed 'such a nostalgic debt to *Shane* that the similarities, scene by scene, become almost parody'. Elsewhere, Cliff Robertson appeared in four episodes of the *Batman* TV series as send-up western villain 'Shame' (the first episode was called 'Come Back, Shame'). In 1966, in the wake of Stevens's *The Greatest Story Ever Told* (1965), *Shane* was re-released by Paramount with the tacky tagline: 'The Greatest Story of the West Ever Filmed!' The same year a TV series, also called *Shane*, lasted one 17-episode season, with David Caradine (later of *Kung Fu*) in the lead and Jill Ireland (Marian), Bert Freed (Ryker) and Chris Shea (Joey).

Following his performance as Wilson, the quick-as-lightning, two-gun pistolero with a point to prove, Palance went on to become one of the great western heavies, especially through cadaverous self-parody in such films as *Compañeros* (1970) and *The Big and the Bad* (1971 – or *Can be Done, Amigo*). *Shane*'s supporting players, Johnson, Cook and Dierkes, all went on to appear in Marlon Brando's influential *One-Eyed Jacks*. In 1953, De Wilde got his own TV series, *Jamie*, but his film career was patchy and he died in a car accident aged 30. Ladd capitalised on his western popularity, with a series of mostly routine entries throughout the fifties, including *Red Mountain* (1952), *The Iron Mistress* (1952 – as Jim Bowie), *The Big Land* (1957) and Delmer Daves's superior *The Badlanders* (1958). Forever the golden-haired epitome of western fairytale heroes, Ladd never equalled his iconic performance as Shane and died in 1964, aged 50, from an overdose of sedatives and alcohol. But he left behind one role, one moment in cinema that will live forever. Shane the loner: the gunfighter with nothing to prove, who can't escape his past or the call of the faraway hills.

7

'I Never Shake Hands with a Left-Handed Draw'

— Johnny Guitar (1954)

Johnny Guitar (1954)
Credits
DIRECTOR – Nicholas Ray
PRODUCER – Herbert J. Yates
STORY – Roy Chanslor
SCREENPLAY – Philip Yordan
DIRECTOR OF PHOTOGRAPHY – Harry Stradling
EDITOR – Richard L. Van Enger
ART DIRECTOR – James Sullivan
MUSIC – Victor Young
Trucolor
A Republic Production
Released by Republic Pictures
110 minutes
Cast
Joan Crawford (Vienna); Sterling Hayden (Johnny Logan,
alias 'Johnny Guitar'); Mercedes McCambridge (Emma
Small); Scott Brady ('The Dancing Kid'); Ward Bond (John
McIvers); Ernest Borgnine (Bart Lonergan); Ben Cooper
(Turkey Ralson); John Carradine (Tom, Vienna's caretaker);
Royal Dano (Corey); Frank Fergusson (Marshal Williams);
Paul Fix (Eddie, roulette croupier); Robert Osterloh (Sam,
card croupier); Rhys Williams (Mr Andrews, railroad boss);
Ian MacDonald (Pete, posse member); Sheb Wooley (Clem,
posse member); Frank Marlowe (Frank, Vienna's bartender);
John Maxwell (Jake, bank guard); Will Wright (Ned,
bank clerk); Trevor Bardette (Jenks, stage driver);
Clem Harvey, Denver Pyle, Rocky Shahan and
Sumner Williams (Posse members)

*   *   *

Director Nicholas Ray had debuted with the noir *They Live by Night* (1948) and went on to make *In a Lonely Place* (1950), the western *Run for Cover* (1955), the iconic *Rebel Without a Cause* (1955) and *The True Story of Jesse James* (1957). He ended his career directing the epics *King of Kings* (1961) and *55 Days in Peking* (1963), both shot in Spain. But in the middle of all this he made a very unusual western with Joan Crawford. Often referred to by critics as 'the great cult western', a 'camp travesty', an 'operatic masterpiece' and a Freudian psychological drama masquerading as a genre piece, *Johnny Guitar* offered a very different view of the American west – home on 'derange'.

Drifting gunslinger Johnny 'Guitar' Logan is summoned from Albuquerque to Vienna's saloon near the town of Red Butte, Arizona. Five years previously Johnny and Vienna had been lovers. Vienna has built a stake there and is waiting for the railroad. The navigators are blasting through the mountains and laying tracks – there'll soon be a thriving town around her saloon. But her association with local outlaw the Dancing Kid and his gang leads the townsfolk in Red Butte, led by Emma Small and John McIvers, to try to force Vienna out. Emma hates Vienna because the Dancing Kid favours her, and Emma loves him. The Dancing Kid's gang rob the First Federal Bank of Red Butte and Vienna is implicated as an accomplice. Emma whips up a posse, captures Vienna and torches her saloon. Johnny manages to save Vienna from a lynching and at the Dancing Kid's mountaintop lair, Emma wounds Vienna and kills the Dancing Kid, before Vienna shoots Emma and leaves with Johnny.

For the strong, focused heroine, who will sit on her claim come what may, Ray cast Joan Crawford. Crawford's real name was Lucille Fay LeSueur; 'Joan Crawford' was chosen for her by a nationwide 'name the starlet' contest. Born in 1904, she was a star by the twenties, but faltered in the forties, until she won the Best Actress Oscar for her comeback movie *Mildred Pierce* (1945), which took $5 million. By the fifties, Crawford's star had again dipped, but Ray provided her with a feisty role as virago Vienna, the saloon owner, of whom one of her employees says, 'I've never seen a woman more like a man.' Crawford looked striking, with her strong jaw line, proud face and elegantly arched eyebrows. Opposite Crawford, as her fanatical adversary Emma, Ray cast 'the world's greatest living radio actress', Mercedes McCambridge, ahead of Crawford's preferred choice, Claire Trevor. An amazing-looking woman, with small intense features and a unique voice, McCambridge had a way of commanding a scene and audience attention – less a performance, more a presence. McCambridge was later nominated for an Oscar in *Giant* (1956), appeared as a menacing biker in *Touch of Evil* (1958) and was the voice of the demon who possesses Linda Blair in *The Exorcist* (1973).

Sterling Hayden had become famous as the 'hoolie' jewel robber in *The Asphalt Jungle* (1950) and was always tough in westerns. In *Timberjack* (1955), a typical vehicle, he wears a deerstalker hat and chequered shirt, and spends his time felling pine trees and rival lumber employees. Hayden had also starred in *Flaming Feather* (1952) as Tex McCloud, a rancher in Canyon Diablo, out to catch a renegade called

'The Sidewinder'. It was filmed on magnificent Arizona locations at Sedona, including Montezuma's Castle, an Indian pueblo embedded in a mountainside at Camp Verde. Hayden later appeared in Joseph H. Lewis's acclaimed cult *noir* western *Terror in a Texas Town* (1958), as Swedish seaman George Hansen, whose farmer father is murdered by all-in-black, steel-handed hired gun Johnny Crale (Ned Young). In the film's famous finale, Hansen faces Crale in the mainstreet of Prairie City and spears him with a seven-foot-long whaling harpoon. As Ray's guitar-playing gunslinger, Hayden plays the role close to parody. Scott Brady appeared in countless westerns throughout the fifties and sixties, and the TV series *Shotgun Slade*. He was cast to great effect in *Johnny Guitar* as the fancy outlaw, the Dancing Kid. His gang consisted of pugnacious Bart Lonergan (Ernest Borgnine), coughing Corey (Royal Dano) and youngster Turkey Ralston (Ben Cooper). Ward Bond, a staunch anti-Communist and leading light of the Motion Picture Alliance for the Preservation of American Ideals (an early version of the House Committee on Un-American Activities) was cast as McIvers, a leading light of the witch-hunting, anti-Vienna posse (Ray's joke is certainly on Bond). According to screenwriter Carl Foreman, a victim of the blacklist, Ward 'The Hangman' Bond 'could smell a Commie-Jew a mile away'. The supporting cast included John Carradine (from *Stagecoach*) as old-timer Tom at Vienna's and early performances by future western regulars Sheb Wooley and Denver Pyle as members of the posse.

Johnny Guitar was filmed on location in late 1953 in Sedona, Arizona, among the sandstone buttes and forested valleys, and at Red Rock Crossing. Vienna's saloon exterior was built especially for the film and later burned down as part of the action. The Dancing Kid's cabin hideout was also constructed, atop a high bluff. Scant town buildings, representing the edge of Red Butte, were built in the locality. The scene of the outlaws' wagon entering town was achieved with optical effects; the buttes were superimposed on the town image by specialists Consolidate Film Industries. The posse's departure from Red Butte was filmed on the Republic western town set. Interiors of Vienna's saloon, the cabin and the bank were filmed at Republic. Vienna and Johnny's conversation on a bridge lit by a picturesque, burnished sunset was filmed on a studio interior, while their buggy ride was in front of a process screen depicting Sedona woodland, though these 'exteriors' stand out compared to the Sedona footage.

On set trouble marred the production. Crawford immediately resented the kudos afforded McCambridge by the crew. Crawford referred to McCambridge as 'an actress who hadn't worked in ten years – an excellent actress but a rabble-rouser. Her delight was to create friction'. When McCambridge delivered a stirring speech to the posse, her performance received a round of applause from the crew. Ray noticed that Crawford was watching from a hilltop in the distance and they later found McCambridge's costumes strewn along the nearby road. Stories abound of Crawford trying to walk out on the production, trying to force Ray to let her co-produce and convincing the director to beef up her role and alter the script, 'I'm Clark Gable,' she told Ray, 'It's Vienna that's got to be the leading part.' 'Poor old rotten-egg Joan,' said McCambridge, years later, 'She was a mean, tipsy, powerful, rotten-egg lady.'

Crawford claimed that McCambridge would deliberately cause tension on set between the actors, 'She would finish a scene, walk to the phone...and call one columnist to report my "incivilities". I was as civil as I knew how to be.' The actresses were getting on so badly that in the final shootout McCambridge's scenes are filmed on location in Sedona, while Crawford's are obviously studio 'exteriors' created on sound stages, matched to the location footage. To make matters worse, Hayden also hated Crawford, noting, 'There is not enough money in Hollywood to lure me into making another picture with Joan Crawford...and I like money.'

The opening shot of *Johnny Guitar* is a pastoral scene of Johnny, a guitar strapped to his back, riding past a butte, which suddenly explodes in a blast of dust and smoke. This is an aptly dramatic beginning and hints at things to come: in Ray's west nothing is what it seems and surprise and effect stalk every scene. The plot of *Johnny Guitar* is an old and familiar one: Vienna owns land which will be even more valuable when the railroad arrives. But it is the settings and performances which lift Ray's drama to another level. Ray had studied architecture under Frank Lloyd Wright and this shows in the interior décor of Vienna's saloon, photographed in opulent Trucolor and designed by James Sullivan, with heavy beams, a long bar, gaming tables, open fireplaces and a scale model of a town and train

Original Italian poster artwork for the release of Nicholas Ray's *Johnny Guitar*, with Joan Crawford as Vienna and Sterling Hayden as Johnny (Picture courtesy of Ian Caunce Collection.)

line – Vienna's vision of the future. One wall of the saloon interior is sandstone, built against the rock. It's strong foundation, immovable like Vienna. Later, when the posse prepares to lynch Vienna, Emma takes a shotgun and shoots the chandelier, which crashes to the floor and torches the saloon – the symbol of Vienna's power in Red Butte. Ray dramatically films the posse thundering through the night as Vienna's dream burns.

The powerful love story between Vienna and Johnny is well played by Crawford and Hayden. Vienna asks for Johnny to strum her something. 'Anything special?' 'Just put a lot of love in.' Johnny starts to play a lament, which obviously is 'their song' and she tells him to play something else – too many memories. Because Johnny had walked out on her five years previously, she has 'learned not to love anybody again'. Johnny wants to know if there's a chance of reconciliation. 'When a fire burns itself out,' says Vienna, 'all you have left is ashes.' In a famous scene, neither can sleep (suffering 'dreams, bad dreams') and discuss their pasts in the parlour. 'How many men have you forgotten?' Johnny asks. 'As many women as you've remembered,' replies Vienna. 'Tell me something nice,' offers Johnny. 'Sure,' says Vienna, 'what do you want to hear?' Johnny asks her to lie, to say that she waited for him, that she still loves him. Vienna tells him all these things. 'Once I would have crawled at your feet to be near you,' she adds, 'I searched for you in every man I met.' Eventually the ambiguity of the scene blurs the truth and lies. 'I have waited for you Johnny,' says Vienna, as they embrace and kiss, 'What took you so long?'

Yordan's cryptic script has some of the best dialogue ever written for a western. The Dancing Kid doesn't like Johnny moving in on Vienna and Johnny enjoys riling the outlaw, asking Vienna, 'What's eating the fancy man?' Their verbal sparring at Vienna's is one of the film's high points. Johnny Guitar tells the Kid his name – 'That's no name,' scoffs the Kid. 'Anybody care to change it?' asks Johnny. 'Can you dance?' enquires Johnny. 'Can you play?' the Dancing Kid quips. Later, Bart, the Kid's bullying sidekick, says, 'I always wanted to shoot me a guitar man.'; 'That's a worthy ambition,' says the Kid. In Vienna's saloon, Emma and McIvers's posse are looking for four stagecoach robbers, her brother's murderers. Johnny witnessed the killing from a hilltop on his way to Vienna's. McIvers questions Johnny, who observes that McIvers has a suspicious mind. McIvers asks why Johnny doesn't carry a gun, ''Cos I'm not the fastest draw west of the Pecos.' At his cabin, the Kid offers to shake hands with Johnny, to which the guitar man sensibly replies: 'I never shake hands with a left-handed draw.'

Emma stokes the fires of hatred for Vienna in Red Butte, calling her 'a railroad tramp' and implying that Vienna and the Dancing Kid are up to no good, 'They both cast the same shadow.' The on-set feuding between the actresses no doubt adds real venom to their confrontations. Vienna stands looking down at Emma and the posse in her saloon, brandishing a pistol, 'Down there I sell whisky and cards. All you can buy up these stairs is a bullet in the head.' During Vienna's lynching, beneath a trestle bridge, she is dressed in a pure white dress, more appropriate for a wedding, while Emma is all in black. None of the posse will crack the whip to scare Vienna's horse, thus hanging her. Emma takes the whip and is about to lash the horse, when

Johnny cuts the rope from above and saves Vienna from the necktie party. Earlier, Vienna observes of Emma that 'He [The Dancing Kid] makes her feel like a woman and that frightens her'. When the Kid grabs Emma in the saloon and dances a jig with her, Emma reels away, the experience of being so close to the object of her obsession too much to bear.

Throughout *Johnny Guitar* there are several barbed digs at McCarthyism, especially its mob ethic – a subtext intended by Ray and Yordan. As Johnny warns Vienna, 'A posse is an animal... it moves like one and thinks like one.' Emma's brother has been killed in the opening hold-up (though it is never established who actually carried this out) and the posse are attending his funeral when the Dancing Kid's bunch rob the bank. Thereafter, the posse are dressed uniformly in formal black funeral suits, while Emma leads them in full mourning attire, adding a stylish dimension to the hunt. 'My men are not killers,' says McIvers, 'They gotta be cold, tired and hungry before they get mad.'; 'How long does that take?' snaps Emma. Although she is hiding wounded outlaw Turkey in her saloon, Vienna goads the mob, as she sits at the piano, 'I'm sitting in my own house, minding my own business, playing my own piano. I don't think you can make a crime out of that.' At the most inopportune moment, the outlaw's boot gives his hiding place away under Vienna's model town – displaying her hypocrisy at the very moment she is deriding the posse's. McIvers tries to convince Turkey to implicate Vienna in the bank robbery – 'You've got a rope around your neck son, you'd better talk' – in the film's clearest voicing of McCarthyism.

Ray stages an explosion of love and hate in the finale, a shootout set in the Dancing Kid's mountain bolt-hole, which can only be accessed through a waterfall (an old series western cliché). Vienna, now dressed in dead outlaw Turkey's bright yellow shirt and red scarf, shoots it out with Emma on the cabin veranda, high above the gorge. When Emma shoots the Kid, she hits him right through the forehead and then plunges off the veranda when shot by Vienna, falling down the steps and into the valley. Her black-clad hunting party huddle around Emma's body, visualising Vienna's summation of the posse earlier as 'vultures waiting for another corpse'.

Vienna and Johnny's love is cemented in the romantic ending. After all the killing, the high emotion and histrionics, they descend the cabin steps together, walk unharmed through the posse and out through the waterfall, before embracing, drenched. The song, 'Johnny Guitar', with music by Victor Young and sung by Peggy Lee (who also composed the non-rhyming lyrics), aptly underscores this sequence:

> Whether you go, whether you stay, I love you
> What if you're cruel, you can be kind, I know.
> There was never a man like my Johnny
> Like the one they called Johnny Guitar.

In late 1953, before *Johnny Guitar* was released, Crawford invited McCambridge to attend the gala premiere of her latest film, *Torch Song*, in an attempt to make it appear their fighting had ceased. To the press McCambridge and Crawford seemed old friends, chatting, smiling, but it later became known that Crawford had asked

McCambridge to show up and pretend they were friends, solely to promote *Johnny Guitar*. Posters for *Johnny Guitar* announced 'Joan's Greatest Triumph' and depicted Crawford in all her glory, in tight trousers, riding boots, bright red or black shirts, scarf and packing a pistol, with the taglines: 'Gun Queen of the Arizona Frontier – and Her Kind of Men' or 'Play Me a Song Johnny... And Put a Lot of Love Into It'. Two different versions of the film's title sequence were prepared – one print has the yellow titles appearing with the Sedona landscape as a backdrop, the other has the same yellow lettering on a deep blue background; both have since shown up on home video and TV.

Johnny Guitar was exhibited to mixed notices and only a fair box office response in May 1954. *Time* said the film was 'a crossbreed of the western with a psychological case history. Somehow, strains of Greek tragedy, Germanic grand opera and just plain better class living have also slipped into the mixture'. *Variety* assumed it was heading 'for spotty returns, even with exploitation', while *Cue* noted that although *Johnny Guitar* was 'strikingly artistic, decoratively imaginative and nearly always absorbing drama', slipping 'swiftly from amorous to murderous', it frequently 'stumbles over its own artiness'. When Alex Cox introduced the film in the *Moviedrome* cult film season on BBC2 TV, he called it 'not an entirely successful film – a bit like a Christmas in July'. It was known as *Johnny Guitar* throughout Europe, except in Germany where it was *Wenn Frauen Hassen* ('When Women Hate') and *Johnny Guitar – Gejagt, Gehaßt, Gefürchtet* ('Hunted, Hated, Feared'). The film was a critical hit in France on its release. In 1966 *Le Western* featured a list of 28 French critics' best westerns and *Johnny Guitar* topped the list, with *Rio Bravo* second. François Truffaut called the film 'beautiful and profound' and noted in his review, 'Never trust appearances. A Trucolor western from humble Republic can throb with the passion of *l'amour fou* or whisper with an evening delicacy.'

Crawford wasn't the first actress to strap on six-guns and play the lead in a western, nor was she the last. Outlaw Belle Starr (or her relatives) has been played by Gene Tierney in *Belle Starr* (1941), Jane Russell in *Montana Belle* (1952), Ruth Roman in *Belle Starr's Daughter* (1947) and Elsa Martinelli in *The Belle Starr Story* (1968). Sam Newfield's *Outlaw Women* (1951), where the town of Los Mujeres was run by gambling queen Iron Mae McCloud (Marie Windsor) and her 'gun girls', has often been cited as an influence on *Johnny Guitar*. In *The Guns of Fort Petticoat* (1957) Audie Murphy schooled a group of women in Indian fighting as though running a night class. Gunslinging saloon owner Jayne Mansfield helped out English gunsmith Kenneth More in *The Sheriff of Fractured Jaw* (1959), a British western shot near Madrid and released in Italy as *La Bionda e Lo Sceriffo* ('The Blonde and the Sheriff'). Jane Fonda starred as outlaw *Cat Ballou* (1965), who turns to outlawry when a development corporation kills her rancher father. *The Shooting* (1966) saw Millie Perkins employing ex-bounty hunter Willet Gashade (Warren Oates) to track the killer of her husband and child, in Monte Hellman's oblique desert-set mystery-western, which also featured a cold performance by Jack Nicholson as hired killer, Billy Spear. In *The Legend of Frenchie King* (1971), a French western, rancher Claudia Cardinale faced outlaw Brigitte Bardot. In the brutal *Hannie Caulder* (1972), poncho-clad Raquel Welch tracked down the three outlaws who raped her and murdered her husband. *The Ballad of Little Jo* (1993) saw Josephine Monaghan (Suzi Amis) posing as a man in order to survive out west, having been ostracised back east by her parents following the birth of her child outside marriage. Madeline Stowe, Andie MacDowell, Drew Barrymore and Mary Stuart Masterson (no relation to Bat) were *Bad Girls* (1994), 'Honky-tonk Harlots' from Echo City turned outlaws on the run, and Sam Raimi's *The Quick and the Dead* (1995) starred Sharon Stone. Salma Hayek and Penélope Cruz have appeared as a Mexican 'Butch and Sundance' in *Bandidas* (2006) and in the bizarre R 'n' B western *Gang of Roses* (2004), the five-strong all-female Rose Gang teamed up to save a town, with featured appearances by singers Lil' Kim, Bobby Brown and Macy Gray.

Two of Roger Corman's four low-budget westerns owed much to *Johnny Guitar*. *The Oklahoma Woman* (1956) cast Peggie Castle as Marie 'Oklahoma' Saunders, a land-grabbing saloon owner in Silver Hill, who wields a bullwhip, wrestles with Cathy Downs (Ford's darling Clementine) and ends up mud-splattered by a lynch mob. 'Downstairs I'm a saloonkeeper,' says Oklahoma, as she tries to seduce a sheriff, 'Up here I'm a woman.' 'There's no denying that,' answers the lawman. In *The Gunslinger* (1956), Rose Hood (Beverly Garland) becomes sheriff of a mud-strewn Texas town when her lawman husband is killed. Landowner Erica Page (Allison Hayes) is waiting for the railroad to arrive to make her rich and hires gunslinger Cane Miro (John Ireland) for protection. Corman figured out that women in the title and on the posters spelled box office (Corman also made *Apache Woman*, *Viking Women and the Sea Serpent*, *The Swamp Women*, *The Last Woman on Earth* and *The Wasp Woman*). Despite sharing themes, Corman's budget filmmaking was the opposite of Ray's painstaking, psychological 'cinema as art', more a 'cinema of action'. Corman would tell his scriptwriters, 'Here on page 20, I'd like to have some violence,' without any motivation or reason being established – purely for pace.

During the fifties TV western bonanza, a 30-minute black and white TV pilot called *Johnny Guitar* appeared in 1959, with William Joyce as Johnny and no sign of Vienna, while Sergio Leone used Ray's film as the plot for *Once Upon a Time in the West* (1968). In 2004 *Johnny Guitar: the Musical* opened in Boston (music and lyrics by Martin Silvestri and Joel Higgins), with song titles including, 'Tell Me a Lie', 'Let it Spin', 'Branded a Tramp' and 'We Had Our Moments'. Perhaps Broadway is the best place for *Johnny Guitar*'s blend of larger-than-life characters, clashing egos and lavish visuals, though no one will ever outgun the original Vienna for riveting charisma.

8

'We'll Fool Saint Peter Yet'

— *Vera Cruz* (1954)

Vera Cruz (1954)
Credits
DIRECTOR – Robert Aldrich
PRODUCER – Harold Hecht
STORY – Borden Chase
SCREENPLAY – Roland Kibbee and James R. Webb
DIRECTOR OF PHOTOGRAPHY – Ernest Laszlo
EDITOR – Alan Crosland Jnr
PRODUCTION DESIGNER – Alfred Ybarra
MUSIC – Hugo Friedhofer
SuperScope/Technicolor
A Hecht-Lancaster/Flora Production
Released by United Artists
94 minutes
Cast
   Gary Cooper (Major Benjamin Trane); Burt Lancaster
   (Joe Erin); Denise Darcel (Countess Marie Duvarre);
   Cesar Romero (Marquis Henri De Labordere); Sarita
   Montiel (Nina); George Macready (Emperor Maximilian);
   Ernest Borgnine (Donnegan); Morris Ankrum (General
   Ramirez); Henry Brandon (Captain Danette); Charles
   Bronson (Pittsburgh); Jack Lambert (Charlie); Jack
   Elam (Tex); James McCallion (Little-Bit); Archie Savage
   (Ballard); Juan Garcia (Pedro, Ramirez's lieutenant); James
   Seay (Abilene); Charles Horvath (Reno); Fetty Clavijo
   (Flamenco dancer in Las Palmas)

*   *   *

The early fifties was a prolific period for actor Burt Lancaster as he bounded acrobatically through a series of massively popular action adventures, set in a variety of historical periods. *The Flame and the Arrow* (1950) saw Lancaster's Lombardy rebel outlaw Dardo demonstrating his archery prowess, modelling some technicolor tights and spouting contemporary-sounding dialogue like, 'Tell da boys I'll meet 'em in da tavern.' *Ten Tall Men* (1951) turned *Beau Geste* into 'Beau Jest', while swashbuckler *The Crimson Pirate* (1952) was his biggest hit, a carnival of acrobatics, romance and action. For *Flame* Lancaster had learned to ride, fire an arrow and sword fight, and had trained for weeks with master acrobat and human cannonball 'Shotsy' O'Brien to the peak of athleticism.

To capitalise on this popularity, producer Harold Hecht and Lancaster's Hecht-Lancaster productions made two westerns with United Artists, both directed by Robert Aldrich. The first was *Apache*, filmed in 1953. Based on the novel 'Bronco Apache' by Paul I. Wellman, it cast Lancaster, not wholly convincingly, as Apache warrior Massai, the last of the renegades, on the run from the army. Made for $1,240,000, it grossed $6 million following its release in the US in June 1954. The next Hecht-Lancaster production was *Vera Cruz*, set in Maximilian's Mexican revolution, the so-called French Intervention (1862–1867), when the Juaristas under Benito Juarez rose against the French invaders. When Hollywood lost its lucrative European audiences during the Second World War, it discovered that films set in Mexico and South America, with stars like Carmen Miranda and Cesar Romero, opened up a whole new market.

Vera Cruz was written by Roland Kibbee and James R. Webb from a story by Borden Chase, though reputedly a full script was never finished. In the aftermath of the American Civil War assorted soldiers of fortune, adventurers and criminals headed south to work as mercenaries. Ex-Confederate Major Ben Trane and scallywag gunslinger Joe Erin hook up when Erin sells Trane a stolen horse. With Erin's mercenary gang, they accept a mission from Emperor Maximilian to escort a coach taking Countess Marie to the port of Vera Cruz, where she can sail for France. Accompanying them will be an imperial escort of lancers, led by Marquis Labordere and Captain Danette. Judging by the deep coach tracks, the countess really is 'worth her weight in gold'; her journey is a ruse by Maximilian to ship $3 million in coin to pay for French reinforcements. Erin sides with the countess, who plans to steal the cache, while Trane is also after a share. Following double and triple crosses, the Marquis makes off with the gold and reaches Vera Cruz, where the funds are to be transported to Europe. Trane and Erin help the Juaristas attack the port, but Erin wants the money for himself. In a duel, Trane has to kill Erin, and donates the fortune to the revolution.

Star Gary Cooper was offered a percentage deal, based on the profits, to appear as Trane. Acting as producer, Lancaster was happy to settle for second billing, as perpetually-grinning Joe; Lancaster spent most of the film showing off his newly acquired $5,000 capped teeth. Sarita (real name Sara) Montiel, a Spanish singing star, was cast as pickpocketing Juarista Nina, and was described in the trailer as a 'temptress and tease…who entices Gary Cooper into her web of intrigue'. She married director Anthony Mann in 1957 and appeared in Samuel Fuller's *Run of the Arrow* (1957). The villainous French characters were played by an international mix: Cesar Romero, a popular actor of Cuban ancestry, appeared as the Marquis (he was later Batman's sworn enemy, the Joker, on TV), Parisian-born nightclub singer Denise Darcel played Countess Marie ('Alluring, free with a kiss or a caress', said the trailer), while martinet lancer Captain Danette was Berlin-born Henry Brandon, or rather Heinrich Von Kleinbach, to give him his real name. Emperor Maximilian was played by George Macready, his trademark scarred right cheek (the result of a car accident) concealed by angled filming and a beard. Erin's gang of gringo mercenaries included several future stars. Charles Buchinsky (who changed his name to Charles Bronson immediately after *Vera Cruz*) portrayed harmonica-playing Pittsburgh. Ernest Borgnine appeared as Donnegan, Jack Lambert was Charlie and Jack Elam played Tex. James Seay played gambler Abilene and stuntman Charles Horvath portrayed tall, Indian-looking Reno. Choreographer Archie Savage, cast as cashiered bluecoat Ballard, performed a couple of hoedowns – he'd just appeared with Lancaster as South Sea Island chief Boogulroo in *His Majesty O'Keefe* (1953).

Vera Cruz was filmed in Mexico from 3 March to 12 May 1954 near arid Cuernavaca, Morelos. Interiors were lensed at Estudios Churubusco, Mexico City. The action was set among plazas, missions, rivers and viaducts – a picture-postcard Mexico of crumbling buildings, giant Teotiaucan pyramids, stone bridges and sleepy adobe villages. These locations looked great in Technicolor and SuperScope, with production design by Alfred Ybarra. Budgeted at $850,000, production costs rose to $1.7 million. One story goes that Bronson and Borgnine left the set in Mexico in their cowboy costumes to buy cigarettes and were arrested by Federales who thought they were real bandits – actually it was Charles Horvath who was mistaken off-set for real outlaw 'Jamarillo'.

Major Benjamin Trane from Louisiana had been an aide to General Beauregard. Erin calls him 'a real southern gentleman', but behind his back confesses, 'I don't trust him – he likes people and you can never count on a man like that.' Erin mistakes Trane for a colonel ('All you southerners are colonels, ain't you?') and later Trane offers his reason for fighting for the Juaristas – he wants the money to rebuild his plantation. He made the mistake of fighting his last action of the Civil War on his own property and his staff are relying on him for their livelihoods. But Trane is a good negotiator and a useful ally to Joe's fast gun.

Lancaster's hero Joe Erin steals the film. Dressed entirely in black, with a black buckled wrist gauntlet, Erin is the most stylish anti-hero of the fifties. He tries to steal the gold at every opportunity, siding with whoever has the upper hand, however temporarily. Unlike idealist Trane, Erin wouldn't give the Juaristas 'the sweat off my brow'. He's a con man, with a streak of black humour, established in his first meeting with Trane. The major limps into a desert cantina on a lame horse and Joe offers him a fresh nag for $100. 'That's mighty hard,' says Trane. 'So's walking,' replies Erin. Trane pays him and shoots his injured horse. 'Three-legged horse bring a price down here.'; 'He was suffering,' says Trane. 'Soft spot, huh?' notes Erin; 'Only for horses,' the major replies. When a squadron of lancers appear, Trane can't work out why their captain is shooting at him. 'That's his horse you're riding,' laughs Erin. Later when Joe saves Trane from a gang of gringo mercenaries, the major asks, 'Soft spot for an innocent man?'; 'No such thing as an innocent man,' answers cynical Joe, who doesn't take chances, trust anybody or do any favours. He learned these lessons from his mentor, Ace Hannah, who shot Erin's father in a stud game. 'Ace lived long enough to know he was right,' says Joe, 'He lived 30 seconds after I shot him.'

Seemingly everyone in Mexico is out to double-cross everyone else. As the emperor notes, if the mercenaries are not killed by Juaristas, they will be bayoneted by his troops. Joe tries unsuccessfully to steal Trane's wallet (later pickpocket Nina steals it instead), though even Trane can be mercenary, 'It's not the wallet, it's the sentiment – I had $12 in it.' On the eve of battle, the Juaristas write down their names, so that the correct title appears on their tombstones. Erin suggests to Trane, 'You write my name, I write yours – we'll fool Saint Peter yet!' As the only mercenary going to Heaven, the major is the film's sole trustworthy protagonist. Erin has no scruples when it comes to gaining an edge. In one scene, with the hired guns surrounded in a plaza by Juaristas, his men take a group of Mexican children hostage and threaten to kill them. The Marquis notes afterwards that it was a fine bluff by Erin – or was he bluffing? 'They're still alive aren't they,' says Trane, unconvinced.

Vera Cruz is the first western to send its mercenary heroes to Mexico and it was also the first Hollywood western to be filmed there. The actual eastern port of 'Veracruz' in the Gulf of Mexico (which the film calls Vera Cruz) was an important

Big Rushmores: Mercenaries Joe Erin and Major Ben Trane in Robert Aldrich's archetypal Mexican Revolution movie; Burt Lancaster and Gary Cooper in *Vera Cruz* (1954).

strategic objective in the revolution. This south of the border setting is echoed in Hugo Friedhofer's evocative score, orchestrated and conducted by Raul LaVista. Even the title sequence is daubed in bright red, like revolutionary slogans on adobe walls. 'La Revolucion' allows Aldrich to stage some frantic action sequences: a Juarista ambush in the narrow village streets and a shootout in the plaza of Las Palmas, when the French escape with the coach to Vera Cruz. The final assault on the city sees the mercenaries offering covering fire with their Winchester repeaters, while the machete-wielding Juarista hordes storm the heavily fortified gates. The French defences include artillery and a Gatling gun, but the Juaristas keep coming – eventually heroic peon Pedro manages to detonate a charge (and unfortunately himself), obliterating the gates. This pyrotechnic finale, the first in a western, was very influential on Mexican Revolution films like *A Professional Gun* (1968), *100 Rifles* (1968), *Cannon for Cordoba* (1970), *Two Mules for Sister Sara* (1970) and *Duck You Sucker* (1971).

Aldrich's action is also highly stylised. In the walled square of a town, the gringos rendezvous with Maximilian's envoy, Marquis Labordere. Erin says they have 17 guns for hire, but rival mercenary Charlie (Jack Lambert) claims to be running the show. Erin steps forward, 'Anything wrong with the count?' Charlie stands firm, while his henchman chips in, 'I string with Charlie.' Erin turns away, then flashily draws his pistol behind his back and shoots Charlie and his sidekick dead. 'Anybody else string with Charlie?' asks Erin. Aldrich called his stylised close-ups of faces 'Big Rushmores', with Lancaster's face dominating the foreground and Cooper in the background. In the final duel between Trane and Erin, the major gives the trickster a chance, 'That old soft spot, eh Ben?' 'Even Ace had one,' answers the major. 'That was Ace's mistake,' notes Erin. But Trane is faster: in a flourish, Joe is able to twirl his pistol and place it back in his holster before toppling into the dust.

Mexico, a country on its knees, is the backdrop to Lancaster and Cooper's sparring. Aldrich isn't very interested in the film's politics, and characters have to make an effort to ensure their message is heard over the gunshots and explosions. Juarista pickpocket Nina notes that, 'It is hard to be a patriot on an empty stomach,' and she is travelling to Vera Cruz because 'there are many people and many pockets'. Erin laughs when he first meets ragtag General Ramirez, dressed no better than a beggar, but later finds himself aligned with the rebels out of necessity. 'We offer you more than money,' says Ramirez to the gunmen, 'We offer a cause.' 'How about that Ben?' grins Joe, introducing the Confederate major, 'This here's our cause expert.' Aldrich uses the scenes at the Emperor's Mexico City palace as comic relief, rather than social comment. The mercenaries arrive, incongruous among the opulent décor, ball gowns and ostentatious Napoleonic uniforms. 'Man,' marvels gunslinger Tex, 'this is the fanciest lodge hall I ever seen.' The hired guns guzzle wine and set about the buffet, shocking the guests with their manners. As a demonstration of their firepower (Winchester repeaters, which are a little early for the post-Civil War period depicted), the mercenaries turn the elegant ball into a shooting contest, with Joe and Ben hitting guards' lance points and snuffing out torches at distance. These contrasts, between rough adventurers and the bourgeoisie, had already been exploited in Lancaster's earlier period adventures, and later became western clichés.

'The Giants Clash in the Biggest Spectacle of them All' read *Vera Cruz*'s posters, depicting the stars face to face, with Lancaster snarling at Cooper. It was premiered in the US during Christmas, 1954. The trailer called Cooper and Lancaster: 'The Quiet Man and the Gunslinger, Fighting Side by Side – And Each Other!' Though it didn't feature in the film, Tony Martin's rendition of the title song 'Vera Cruz' was released by RCA as a tie-in. The song is even billed in the credits, with music by Friedhofer and lyrics by Sammy Cahn. *Vera Cruz* took $4.6 million in the US and $9 million overall, making it the fourth biggest earning western of the fifties. Cooper, with his percentage deal, made $1 million from it. *Vera Cruz* went on general release on 12 January 1955. The MPAA complained that Lancaster mouths 'You dirty son of a bitch' to Cooper, with the last word drowned out on the soundtrack by a fanfare announcing Maximilian's arrival, but it was left in the final cut of the film.

Andrew Sarris called *Vera Cruz* 'elegant escapism', while a French reviewer said the release of Aldrich's *Apache*, *Vera Cruz* and *Kiss Me Deadly* was 'the single most exciting cinematic event of the mid-fifties'. The *New York Times* complained that the film was a 'big, noisy, badly-photographed melodrama'. The UK's *Picturegoer Film Annual* 1955–1956 called Lancaster 'a whale of a wicked fellow', while commenting on the even-handedness of the action: 'If Cooper gets a spot of glory to himself in one scene, Lancaster gets a spot in the next … and (they) have a glorious time outdoing each other'. But many critics found the unrelentingly cynical tone too much. *MAD* magazine parodied the film's unbelievable action, with 'Burt Lambaster' having time to shave and wash before falling over dead after his shootout with 'Gary Chickencooper'. And despite a lengthy 'thank you' to the 'people and government of Mexico' and the Mexican film industry at the end of the film, the Mexicans were very unhappy with the way their countrymen were depicted. This resulted in the formation of a strict Mexican censor board, which would rigorously vet productions wishing to be filmed in their country.

Aldrich returned to Mexico to make the $3 million *The Last Sunset*, an incestuous psychological western, in 1961. The relationship between black-clad singing psychopath O'Malley (Kirk Douglas) and chunky sheriff Dana Stribling (Rock Hudson) during a cattle drive from Mexico to Texas was clearly influenced by *Vera Cruz*'s heroes. Aldrich's mixture of excess, romance and cynicism didn't quite work, but the finale, a stylised duel in the riverside town of Crazy Horse (the film was based on Howard Rigsby's novel 'Sundown at Crazy Horse'), is memorable. O'Malley courts Missy (Carol Lynley), the daughter of his ex-wife Belle (Dorothy Malone), until the unfortunate revelation that he's fallen for his own daughter. Destroyed, O'Malley commits suicide by facing Stribling with an unloaded Derringer.

Vera Cruz's Maximilian-era Mexican setting was used in several other westerns. *Mutiny at Fort Sharpe* (1966) features French cavalry straying across the border and finding themselves caught between hostile Indians and inhospitable Confederates, led by grouchy Broderick Crawford. 3,000 Navajos apparently surround the fort, though we only ever see about 30 – the excuse is that they're 'attacking in waves'. *Major Dundee* (1965) and *The Undefeated* (1969) had Unionists and Confederates united in Mexico, *Two Mules for Sister Sara* (1970) starred Clint Eastwood as an

American mercenary helping the Juaristas, while spaghetti westerns *Adios Sabata* (1970 – *The Bounty Hunters* in the UK) and *They Call Me Hallelujah* (1971) parodied *Vera Cruz* – both dealt with the secret transportation of government gold or jewels. Sergio Leone admitted using the relationship between Trane and Erin as the basis for *For a Few Dollars More* (1965), with Lee Van Cleef as Carolina Colonel Mortimer and Clint Eastwood as his bounty-hunting competitor Manco. Louis Malle also used *Vera Cruz* as his template for *Viva Maria!* (1965), with Brigitte Bardot and Jeanne Moreau as revolutionaries fighting in Central America.

A couple of fifties westerns used Mexico as a setting, though usually during the 1910–20 revolution instigated by Francisco Madero to overthrow Porfirio Diaz's regime, where bandit rebels Pancho Villa and Emiliano Zapata battled General Huerta. Villa's followers fought for 'Villismo' (their ideology) in the north, while Zapatistas struggled to install 'Zapatismo' in the south. *The Treasure of Pancho Villa* (1955) starred Rory Calhoun as Tom Bryan, a bank-robbing mercenary in 1915 Mexico, who liberates funds for Villa. Wanting to retire, he takes one more job: the assault on an artillery-equipped military train transporting government gold. For the train attack, Bryan fires his machine-gun 'La Cucaracha' from the hip without the aid of a tripod (a common but inaccurate feature of many turn-of-the-century Tex-Mex westerns) and in the finale takes on the Federales from behind a barricade of gold sacks. *Bandido!* (1956) saw Robert Mitchum's white-suited gunrunning mercenary Wilson, with a suitcase filled with grenades, arrive at a besieged town by taxi then calmly check into a hotel, as bullets whiz by. Both films were shot in Mexico and co-starred Mexican actor Gilbert Roland as a Villista leader.

In 1966 Lancaster returned to the Mexican Revolution for *The Professionals*, directed by Richard Brooks. Four specialists are hired for $10,000 apiece by railroad tycoon J.W. Grant (Ralph Bellamy) for a nine-day, 'mission of mercy': to rescue his kidnapped Mexican wife Maria (Claudia Cardinale) from Villista revolutionary Captain Jesus Raza (Jack Palance). The quartet of professionals are philandering dynamiter Bill Dolworth (Lancaster), tracker, scout and bowman Jacob Sharp (Woody Strode), ace wrangler Hans Ehrengard (Robert Ryan) and munitions expert Henry Rico Farden (Lee Marvin). Mercenaries Farden and Dolworth have fought alongside Raza in the past and Farden's wife was killed by the ruthless 'Colorados' (Mexican government soldiers). Once again they find themselves heading into the Painted Mountains of northern Mexico to fight – this time 'strictly for cash'. They manage to rescue Maria, and Raza gives chase, but it becomes apparent that they are lovers. The mercenaries return to Texas, discovering that the whole operation was a ruse by Grant: Maria had run away to Raza – there never was a ransom note or a kidnapping. The professionals have been had and they return Maria to her lover. 'You bastard,' snorts Grant, the real kidnapper, 'Yes sir, in my case an accident of birth,' replies Farden, 'But you sir, you're a self-made man.'

The Professionals was filmed in October 1965 on location in the Death Valley National Monument, the Valley of Fire State Park, Nevada, and on a railroad line east of Indio, California – the rail spur, owned by the Kaiser Steel Company, was used for the scenes where the professionals prepare for their attack. Coyote Pass, near

'The Cemetery of Nameless Men', was the chasm rigged with dynamite for the mercenaries to make their escape. The Death Valley locations, photographed by Conrad Hall, offered an interesting geology – they were used by NASA to replicate the conditions for moon landings. Brooks's film, based on the novel: 'A Mule for the Marquesa' by Frank O'Rourke, inspired many Mexican Revolution movies, particularly *The Wild Bunch*. With its train attacks, roving Mexican bandidos, modern 'hardware', big explosions and Jack Palance's ruthless performance as Raza, 'The bloodiest cut-throat in Mexico' (who shoots Colorados prisoners in the back and executes their officers from telegraph poles), *The Professionals* looks like an Italian western, but no examples of the European genre had been released in the US by 1965.

Lancaster, as Dolworth 'the whirliest dervish of them all', again upstages his gringo co-stars and gets all the best lines, 'Nothing's harmless in the desert, unless it's dead,' he warns. Having watched Sharp's accuracy with a bow and arrow, he comments, 'Makes you wonder how we ever beat the Indians.' 'Go to Hell,' Maria tells Dolworth, when she doesn't want to be rescued. 'Yes ma'am,' quips Dolworth, 'I'm on my way.' At one point, the explosives expert offers his gospel according to nitro-glycerine, 'Then dynamite, not faith, will move that mountain into this pass. Peace brother.' Locked in a duel with Raza in a canyon, the Mexican tells Dolworth that the revolution is like a love affair, which eventually becomes 'lust but no love, passion but no compassion'; 'Nothing is for always,' Dolworth tells the idealist, 'except death.' These professionals, with their terse dialogues, military precision, pump-action shotguns, machine-guns and flair with dynamite kept audiences rapt. *The Professionals* took $8.8 million on its release in November 1966, putting it in the top ten earning westerns of the sixties. Dolworth perfectly captures the essence of films like *Vera Cruz* and *The Professionals*, which deploy the Mexican Revolution in the name of action entertainment: 'Maybe there's only one revolution – the good guys against the bad guys. The question is, "Who are the good guys?"'

9

'I Came a Thousand Miles to Kill You'

— *The Man from Laramie* (1955)

The Man from Laramie (1955)
Credits
DIRECTOR – Anthony Mann
PRODUCER – William Goetz
STORY – Thomas T. Flynn
SCREENPLAY – Philip Yordan and Frank Burt
DIRECTOR OF PHOTOGRAPHY – Charles Lang
EDITOR – William Lyon
ART DIRECTOR – Cary Odell
MUSIC – George Duning
CinemaScope/Technicolor
A Columbia Production
Released by Columbia Pictures
101 minutes
Cast
    James Stewart (Captain Will Lockhart); Arthur Kennedy (Victor 'Vic' Hansbro); Donald Crisp (Alec Waggoman); Cathy O'Donnell (Barbara Waggoman); Alex Nicol (Dave Waggoman); Aline MacMahon (Kate Canaday); Wallace Ford (Charley O'Leary); Jack Elam (Chris Boldt); John War Eagle (Frank Darrah, mercantile storekeeper); James Millican (Sheriff Tom Quigby); Gregg Barton (Fritz, Barb rider); Boyd Stockman (Spud Oxton, Barb rider); Frank DeKova (Padre of Coronado); Eddy Waller (Doctor); Jack Carry, Frosty Royce, Bill Catching and Frank Cordell (Mule drivers)

*   *   *

In the 1950s, director Anthony Mann and star James Stewart made eight films together, five of which were westerns: *Winchester '73*, *Bend of the River*, *The Naked Spur*, *The Far Country* and *The Man from Laramie*. In contrast to Stewart's boyish innocence in such films as *The Philadelphia Story* (1940) and *It's a Wonderful Life* (1947), his western heroes were driven by justice, revenge or greed – and sometimes all three.

In *Winchester '73* (1950), Lin McAdam (Stewart) arrives in Dodge City to take part in the Independence Day Centennial Rifle Shoot, a competition to win a 'One of a Thousand' Winchester Rifle, a flawless edition of 'The Gun that Won the West'. But he's also there to catch gunman Dutch Henry Brown (Stephen McNally). McAdam wins the competition, but Dutch steals the gun, which passes through various people's ownership as McAdam follows Dutch across the west. Dutch is actually Matthew McAdam, Lin's brother; but when Dutch became an outlaw, he shot their father – the man who taught them how to shoot in the first place.

Mann uses this tightly plotted Winchester pass-the-parcel on which to pin his tale of revenge. Dan Duryea's turn as two-gun outlaw Waco Johnny Dean, a grinning lunatic, steals the film, while Stewart easily settles into his new tough cowboy persona, especially in the scene with Waco, when he almost breaks the outlaw's arm in a fistfight in the Tascosa saloon (filmed on location at Old Tucson, Arizona). As screenwriter Borden Chase noted, there were some titters in the audience in 1950 seeing lightweight Stewart's name in a western, 'But once he smashed Duryea in the bar, there would be no more snickering'. Stewart was the first star to work for a percentage of the profits and the film is largely responsible for the renewed popularity of adult-themed westerns in the early fifties, when television, cheapies and singing cowboys monopolised post-war audiences.

Mann's *Bend of the River* (1952 – *Where the River Bends* in the UK), adapted from the novel 'Bend of the Snake' by Bill Gullick, saw guide Glyn McLyntock (Stewart) leading a wagon train through Oregon to build a new life as part of a farming community. But as winter approaches their promised supplies haven't arrived from Portland. McLyntock returns to town and finds there has been a gold strike and inflation has rocketed; the town is iniquitous and the supplies are impounded. McLyntock, with Cole Garett (Arthur Kennedy), a man he has saved from lynching, gather a bunch of ruffians to transport the four supply wagons. The journey is arduous. Realising they can make more money selling the supplies to prospectors, the gang leave McLyntock to die. He survives, trails his betrayers and kills them, beating Garett in a fistfight in the swirling waters of the Snake River, before delivering the supplies to the settlers.

Here Mann begins to use landscapes more effectively. He filmed for six weeks in the locality of Mount Hood in Oregon and on the Sandy River. One of the most memorable sequences depicts the trip upriver by paddle steamer, the 'River Queen'. The scenes of the wilderness, pine forests, rocky trails and raging torrents add an elemental quality to Stewart's tormented character. McLyntock is an ex-Missouri border raider, like Garett, who was almost lynched (McLyntock hides his scar beneath a neckerchief). McLyntock wants to forget his past, to prove that people can change. Garett has no hope of redemption and McLyntock, having given him the benefit of the doubt, is forced to kill him. The action is violent, further enhanced by Stewart performing most of his own stunts. The supporting cast includes Jay C. Flippen as settler Baile, Rock Hudson as gambler Trey Wilson, and heavies Harry Morgan, Royal Dano and Jack Lambert as the untrustworthies hired to haul the wagons over the mountains. But again it is the villain, played by Kennedy, who hits the mark: a man who initially seems a romantic drifter 'following the stars', but really is an unreformed killer, pursued by tin stars.

For *The Naked Spur* (1953), Stewart and Mann further punished Stewart's demented western hero, here bounty hunter Howard Kemp, who is a man driven to hunt men for money due to misfortune. He went to fight in the Civil War and returned to find that his wife had sold their farm and run off with another man. He wants the $5,000 reward to reclaim his land. With the help of Jesse Tate, an old prospector (Millard Mitchell) and Roy Anderson (Ralph Meeker), a dishonourably discharged cavalry lieutenant, Kemp apprehends wanted outlaw Ben Vandergroat (an unshaven, sneering Robert Ryan) and his girl, Lina Patch (Janet Leigh). But Ben preys on the group's weaknesses. Kemp catches a bullet in his right leg and Ben torments him about his unfaithful wife. Ben tells Tate he knows where a fortune in gold lies hidden in a mine and convinces Lina to distract ladies' man Anderson. In the course of their gruelling journey, Ben grinds the spur in the wound he's opened within the group. In the finale, he escapes and kills Tate, but is shot by Anderson, who in his attempt to retrieve the valuable corpse from the rapids, is killed by a drifting log. Kemp, consumed with hatred for Ben and himself, breaks down, buries Ben's body rather than cashing it in and rides off with Lina.

The Naked Spur is Mann and Stewart's most demonic western, enacted with a minimal cast in the spectacular Rocky Mountains of Colorado. The violence and drama is as jagged as the landscape (it was rated 'A' in the UK, after it had been pruned for violence). Whether Kemp is maniacally screaming his wife's name in delirium or gritting his teeth, whilst dragging his wounded leg behind him, so as not to slow the group down, he is a cowboy on the brink of a nervous breakdown. There is a wild look in Stewart's eyes and a tightness in his face that had hitherto been only glimpsed in his more intense moments (for example, when he tried to knife Jack Lambert's ruffian, Red, or when he's left behind on Mount Hood, in *Bend of the River*). This embittered hero is right at home in Mann's twisted west, where the psychological torture, the unexpected and shocking death of Tate, or a spur thrown by Kemp into Ben's face, anticipate the outright brutality of *The Man from Laramie*.

The Mann-Stewart team followed *Spur* with the drama *Thunder Bay* (1953), *The Glenn Miller Story* (1954 – with Stewart as the title bandleader) and another western, *The Far Country*, though it had been filmed 18 months earlier and was held back by the producers until 1955. Set on the US–Canadian border during the Klondike gold rush in Yukon Territory, Mann's vivid locales (the rough town of Skagway, the nascent prospectors' settlement of Dawson) were recreated in Jasper

National Park, Alberta, Canada. The film includes some of the most powerful moments of the series, especially the ambush on Ben (Walter Brennan) and Jeff (Stewart) as they try to escape by raft from Gannon (John McIntire), a top-hatted, self-appointed Judge Roy Bean character. Also of note are Ruth Roman's performance as saloon-chain owner Ronda Castle, Jay C. Flippen as a drunken sheriff, Jack Elam as a sloth-like deputy and Robert Wilke as slimy hired gun Matt Madden, given to

His gun hand bandaged, Will Lockhart takes on the Waggoman clan single-handed; James Stewart as *The Man from Laramie* (1955).

provoking helpless opponents. In one scene, Madden picks on a prospector, then spits at him, before shooting him dead. *Far Country* was followed by the autobiographical *Strategic Air Command* (1955 – Stewart had risen to colonel in the air force during the war), before the team embarked on their most ambitious western, *The Man from Laramie*, based on the *Saturday Evening Post* story of the same name, by Thomas Flynn.

Adapted for the screen by Philip Yordan and Frank Burt, *The Man from Laramie* told the story of freighter Will Lockhart, who arrives in the New Mexican pueblo of Coronado to deliver mercantile supplies. There, he falls foul of the Waggoman family: patriarch Alec, his wild son Dave and his adopted son Vic Hansbro. For allegedly trespassing, Lockhart's wagons are upturned and burned, and his mule team slaughtered, while later Dave cripples Lockhart by shooting him in his gun hand. Lockhart is sheltered by local rancher Kate Canaday and develops a relationship with Barbara Waggoman, a cousin of the dynasty. But Lockhart's objective in Coronado is to find out who is selling repeating rifles to the Apaches. Lockhart is an army officer and his brother had been killed months before at the Dutch Creek Massacre, on Waggoman land. Dave and Vic are running guns to the hostiles and Alec finds out. Vic kills Dave and tries to kill Alec, but Lockhart forces Vic to destroy the wagonload of rifles, cached in the high country. In retribution, the Apaches kill Vic, leaving Lockhart to return to Laramie, his brother avenged.

Stewart was yet again cast as the hero, the noble-sounding Will Lockhart. He wore virtually the same costume for each of his Mann westerns (chaps, turned-up denims and a short leather or corduroy jacket) and always the same lucky hat, which he kept in a vault between films. He also always rode the same horse, his beloved Pie, which he hired from a wrangler's daughter. 'He's a great horse,' Stewart recalled, 'almost human. I'm sure he can read the script.' Years later, Henry Fonda presented Stewart with a painting of Pie when they worked together on *The Cheyenne Social Club* (1970), shortly before the horse's death.

The supporting cast was a strong one, with Mann casting 75-year-old, London-born Donald Crisp as the cattle baron, Alec Waggoman. Alec is losing his eyesight and Crisp movingly played the atypical role; Crisp had won a Best Supporting Actor Oscar for *How Green Was My Valley* (1941). Wallace Ford (real name Samuel Jones Grundy, born in Bolton) had been Randolph Scott's sidekick Andy West in *Coroner Creek* (1948), among many other supporting roles. In *Laramie* he played half-Apache muleskinner Charley O'Leary, who rendezvous with Lockhart at regular intervals throughout the action to inform him of developments in the gunrunning subplot. Aline MacMahon had made a name for herself playing grandmas, nanas and matrons, and was ideally cast as tough, independent rancher Kate, while Cathy O'Donnell (as love interest Barbara) had been a regular in *films noirs*, notably *They Live by Night* (1949). Arthur Kennedy, as Vic, had appeared in *Bend of the River* and as a vengeful cowboy in Fritz Lang's cult classic *Rancho Notorious* (1952), while Alex Nicol went completely over the top as wild-eyed, uncontrollable Dave. Jack Elam provided another of his shifty cameos, as local ne're-do-well Chris Boldt, who ends up being knifed in a back alley: a typical Elam demise.

The Man from Laramie was filmed on location in New Mexico, with interiors at Columbia Studios. Filming commenced on 29 September 1954 for 28 days on location and wrapped in Hollywood on 16 November. The Pueblo Indian settlement of Coronado was shot in the actual pueblo of Tesuque, with its adobe mission, town square and flat-roofed log and mud dwellings. A picturesque, torch-lit wedding was staged on a studio interior, as was the interior of 'Waggoman's Mercantile'. All location filming, on 18 separate sites, was within 100 miles of Santa Fe, with 14 electric poles and many TV aerials being removed to give authenticity to the 1870s settings. The Waggoman's Barb Ranch, with its grand corral gate and windmill, was built 32 miles from Santa Fe and Kate's Half Moon cattle ranch, incorporating trees and a watering hole, was built at the 90,000 acre Jarrett Ranch, near the old mining town of Bonanza. The scene where the Barb riders torch Lockhart's wagons at the 'salt lagoons' was filmed at White Sands. The shoot was tough, with Stewart, Nicol and Kennedy performing most of their own riding and stunts.

Winchester '73 had been shot in black and white, Mann's subsequent westerns in Technicolor, but *Laramie* was his first in CinemaScope. The photography, by Charles Lang, is expansive, with the six-mule wagon teams wheeling around the cattle pens into Coronado town square, Lockhart's men shovelling salt on the desolate snow-white flats or Barb riders ranged across the rocky sierras, beneath magnificent Michelangelo skies. There is hardly a scene in the film that isn't cramped and compromised for TV showings; as the trailer stated: 'Big as Life in life-sized CinemaScope'. It is a western, like *Forty Guns*, *The Big Country*, *Ride Lonesome*, *The Magnificent Seven* and *Once Upon a Time in the West*, that must be seen in widescreen.

Yordan and Burt's story, as well constructed as a mystery thriller, is unrecognisable as the familiar 'who's running guns to the Apache?' The film should actually be called *The Man from Fort Laramie* and there are many clues to Lockhart's real identity and purpose. In the opening sequence, Lockhart pauses by the burnt-out remains of the cavalry patrol massacred at Dutch Creek: a scattering of belongings, an ensign and wagons in ashes. He picks up a cavalry hat, lost in reminiscence. 'Standing there thinking about it won't bring him back,' says muleskinner Charlie, breaking the mood. 'No, but it reminds me of what I came here to do,' answers Lockhart. 'Hate's unbecoming in a man like you,' continues Charlie, 'On some men it shows.' The ex-scout recognises in Lockhart a military manner and it's later revealed that Lockhart is a captain.

Like *Bad Day at Black Rock*, released the same year as Mann's film, a stranger arrives in a town that hides a guilty secret. The stranger asks awkward questions, getting few answers: in *Laramie*, everyone, except Barbara and Kate, want him out of town. Alec pays him $600 in damages and Sheriff Quigby pushes him to leave town – as Vic says: 'Pick some other place to roost.' But Lockhart hangs around, until the incendiary Coronado atmosphere can't contain its secret any more. 'I came a thousand miles to kill you, Hansbro,' Lockhart tells Vic. 'I never did anything to you,' blurts Vic. 'I guess,' hisses Lockhart, 'a man has a right to know what he's gonna die for,' and recounts the tale of the Dutch Creek Massacre, perpetrated by Apaches armed with Winchesters. Vic is as guilty as if he'd pulled the trigger himself.

The Man from Laramie is the most violent fifties western, though it only features three killings in the entire film. None are perpetrated by Stewart, with Lockhart revenging his brother's death without having to kill anyone. Vic knifes Chris Boldt (though Lockhart is blamed), Vic shoots dangerous Dave (when the hothead wants to let the Apaches loose on the Half Moon) and the Apaches kill Vic with three shots from a repeating rifle he sold to them, and an arrow in the back for good measure. But Lockhart still has to suffer for his vengeance. Out at the salt flats, Dave calls Lockhart's men a 'bunch of thieves'. For trespassing and stealing salt, Lockhart is roped by Barb rider Spud (stuntman Boyd Stockman) and dragged headfirst through a campfire. Later Lockhart strides towards Dave in the Coronado plaza, a long camera dolly-out of Stewart (and his pent-up scream of 'Dave!') intensifies and then releases the tension. Lockhart attacks the punk, then finds himself accosted by Vic, beneath trampling horses' hooves and through the cattle pens, photographed amid the confusion of sunlight and swirling dust.

All previous brutality is surpassed with the most famous scene in the film, when Dave shoots helpless Lockhart through the palm, with a pistol, at point blank range. Mann's camera focuses on Stewart's face throughout the ordeal, as his eyes roll in pain and he spits, 'Why you scum.' Alex Nicol wanted to 'play that scene as cool as I could, to increase the sense of menace', but Mann and Stewart vetoed it. Instead, Nicol ran around in circles, 'whipping up as much anger as I could', before the explosive scene. As the actor noted, 'I went at it like a lunatic ... with more fury than any other scene in my entire career.' Offset against such manic sadism, there are also several moving moments in the film, as in the scenes where Vic returns with Dave's body over a saddle, through the grand Barb corral gateway (a scene Mann was particularly pleased with), and the subsequent cortege and funeral in Coronado.

In the sixties, Mann was working on an adaptation of Shakespeare's *King Lear* out west, to be called *The King*. But already in *The Man from Laramie* he had touched on such dynastic themes, with the character of patriarch rancher Alec Waggoman, even to the extent that he's going blind, like Shakespeare's Gloucester. Alec is also haunted by a recurring dream, where 'a stranger comes into my home' and kills Dave. Lockhart replies, 'I'm not the man in your dream.' Later, Alec realises the truth, 'He didn't come from far away to kill my boy. He was right here in my house, pretending he loved me like a son.' Woven into this classical tragedy is the tale of two sons, one good, one bad, echoing *Winchester '73*. Here Waggoman's worry is who will be left in charge when he can't oversee his spread – Dave's no rancher and Vic isn't his son. Blood is thicker than water and Vic will never be a Waggoman. As Alec tells him, 'Liking and loving aren't the same.' Vic forced Dave into joining his gunrunning scheme and kills him when Dave loses control.

All the Mann–Stewart westerns were big hits in the US and UK. *Bend of the River* was high up in the 1952 grosses with *High Noon* and *Son of Paleface* (taking over $2 million), while *Winchester '73* took $2.5m in 1950, and *The Naked Spur* was a top earner, with *Shane* and *Hondo*, in 1953. But *The Man from Laramie*, along with *Bad Day at Black Rock*, was the high-grossing western of 1955 and Stewart was at the top of the box-office charts in the US as a result, toppling John Wayne. The UK BBFC passed the film in August 1955 as a 'U' certificate, after cuts had been made, and the film was very successful. Posters read: 'This is the Man from Laramie, straight from one of the most powerful adventures stories the *Saturday Evening Post* ever ran' and 'He Came a Thousand Miles through Teeming Dangers, to Kill a Man He'd Never Seen!' The trailer saw Stewart relaxing on set in Tesuque, reading a copy of the *Saturday Evening Post*: 'The Man who was Magnificent in *The Glen Miller Story* ... who was Unforgettable in *Rear Window* ... Terrific in *Strategic Air Command*, now tops all past triumphs as *The Man from Laramie*'. The action-filled trailer also played-up the Indian fighting subplot (they actually only appear for a couple of scenes at the end). The film remained Stewart's favourite western, and of all his performances, he only preferred *It's a Wonderful Life*.

The superior score, by George Duning, was atmospheric, while the title song, with music by Lester Lee and lyrics by Ned Washington, landed in the UK hit parade. In the film it is performed by an unnamed chorus, but two cover versions were released, one by Al Martino which reached No. 19, the other by future radio DJ Jimmy Young. Young's version gave him his second No. 1 on 14 October 1955, and it stayed on top for four weeks, its popularity ensured by its singalong, simple refrain:

> The Man from Laramie, though he was friendly to everyone he met
> No one seems to know a thing about him – he had an air of mystery
> He was not inclined to speak his mind, the man from Laramie

The end titles feature a jauntier reprise, with added lyrics including:

> Everyone admired the fearless stranger, danger was his speciality
> So they never bossed or double-crossed the man from Laramie

'I came a thousand miles to kill you.' Captain Will Lockhart (James Stewart) takes revenge on gunrunner Vic Hansbro (Arthur Kennedy) in Anthony Mann's CinemaScope western *The Man from Laramie* (1955).

Several cattle baron epics followed *Laramie*'s expansive lead. The best was the Technirama *The Big Country* (1958), with its extended, quarrelling families and landscapes that seem to stretch forever. In *Backlash*, made the year after *Laramie*, the hero (Richard Widmark) is on the trail of the man who betrayed his father, killed by Apaches in the Gila Valley Massacre. At the 'Diamond C', he encounters Major Carson (who looks exactly like Alec Waggoman), a rancher who keeps in check his short-tempered, leather-jacketed hired gun, jumpy Johnny Cool (William Campbell). *Shoot Out at Medicine Bend* (1957), starring Randolph Scott, borrowed plot elements from *Laramie* (here faulty ammunition causes the death of Scott's soldier brother), while Scott's heroes in his films with Budd Boetticher are clearly driven by the same obsessions as Stewart's.

Laramie was the last Mann–Stewart collaboration. They were supposed to make *Night Passage* (1957), the first production in Technicolor's Technirama format, but Mann pulled out at the last minute, citing an incoherent script. The resultant film, directed by James Neilson, exhibits several Mann-erisms: the impressive scenery (here a railroad through spectacular forests and mountains near Durango, Colorado), the ambivalent hero (Stewart's trouble-shooter, Grant McClain) and a well chosen supporting cast, including Dan Duryea as outlaw Whitey Harbin, with his gang: the Utica Kid (baby-faced Audie Murphy), Concho (Robert J. Wilke) and Shotgun (Jack Elam). The plot features McClain hired to deliver $10,000 by train, from Junction City to the railhead, to pay off Irish railroad workers. A long, slow haul for the most part, *Night Passage* is redeemed by the exciting finale (a gunfight at a mill, with mining cable cars on pulleys) and the revelation that McClain and Utica Kid are brothers (as in *Winchester '73*). Stewart particularly wanted to make the film, as it gave him the opportunity to squeeze two featured musical numbers ('Follow the River' and 'You Can't Get Far Without a Railroad') out of his accordion. Elam said of the film, which was fraught with production problems and general bad atmosphere, 'It was a payday, but I could have done without it.' Stewart was so incensed with Mann's desertion that they never worked together again.

Instead, Mann went on to make *The Tin Star* (1957), with Stewart's old friend, Henry Fonda as a bounty hunter, and then *Man of the West* (1958), based on the novel 'The Border Jumpers' by Will Brown. Gary Cooper was cast as Link Jones, an ex-outlaw. While travelling by train from Crosscut to Fort Worth, he is embroiled in a hold-up by his old gang, the Tobin Bunch, led by 'Uncle Dock', and finds himself a wanted man once more. Dock plans to rob the Bank of Lasso of its gold deposits, but when they arrive they discover that the gold is played out and the settlement's a ghost town. Link must lay these ghosts to rest in order to live a peaceful life. The 'brother versus brother' conflict, so central to earlier Mann–Stewart westerns, is now evinced in paternal discord.

The sadistic Tobin gang, who would 'run you down and cut you into little chunks', featured Jack Lord (later of TV's *Hawaii Five-O*) as Cousin Coley, Robert Wilke (none-too-bright Ponch), John Dehner (Cousin Claude), and Royal Dano (the mute, Trout). Julie London (of 'Cry Me a River' fame) was Cooper's companion, Billie. The most memorable performance is Lee J. Cobb as the ranting Dock Tobin, a monster of a man, amoral and demented. His rosy reminiscences of taking off the top of a man's head with a gunshot remind his nephew Link why he left the gang originally. The atmospheric score deployed marimba and strings, and the great location photography (in CinemaScope and gritty DeLuxe Color) add to the film's success.

Mann only made one more western, a cramped, mostly studio-bound remake of 1931's epic *Cimarron* in 1960, which recreated the famous Cherokee Land Rush sequence: here the careering wagons and thundering horses compete with such bizarre sights as a penny farthing and a *Goodies*-style three-seater tandem. But *The Man from Laramie* remains the finest Stewart-Mann collaboration and one of the most significant fifties westerns in the development of obsession, redemption and violence that became the key ingredients of the genre in the mid-sixties. As Mann summed up the film's extremes, 'I wanted to recapitulate my five years with Jimmy Stewart. I reprised themes and situations by pushing them to their paroxysm.' As paroxysms go, this is one of the best.

10

'That'll Be the Day'

— *The Searchers* (1956)

The Searchers (1956)
Credits
DIRECTOR – John Ford
EXECUTIVE PRODUCER – Merian C. Cooper
ASSOCIATE PRODUCER – Patrick Ford
STORY – Alan LeMay
SCREENPLAY – Frank S. Nugent
DIRECTOR OF PHOTOGRAPHY – Winton C. Hoch
EDITOR – Jack Murray
ART DIRECTORS – Frank Hotaling and James Basevi
MUSIC – Max Steiner
VistaVision/Technicolor
A C.V. Whitney Pictures Production
Released by Warner Bros
119 minutes
Cast
    John Wayne (Ethan Edwards); Jeffrey Hunter (Martin
    Pauley); Vera Miles (Laurie Jorgensen); Ward Bond (Captain
    the Reverend Samuel Johnson Clayton); Natalie Wood
    (Debbie Edwards); John Qualen (Lars Jorgensen); Olive
    Carey (Mrs Jorgensen); Henry Brandon (War Chief Scar);
    Ken Curtis (Sergeant Charlie MacCorry); Harry Carey Jnr
    (Brad Jorgensen); Antonio Moreno (Emilio Gabriel
    Fernandez y Figueroa); Hank Worden (Mose Harper); Lana
    Wood (Debbie, aged 11); Walter Coy (Aaron Edwards);
    Dorothy Jordan (Martha Edwards); Robert Lynden (Ben
    Edwards); Pippa Scott (Lucy Edwards); Pat Wayne
    (Lieutenant Greenhill); Cliff Lyons (Colonel Greenhill); Bill
    Steele (Ed Nesby); Beulah Archuletta (Wild Goose Flying in

the Night Sky, alias 'Look'); Jack Pennick (Sergeant at snowbound army post); Peter Mamokos (Jerem Futterman); Chief Thundercloud (Comanche Chief); Chuck Roberson (Ranger); Away Luna, Exactly Sonnie Betsuie, Feather Hat Jnr, Percy Shooting Star, Billy Yellow, Bob Many Mules, Many Mules Son, Harry Black Horse, Jack Tin Horn, Pete Grey Eyes, Smile White Sheep and Pipe Line Begishe (Nawyecka Comanches)

*   *   *

Critics often noted that John Wayne only had two expressions – with and without his hat – but with his performances for John Ford and Howard Hawks, he proved that he had greater dramatic range than many observers claimed. Ford's *The Searchers*, their greatest joint achievement, saw Wayne giving the finest portrayal of his career, as the vengeful contradiction named Ethan Edwards.

Prior to *The Searchers* Wayne made the interesting *Hondo* (1953), shot in Utah and the Mexican desert by Batjac Productions (Wayne's own company). It was based on Louis L'Amour's novel 'A Gift of Cochise'. The film tells the story of a part-Indian US cavalry dispatch rider, Hondo Lane (Wayne) and his dog Sam (played by Lassie), and Hondo's relationship with homesteader Angie Lowe (Geraldine Page) and her son, Johnny. It's 1870, and the area is terrorised by Apache Vittorio (Michael Pate), so Hondo and the cavalry lead the settlers to safety in an exciting circled wagon attack finale, choreographed by stunt co-ordinator Cliff Lyons. *Hondo* was made in 3-D and the 'in-your-lap' action scenes highlight this. It was publicised as 'Hondo: the most exciting man you'll ever meet'. Ford reputedly directed two shots of *Hondo*, with the cavalry troop riding in columns of two's, while he visited Wayne in Mexico. The cast also features Ward Bond and future *Gunsmoke* star, six-feet-six-inch tall James Arness, as army scouts Buffalo Baker and Lenny (Wayne was offered the lead in *Gunsmoke* in 1955 but recommended Arness instead, making him a star). *Hondo* depicts the larger-than-life Wayne persona – the walk and drawl – in extremis and took $4.1 million in the US.

With its roots in the true story of the kidnapping of Cynthia Ann Parker (later the mother of war chief, Quannah Parker) from Parker's Fort by Comanches in 1836, Ford used Alan LeMay's novel *The Searchers* as the basis for his next Wayne movie. In the book, the hero Ethan Edwards is called Amos and the plot is more straightforward than that of the film. Ford developed the screenplay with Frank S. Nugent during early 1955, setting the story in 1868 Texas, and took the idea to Warner Bros, who agreed to provide the $2.5 million budget.

A Nawyecka Comanche band led by Chief Scar attack Aaron Edwards's Texan homestead, killing Aaron, his wife and 14-year-old son, and kidnapping their daughters, teenage Lucy and 11-year-old Debbie. Ethan, Aaron's younger brother, recently returned from the Civil War, joins the party of Texas Rangers on the raiders' trail. Martin Pauley, Aaron's part-Cherokee adopted son, and Brad Jorgensen,

Lucy's beau, also ride along. Ambushed by the Comanche, the Rangers turn back, leaving Ethan, Martin and Brad to continue. Brad dies when he rushes the Comanches' camp, after Lucy is found murdered. Martin and Ethan continue their search for five long years, eventually trailing the nomadic Comanche to New Mexico. There they come face to face with Scar and see Debbie, now living as one of Scar's squaws, but are forced to leave without her. When fate brings the Nawyeckas into the vicinity of Edwards's farm once again, Ethan, Martin, the Rangers and the US Cavalry attack the village, but not before Martin has rescued Debbie. In the attack, Martin kills Scar and Ethan scalps him, before the searchers bring Debbie home.

Ford cast Wayne as Ethan, while teen heart-throb Jeffrey Hunter (whose real name was the rather less snappy Henry Herman McKinnies Jnr) was cast as his companion, Martin Pauley, described in Nugent's script as having 'Indian-straight hair and a white man's eyes'. Hunter closely resembled a young Henry Fonda. He appeared as the council for the defence in Ford's *Sergeant Rutledge* (1960), as Jesus Christ in *King of Kings* (1961) and as Captain Pike in the pilot for TV's *Star Trek* (1966), before his premature death in 1969. Natalie Wood was cast on the back of her Oscar-nominated performance in *Rebel Without a Cause* (1955), as Debbie, while Natalie's little sister Lana, played Debbie aged 11 in the opening scenes. Ford regular Ward Bond played Captain the Reverend Clayton: 'The Good Book in One Hand – and a Gun in the Other', claimed the posters. Hank Worden played old coot Mose Harper, the simpleton wanderer who wants nothing more than a roof over his head and a rocking chair by the fire. Harry Carey Jnr played Brad (his mother, Olive, played his screen mother, Mrs Jorgensen), while he noted that on set Wayne 'didn't kid

'Just as sure as the turning of the earth': John Wayne as the unstoppable Ethan Edwards, forever in pursuit of Debbie, in John Ford's *The Searchers*.

around... like he usually would. Ethan was always in his eyes.' Carey Jnr fell out with Ford over the start date on the actor's next assignment (*The Mickey Mouse Club*) and Ford didn't speak to him for the next five years. Look, a Comanche woman whom Martin accidentally marries during his journey, was played by Beulah Archuletta, while Chief Scar was Berlin-born, blue-eyed Henry Brandon, from *The Paleface* (1948) and *Vera Cruz* (1954).

Ex-beauty queen Vera Miles had appeared in the massively successful 3-D western *The Charge at Feather River* (1953), but only her roles for Ford (Laurie in *The Searchers* and *The Man Who Shot Liberty Valance*'s wife, Hallie) and Hitchcock (in *The Wrong Man* [1957] and *Psycho* [1960]) put her talent to good use. Comic relief Ken Curtis, previously a fixture in the Sons of the Pioneers and a series cowboy in his own right, plays Laurie's drawling suitor, Ranger Sergeant Charlie MacCorry, who arrives at Jorgensens' a-courtin' with his 'geetar' and mouths the enticing opener, 'Say, I brung yuh some boiled sweets.' Later his irritating laugh ('Haw! Haw! Haw!') and his request of Martin, 'I'll thank you to unhand my fi-an-see,' show Curtis at his best. He had married Ford's daughter Barbara in 1952 and had small roles in many of his father-in-law's films. He also played grizzled Festus in TV's *Gunsmoke*.

The first part of filming began in March 1955 in Colorado at Gunnison, with the 7th Cavalry fording an iced-up river and herding Comanches back onto the reservation. The snow-riding scenes featured Ethan and Martin. A buffalo herd was filmed at Elk Island National Park, in Edmonton, Canada. Preparation for the second part of the shoot, in Monument Valley, commenced during the winter rains of early 1955, where joiners constructed two homesteads from scratch: Jorgensens' in wood at Mitchell Butte and Edwards's in adobe at Sentinel Mesa. The crew erected a village to house the Warner Bros Location Department; in all there were 258 cast and crew. At a crossroads in the camp, a signpost read: 'Hollywood Bvd' and 'Vine St'. Tracks were laid for complicated camera dollies, and camera cars were rigged with scaffolding to accommodate the heavy shooting equipment.

The next part of the production began on 16 June in Monument Valley. The first scene shot was Ethan's return, framed between Gray Whiskers and Mitchell Butte. Several riding scenes were shot in the valley (the Rangers' dash to the river, the attack on Scar's village at the canyon confluence called the 'Seven Fingers of Brazos'), as part of Ethan and Martin's travelogue, depicting Castle Rock, the Mittens, Sentinel Mesa and the Stagecoach. On set, Wood recalled how her sunbathing in a swimsuit offended the local Navajos. During the famous scene when Ethan rants at Martin and Brad, following the discovery of Lucy's naked body, filmed very early in the morning, the camera mysteriously stopped running and the actors had to repeat the scene. Only later did it become apparent that Ward Bond had unplugged the camera to connect his electric razor for a morning shave. When Brad suicidally attacks the Comanches in the middle of the desert, Gray Whiskers and Mitchell Butte are in the background (geographically, Brad's home is actually by Mitchell Butte). Ethan and Martin camp beside Sand Creek, with its distinctive dunes, an area called Sand Springs. The New Mexican desert and Comanche camp scenes were shot near the Totem Pole and Yei Bi Chei rock formations and the searchers later shelter in Victory Cave. When the

Rangers discover Jorgensen's slaughtered cattle and realise that Scar is on a murder raid to attack the farms, Monument Valley's North Window (Elephant Butte, Cly Butte and Camel Butte) appears as a backdrop. As the Rangers prepare for the final attack, they are photographed before the Mittens and Merrick Butte. The second unit filmed the river battle, staged on the San Juan River. The famous last shot, of Wayne walking away from Jorgensen's door, was shot on 3 July. Wayne had a major hangover. His pose, arms crossed, was in tribute to western star Harry Carey Snr, who often affected the same stance – Olive Carey, his widow, played Mrs Jorgensen in the scene and was deeply moved by the tribute.

Local Navajos, including Feather Hat Jnr, Percy Shooting Star, Smile White Sheep, Bob Many Mules and Many Mules Son, played Comanches, with stuntmen in make-up doubling for warriors to perform jumps and horse falls. These bursts of action – in particular the Rangers' charge for the river and the final attack on Scar's village – were what Ford referred to as 'Bustin' 'em up'. Cameras were buried in pits for the riders to vault and the horses were protected by having bandaged kneepads wound around their legs. Stuntman Chuck Roberson doubled for Scar in the riding scenes and also had a cameo as the Ranger who was told to take his spurs off at the wedding ceremony. A stuntman doubled for Hunter when he dropped off a promontory ('Ford Point') into Scar's camp in the moonlit valley below. The Monument Valley shoot was completed on 13 July.

The Totem Pole and Yei Bi Chei stand proud in Monument Valley, the location used for War Chief Scar's New Mexican camp in *The Searchers*. (Photograph courtesy Victoria Millington and Mark Chester.)

The crew then worked in Hollywood for the final section of filming, lensing interiors and studio 'exteriors', filmed on sound stages at RKO-Pathé (the *New York Times* complained that these sets looked like 'sporting-goods store window' displays). These included the misty river scenes, snowy close-ups of Wayne and Hunter, the campsite ambush by crooked trader Futterman and company, Debbie hiding in the graveyard from Scar, and Scar's night-time camp prior to the final raid. Principal photography took 49 days, with the film wrapping on 13 August. The last scenes filmed were in Bronson Canyon when Wayne corners Debbie in a cave, and Wayne's 'turning of the earth' speech in the snow, on Stage 15's studio interior. Post-production was wrapped up in January 1956.

Ford's west is a desolate, lonely land, where receiving two letters in a year is cause for celebration. The life of the homesteaders offers only hardship, with scant reward, and is evidence of cynicism creeping into Ford's west for the first time. Of the two families depicted in the film, one is wiped out by Comanches, the other lose their son. Mrs Jorgensen notes, 'Someday this country is gonna be a fine, good place to be. Maybe it needs our bones in the ground before that time can come.'

Ethan is the most complicated character Wayne was ever asked to play – a racist, who is also capable of tenderness, a killer who acknowledges unspoken love. Ethan returns from the Civil War three years late and it's hinted that he may be a wanted man. A Confederate, he's carrying 'Yankee dollars, fresh minted' and a ranger notes he fits 'a lot of descriptions'. In Nugent's screenplay, it is made explicit that Ethan has been fighting in Mexico – the coins and medal Ethan own are consistent with the Maximilian-era Mexican Revolution. Later, when ambushed, Ethan shoots crooked Futterman and his two associates in the back, an unthinkable action for the usual Wayne screen hero, suggesting he's outside the law.

Ethan's desire for revenge and his hatred of the Comanche is his motivating force throughout. One of the reasons for his quest is revenge for the death of Martha, with whom he was in love. From the visceral moment when Ethan throws the scabbard off his rifle in a tempestuous arc (when he first sees his brother's burning farm) Ethan is only just in control of his actions. He interrupts prayers at the Edwards's family funeral, to hasten their departure in pursuit of Scar, snapping, 'Put an Amen to it.' At a Mexican cantina, Ethan finds out where Chief Cicatriz is camped. Wayne throws his glass of tequila onto a stove, the whoosh of flames accentuating Wayne's delivery of the line, 'Cicatriz is Mexican for Scar', which visualises Ethan's burning thirst for vengeance.

Ethan's attitude to Comanches is bordering on racism. In one scene, Ethan encounters a herd of buffalo and proceeds to shoot as many as possible, reasoning that by killing them he's depriving the tribe of food. When the posse find a dead Comanche buried under a slab of sandstone, ritually laid out in death, Brad bashes the corpse with a rock. Ethan draws his pistol to finish the job, shooting the Comanche's eyes out. As Old Mose informs us, with no eyes the warrior can't enter the spirit world and must wander forever 'between the winds'. At the river battle, Ethan continues to blast his Winchester at Scar's warriors, even after they have been routed. At his most demented, Ethan breaks the news to Brad that the person Brad can see in the Comanche camp in a blue dress isn't Lucy, but a warrior in Lucy's dress. Ethan found Lucy on the trail, wrapped her in his Confederate coat and buried her with his own hands. Brad begins to ask if she had suffered, 'What'd you want me to do?' screams Ethan, 'Draw you a picture, spell it out? Don't ever ask me, long as you live, don't ever ask me more.'

The fatalistic, endless search is reinforced by Ethan's repeated mantra, 'That'll be the day'. In the snowscape whiteout, when he and Martin are forced to turn back to Texas for the first time, Ethan says through gritted teeth, 'We'll find 'em, just as sure as the turning of the earth.' The middle section of the search is narrated by Martin, which balances Ethan's excesses. Twice the searchers return to the Jorgensens' farm, the trail cold, until clues send them off again. Martin's first return sees Laurie rushing to kiss him and Martin commenting, 'I fairly forgot how pretty she was.' By the second time he returns, she is engaged to Charlie MacCorry. The resulting punch-up between Martin and Charlie is Ford at his most slapstick. But even when Wayne isn't centre stage, his character dominates the piece, interrupting these romantic subplots with his single-mindedness.

In the course of the journey, Ethan also does a lot of searching within himself. In the finale, after spending five years looking for Debbie and having found that she is now a Comanche in all but blood, Ethan aims to shoot her, but Martin stands between them and Scar's ambush curtails the execution. Later Ethan corners Debbie in a cave and lunges at her. But instead of throttling her, he takes her in his arms, cradling her: 'Let's go home Debbie.' In the shooting script, based on LeMay's book, it is Debbie's resemblance to Martha that saves her life. Amos (Ethan) puts a pistol to Debbie's head, 'I'm sorry girl, shut your eyes,' before at the last moment he reconsiders, adding, 'You sure favour your mother.'

The music by Max Steiner is the best Ford film score, from the opening brass and drums that later becomes the 'Comanche theme', to the lilting instrumental version of the Civil War ballad 'Lorena'. Elsewhere the score ranges from comedy themes to the use of 'Garryowen', when the cavalry herd captive Comanches. Ken Curtis serenades Laurie with a strummed 'Gone again, Skip to My Loo My Darlin'' and Stan Jones wrote the lyrics to the title song 'The Searchers':

> What makes a man to wander? What makes a man to roam?
> What makes a man leave bed and board and turn his back on home? Ride away.

At the end of the film, the lyrics reflect a change in Ethan, still a wanderer, but with his ghosts laid to rest:

> A man will search his heart and soul, go searching way out there
> His peace of mind, he knows he'll find, but where, oh Lord, Lord where? Ride away.

The repeated 'ride away' accompanies the famous final shot of the film, as Ethan returns Debbie to the Jorgensens' ranch. Ford films the scene through the door, framed in darkness. As each person passes through the portal they become silhouettes, then vanish into the shadows. Mr and Mrs Jorgensen and Debbie enter, then Ethan steps aside to allow Laurie and Martin past. Ethan pauses, a lopsided stance, watching, brushed by the prairie wind. Then he turns and walks aimlessly away from the house. The door closes, condemning him forever to wander between the winds, forever searching: 'But where oh Lord, Lord where?'

During post-production, a scene depicting the Washita River massacre by Custer was cut from the film, and a meeting between Ethan and Custer (played by Peter Ortiz) was also excised. All that remains is the aftermath of the massacre (where Look is discovered dead in a tepee) and the cavalry shepherding hostiles into custody. A clue to the abridgements is the sudden change in climate – one minute Ethan and shirtless Martin are in Monument Valley, beside a river, the next they're in snowbound Edmonton, watching a buffalo herd, with an explanatory line from Hunter detailing a week-long snowfall.

The Searchers was released in the US on 25 May 1956. Posters featured the classic shot of Wayne and Hunter astride their horses in Monument Valley beneath a blazing sunset, with the tagline: 'He had to find her … he had to find her …' Ethan's supposed racism came in for criticism, with *Variety* noting that 'Wayne is a bitter, taciturn individual … and the reasons for his attitude are left to the imagination of the viewer'. *Look* magazine called Scar 'the screen's most wicked, unregenerate Indian in a long time' and the film 'the most roisterous since *Shane*'. The trailer, which includes shots of Ethan riding towards Aaron's ranch not included in the film, plugged: 'Adventure … From the Sand-Choked Deserts of Arizona to the Snow-Swept Plains of Canada'. Ethan's true character is distorted as having 'a rare kind of courage, that simply keeps on and on, far beyond all reasonable endurance … never thinking of himself as martyred, never thinking of himself as brave'. In the UK the film was rated 'U' in April 1956. *The Searchers* was also the first film to use a promotional 'Making of' documentary, screened over four weeks on the *Warner Bros Presents* TV show. Host Gig Young is joined in the studio by Hunter and Wood, who appears in her Comanche costume and gives the audience a guided tour of the Navajo Reservation. 'Welcome once again to the land of the Navajo,' says Young in one segment, obviously standing in front of a studio backdrop of Monument Valley.

The Searchers is the third most successful western of the fifties (after *Shane* and *The Tall Men* [1955]), taking $4.9 million. In France the film was called *La Prisonnière Du Désert* ('The Prisoner of the Desert'), in Germany *Der Schwartze Falke* ('The Black Falcon') and in Italy *Sentieri Selvaggi* ('Wild Paths'). In the UK, pop band The Searchers (of 'Needles and Pins' fame) named themselves after Ford's movie, while Buddy Holly borrowed Wayne's catchphrase 'That'll be the day' as the title for his 1957 hit. In February 1962, Wayne named his son John Ethan. Ford won six Oscars throughout his career, but none were for his westerns. Wayne won one for his eccentric turn as one-eyed marshal, Rooster Cogburn in *True Grit* (1969). Both should have won for *The Searchers*, but it wasn't even nominated in any category. *The Searchers* remains Ford's masterpiece.

In later years, Ford was familiar to the public as a cantankerous old man, with his distinctive slouch hat, eye patch and cigar. He continued to make films, mainly westerns, but only once did he equal the power of *The Searchers*. *The Horse Soldiers* (1959) was a middling Civil War tale, with Wayne in the lead. *Two Rode Together*

(1962), starring James Stewart and Richard Widmark, was pantomime Ford, a ponderous, *Searchers*-inspired tale of a marshal and a cavalry officer seeking white captives, this time held by Comanche Quannah Parker (Henry Brandon again). As an in-joke, Parker refers to Widmark's officer as 'Natani Nez' (Ford's own nickname from the Navajo, given to him during the filming of *Stagecoach*, meaning 'Tall Leader'). Ford called the film, 'the worst piece of crap I've done in twenty years'. Ford's 22-minute 'The Civil War' segment of *How the West Was Won* (1962), with Wayne as General Sherman, was better, but only a small part of a sprawling, five-episode soap-opera western in three-screen Cinerama, which grossed $20 million in the US. Wayne had also played Sherman in an episode of *Wagon Train* called 'The Colter Craven Story', directed by Ford in 1960 (Wayne was billed under the pseudonym 'Michael Morris'). Ford returned to Monument Valley for some action footage in *Sergeant Rutledge* (1960 – which used the Three Sisters location) and much of *Cheyenne Autumn* (1964), the last of the seven films, was shot there. Both were apologetic westerns – the first for the Hollywood western's treatment of black Americans, the second for its treatment of Native Americans – from a director who used to claim, 'I've killed more Indians than Custer.'

The one great film Ford made in this period, before his retirement from films in 1966, was *The Man Who Shot Liberty Valance* (1962). Here the myths of the west are shown to be lies, with dude eastern attorney of law Ransom Stoddard (James Stewart) forging a political career because he's 'the man who shot Liberty Valance' – Valance is a wild, whip-wielding hired gun, working for the cattlemen, played by Lee Marvin. The man who actually shot him was Tom Doniphon (John Wayne), hiding in the shadows across the street. Told in flashback, with Senator Stoddard and his wife (Vera Miles) returning to Shinbone for Doniphon's funeral, *Liberty Valance* is Ford's most cynical western, shot almost entirely on studio sets and the

The man who really shot Liberty Valance: John Wayne as Tom Doniphon, in a publicity shot for John Ford's 1962 western.

Paramount western street. Here Ford's iconic *Stagecoach* is a dust-covered hulk, obsolete in the new civilised west, while Wayne's hero tries to kill himself by burning down his own house. When the truth is revealed by Stoddard, a newspaperman tears up the story, 'This is the west, sir. When the legend becomes fact, print the legend.' Wayne and Stewart's contrasting screen images work well. As Stewart noted, 'People identify with me, but dream of being John Wayne.'

In *The American West of John Ford* (1971) documentary, Ford returned to Monument Valley for the last time. Wayne calls him 'Pappy' or 'Coach' throughout and introduces the show, standing at 'Ford Point' in Monument Valley, a place where Ford placed his camera so often that it was named in his honour. Ford directs a Wayne horse fall (doubled by Chuck Roberson), then director and star remember the old days. 'Memories come back,' says Ford of their reminiscences. For all Ford's irascible bluster, it is a very moving moment. In voiceover, Ford muses, 'I never felt important, or that I was a career director, or a genius, or any other damn thing... when I pass on, I want to be remembered as John Ford, a guy that made westerns.'

11

'There's a Hundred More Tombstones'

— *Gunfight at the O.K. Corral* (1957)

Gunfight at the O.K. Corral (1957)
Credits
DIRECTOR – John Sturges
PRODUCER – Hal B. Wallis
STORY – George Scullin
SCREENPLAY – Leon Uris
DIRECTOR OF PHOTOGRAPHY – Charles Lang Jnr
EDITOR – Warren Low
ART DIRECTORS – Hal Pereira and Walter Tyler
MUSIC – Dimitri Tiomkin
VistaVision/Technicolor
A Paramount Production
Released by Paramount Pictures
122 minutes
Cast
  Burt Lancaster (Marshal Wyatt Berry Stapp Earp); Kirk
  Douglas (John Henry 'Doc' Holliday); Rhonda Fleming
  (Laura Denbow, the gambler); Jo Van Fleet (Kate Fisher);
  John Ireland (Johnny Ringo); Lyle Bettger (Joseph Isaac 'Ike'
  Clanton); Frank Faylen (Sheriff Cotton Wilson); Earl
  Holliman (Deputy Charlie Bassett); Ted De Corsia (Shanghai
  Pierce); Dennis Hopper (Billy Clanton); Whit Bissell (John P.
  Clum, 'Tombstone Epitaph' editor); George Mathews (John
  Shanssey, Griffin saloon owner); John Hudson (City Marshal
  Virgil Earp); DeForest Kelly (Deputy Morgan Earp); Martin
  Milner (James Earp); Kenneth Tobey (Bat Masterson); Lee
  Van Cleef (Ed Bailey); Joan Camden (Betty, Virgil's wife);
  Olive Carey (Mrs Clanton); Nelson Leigh (Mayor Kelly, of
  Dodge City); Jack Elam (Tom McLaury); Mickey Simpson

(Frank McLaury); Lee Roberts (Finn Clanton); Don Castle
(Shorty, the drunk); Charles Herbert (Tommy, Virgil's son);
Harry B. Mendoza (Frank Loving, Dodge City dealer);
Tony Merrill (Mario, the barber); Bing Russell (Harry,
Griffin bartender)

*   *   *

Even though he has directed films in other genres, notably the Second World War adventure *The Great Escape* (1963), ex-documentary filmmaker John Sturges is forever associated with westerns. He directed the Randolph Scott vehicle *The Walking Hills* (1949), followed by *Escape from Fort Bravo* (1953), then had great success with the modern western *Bad Day at Black Rock* (1955), shot at Lone Pine and in the Alabama Hills, California. It starred Spencer Tracy as John T. McCready, a one-armed war veteran in a black suit, who gets off the interstate 'Streamliner' to present a medal to the Japanese father of the young soldier who saved McCready's life, but lost his own. The local slobs who hang around the Black Rock Bar & Grill (including Lee Marvin, Robert Ryan and Ernest Borgnine) killed the man when they got 'patriotic drunk'. In this west of slot and pinball machines, jeeps and baseball caps, Ryan's thug tells McCready that strangers are always seeking something out west, 'To the historians it's the old west, to the book writers it's the wild west, to businessmen it's the undeveloped west – but to us this place is our west and I wish they'd leave us alone.'

Sturges followed this with *Backlash* (1956), based on a novel by Borden Chase, starring Richard Widmark. Widmark played Jim Slater, a man trying to solve the mystery of the Gila Valley Massacre, where the Apaches killed five prospectors and stole their $60,000 haul. It was of note for its great Arizona location work (including the distinctive cactus beds of the Saguaro National Park) and the finale was shot at Old Tucson Studios, in the adobe corral, with its low, wind-weathered walls and mission bell tower. In fact this town set, shot from different angles, impersonated all three settlements in the film: Silver City, Tucson and Sierra Blanca.

Sturges reused the same set in his next film, this time as the mythical frontier town of Tombstone, Arizona, site of the infamous O.K. Corral. Written by best-selling novelist Leon Uris, and based on the *Holiday* magazine article 'The Killer' by George Scullin, *Gunfight at the O.K. Corral* told the story of Dodge City Marshal Wyatt Earp. When he tracks wanted men Ike Clanton and Johnny Ringo to Ft Griffin, Texas, they elude him. While in town, Wyatt saves gambler 'Doc' Holliday from a lynching and the two become friends. Returning to Dodge, Wyatt and Doc keep the peace, but the arrival of Doc's girl, Kate, and a gambler, Laura Denbow, cause problems for both men. Kate runs off with gunman Johnny Ringo, while Wyatt falls for Laura. About to retire with Laura to California, Wyatt learns his brother Virgil needs help in Tombstone, where he is marshalling. The Clanton clan are running stolen cattle through town and are about to wrest control from the lawmen. Wyatt is appointed Tombstone city marshal and determines to run the Clantons out. Tensions and murders escalate until in a final shootout near the O.K. Corral, the Earp brothers Wyatt, Morgan and Virgil, plus Doc, face the six-man Clanton gang in a duel to the death.

Paramount producer Hal Brent Wallis considered several actors for Wyatt, including Van Heflin, Humphrey Bogart, Richard Widmark and even Jack Palance, before settling on Burt Lancaster. After some deliberation, Kirk Douglas eventually took the Doc Holliday role. Douglas was no stranger to westerns, scoring hits as *The Indian Fighter* (1955) and Dempsey Rae, the *Man Without a Star* (1955). He later appeared as Brendan O'Malley, the black-clad anti-hero of Robert Aldrich's *The Last Sunset* (1961). With A-list stars, it was clear *Gunfight* was going to be a big-budget treatment of America's most popular gunfighting hero. The stars got on well together, even though top-billed Lancaster would occasionally hide Douglas's shoe lifts before their scenes together. The supporting cast was filled with fine actors. Redheaded Rhonda Fleming, as savvy gambler Laura Denbow, had appeared in such films as *The Redhead and the Cowboy* (1951 – as a confederate spy) and *Those Redheads from Seattle* (1953). *Gunfight* remains her best performance. Theatre actress Jo Van Fleet (cast as Kate Fisher) had won a Best Supporting Actress Oscar for her debut as a madam in *East of Eden* (1955). Kenneth Tobey had a cameo as Derby-wearing Marshal Bat Masterson; Frank Faylen was suitably lily-livered as Sheriff Cotton Wilson. Dennis Hopper, cast as Billy Clanton, brought a little of his one-time friend and co-star James Dean's Method style to the frontier. Lyle Bettger

Packing shotguns and six-guns in Paramount Studio's western street, Doc Holliday (Kirk Douglas) and the Earps – Wyatt (Burt Lancaster), Virgil (John Hudson) and Morgan (DeForest Kelly) – head for the *Gunfight at the O.K. Corral* (1957).

was typecast as Ike Clanton (he'd been a great villain, teamed with Hugh O'Brian, in *Drums Across the River* [1954]), while heavies John Ireland, Jack Elam and Lee Van Cleef lurked menacingly. Ireland had previously played Billy Clanton in *My Darling Clementine* and here appeared as villainous Johnny Ringo.

Shooting commenced on 12 March 1956. The desert western town set was authentically in Arizona, at 'Old Tucson' Studios, 201 South Kinney Road, Tucson. The set was built for a small fortune in 1940 by Columbia Pictures for Wesley Ruggles's *Arizona*. It can be seen in *Gunfight's* opening scene, when Ed Bailey and his cohorts ride into Ft Griffin, and later for some of the Tombstone scenes, including the final gunfight. The riding shots, the title sequence and the 'Boot Hill' scenes were shot in the yellowing grassland of Elgin, Arizona. The Dodge City street scenes (plus some of the Tombstone shots) were filmed on the western street set at Paramount Studios. Behind the set was the vast 'Blue Sky' wall, which had a mountain backdrop painted on it, to hide the rest of the studio from view. Interiors were also shot at Paramount. In the finale, the Earp boys and Doc stride down the Paramount street, past a big fake Saguaro, vanish down an alley, and seamlessly emerge on the edge of town at Old Tucson, approaching the adobe ruin of the O.K. Corral. The gunfight was filmed last in Old Tucson, between 11 and 14 May. The film was completed on 17 May. The death of Billy Clanton was shot in the studio interior of Fly's Photographic Gallery – it was also actor Hopper's twentieth birthday.

Like *My Darling Clementine*, Stuart Lake's much-mythologised biography 'Wyatt Earp, Frontier Marshal' was used as the basis for the story. Lake worked on early drafts of the script until he was fired by Paul Nathan, Paramount's head of publicity, who called him, 'a tired old man…and a big phoney to boot'. Sturges claimed in 1962, 'Western characters must not be glamorised. I'm a westerner myself and I can tell you I don't go for all that Stuart Lake baloney.' But Sturges's film is as skewed as any other Hollywood version of the O.K. Corral. The participants in the O.K. Corral are correct for the Earp faction (although all the real Earps had moustaches), but the actual Clanton line-up was Ike and Billy Clanton, the two McLaurys, Tom and Frank, and Clanton associate Billy Claibourne. In the film, Ike and Billy Clanton and the McLaury brothers are present, but the mysterious Clanton brother 'Finn' also tags along (Phineas Clanton wasn't present). The film version makes the further addition of Johnny Ringo to the Clanton faction. Ringo was certainly associated with the Clantons and was involved in the later shotgun murder of Virgil, but he was nowhere near the O.K. Corral on 26 October. Also, it was Sheriff Behan of Cochise County who fought over a woman with Wyatt (named Sadie, later Wyatt's wife), rather than the Holliday and Ringo subplot, over Kate Fisher. Fisher was actually a prostitute named Katherine Elder, better known as 'Big Nosed Kate Fisher'. Sheriff Behan is replaced in Uris's scenario by Sheriff Cotton Wilson, a fictitious lawman. James Earp was actually the oldest brother, not the youngest (he had fought in the Civil War), and wasn't killed in ambush prior to the O.K. Corral. The gunfight itself took place in the afternoon (here it is sun-up), Ike fled the gunfight, hid in a Mexican dancehall and survived (Sturges has Wyatt blow his head off with a shotgun), while it was Claibourne who sheltered in Fly's Photographic

Studio with Behan, not wounded Billy Clanton. Otherwise, the film is exactly how it happened.

Gunfight at the O.K. Corral offers a comic-strip version of American history, populated by western cardboard cut-outs in the classic Hollywood mould. Lancaster's portrayal of Wyatt Earp is irritatingly self-righteous. Doc refers to him throughout as 'preacher', Kate calls him 'Mr Virtue' and gambler Laura notes when he puts her in jail, that he needs a new halo: 'The one you're wearing's too tight.' *Time* said that Lancaster's stoic demeanour 'looks like a man who is heading for nothing better than the electric chair'. It is certainly one of the actor's more subdued performances, a far cry from his exuberance in *Vera Cruz*. Wyatt is also given an added motivation of revenge for the final shootout, with the murder of his kid brother, James, justifying his actions and the death of the partly sympathetic Billy Clanton, a typically misunderstood fifties teenager.

Dimple-chinned Douglas gives the film's best performance, as tubercular, gambling ex-dentist, Doc, the fallen Southern gentleman with 'a reputation'. He became a gambler when 'my patients didn't like my coughing'. In Doc's introductory scene, he drunkenly throws switchblades into his hotel room door, while Kate goads him about Southern 'Magnolia drippin'', the Georgia plantation and 'his lily-white friends', who since the Civil War no longer exist. His rasping cough, heavy drinking and nocturnal socialising style him a doomed romantic: Doc really doesn't care if he lives or dies. 'Everyone puts such an outlandish value on my life,' he notes – everyone except him. In the effective opening, three riders arrive in Ft Griffin to put Holliday on ice. The scenes echo the beginning of *High Noon*. In a duel in Shanssey's saloon, Ed Bailey (Lee Van Cleef) tries to plug Doc in the back with a Derringer hidden in his boot, but Doc's practice in his hotel room pays dividends when his blade hits Bailey in the chest.

Following such a vigorous opening, the first half of *Gunfight at the O.K. Corral* veers off tack, concerned as it is with Wyatt's activities in Dodge City. The film has a stagey look, with much of the action in medium shot. Even worse, all three bar rooms in the film have the same layout – a door at background right, the bar on the left, and look like they were filmed on exactly the same set, redressed; the same problem occurs with the numerous hotel rooms. *Gunfight* often has an urban feel (Shanssey, a saloon owner played by George Mathews, has a raspy voice, like a *film noir* cop or gangster), but unlike *High Noon* or *Rio Bravo*, there is little tension until the finale. The Clantons are nondescript as villains and don't liven up the film half as much as Old Man Clanton and his sons in *My Darling Clementine*. The few excursions out of town include awkward romantic interludes between Wyatt and Laura, but when Wyatt travels to clean up Tombstone, Laura vanishes from the movie, never to return, as Sturges forgets her and rushes towards his big finish.

The actual O.K. Corral fight lasted about 30 seconds, but Sturges wrings further mileage out of his climax and its build-up. It was filmed in VistaVision, which is inferior to CinemaScope for confrontations and duels (it was Paramount's own patented widescreen process). VistaVision's screen ratio is only 1.85:1, as compared with CinemaScope's 2.35:1, width to height. Even so, Sturges arranges his posturing protagonists well for maximum impact, and the shootout justifies the entire film, as it had to. A draft sketch exists, reputedly by Sturges, of the layout for the final gunfight. It features the geography of the junction of Freemont and Third Street, and the lettered positions of various combatants – the Earps' approach down Freemont, the Clantons gathered around a covered wagon – and is a reasonably accurate diagram of the historic fight. It bears no relation whatsoever to what ended up on screen.

To take advantage of the Old Tucson set, with its desert locale, mountain backdrop, cacti, lean-to shacks, adobe walls and rickety bridge over a dry water course, Sturges choreographed his own version of the firefight, in the best tradition of western fiction. The Earps, in funereal suits and packing shotguns, approach from the edge of town, with the Clantons holed up behind a covered wagon. Attempting to cross the bridge, the lawmen come under fire and take cover in the gully. As the fight proceeds, dynamic Lancaster comes alive, bolting from cover, diving behind low adobe walls and letting fly with his 'scatter gun'. The Clantons's wagon catches fire, Frank McLaury emerges aflame, Cotton Wilson is shot down by Ike as he tries to escape and the Clantons manage to wound both Virgil and Morgan. But Doc and Wyatt do the most damage, and soon both McLaurys and two Clantons are dead. Billy, wounded, flees to Fly's Gallery, while Doc kills Ringo with venom, putting four bullets into his corpse. It's pure fiction, but makes a great action sequence and ensured the film's popularity.

Gunfight at the O.K. Corral was released in the US in May 1957. Posters made the most of the titanic pairing of Lancaster and Douglas: 'The Strangest Alliance This Side of Heaven Or Hell!' between the 'famed lawman' and the 'most feared of gambler-badmen'. In the US it was one of the top westerns of the year, taking $4.7 million on its first release and $11 million in all; it was Lancaster's last real blockbuster and the fifth most successful western of the fifties. The *New York Times* called it, 'the old gambling, boozing, boasting, shooting type of western – not *High Noon*'. The same production team (Sturges, producer Wallis, photographer Lang, star Douglas) immediately embarked on *Last Train from Gun Hill* to cash in on its popularity. In the UK *Gunfight* gained an 'A' certificate, following some cuts in March 1957 and was a hit there too. It was also popular in Europe, particularly in Italy, where it was released as *Sfida all'O.K. Corral* ('Challenge at the O.K. Corral'). In Spain it was *Duelo de Titanes* ('Duel of the Titans'), in Denmark *Scheriffen fra Dodge City* ('Sheriff from Dodge City'), while in Germany it was simply *Blutsbrüder* – 'Blood Brothers'.

Frankie Laine's title song, which appears throughout the film as a running commentary, was very popular. Written by Dimitri Tiomkin and Ned Washington, its whistled refrain and clip-clop rhythm whittles at the nerves. Singers like Laine and Tex Ritter used to make personal appearances dressed in cowboy outfits. Laine's other western hits include the title songs for *Man without a Star* (1955), *3:10 to Yuma* (1957), *Bullwhip* (1958), the parodic *Blazing Saddles* (1974 – 'He rode a blazing saddle, he wore a shining star. He made his blazing saddle, a torch to light the way') and his most famous song – the theme from the TV series *Rawhide* (1959–1966).

In the world of sixties sci-fi TV, which saw the 'Living in Harmony' episode of Patrick McGoohan's *The Prisoner* transport Number 6 from his Portmeirion

Italianate village to the western town of Harmony, DeForest Kelly, who had played Morgan Earp in *Gunfight*, returned to the O.K. Corral in the eerie *Star Trek* episode 'Spectre of the Gun'. Captain Kirk, Spock, Scotty, Chekov and Doc Bones McCoy (Kelly) are teleported into Tombstone 1881 and are mistaken for the Clantons. *Dr Who* also found himself in Tombstone *circa* 1881, in the episode 'The Gunfighters'.

Sturges made a violent sequel to *Gunfight* in 1967, called *Hour of the Gun*, with James Garner as Earp and Jason Robards as Holliday. The film opens in fine style with a much more accurate rendering of the O.K. Corral, with Ike (Robert Ryan) surviving and the McLaurys and Billy Clanton biting the dust. We then see Virgil ambushed and Morgan killed, in a memorable shotgun ambush that propels him across the baize as he takes a billiard shot. Earp and Holliday (still coughing after a spell in the Glenwood Springs Sanatorium) embark on a fictitious chase to Mexico to round up the culprits, supposedly for 'Arrest and Conviction', but Wyatt executes each one, including Ike. Although more effort was taken here with historical accuracy, Clanton didn't hide out in Mexico and wasn't killed by Earp; he was shot in Bonita, Arizona in 1887 by Deputy Sheriff Brighton, after rustling cattle. Filmed around Durango in Mexico and with an effective Jerry Goldsmith score, *Hour of the Gun*'s cynical, vengeful tone is an interesting shift a decade after Sturges's comic book version of the protagonists. As the posters claimed: 'Wyatt Earp – hero with a badge or cold-blooded killer?' Via Garner's grim performance, he is definitely the latter.

Interest in the most famous western lawman and the O.K. showdown continues. In the real Tombstone, you can pay to visit the site of the gunfight and even see daily re-enactments, while local attractions include 'Big Nose Kate's Saloon'. The community dubbed 'The Town Too Tough Too Die' now keeps itself alive with tourism.

12

'I Bet That Rattler Died'

— *Forty Guns* (1957)

Forty Guns (1957)
Credits
DIRECTOR, PRODUCER AND SCREENPLAY – Samuel Fuller
DIRECTOR OF PHOTOGRAPHY – Joseph Biroc
EDITOR – Gene Fowler Jnr
ART DIRECTOR – John Mansbridge
MUSIC – Harry Sukman
CinemaScope
A Globe Enterprises Production
Released by 20th Century-Fox
79 minutes
Cast
   Barbara Stanwyck (Jessica Drummond); Barry Sullivan
   (Griff Bonell); John Ericson (Bronky Drummond); Gene
   Barry (Wes Bonell); Robert Dix (Chico Bonell); Dean Jagger
   (Sheriff Ned Logan); Eve Brent (Louvenia Spanger); Hank
   Worden (Marshal John Chisum); Jidge Carroll (Barney
   Cashman); Paul Dubov (Judge Macy); Ziva Rodann (Rio);
   Gerald Milton (Shotgun Spanger, the gunsmith); Neyle
   Morrow (Wiley); Chuck Roberson (Howard Swain); Chuck
   Hayward (Charlie Savage); Eddie Parks (Tombstone Sexton);
   Sandra Wirth (Saloon girl in street eyeing Chico)

*   *   *

Samuel Fuller had an extraordinary life, as recounted in his autobiography, *A Third Face: My Tale of Writing, Fighting and Filmmaking*. From the age of 17, he worked as a journalist on the San Diego Sun, rode freight trains, wrote pulp fiction and after a stint in North Africa and Europe fighting in the US First Infantry Division ('The

Big Red One'), he became a director in 1949, aged 38. His debut was the western *I Shot Jesse James*, starring John Ireland as Bob Ford (James's assassin) and in 1951, Fuller arrived at 20th Century-Fox. As Fuller recalls, he had a meeting with chief of production Darryl F. Zanuck who decided to take a chance on Fuller's raw style of B-movie cinema, without worrying too much about profitability. Fuller made seven films for Fox: *Fixed Bayonets* (1951), *Pickup on South Street* (1953), *Hell and High Water* (1954), *House of Bamboo* (1955), *China Gate* and *Forty Guns* (both 1957), and *The Crimson Kimono* (1959).

Prior to *Forty Guns*, Fuller directed *Run of the Arrow*, the first film for his own Globe Enterprises, released by RKO in 1957. *Arrow* tells the story of Confederate sharpshooter Private O'Meara (played in surly fashion by Rod Steiger), who fired the last bullet of the Civil War. Hating post-Civil War society and disowned by his mother, he heads west, where he meets Sioux army scout Walking Coyote (Jay C. Flippen). He also survives the 'Run of the Arrow', a Sioux endurance test at the hands of renegade Crazy Wolf. O'Meara joins the Sioux tribe, taking Yellow Moccasin (Sarita Montiel) as his wife and adopting Silent Tongue, a mute boy, as their son. But the arrival of the army to build Fort Abraham Lincoln causes friction with the Sioux and puts O'Meara's allegiances in the firing line.

Run of the Arrow was filmed in CinemaScope and Technicolor in St George, Utah. Despite a jumpy narrative and Steiger's variable Irish accent, Fuller's set pieces and cinematography are memorable (with several elaborate tracking shots, pans and cranes). For the 'Run of the Arrow' barefoot sprint challenge, O'Meara is given an arrow's flight distance head start from a drunken war party of screaming Sioux. The final attack and torching of the half-built Fort Abraham Lincoln is Fuller at his economical best, with swirling smoke and deft editing concealing his thin budget. There are many references to US history in the film, with Brian Keith, as moderate cavalryman Captain Clark, trying to convince O'Meara that his principle allegiance should be to the United States. *Arrow* remains an interesting cult film, but not up to the standard of Fuller's next excursion west.

Fuller directed, produced and wrote *Forty Guns*, under the working title 'Woman with a Whip'. In his scenario, Griff Bonell, a peace officer, and his two brothers, Wes and Chico, arrive in Tombstone to serve a warrant for Howard Swain, wanted for mail robbery. Swain is one of forty riders employed as hired hands by Jessica Drummond at the Dragoons ranch. The Bonells come into conflict with Jessica and her wild brother, Bronky. Swain is murdered in custody by Charlie Savage, another of Jessica's men, who is later shot by Chico. Crooked Sheriff Logan, who loves Jessica, sees that she is falling for Griff; she eventually pays Logan off, who in despair hangs himself. Wes decides to settle down, becomes town marshal and marries local gunsmith Louvenia, but on their wedding day, Bronky shoots him dead. Jessica's empire is crumbling and Bronky finds himself in Tombstone jail. But Bronky breaks out and takes his sister hostage; in a showdown, Griff wings Jessica before killing Bronky in cold blood.

With Fox's backing, Fuller headlined an excellent cast. Marilyn Monroe wanted the role of Jessica Drummond, but lost out to Barbara Stanwyck. Stanwyck (real name

Ruby Stevens) worked on Broadway, then moved into movies in 1927. Her most famous film was the *noir*, *Double Indemnity* (1944), where she played murderess Phyllis Dietrichson, with a $100,000 'double indemnity' insurance policy on her husband; that same year Stanwyck was named as the highest paid woman in the US. Though her earning power waned in the fifties, she starred in several westerns, which proved popular: Anthony Mann's *The Furies* (1950), *Cattle Queen of Montana* (1954), *The Violent Men* (1955) and *The Maverick Queen* (1956). These roles, as a cattle baron's ambitious daughter, a battling rancher, a cattle baron's mistress and an outlaw in league with Butch Cassidy and the Sundance Kid, established Stanwyck as a strong female western lead, which Fuller exploited in *Forty Guns*.

Barry Sullivan was cast as tough lawman Griff Bonell. 'Griff' is named after Griffith, a GI Fuller became friendly with. A landmine victim, he died in hospital having had his arms and legs amputated. The name 'Griff' appears in several Fuller films in honour of the soldier's courage. Sullivan, who more often appeared in gangster movies, appeared as film director Fred Amiel in *The Bad and the Beautiful* (1952) and had just starred with Stanwyck in *The Maverick Queen*. He later played cattleman Chisum in *Pat Garrett & Billy the Kid* (1973). Gene Barry and Robert Dix gave good performances as Griff's brothers, Wes and Chico. Wes decides to settle in Tombstone, while Griff is determined that Chico, the youngest, will never be 'Griff's third gun'; he must head west to their parents' spread in California.

Dean Jagger, who had played the title role in *Brigham Young* (1940), had appeared opposite Robert Mitchum in Raoul Walsh's *noir* western *Pursued* (1947) and had portrayed useless sheriff Tim Horn in *Bad Day at Black Rock* (1955). He was cast as equally useless Sheriff Logan. Beautiful Eve Brent, as Wes's gunsmith lover, Louvenia, later played Jane (to Gordon Scott's Tarzan) in two 1958 jungle adventures. John Ericson, with his broad shoulders and swept-back quiff, summoned in unruly Bronky the intensity of a young Brando. A bronco, or 'bronc' is a wild horse or mustang, who must be broken or 'busted'. Jessica recalls how their mother died giving birth to Bronky and how she then raised him. There are references in Fuller's story suggesting Bronky must be 'broken' or his philandering with local women will result in 'a calf in every corral'. Jidge Carroll, a well-known singer, appeared as Barney Cashman and performed the film's two featured ballads. Ziva Rodann (as Rio, Bronky's lover) went on to play Kirk Douglas's murdered wife in *Last Train from Gun Hill* (1959). Hank Worden had a brief cameo as ageing Marshal Chisum who is blinded by Bronky. Stuntman Chuck Roberson (also called 'Bad Chuck Roberson') played Griff's mark, Swain (he'd appeared in Fuller's *Run of the Arrow* as the soldier who falls into the quicksand trying to save Silent Tongue) while Chuck Hayward, another stuntman, played Dragoon's rider Charlie Savage. With so many western regulars in the cast, audiences expected a regular western, but Fuller was planning anything but.

The town of Tombstone, Cochise County, Arizona was the 20th Century-Fox backlot town set. The same locale, with its rising street, also appears in other Fox westerns: *The Ox-Bow Incident* (1943), *Broken Arrow* (1950), *Man With the Gun* (1955), *The Proud Ones* (1956), *The Comancheros* (1961) and was Northfield, Minnesota, in *The True Story of Jesse James* (1957). It was also transformed into

the mud-strewn gold mining town of Nome, *circa* 1900, for *North to Alaska* (1961).
Forty Guns' location scenes were shot in the arid Californian valleys, while the interior
of Jessica's ranch house was the redressed Tara set from *Gone With the Wind*. For
the scene when Griff and Jessica are caught in open country in a tornado, special
effects created an authentic swirling windstorm. A black twister (a photographic
effect) loomed across the landscape, while the ferocious wind (actually huge
propellers on set) blew dust, straw, tumbleweeds, planks of wood and a buggy across
the screen. When stuntmen refused to be filmed in the storm, Stanwyck herself
performed the scene where she is dragged by her stirrup, three times. According to
Fuller, she didn't complain once.

Forty Guns was photographed in black and white CinemaScope by Joseph Biroc.
Like Akira Kurosawa, Fuller displays a mastery of the monochrome widescreen frame,
which is demonstrated well in the film's wordless pre-title sequence. The Bonell
brothers' buggy moves through a valley in rolling hill country, the black shadow of
a cloud passing ominously across the landscape. Thunder rolls in the distance, but
it isn't a storm approaching – it's the pounding hooves of Jessica and her 'forty
thieves'. Jessica, dressed in black and mounted on a white stallion, is followed by a
black snake of riders, tearing out of the emptiness in a cloud of dust. They split from
their column of two's formation, to ride either side of the buggy, spooking Bonell's
team – Fuller films part of this from beneath the wagon chassis, through the team's
stamping hooves. When the riders have passed, the three brothers look in awe at
the departing dust cloud, before Fuller cuts to Stanwyck, riding her horse at full
throttle, as the racing title music begins, with 'SAMUEL FULLER'S *FORTY
GUNS*' emblazoned across the widescreen.

Elsewhere, Fuller uses tracking shots and cranes for complicated set-ups. Two
long dialogue scenes in Tombstone's main street are filmed in continuous takes. In
the first, the camera starts inside a first-floor hotel room, follows the Bonells onto

'God Has His Arms Around Me': Gunsmith Louvenia (Eve Brent) mourns her
husband's murder in Sam Fuller's stylish, gothic western *Forty Guns* (1957).

the balcony, descends the stairs, then tracks ahead of them up the street, as they discuss business with Logan. The camera pauses when Griff sends a telegram and then captures Jessica and her riders roaring past to release Bronky from jail. A thousand feet of dolly track was laid up the Fox street, the longest dolly shot in the history of the studio. In the second scene, Chico boards the stage, which pulls off up the street. Wes and Griff walk alongside the coach, chatting, then Wes picks up a rifle from the gunsmith's, as he and Griff prepare to face gunman Charlie Savage who has been reported waiting in the undertaker's alley for a showdown. Again, the whole set-up is one take.

Elsewhere there are overhead shots, *noir*-ish shadows and in two scenes blurred point-of-view shots demonstrating Marshal Chisum's fading eyesight. Fuller fully exploits CinemaScope's wide format, with characters positioned on the periphery of the frame. For the most famous scene in the film, Griff Bonell's trademark 'walk' when he faces drunken Bronky, Fuller's style reached new heights. Bonell's reputation precedes him. He strides up the street and Bronky's henchman Charlie notes, 'There's only one man walks like that,' before skedaddling. Fuller cuts from Bronky's unholstered pistol to Griff's striding feet and steely eyes. Bronky stands paralysed, too overawed to react, until Griff is so close that he knocks the troublemaker out with his pistol, dumping his body in a wheelbarrow and trundling him off to jail.

With its 1880s Tombstone setting and three lawman brothers arriving in town, *Forty Guns* resembles Fuller's take on *My Darling Clementine*. Certainly the Bonells' matching black suits and Wes's murder owe much to the historical Earps, while crooked County Sheriff Logan recalls Sheriff John Behan's involvement with the Clantons. Fuller even names the photographer at Wes's wedding Fly, after 'Camillus S. Fly's Photographic Gallery', in Tombstone. When the lawmen kill assassin Charlie Savage his corpse is put on display in the undertaker's window with placards: 'Murdered by Bonell Brothers' and 'Shot in Back of Head', as depicted in period photographs (three Clanton corpses were displayed in a hardware store window). The Clanton faction are now Drummond's much more formidable forty guns, Old Man Clanton becomes Jessica and live-wire troublemaker Billy Clanton is the model for Bronky.

Jessica Drummond is one of the most powerful female roles in the genre. Her escort symbolises her power in Cochise County, which she rules through corruption. For dinner at the Dragoons's mansion, she presides at the head of a long table with 20 gunmen sitting either side – when Griff arrives to apprehend Swain, she wants to talk to Griff in private and the riders rise en masse, adjourning to the next room. Jessica and Griff's relationship is initially mutual dislike. She calls Griff 'a legal killer for hire'. When they visit her childhood home, she recalls that a rattlesnake bit her when she was 15; 'I bet that rattler died,' snipes Griff. Later, as they shelter together from a tornado on the prairie, they become closer. 'This is the last stop Griff,' Jessica tells him, 'the frontier is finished. There'll be no more towns to break, no more men to break – time you started to break yourself. You don't want the only evidence of your life's work to be bullet holes in men.' He's already told her how difficult his job is, 'In my heart I've always asked for forgiveness before I killed, just like an Indian asking forgiveness from an animal before the slaughter.' Now, as her empire teeters on collapse, she asks him to run the Dragoons, 'I need a strong man to carry out my orders', 'And a weak man to take them,' he concludes.

Fuller's other love subplot has Wes the shootist falling for his perfect woman – a gunsmith (the alternative ideal would be an undertaker's daughter, but that scenario never occurred). 'She even looks good in overalls…she's built like a 40.40,' muses Wes to Chico, comparing Louvenia to a custom-made rifle. Louvenia measures him for a new gun, a good excuse for them to spend time together, 'You've got a high cheekbone and low shoulder,' she admires. Wes begins to wonder about settling down, 'This kind of rifle's worth hanging around for.' Wes looks at Louvenia through a gun barrel, her face framed by the spiralled rifling, then Fuller cuts to them kissing. 'I've never kissed a gunsmith before,' says Wes, 'Any recoil?' offers Louvenia.

Forty Guns has often been accused by critics of being little more than a rough-edged exercise in style, but it works in the film's context, with abrupt climaxes and high-riding emotions, juxtaposing love and sudden death. In Jessica's parlour, jealous Logan tries to kill Griff, but misses. Jessica wants rid of the meddling sheriff and pays him off. Alone again, Jessica tells Griff, 'What's happened between us is like war – easy to start, hard to stop.' She continues, 'I never knew how to like anybody until I knew how to love and I like you Griff.' Their kiss is interrupted by an odd banging noise, like heavy, lopsided footsteps. They investigate and find broken Logan in an adjacent room, hanged, his boot heels hitting the wall. The conclusion of Wes and Louvenia's romance is equally hard-hitting. On their wedding day, as Griff leans to kiss the bride, Bronky rides by and shoots Wes. When Bronky is arrested, he tells Griff, 'You're lucky you kissed the bride, or else my bullet would have been in your head.'

'Not Suitable for Children': Australian 'daybill' publicising Samuel Fuller's *Forty Guns* (1957); Bronky Drummond (John Ericson) uses his sister Jessica (Barbara Stanwyck) as cover, in the film's unexpected climax. (Picture courtesy of Ian Caunce Collection).

Wes collapses dying on his wife of seconds, rice still in his hair. The following scene, a tracking shot, depicts Louvenia standing on a hilltop in full mourning attire, with Jidge Carroll nearby, singing the hymnal 'God Has His Arms Around Me'.

In Fuller's pessimistic ending, vetoed by Fox, Griff was to have killed Jessica and Bronky with the same bullet, even though Griff is in love with her. As filmed, Bronky uses Jessica as a human shield, goading Griff to shoot her. He does and Jessica falls, enabling Griff to execute Bronky in a hail of bullets. 'I'm killed, Mister Bonell, I'm killed,' screams Bronky, on his knees, gutshot, as Griff continues to empty his pistol. Griff then walks past the two bodies, saying emotionlessly, 'Get a doctor – she'll live.' A tacked-on epilogue has Jessica apologising to Louvenia for the death of Wes ('You have one thing in your favour Mrs Bonell – youth') and then running up the street to catch Griff's departing buggy, leaving with him for California, a more conventional and acceptable ending to an unconventional story.

Forty Guns is notable for Fuller's unusual use of the two featured songs. 'High Ridin' Woman' (by Harold Adamson and Harry Sukman) is sung by Jidge Carroll at two points on screen: as he walks through the streets carrying pails of water to his bathhouse and later as Jessica and Griff leave town. A lilting ballad introducing Jessica, it includes the lyrics:

She's a high-ridin' woman with a whip, she's a woman that all men desire
She commands and men obey; they're just putty in her hands so they say.
When she rides and the wind is in her hair. She has eyes full of life, full of fire
But if someone could break her and take her whip away
You may find that the woman with a whip is only a woman after all

The lament, 'God Has His Arms Around Me' by Adamson and Victor Young, sung by Carroll during Wes's funeral, is more effective:

Although the way before me, may be a road that's stormy
God has his arms around me, I'm not afraid
And though I stumble blindly, I see a light that's kindly
I feel his love surround me, his tender touch has found me
God has his arms around me, I'm not alone.

Sukman also composed and conducted the score, which is frequently as melo-dramatic as the action. The title music is a riding theme, which incorporates the melody of 'High Ridin' Woman', while the ominous, march-like accompaniment to Griff Bonell's 'walk' is laced with staccato strings and electric guitar.

Advertising posters featured the forty riders kicking up a tornado, with Stanwyck and Sullivan caught in the eye of the storm. *Forty Guns* was released in the US at 79 minutes, but pruned by a minute in the UK in October 1957, to gain an 'A' certificate. The film wasn't a success in the US, with reviewers largely ignoring it. *Village Voice* called it 'the most phallic western ever made'. Fuller has since discussed the film in his autobiography in the chapter 'Stuffed with Phalluses', and singles it out as one of his favourites, 'I'd really hit my stride'. *Movies on TV*'s review was typically nonplussed: 'The *Forty Guns* of the title must go off forty times each in this literal shoot-em-up…it seems the entire cast is either shooting or being shot at during every scene.' As with many widescreen westerns, pan-and-scan TV showings have destroyed Fuller's CinemaScope compositions (which often result in western streets featuring cropped signs for 'RIFF'S OFF' or 'ALOO'). Some TV prints even abridge Fuller's final shot, ending before Jessica reaches Griff's buggy, giving the impression that she runs after him, but he doesn't stop for her. DVD releases are now uncut, in the original CinemaScope format.

In Europe in the late fifties *Forty Guns* was very influential. In France it was dubbed a masterpiece and promoted Fuller to cult *auteur* status; Jean-Luc Godard paid homage to the famous shot of Eve Brent through the rifled gun barrel. In *Breathless* (1959), Patricia Franchini (Jean Seberg) looks through a rolled up Renoir poster at her lover Michel Poiccard (Jean-Paul Belmondo), who is posing with a Gauloise; Godard then cuts to a close-up of them kissing.

Hysterical 'cleaning up the town' westerns reached their zenith with Edward Dmytryk's *Warlock* (1959), which lacks Fuller's fast pacing, but had plenty of style and a bizarre atmosphere. Fancy gunfighting team Clay Blaisdell (Henry Fonda) and Tom Morgan (Anthony Quinn, as his club-footed partner) are hired by the citizens of Warlock to face a bunch of rowdy cowboys operating from the San Pablo ranch. After the death of his brother, former outlaw Johnny Gannon (Richard Widmark) decides to take the sheriff's star in opposition to Blaisdell and Morgan, who in pacifying the town begin to overstep their authority. Their partnership breaks up when Blaisdell falls for Miss Jessie, then Blaisdell is forced to shoot Morgan when he runs amuck. During a thunderstorm, Blaisdell lays his friend's corpse out on a roulette table in the French Palace Saloon, then torches it, sending Morgan off in style.

Filmed at Fox Studios on the same town set as *Forty Guns* (with location scenes in Moab, Utah) in CinemaScoped Technicolor, *Warlock* is one of several celebrated westerns starring Richard Widmark, though his role as Jonathan 'Comanche' Todd in Delmer Daves's *The Last Wagon* (1956) remains his best. Dapper, black-suited Fonda carries a pair of gold-handled pistols. The film's French title was *L'Homme aux Colts D'Or* ('The Man with the Golden Colts'), while in Italy it was *Ultima Notte a Warlock* ('Last Night in Warlock'). Morgan is known by the dime novel nickname 'The Black Rattlesnake of Fort James' ('a very poetic image' notes Quinn). These two hired 'lawmen' are most unusual for fifties westerns: Morgan actually seems to be in love with Blaisdell, the only man who doesn't see him as 'a cripple'. An excellent supporting cast is headed by Dorothy Malone, as vengeful widow Lily Dollar. Directed in fine style, *Warlock* fully deserves its reputation as an intelligent, dramatically powerful western.

Forty Guns was Stanwyck's last film for five years and she only returned to the big screen for three more movies: *Walk on the Wild Side*, *Roustabout* and *The Night Walker*. In the sixties Fuller wanted to cast her as Eva Peron, but the project never materialised. Stanwyck enjoyed a new audience playing Victoria, matriarch of the Barkley family, in the popular ATV western series *The Big Valley* (1965–1969). Interviewed on set in 1967, Stanwyck told a reporter, 'I've always loved westerns. Victoria Barkley is a wonderful woman to play. She's just what I've been looking for.' Tough Victoria is cast from the same mould as Jessica Drummond.

In the early sixties, Fuller was left without studio backing and worked on lower-budget films, including *Underworld USA* (1960), *Merrill's Marauders* (1962), *Shock Corridor* (1963) and *The Naked Kiss* (1965). In 1972, he began filming *The Deadly Trackers* in Spain, with Richard Harris (an adaptation of Fuller's screenplay 'Riata'), but Warner Bros closed the production down and the film was eventually shot in Mexico by Barry Shear. Fuller's autobiographical masterpiece *The Big Red One* (1980) is by far the best of his later works. In a 1996 British Film Institute documentary, *The Typewriter, the Rifle and the Movie Camera*, fans Jim Jarmusch, Martin Scorsese and Quentin Tarantino celebrated Fuller's career. He is among the great film directors, with a unique style: journalistic in its approach to realism, sentimental in its depiction of love and totally convincing as great cinema.

13

'There's Some Things a Man Just Can't Ride Around'

— *Ride Lonesome* (1959)

Ride Lonesome (1959)
Credits
DIRECTOR – Budd Boetticher
EXECUTIVE PRODUCER – Harry Joe Brown
PRODUCERS – Budd Boetticher and Randolph Scott
WRITTEN BY – Burt Kennedy
DIRECTOR OF PHOTOGRAPHY – Charles Lawton Jnr
EDITOR – Jerome Thoms
SET DECORATOR – Frank A. Tuttle
ART DIRECTOR – Robert Peterson
MUSIC COMPOSER AND CONDUCTOR – Heinz Roemheld
CinemaScope/Eastman Color
A Ranown Production
Released by Colombia Pictures
74 minutes
Cast
 Randolph Scott (Ben Brigade); Pernell Roberts (Sam Boone);
 Karen Steele (Mrs Lane); James Best (Billy John); Lee Van
 Cleef (Frank, Billy John's brother); James Coburn (Whit);
 Dyke Johnson (Charlie, Frank's henchman); Boyd Stockman
 (Mascalero Apache chief); Bennie E. Dobbins, Roy Jenson
 and Boyd 'Red' Morgan (Frank's gang); Chief Tahachee
 (Mascalero Apache)

*   *   *

In the fifties, a group of westerns were made that came to be known as the Ranown series, so-called because the production company was the Ranown Pictures Corporation – fronted by star Randolph Scott and producer Harry Joe

Brown. The director of the series was Budd Boetticher and most of the scripts were written by Burt Kennedy. Epitomising the series was a trio of classic films: *The Tall T* (1957), *Ride Lonesome* (1959) and *Comanche Station* (1960), which shared locations, themes and the formidable Boetticher–Scott–Kennedy trio.

Oscar 'Budd' Boetticher travelled to Mexico in the thirties, becoming a matador, and was later technical adviser on *Blood and Sand* (1941). Always fascinated by the arena, he directed two bullfighting movies, *The Bullfighter and the Lady* (1951) and *The Magnificent Matador* (1955). Harry Joe Brown was a producer at Warner Bros who oversaw a number of Randolph Scott westerns, under the banner of the Producers-Actors Corporation in partnership with Scott. They later formed Scott-Brown Productions and their first foray under the Producers-Actors Corporation was *Coroner Creek* (1948).

A western star since the thirties, Scott remained popular in churned-out westerns throughout the fifties, though his last appearance in the box-office stars top ten occurred in 1953. He starred in *Ten Wanted Men* (1955), produced by Scott-Brown, with a strong supporting cast which included Dennis Weaver as the sheriff, Richard Boone as the land-grabbing villain and Denver Pyle, Leo Gordon and Lee Van Cleef among Boone's hired guns, the wanted men of the title. *The Stranger Wore a Gun* (1953) pitted Scott against up-and-coming heavies Lee Marvin and Ernest Borgnine. In *Tall Man Riding* (1955) Scott faced a nervous Castillian villain, who is asked about his loss of appetite and replies, 'I can't eat anything when something's eatin' me.'

Scott also made a series of westerns with director Andre De Toth, which hinted at Scott's persona in his Ranown series; De Toth noted that Scott cared more about golf than acting, but was an astute businessman. In De Toth's *The Bounty Hunter* (1954), black-clad Jim Kipp (Scott) is introduced tracking a fugitive. When he collects the reward, he is asked for the reasons why he became a bounty killer. Mercenary Kipp leafs through the dollar bills, 'I'm counting the reasons … and they're ten short.' Pinkerton detectives hire reliable Kipp to trail a trio of train robbers, despite having no leads. Kipp, bemused, outlines his mission, 'Three men nobody saw got away with $100,000 that they haven't spent – you don't know what they look like or where they are and you want me to find them?' Nevertheless, he trails them to the town of Twin Forks, where the trio now reside behind masks of respectability. An unwelcome stranger, Kipp asks questions, attends church and generally unsettles the locals, while residents with guilty consciences begin to quietly sidle out of town.

In 1956 the Ranown series got underway with *Seven Men from Now* (1956), produced not by Brown, but by Batjac, John Wayne's production company (in fact Wayne was to star, but made *The Searchers* instead). Its success ensured that it was swiftly followed by *The Tall T* (1957), *Decision at Sundown* (1957) and *Buchanan Rides Alone* (1958). *Seven Men from Now*, based on Burt Kennedy's own novel, established the central motifs of revenge, obsession and violence that were central to the series, with Scott as avenger Ben Stride. It also introduced the first in a carnival of monstrous villains that Scott was pitted against: here Payte Bodine (played by John Larch) and Bill Masters (Lee Marvin).

The Tall T, based on the classic novelette 'The Captives' by Elmore Leonard (published in Argosy in 1955), continued the series in even more taut fashion. 'T is for Terror!' announced the posters. Leonard was one of the most popular western fiction writers, although he's better known now for crime novels. His stories *Hombre*, *Valdez is Coming* and *3:10 to Yuma* have all been filmed. In *The Tall T*, Pat Brennan (Scott) loses his horse in a bull-riding rodeo bet and ends up hitching a ride on the Contention to Bisbee stagecoach, which is attacked by a trio of bandits: Frank Usher (Richard Boone), Billy Jack (Skip Homeier) and Chink (Henry Silva). Laying in wait at the Sasabe way station, they have dumped the station man and his little son down a well. They take passenger Doretta Mims (Maureen O'Sullivan), the daughter of a wealthy copper magnate, hostage and demand a $50,000 ransom. Brennan manages to save her, eventually killing the three men. Before the final confrontation, which ends with Usher being shot in the face, Brennan tells her, 'I'm going to finish this once and for all – some things a man can't ride around.' *Decision at Sundown* recalled the obsessions of *The Man from Laramie* with Scott avenging the death of his wife (as in *Seven Men from Now*). The jokey *Buchanan Rides Alone*, based on the best-seller 'The Name's Buchanan' by Jonas Ward, is very different in tone to the other films. Arriving in the border town of Agry (the Old Tucson western set), drifter Buchanan (Scott) finds it ruled by the squabbling, greedy Agry clan. Posters announced 'Big man! Big Gun! Big Excitement!' What they failed to mention was 'Big Laughs'. Though future Sam Peckinpah regular L.Q. Jones (as cowpoke Pecos) is violently shot out of his saddle, for the most part the action is played for rough comedy, as in the sequence where Scott breaks a villain's toe with the butt of his Winchester.

The next film in the series was *Ride Lonesome*. While escorting renegade murderer Billy John to Santa Cruz to be hanged, bounty hunter Ben Brigade arrives at Wells Junction, a remote swing station. There he finds Boone and Whit, two lawless drifters, and Mrs Lane, the station attendant's wife. Mascalero Apaches are on the warpath and Mr Lane is missing. When the westbound stage arrives with the driver and passengers massacred, the group decide to head for Santa Cruz. Whit and Boone have their eyes on Billy, as an offer of amnesty is being issued for the outlaw's capture. But Billy's ruthless brother Frank from Valverde is on their trail with his gang. Even though Brigade knows this, their progress to Santa Cruz is slow. It becomes obvious that Brigade has a score to settle with Frank: Billy is the bait. As they near Santa Cruz, Brigade, Boone and Whit face Frank's gang in a forest clearing, near a hanging tree – the same tree where Frank lynched Brigade's wife years before. Having killed Frank, Brigade allows Boone and Whit to take Billy into town to collect their amnesty.

With craggy Scott established as Brigade, the buckskinned lead, Boetticher went on to assemble yet another compact cast in support. James Coburn made his film debut as gangly Whit, teamed with cocky tough guy Pernell Roberts (Adam Cartright from TV's *Bonanza*) as Sam Boone. James Best played Billy John, the snivelling renegade with a feather in his hat who is handcuffed for almost the entire movie. A veteran of *Winchester '73* (1950) and *The Left Handed Gun* (1958), one of Best's most memorable roles was as an outlaw pitted against the Chandler Detective Agency in

Last of the Badmen (1957), a low-budget, fast-moving Allied Artists western, which was almost ruined by its *Dragnet*-like narration. Best's most famous role remains Sheriff Roscoe P. Coltrane in the popular seventies TV series *The Dukes of Hazzard*. Lee Van Cleef, usually a background supporting player, had one of his meatiest roles as Frank, the killer on the loose. Bombshell Karen Steele, Boetticher's then wife, had appeared in *Decision at Sundown* and *Westbound*. In *Ride Lonesome*, her immovable platinum blonde hair, sculpted conical bustier and tiny waist recalled fifties pin–up Mamie Van Doren rather than Cattle Kate. She would also appear in Boetticher's non-western *The Rise and Fall of Legs Diamond* (1960), before the couple went their separate ways. Boyd 'Red' Morgan was responsible for the stunts in the film, and had a small role as one of Frank's gang. Stuntmen Bennie E. Dobbins and Roy Jenson played the rest of the gang, and Dyke Johnson (later of *Comanche Station*) was fourth henchman, Charlie.

Boetticher shot the entire film on location in the wind-weathered Alabama Hills and around Lone Pine, California, at the foot of the High Sierra, with the 14,494 feet high Mount Whitney as a backdrop. The location had been used for hundreds of westerns (including *Seven Men from Now* and *The Tall T*) and also for Humphrey Bogart's *High Sierra* (1941). Other footage was shot on Movie Flats, an open plain, and at the nearby Owens River, where the forest climax was shot. The Alabama Hills and the flats can be seen to excellent effect in *Guns of Hate* (1948), a black and white RKO quickie featuring Tim Holt, and Scott's own *Hangman's Knot* (1952). Here the hills are the setting for Scott's gang of Confederate renegades to steal a quarter of a million in Union bullion, in the film's opening ambush.

Many fifties westerns became bogged down indoors; Boetticher and Kennedy don't allow this – there isn't a single interior shot in *Ride Lonesome*. Nor are there any studio 'exterior' process shots, with their give-away black outlines around the actors' silhouettes and mismatched, back-projected scenery. *Ride Lonesome* was shot by outdoor cameraman Charles Lawton Jnr, who also lensed *Jubal, 3:10 to Yuma* (both for Delmer Daves), *Man in the Saddle, Hangman's Knot, The Tall T* and *Comanche Station*. The graininess of his Eastman Color photographic stock captures the lunar rock formations, the details of dusty costumes and frontier minutiae, emphasising beadwork on saddles, authentic firearms and props, and the harsh settings – the battered swing station and a ruined adobe corral surrounded by salt flats. This rugged cinematography, when coupled with the vast widescreen of the sparsely populated CinemaScope vistas, makes for some of the finest looking western cinema of the fifties.

Ride Lonesome is a supreme example of Kennedy's terse style, influenced by the Mann-Stewart westerns, especially *The Naked Spur* (1953). Scott, tight-lipped and resolute, exchanges clipped dialogue with Best, Steele, Roberts and Van Cleef. The cosy campfire chats that punctuate the prosaic travelogue, with Brigade complementing Mrs Lane on her fine coffee, contrast with the harshness of their desert journey. 'You just don't seem like the kind that would hunt a man for money,' observes Mrs Lane. 'I am,' is Brigade's brusque reply. Brigade's comments about the rejuvenating effect of the morning sun on an injured horse show rare perception for the genre, fully justifying Boone's comment that Brigade 'doesn't act like a man who makes a living killing'. Later Boone utters the most famous line of the Ranown series, a comment on the protagonists' destiny. He plans to kill Brigade, to make sure he earns his amnesty. When questioned by Mrs Lane why he has to

Randolph Scott, the reliable man with a gun, became one of the stalwarts of the genre, particularly in the Ranown series directed by Budd Boetticher. Here he poses for publicity with a Colt .45 Peacemaker – 'the gun that won the west'.

see this through ('We could bury Brigade and live happily ever after,' she says bitterly), Boone answers, 'There's some things a man just can't ride around.'

Kennedy and Boetticher made many of their villainous characters roguish and treacherous, rather than brutal. Here both Boone and Whit are likeable, though Frank is the vilest villain of the Ranown series. When Boone and Brigade first meet, Boone muses, 'Fancy running into you in all this empty,' when in fact he has heard about the amnesty which will enable him to return to his ranch at Socorro and not spend his life, 'Going all dead inside when you see a man wearing tin on him.' Boone's conversations with Mrs Lane are loaded with sexual innuendo, while Boone and Whit have a happy-go-lucky relationship, well played by macho Roberts and loping Coburn. Boone tells Whit, his riding partner for five years, that he'll be his partner on the farm. 'How come?' asks elated Whit. ''Cos I like you Whit.' 'Why, I never knew that.' These drifters on the run from the law are not to be confused with cold-hearted killers like Frank. When Frank confronts Brigade at the climax, he says that Brigade's wife's murder was so long ago, 'I almost forgot.'; 'A man can do that,' answers Brigade.

Through Kennedy's deft narrative touches, we aren't sure of Brigade's integrity – we only trust that he is the hero because he's played by Randolph Scott. His actions are often morally marginal and his motives hazy. At the outset of *Ride Lonesome* he appears to be a bounty hunter, cashing in blood money, concealing his real motivation from the group (and the audience), even though he tells Billy, 'I'd hunt you free.' Though many filmmakers of westerns took shortcuts to give depth to the hero, cheaply using the death of a family member, usually the hero's wife, as a plot device, Kennedy's scripts never feel manipulative. There is a soulfulness and obsessiveness to Scott's vengeful characters that reinforce their sense of loss. As represented by *Ride Lonesome*'s elliptical title, no matter how many travelling companions Brigade has, he always rides alone.

The film incorporates clichéd western ingredients – Indians on the warpath, chases, smoke signals boding ill and a dramatic moment when the stagecoach crashes into the corral at the station with all on board dead, the driver pinned to his seat by a war lance. The music, by Heinz Roemheld, further reinforces these clichés. The amiable, jaunty clip-clop with clarinet and flute for the group's meandering ride to Santa Cruz (where the outcrops of the Alabama Hills do seem to crop up an awful lot), a romantic violin for campfire chats, the Mascaleros' familiar 'Indian theme' with pounding drums and brass, and the ominous, thundering 'riding theme' that accompanies Frank's pursuit.

A *High Noon* scenario is described by Brigade as the trigger for his vendetta: he was once sheriff of Santa Cruz and put Frank in Yuma prison for murder. Released early, Frank kidnapped Brigade's wife while the sheriff waited in town for a showdown and then lynched her from the hanging tree. Halfway through *Ride Lonesome* the truth dawns on Frank, 'It ain't the money Brigade wants, not the money at all. I did him a hurt once, long ago. So long ago I almost forgot.' The final showdown between Frank and Brigade takes place in a forest glade beside the fateful hanging tree, which is shaped like a cross. With handcuffed Billy perched in the saddle, his head in a noose, Brigade tells Frank, 'Sit there and watch your brother hang,' but Frank forces a confrontation and is killed. As Boone, Whit and Mrs Lane ride on to Santa Cruz, a pall of black smoke rises above the forest; Brigade has symbolically torched the tree, his vengeance satiated.

Ride Lonesome was released in the US in February 1959, and was greeted by critics and audiences as another solid but successful Scott-Boetticher western. Poster advertising heralded 'This Is The Man Called Brigade' and offered 'Scorching Action All The Way', with key art featuring Scott, a sultry-looking Steele brandishing a Winchester and two hands handcuffed together. In the UK it was passed 'U', though recent UK TV showings have removed most of the horse stunts, in particular several Apache horse falls during the ambush at the adobe ruin, with the resultant jump-cuts making nonsense of some of the action. Brigade now appears to shoot Mrs Lane's mount (he actually fells an Apache), while Brigade's own horse fall after he leaps the abode wall to safety, is also missing. In Spain *Ride Lonesome* was called *Cabalgar en Solitario* ('Ride Alone') and *El Secreto Del Jinete* ('The Secret of the Rider'). In France it was *La Chevauchée de la Vengeance* ('The Ride of Revenge'). In Italy the Ranown films were often completely retitled: *The Tall T* was *I Tre Banditi* ('The Three Bandits') and *Seven Men from Now* was called *I Sette Assassini* ('The Seven Murderers'); *Ride Lonesome* was called *L'Albero della Vendetta* which evocatively translates as 'The Tree of Revenge'.

Following *Ride Lonesome*, Scott and Boetticher released *Westbound* (1959) through Warners, though it had actually been filmed before *Lonesome* in 1957. Kennedy didn't write the script, Brown didn't produce it, and this is evident in the finished film, a Civil War 'mission' movie, with Unionist Scott assigned to set up a stage line in Confederate Julesburg to transport Yankee gold shipments. Town-bound for the most part (with the Warners western backlot as Julesburg), only the presence of Karen Steele at her most tomboyish as Jeannie, who converts her farm into a stage station, and a vicious turn by B-movie hardman Michael Pate as hired gun Mace, are of note.

The last film of the Ranown series, *Comanche Station* (1960) shares many themes with *Ride Lonesome* and is similarly structured around a disparate group on a journey, though here the villains ride with Scott's hero. Scott, as ex-army major Jefferson Cody, appears to be a Comanchero, cashing in captive women held hostage by the Comanches for the bounty money. Scott trades goods for Nancy Lowe (Nancy Gates), to collect the $5,000 reward offered by her husband. Three outlaws, Cody's old army colleague Ben Lane (Claude Akins) and his sidekicks, Frank (Skip Homeier) and Dobie (Richard Rust), also aim to cash the reward. But the Comanches are on the warpath following an attack on their camp by scalphunters – it is only Cody and Mrs Lowe who make it back to civilisation in Lordsburg. When Mrs Lowe arrives home, she sees her little son and her blind husband waiting for her; there must have been a good reason why her husband hadn't gone after her himself. 'I always figured there was,' says Cody, who doesn't take the reward. Cody's own search is for his wife, lost years before to the Comanche, a quest he never quits. He rides off, the plot coming full circle, as he goes back into the sierras with a pack mule in tow, to meet another band of Indians and save another white captive.

In *Comanche Station*, the action is even more explicit: Cody uses a Comanche as a human shield to stop arrows, the station man arrives with a grisly arrow protruding from his chest and Dobie is dragged by his stirrup after he has been shot by double-crossing Lane. Posters called it 'The One-Man War Against the Comancheros'. Boetticher reuses *Ride Lonesome*'s plot, redeploys musical cues (which are more sombre than the earlier clippety-clop themes) and several of the Lone Pine settings. A way station (the 'Comanche Station' of the title), the Alabama Hills (a Comanche camp), Movie Flats (where Scott is chased by six Comanche riders) and the river all reappear. Even the woodland clearing with the distinctive hanging tree is here; this time the glade is flooded with water. In *Comanche Station* the Native American characters are also more true to life than usual, even if the Comanches do sport inaccurate Mohican hairstyles. The film was called *La Valle dei Mohicani*, 'Valley of the Mohicans', in Italy.

Writer Kennedy went on to be a highly successful director, scoring hits with such films as *The War Wagon* and *Support Your Local Sheriff!*, while Boetticher's later career was marred by tragedy. In 1960 he made *The Rise and Fall of Legs Diamond*, then returned to Mexico with his new wife Debra Paget to make *Arruza*, a documentary about his close friend, the bullfighter Carlos Arruza. Unfortunately, as often happens with American projects filmed in Mexico, the documentary took on an all-consuming life of its own, and swallowed Boetticher's marriage and all his money. He went to jail for a week and ended up suffering from malnutrition and a lung ailment. Then bullfighter Arruza and most of Boetticher's crew were killed in a horrific automobile accident. Seven years later, Boetticher returned to Hollywood with a print of the film, which was eventually released in 1971. Boetticher also wrote the story on which Don Siegel's *Two Mules for Sister Sara* was based. He was reputedly very unhappy with the way his scenario, originally a gritty, funny story in the manner of his work with Kennedy and Scott, was turned into a spaghetti western-style star vehicle for Clint Eastwood. In 2005 Boetticher fan Eastwood produced a documentary on the director's career called *A Man Can Do That*. In the late sixties, Boetticher and Audie Murphy planned to make a series of films together, but following *A Time for Dying* (1969), the series was curtailed abruptly in 1971 when Murphy was killed in a plane crash.

Boetticher's films with Scott are now regarded as a key creative partnership, in the same vein as Ford and Wayne, Eastwood and Leone, and Mann and Stewart. Scott's granite features are an enduring image of the western; much of his other output was inconsistent, but his popularity remained. His iconic genre status is immortalised in *Blazing Saddles* (1973). When Sheriff Bart (Cleavon Little) tries to persuade the people of Rock Ridge to give him 24 hours to save their town, they initially refuse. 'You'd do it for Randolph Scott,' ventures Bart. The townsfolk respectfully remove their hats, as a chorus of 'Randolph Scott!' hallelujahs on the soundtrack. But Scott will always be best remembered for creating, with Boetticher and Kennedy, a timeless hero with steadfast integrity. A man can do that.

14

'I'd Hate to Have to Live on the Difference'

— *Rio Bravo* (1959)

Rio Bravo (1959)
Credits
DIRECTOR AND PRODUCER – Howard Hawks
STORY – B. H. McCampbell
SCREENPLAY – Jules Furthman and Leigh Brackett
DIRECTOR OF PHOTOGRAPHY – Russell Harlan
EDITOR – Folmar Blangsted
ART DIRECTOR – Leo K. Kuter
MUSIC – Dimitri Tiomkin
Technicolor
An Armada Production
Released by Warner Bros
141 minutes
Cast
    John Wayne (Sheriff John T. Chance); Dean Martin (Deputy
    Dude); Ricky Nelson (Colorado Ryan); Angie Dickinson
    (Feathers); Walter Brennan (Deputy Stumpy); Ward Bond
    (Pat Wheeler); John Russell (Nathan Burdette); Pedro
    Gonzales-Gonzales (Carlos Robante); Estelita Rodriguez
    (Consuela Robante); Claude Akins (Joe Burdette); Malcolm
    Atterbury (Jake the stage driver); Harry Carey Jnr (Harold);
    Walter Barnes (Charlie, the bartender); Bob Steele (Matt
    Harris, Burdett gunman); Bing Russell (Man murdered in
    El Toro Rojo cantina); Joseph Shimada (Burt, Chinese
    undertaker); Gordon Mitchell (Man in green shirt); Bob
    Terhune (Bartender); Riley Hill (Burdette messenger);
    Jose Cuchillo (Pedro); Ted White (Bart); Yakima Canutt,
    Fred Graham, Tom Monroe, Chuck Roberson and Dean
    Smith (Burdette's gang)

Since *Red River* in 1948, Howard Hawks had made a variety of films, including *I Was a Male War Bride* (1949), *The Thing from Another World* (1951), *Gentlemen Prefer Blondes* (1953) and the disastrous *Land of the Pharaohs* (1955). No one could ever accuse Hawks of being less than eclectic. For his next film, *Rio Bravo*, Hawks retained the central character dynamic from *Red River*, with John Wayne cast as the lead, alongside scene-stealing co-stars. 'I determined to go back and try to get a little of the spirit we used to make pictures with,' said Hawks, 'In *Rio Bravo* I imagine there are almost as many laughs as if we had started out to make a comedy.'

In the border town of Rio Bravo, Presidio County, Texas, Sheriff John T. Chance has imprisoned Joe Burdette, the brother of local rancher Nathan, for cold-bloodedly murdering a cowboy in the El Toro Rojo cantina. In retribution Nathan bottles up the town and lays siege to the jail. Chance, aided by his drunken deputy Dude, young gunslinger Colorado Ryan and jumpy old deputy Stumpy, repels all attempts at springing Joe. A Mariachi band in the pay of Burdette plays a mournful trumpet 'Deguello' from a saloon across the street, to psyche-out the lawmen. Chance is attracted to Feathers, a drifting gambler staying in town, while Dude battles to regain his self-respect and kick the bottle. Finally, Burdette's men capture Dude and offer his life in exchange for Joe's. At the dawn rendezvous near Burdette's warehouse, a shootout ensues. Joe is recaptured and Chance, Dude, Colorado and Stumpy rout Burdette's gang with dynamite, restoring peace to Rio Bravo.

Based on a short story by B. H. McCampbell, *Rio Bravo* was written for the screen by Jules Furthman and Leigh Brackett. Furthman had worked on *The Outlaw* (1943) for Hawks, while Brackett was a writer of sci-fi fiction and mysteries. Hawks went to Warner Bros with the idea for the film, so he could produce for his own company, Armada, in a 50–50 deal for the profits.

For the central role of John T. Chance, Hawks cast John Wayne. Amassing funds for his soon-to-commence *The Alamo*, ten years in the planning, Wayne agreed to star as the siege-bound sheriff for $750,000. The construction of the vast 'Alamo Village' set at Bracketville, Texas took two years and $1.5 million of United Artists' money. Throughout the making of *Rio Bravo* Wayne kept an eye on progress and the project is referenced in the film: the name of the hotel where Feathers lives and works is the 'Hotel Alamo Dining Room and Bar'. Hawks tried to cast Montgomery Clift, from *Red River*, as Dude, but Clift refused. Instead Hawks hired a rather unusual choice in Dean Martin, nicknamed 'Dino', a popular crooner known as the straight man in his partnership with Jerry Lewis, the most financially successful comedy team the world had ever known. When they split in 1956, no one thought Martin stood a chance of becoming a proper actor. He had had several hit LPs and the massive singles 'Memories are Made of This' and 'Volare'. He later became part of Frank Sinatra's sixties Rat Pack. Despite having practice with his boozy stage act, Martin's sodden Dude was, according to his wife Jeannie, the most difficult role of his career, 'his biggest stretch'.

Pop singer Ricky Nelson was cast as Colorado to attract the teenybopper audience. Ward Bond appeared as Pat Wheeler, Colorado's boss, whose murder causes the youngster to side with Chance. Bond was currently starring on TV in the *Wagon Train* series and Hawks cast him as a freighter leading a wagon train into town (it was Bond's last film). Harry Carey Jnr was originally employed on the film, but allegedly arrived on set drunk and was fired, although his name is still in press books and the title sequence. Walter Brennan played gimpy Deputy Stumpy; he'd also played jail keeper Jake in *The Proud Ones* (1956), though in that film he was killed during a jailbreak. John Russell, who played villain Nathan, was currently appearing in *The Lawman* TV series and later starred as evil Marshal Stockburn in Clint Eastwood's *Pale Rider* (1985). Angie Dickinson had previously acted in several Westerns, including *Man with the Gun* (1955). She had also dubbed the voice of Yellow Moccasin (the Sioux squaw played by Sarita Montel) in *Run of the Arrow*

(1957). Claude Akins was memorable as hostage Joe Burdette, the gunman with a sickly ear-to-ear grin. Joe Byrne was Nelson's stunt double, Joe Grey doubled Martin (and appeared as a card player) and Wayne's regular double, Chuck Roberson, also appeared. Wayne's boyhood friend Bob Steele, a cowboy hero from the thirties and forties, was Burdett henchman Matt Harris in a huge, incongruous thirties-style black Stetson.

Even though it was set in Texas, *Rio Bravo* was shot by Hawks from May to July 1958 on location in Arizona. It was budgeted at $1,950,000, with Hawks receiving $100,000. The clapboard border town of Rio Bravo was the set at Old Tucson Studios. It consisted of a rickety bridge over a dried-up

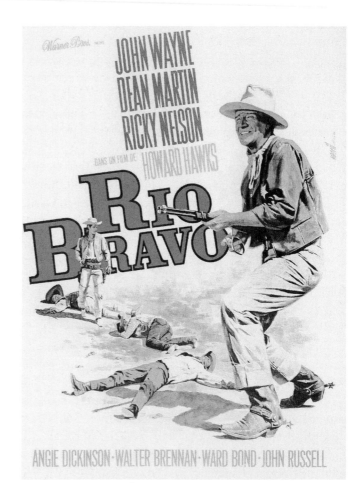

Original poster for the French release of Howard Hawks' *Rio Bravo* (1959) by master poster artist Jean Mascii, with John T. Chance (John Wayne) springing into action.

riverbed and 84 buildings, ranging from timber-framed, false-fronted saloons and stores, to Mexican adobe and stucco hovels – a typical mixture of cultural architecture in a border town. It had been built scaled down in size to increase the actors' stature. Burdette's creek-side warehouse was specially built nearby (the location had been used for the finale of *Gunfight at the O.K. Corral*) and was the setting for *Rio Bravo*'s hostage exchange. Interiors for Chance's jail office (with its pot-bellied stove and hefty timber shutters), the Alamo Hotel and two saloons were also created. The El Toro Rojo cantina deployed Mexican matador décor of ornamental bulls' horns, bullfighting paintings and posters ('Corrida De Toro'), with a barber in the corner, while Burdette's saloon is slightly more upmarket, boasting a pool table. Although shooting conditions on location were hot and tough, filmmakers working in Old Tucson often stayed at the Ramada Hotel in Tucson, 13 miles away. *Rio Bravo* was lensed by Russell Harlan, from *Red River*, in a 1.85:1 screen ratio (rather than 'scope), which increases the camera's intimacy with the characters.

Rio Bravo was Hawks and Wayne's answer to two liberal 'go it alone' westerns they detested: *High Noon* and *3:10 to Yuma* (1957). In *Rio Bravo* Chance refuses help and is only interested in working with professionals. Burdette has 30 or 40 guns and any help from 'well-meaning amateurs – worried about their wives and kids' would simply be giving Burdette's men more targets. *Rio Bravo* is not concerned with cynical isolationism but with comradeship, morality and self-esteem. Sheriff Chance is just doing his job: his salary isn't mentioned (as the meagre lawman's wage is often quoted in other westerns), while he should really be on danger money.

The celebrated opening scenes of *Rio Bravo* start the ball rolling in economical style. Dude sneaks into the El Toro Rojo cantina, desperate for a nerve-steadying whisky, but he's broke. Leering Joe spots Dude and mockingly tosses a dollar into a spittoon. Dude is about to retrieve the coin when Chance kicks the spittoon away, flashing him a look of utter contempt. Dude knocks Chance out, but in the fracas, Joe shoots an unarmed bystander (played by Bing Russell, actor Kurt's father). The killer swaggers on down the street to Burdette's saloon, but Chance, regaining consciousness, follows. With help from Dude, Chance apprehends Joe, laying him out with his carbine. As the two lawmen drag Joe's unconscious body out of the bar, a slow drum begins on the soundtrack and Hawks cuts to the murdered cowboy's funeral cortege making its way through Rio Bravo to Boot Hill the following day.

Wayne gives one of his finest performances as Chance, a tough man in a tight spot. When Wheeler hears what constitutes Chance's line-up he scoffs, 'A lame-legged old man and a drunk – that's all you got?' 'That's what I got,' corrects Chance. 'If I ever saw a man holding a bull by the tail,' Wheeler replies, 'You're it.' As Feathers says of Chance's initial, 'T [is] for Trouble'. Wayne's performance as Chance is where his sixties 'John Wayne' persona begins – the big man, the brawler with the fast gun and the iron fists – which reappeared in much of his post *Rio Bravo* output. As in *Hondo*, Wayne uses a distinctive Winchester carbine with an outsized lever arm – Ringo's gun from *Stagecoach*, which also appeared in the TV series *The Rifleman*. He also wears the button-fronted placket shirt, the so-called bib shirt that he wore in nearly all his later westerns, and his 'Red River D' belt buckle. On more than one occasion, Chance sneaks into the action through the back door, a shift in Wayne's heroic screen persona – the older he gets, the craftier he has to be to gain an edge over the opposition.

For the first hour and 15 minutes, Dude looks rough – unshaven in his battered, threadbare clothes, he describes himself as 'an expert on saloons'. Booze has a grip on him and he is a shadow of his former self, due to an ill-fated love affair. Since then he's been hiding inside a bottle and has the shakes so bad he can't hold a gun, nor roll a cigarette. Wayne keeps handing Martin ready-rolled smokes, a gesture that was improvised on set. The Mexicans have christened Dude 'Borachón' ('Drunk'). As he sits in a chair, cooped up in the office, nerves shredded, he thumps a nerve twitching in his leg, like a Dr Strangelove of the west. Stumpy's chattering doesn't help, almost driving Dude back to drink. 'Think you invented the hangover?' Chance says of Dude's moaning, 'I could sure take out a patent for this one.' Martin's mannerisms – nervously rubbing his chin, wetting his lips, tasting the whisky he can't afford – add to his fidgety performance.

When Dude emerges from his stupor, Chance gives him back his laundered clothes and gunbelt. Now Dude looks exactly like a clean-shaven TV cowboy. The siege wears on Dude's nerves and when Burdette's men ambush him, he quits as deputy exclaiming, 'A man ought to have sense enough to know when he's no good no more.' 'Sorry don't get it done, Dude,' answers Chance. Colorado replaces Dude as deputy. 'Is he as good as I used to be?' asks Dude. 'It'd be pretty close,' answers Chance, 'I'd hate to have to live on the difference.' At a crucial moment, as the ominous 'Deguello' wafts across the street, Dude is galvanised: he looks at the glass of whisky he has just poured and tips it steadily back into the bottle, his tremor gone, 'Didn't spill a drop,' says Dude, with relief rather than triumph.

Fast-gun Colorado, a man who is 'So good he doesn't feel he has to prove it', replaces quitter Dude, just as Ricky's rock 'n' roll was supplanting Dino-style crooning on the Billboard chart. Initially Colorado won't be drawn into the conflict, until the death of his mentor Wheeler, reasoning that he's already getting shot at and 'I might as well get paid for it.' Lightweight Nelson isn't a great actor and struts around like he's still got the coat hanger in his shirt, but even his inexperienced performance passes muster, so good are Wayne, Martin and especially Brennan.

Stumpy is a familiar Brennan portrayal, very similar to Groot in *Red River*, with a hiccuping high-pitched laugh and sayings like, 'Jumpin' Jeehoosefats!' Stumpy is lame in one leg – publicity worsened this to 'no teeth, one leg, but all the rest was guts'. Armed with a scattergun, he spends the entire film locked up in the gloomy jail, guarding Joe. He says that he feels 'Like a gopher or a burrowing owl or something…when I went outside I could hardy see in the daylight'. Stumpy has a personal score to settle with the Burdettes, who stole his 460 acres of land. The tense old timer tackles his own nerves by talking constantly which is a strong contrast to Wayne's stoicism.

Wayne gives a softly spoken performance and only raises his voice when he ruffles Feathers. Their wary courtship is what makes *Rio Bravo*'s script a classic. Feathers is a gambler's widow, who is wanted in connection with her deceased husband's illegal dealings. She is an integral part of the *Rio Bravo* dynamic, revealing her strength of character, and the antagonistic love affair makes for some sharp exchanges. Their first meeting immediately puts Chance on the defensive, embarrassed: Mexican hotellier Carlos is showing Chance a pair of bright red bloomers he has bought for his wife, Consuela. 'Those things have big possibilities,' says Feathers, 'but not for you.' Suspecting Feathers of cheating at cards, Chance tells her to leave town and stop gambling, but she refuses, 'That's what I'd do if I were the kind of girl you think I am.' They grow closer, with Chance admitting that if he wasn't in 'this mess' things might be different between them. 'That's all I wanted to hear,' she replies, kissing him once, then again more passionately, 'I'm glad we tried it a second time,' she smiles, 'It's better when two people do it.' Finally, Chance sees Feathers in the brief corset and stockings she intends to wear while performing a song downstairs in the Alamo ('You need a rig like that to sing?', 'You haven't heard me sing.'). He refuses to let her appear so revealingly in public and threatens to arrest her. Feathers says Chance has the funniest way of saying, 'I love you,' but, 'It means the same thing.'

A series of memorable action sequences sustain *Rio Bravo*'s tension. In contrast to the finely drawn heroes, the villains are faceless. Burdette was described in advertising as 'the knife poised at the throat of Rio Bravo' and Burdette's gunmen are an ever-present danger, with $50 gold pieces the price of a life in Rio Bravo. 'That's earning money the hard way,' says Chance. In one scene, Dude and Chance track Wheeler's assassin to Burdette's saloon. They are unable to find the culprit and barman Charlie jokes, 'Dude, you been seeing things again?' Then blood begins to drip into a beer glass on the bar, telling Dude the gunman is hiding up in the loft, whereupon the lawman spins and shoots the killer dead. Dude is regaining his self-esteem – he even forces a Burdette henchman to retrieve a dollar coin from a spittoon. Later, outside the Alamo Hotel, three gunmen have the drop on Chance and Colorado, until Feathers throws a plant pot through the hotel window, distracting the gunmen and enabling the lawmen to get the upper hand. In the final hostage exchange, Colorado, Stumpy and Chance take cover in the stable and nearby adobe ruins, opposite Burdette and his gang in their sturdy warehouse. Stumpy finds a box of dynamite in Wheeler's freighters, 'Can you shoot near as good as you say you can?' asks Stumpy. 'Can you throw?' replies Chance. 'Near as far as you can shoot!' They work as a team, with Chance shooting the dynamite sticks. The Burdette warehouse is destroyed and the gang apprehended, in what is, for its brevity, something of an anticlimax.

Rio Bravo's music was composed by Dimitri Tiomkin. His 'Deguello' is another Alamo reference; at the Battle of the Alamo, the 'Deguello' or 'the cut-throat's song' (a plodding guitar and trumpet dirge) was a sign from the Mexicans that there would be no quarter given to the losers. With Martin and Nelson on board it seemed natural for them to sing. The musical showcase in the jailhouse, which is the defenders' answer to the droning 'Deguello', is *Rio Bravo*'s most criticised scene. Seen as an opportunistic ploy by the film's producers to capitalise on Nelson's recent No. 1 single 'Poor Little Fool', the two numbers – 'My Rifle, My Pony and Me' and the up-tempo, rockabilly 'Cindy' – delineate the generational relationship between

The hat, the Winchester carbine and the 'Red River D' belt buckle: the John Wayne trademarks, depicted here in a studio publicity portrait for Howard Hawks' *El Dorado* (1967).

the protagonists. Dino, reclining on his bunk, puffing on a cigarette and with his hat brim tilted low, is the epitome of lounge cool, western-style. Rock 'n' roller Nelson strums his guitar and wobbles his head, while hillbilly Brennan toothlessly beams between saws on a harmonica and joins in the chorus. Only Wayne remains aloof, smiling benignly from a safe distance.

Martin recorded 'Rio Bravo' (which is mainly used as an instrumental in the actual film) and 'My Rifle, My Pony and Me' on 15 September 1958 for release as a 45rpm single on Capitol Records. The melody to 'My Rifle' is actually 'Settle Down' from *Red River* with different lyrics. Martin also recorded a duet of 'My Rifle' with Ricky Nelson (as performed in the film) in January 1959 for Warner Brothers, which was released as a one-sided promotional 45 rpm in February. 'Deguello' (mistakenly billed as 'De Guello') was also released as a tie-in. Written by Tiomkin and lyricist Paul Francis Webster, 'My Rifle, My Pony and Me' is close to parody:

> The sun is setting in the west, the cattle go down to the stream
> The redwing settles in the nest
> It's time for a cowboy to dream
> Gonna hang my sombrero, on the limb of a tree
> No more cows to be ropin'
> No more strays will I see
> Round the bend, she'll be waiting
> For my rifle, my pony and me

Rio Bravo was released in the US in March 1959. Posters displayed the line: 'John Wayne, the big guy with the battered hat…and Dean Martin, the ragged woman-wrecked cast-off called Dude…and Ricky Nelson, the rockin' babyfaced gunfisted kid…and time was running out through bullet holes at Howard Hawks's *Rio Bravo*'. Ad material boasted: 'And Dean and Ricky sing too!', while other taglines include: 'You've seen nothing like 'em together…and in the heat and hate of *Rio Bravo* nothing can tear 'em apart!' Feathers was described as: 'the one girl who could give the big guy a hard time', while Wheeler was 'a chunk of solid granite now crumbling with age'. 'It's a once-in-a-lifetime combination of today's hottest star names' declared the trailer, which featured a specially filmed version of the musical interlude, with Nelson turning to camera and saying, 'This has been one of the few peaceful scenes from the picture,' before introducing the cast. 'Tell 'em about Ricky Nelson,' adds Martin from off-camera, 'Oh, yea,' says Nelson, 'That's me…come and see it.'

Variety called it 'somewhat long', but it was still 'one of the better class oaters of the year'. The *New York Daily News* said that, 'it looked as though Dean Martin can start calling himself an actor…in a difficult characterisation, deftly realised'. Reviewer 'G. Cain' (actually Cuban poet Guillermo Cabrera Infante) retitled the film 'Lost Weekend On the Range' and moaned that other critics had given it 'a thumbs-down at sundown'. *Saturday Review* called it 'as standard fare as has ever turned up on the Hollywood menu', but praised Wayne and Martin. *Cue* liked the 'rollicking western built along familiar suspense plot lines' and the *New York Times* dubbed it 'well-made but awfully familiar'. *Punch* saw 'shameless hokum' and the *London*

Observer noted that it was 'based on a short story and feels as if it were. The film starts with a fine burst of action, dwindles off and long before the end becomes confused and repetitious.' With *Auntie Mame* (a Broadway adaptation), *Hercules* (starring muscleman Steve Reeves) and *The Nun's Story* (with Audrey Hepburn), *Rio Bravo* was a hit for Warners. It was also one of Wayne's most successful films, taking $5.75 million in the US, and was the 11th biggest grosser of 1959 – the highest-grossing western on the list at a time when TV westerns were starting to take their toll on box-office receipts.

A *Rio Bravo* novel by Leigh Brackett was published, which is a faithful adaptation of the screenplay and shouldn't be confused with *Rio Bravo* by Gordon Shirreffs published in 1957, a tough western concerning a cavalry troop on the trail of Chiricahua Apache chief Asesino. In the UK *Rio Bravo* was passed with minor cuts to gain a 'U' certificate. It was released as *Rio Bravo* everywhere except in Italy, where it was called *Un Dollaro D'Onore* ('A Dollar of Honour', with reference to the coin's retrieval from a spittoon). This retitling was to avoid confusion with John Ford's *Rio Grande*, released in Italy as *Rio Bravo*. In the Italian artwork Dickinson featured prominently in her corset.

Hawks's film has been remade by John Carpenter as *Assault on Precinct 13* (1976), which had cops besieged in their station by gangs of street crazies. Carpenter, who cites Hawks as his favourite director, edited the film under the pseudonym 'John T. Chance'. Carpenter also remade Hawks's *The Thing from Another World* (1951) as *The Thing* (1982), another story concerning an embattled confined group, albeit facing a markedly different threat. On one episode of TV's *The Dean Martin Show*, a western saloon sketch features Don Rickles as a barman (wearing the same style cowhide waistcoat as Claude Akins in *Rio Bravo*). During the sketch Martin pokes fun at his Dude persona, ordering milk, then questioning whether he's reading the right cue card. Rickles cracks that Martin 'deserves an Academy Award for saying that line'. On another edition of the TV show, Martin duetted with Wayne on 'Everybody Loves Somebody Sometime', with Wayne dubbed by Frank Sinatra.

Hawks had so many ideas for *Rio Bravo* that he was able to redeploy them in two sequels. Based on a short story called 'The Stars in their Courses' by Harry Brown, but again co-scripted by Leigh Brackett, *El Dorado* (1967) cast Wayne as hired gun Cole Thornton who helps J.P. Harrah (Robert Mitchum), the alcoholic sheriff of El Dorado; Harrah is known locally as 'a tin star with a drunk pinned on it'. El Dorado is in the grip of a water rights feud between the MacDonald clan and rich landowner Bart Jason. Initially hired by Jason, Thornton, with the help of young gun Mississippi (James Caan) and old-timer Bull Thomas (Arthur Hunnicutt), helps Harrah pacify the town. The same Old Tucson town set is employed, with location scenes lensed near Señorita Creek, between Nogales and Patagonia, the Amado ranch house and the cactus beds of Avra Valley, while TV's *High Chaparral* set appeared as Bart Jason's ranch. One notable addition is heavy Nelse McCloud (Christopher George), hired by Jason in the wake of Thornton's defection.

Advertised as 'It's The Big One With The Big Two', *El Dorado* is a star vehicle for Wayne, though Mitchum, nursing a permanent hangover, steals the picture. He woozily arrives late for a shootout and a local comments, 'What you do ... stop off for a drink?' while later Harrah drawls to Thornton, 'I may be a drunk. I may not be able to load my own gun. But I don't need you to tell me how to do my job.' There are several replays of *Rio Bravo*-esque situations (nightly patrols, jokes about drunken pushover Harrah's cleanliness, fugitives hiding in a bar), though Maudie (Charlene Holt) is no substitute for Feathers. The *Monthly Film Bulletin* noted that 'The formula of John Wayne, plus a drunk, greenhorn and ancient against the bad men is a good one, and Hawks manages the variations so cunningly that it works all over again'.

Though *Rio Lobo* (1970) is indebted to *Rio Bravo* (Wayne assembles the usual rag-tag bunch of misfits), this time no one gets drunk and the violence is laid on thick. Following a Civil War train hold-up by Confederates, Union Colonel Cord McNally (Wayne) takes it personally: his adopted son was one of the casualties. With the cessation of hostilities he goes after the culprits, convinced a Unionist sold information to the rebels about the bullion shipment. McNally fetches up in Blackthorn, Texas (the Old Tucson set) and finds out that Marshall Tom Hendricks (Mike Henry) and his deputy (Jim Davis – later Jock Ewing in *Dallas*) are landgrabbing in the nearby town of Rio Lobo (Old Tucson again), in league with villainous Ketchum (Victor French). McNally sides with a couple of young demobbed Confederates, 'Frenchie' Cardona (Jorge Rivero) and Tuscarora Philips (Chris Mitchum, son of Robert), while striking Jennifer O'Neill appears as Shasta Delaney and Jack Elam grandstands as Old Man Philips. Twitchy, wild-eyebrowed Elam is the best aspect of the film, with his Jew's harp and hair-trigger shotgun with both hammers wired back.

In *Rio Lobo*, the lack of the *Rio Bravo* magic is as obvious as ageing John Wayne's acrobatic stunt double. The violence, for once in a Wayne film, is excessive: the opening train robbery is particularly vicious; greased rails were used to stop the train on an incline and a hornets' nest was dropped into the bullion car to disperse the guards. Wayne took the role on the basis of working with Hawks and Yakima Canutt, hired as second-unit director, without ever having read the script and unfortunately it shows. On its release, with the tagline: 'Give 'Em Hell, John', *Variety* noted, '*Rio Lobo* is the sort of western that Wayne and Hawks can do in their sleep'. *Rio Bravo*, Hawks' finest western, gives the impression of such effortlessness, but it's simply that, when on form, Hawks and Wayne were such a great team. Bravo indeed.

15

'We Deal in Lead, Friend'

— *The Magnificent Seven* (1960)

The Magnificent Seven (1960)
Credits
DIRECTOR – John Sturges
PRODUCER – John Sturges
ASSOCIATE PRODUCER – Lou Morheim
STORY – Shinobu Hashimoto, Hideo Oguni and Akira Kurosawa
SCREENPLAY – William Roberts, Walter Newman and Walter
    Bernstein
DIRECTOR OF PHOTOGRAPHY – Charles Lang Jnr
EDITOR – Ferris Webster
ART DIRECTOR – Edward Fitzgerald
MUSIC – Elmer Bernstein
Panavision/DeLuxe Color
A Mirisch–Alpha Production
Released by United Artists
128 minutes
Cast
   Yul Brynner (Chris); Eli Wallach (Calvera); Steve McQueen
   (Vin); Horst Buchholz (Chico); Charles Bronson (Bernardo
   O'Reilly); Robert Vaughn (Lee); Brad Dexter (Harry Luck);
   James Coburn (Britt); Vladimir Solokov (Old man in
   Ixcatlan); Rosenda Monteros (Petra); Jorge Martinez De
   Hoyos (Hilario); John Alonso (Miguel); Pepe Hern (Tomas);
   Whit Bissell (Chamlee, the undertaker); Val Avery (Henry,
   travelling corset salesman); Bing Russell (Robert, Henry's
   friend); Rico Alaniz (Sotero, Ixcatlan spokesman); Robert
   J. Wilke (Wallace); Joseph Ruskin (Filene, at rail depot);
   Valentin De Vargas (Cirillo, Calvera's lieutenant); Larry
   Duran (Santos, Calvera's henchman); Mario Navarro

(Mexican boy); Alex Montoya (Bandit); Roberto Contreras
(Villager) with Natividad Vacio, Enrique Lucero and
Danny Bravo

*   *   *

Since *Gunfight at the O.K. Corral*, Sturges had made the underrated western *The Law and Jake Wade* (1958). Despite its awful title it was a tautly scripted $20,000 treasure hunt. Sturges followed this with *Last Train from Gun Hill* (1959), a *3:10 to Yuma*-inspired tale with Kirk Douglas as Matt Morgan, a marshal on the trail of his wife's killer. The culprit is scar-face Rick (Earl Holliman), the son of Morgan's best friend, Gun Hill rancher Craig Belden (Anthony Quinn). Morgan vows to take Rick out on the nine o'clock train. Sturges then directed *Never So Few* (1959), with Steve McQueen. Here a group of American soldiers, led by Frank Sinatra, help 600 guerrillas hold off 400,000 Japanese soldiers in Burma – odds that were paralleled in Sturges's next western, an adaptation of Akira Kurosawa's Japanese adventure, *Seven Samurai* (1954).

In *Seven Samurai*, a much-praised international hit, Kambei (Takashi Shimura) recruits masterless samurai to help defend a peasant village from bandits, including youngster Katsushiro (Ko Kimura), Shichiroji (Daisuke Kato), Gorogei (Yoshio Inaba) and Heihachi (Minoru Chiaki). The great swordsman Kyuzo (Seiji Miyaguchi) and a ruffian, Kikuchiyo (Toshiro Mifune), also join the group. After the battle, only three survive: Katsushiro stays in the village with his girl, while Kambei and Shichiroji depart. A year in the making, Kurosawa's film is a masterpiece of human drama, highlighted by evocative black and white photography by Asakazu Nakai and a moving score by Fumio Hayasaka. On its release in the US in November 1956, one version of the film was retitled *The Magnificent Seven*.

In Sturges's remake, bandido Calvera is raiding Mexican villages, pillaging the harvest from the already-poor inhabitants. The villagers of Ixcatlan decide to stand up to the bandits and send three emissaries, Hilario, Miguel and Tomas, to the US border to buy guns. In the Texas town of Los Toritos, they meet Chris, a down-on-his-luck gunman, who suggests they hire men: 'Nowadays men are cheaper than guns.' 'It would be a blessing if you came to help us,' plead the villagers. 'Sorry, I'm not in the blessing business.' But Chris is convinced when he hears that their children are starving. He recruits six more gunmen for $20 apiece, in return for six weeks' work 'shooing some flies away from a village': Vin, Harry Luck and his friend O'Reilly, Britt, Lee and young Mexican gunslinger Chico. They ride to Ixcatlan, help the peons build defences against the bandits ('civic improvements') and enjoy village life. Following a confrontation, the seven think they have seen off the bandidos, but Calvera's gang capture the mercenaries and run them out of town. The gunmen vow to save the peons, taking on the bandits in a pitched gun battle. Harry Luck, Lee, Britt and O'Reilly are killed, but the bandits are routed and Calvera is slain. Chico stays on in Ixcatlan with local girl Petra, while Chris and Vin ride away, 'Only the farmers won. We lost,' notes Chris, 'We always lose.'

Although Yul Brynner claimed it was he who bought the rights to *Seven Samurai*, it was producer Lou Morheim who paid $250 for them; Anthony Quinn was interested and would star as Chris, with Brynner directing and Morheim producing. Eventually Morheim was ousted from the production, receiving an 'associate producer' credit, and Brynner was going to star, with Quinn as Vin and Martin Ritt directing. Ritt hired Walter Bernstein to adapt the screenplay, but when the property shifted to Mirisch Productions at United Artists, via Brynner, Sturges was brought in as director and producer. Quinn, now not involved in the film at all, sued Brynner and United Artists for $650,000, but lost. Sturges then hired his own writer, Walter Newman, to work on the screenplay.

Cast in the lead role of Chris was shaven-headed, Russian-born Yul Brynner, best known as the King of Siam in the musical *The King and I* (1956). His trademark baldpate was a result of this role, though in *Magnificent Seven* he only appears in one scene without his hat (while digging a defensive ditch). 'There are only two clean things about him,' noted Brynner on the UK TV show *Parkinson*, 'His gun and his soul.' For the role of Calvera, Sturges cast Brooklyn-born actor Eli Wallach, who hadn't ridden a horse before, let alone appeared in a western. The Mexican actors playing his 35-strong bandit gang took Wallach under their wing and looked after him throughout the shoot.

Replacing Quinn as Vin, Steve McQueen had appeared on TV in an episode of *Trackdown* called 'The Bounty Hunter', as Josh Randall, a tracker packing a sawn-off Winchester rifle in a holster. He was so popular that in 1958 he got his own spin-off series *Wanted: Dead or Alive*, which led to B-movie roles, including *The Blob* (1958). Sturges was a fan of *Wanted: Dead or Alive* and cast him in *The Magnificent Seven* as a result. According to his contract, McQueen couldn't take any time off the TV series, so faked a car accident with his wife Niele, to enable him to make *Magnificent Seven*, a role for which he received $100,000, his highest fee thus far.

Britt, Lee, Vin, Chris, Chico, O'Reilly and Harry Luck relax on the Mexican border-town set, during the making of *The Magnificent Seven* (1960). Horst Buchholz's name is spelt 'Bucholtz' on his chair and 'Bucholz' in promotional trailers, though it is spelt correctly in the film's title sequence.

Berlin-born Horst Buchholz was an unusual choice for Chico, though he was popular in Europe and a useful asset on billboards there. His 'young gun' persona echoed Ricky Nelson in *Rio Bravo* and the role of Chico is an amalgamation of Katsushiro (the love story subplot) and Kikuchiyo (his quick temper and farming roots) in *Samurai*. Brad Dexter, as treasure-hunting trickster Harry Luck, had some supporting roles (including a cigar-smoking heavy in *Last Train from Gun Hill*) and was later friends with Frank Sinatra – in 1964 he saved Sinatra from drowning. Urbane Robert Vaughn was cast as fancy gunslinger on the run, Lee. Muscle-bound Charles Bronson, as denim-clad Mexican-Irishman Bernardo O'Reilly, received $50,000 for his role. He had appeared in many westerns (including the bounty-hunting lead in *Showdown at Boot Hill* [1958]) and already knew Sturges, while lanky James Coburn took the role of knife-thrower Britt, after Sterling Hayden and John Ireland pulled out. Britt, the last role cast in February 1960, was based on master sword fighter Kyuzo in *Samurai* – Coburn got a phone call from Sturges: 'Okay Jim, come on over and pick up your knives.'

With a $2 million budget, *The Magnificent Seven* was lushly photographed in Panavision and DeLuxe Color by Charles Lang Jnr (from *The Man from Laramie* and later *One-Eyed Jacks*). Filming began on 1 March 1960 and lasted for eight weeks. The Mexican town of Ixcatlan was built near Cuernavaca, in Morelos, Mexico, with its church and bell tower, low adobe brick walls, brush *ramadas* (lean-to's), plaza and fountain, set in corn fields, with a magnificent mountain backdrop. The *arroyo* riverbeds, shaded by trees, were used for other location scenes. Brynner got married to his fiancée Doris on location in 'Ixcatlan' and the fiesta featured in the film is part of their celebrations, with garlanded flowers, fireworks, bunting, costumed Mexican pueblo dancers and a parade. Los Toritos, the Tex-Mex border town, was also built near Cuernavaca, its long street rising to the gates of Boot Hill. Interiors, including Chris's Toritos hotel room, a saloon and other village dwellings were filmed at Estudios Churubusco, Mexico City. A couple of exterior night-time camp sequences were also filmed on sound stages there, including the scene where the seven decide to go back and save the village.

Filming in Mexico proved problematic. The censor had the final say on the depiction of the Mexican characters in the film, with dialogue such as 'Hire gunfighters', 'Gunfighters are expensive', 'Find hungry gunfighters' being axed. Hence the villagers in the film travel to Texas to buy guns. As a filmmaker, Sturges noted of Mexico, 'it's okay as long as you are making movies about an American or about a boy and his dog.' Sturges and his troupe had Mexican counterparts assigned to shadow them while they shot the film. That is why there are Mexican equivalents listed for many of the crew in the title sequence (for example Jaime Contrarez for assistant director Rob Relyea). Rewrites were required and Newman was already busy, so William Roberts was brought in to alter the script on set – enough to earn himself a co-writer's credit. Newman, disgusted, asked for his name to be removed from the film. After so many contributions, the only name that appears in the credits is Roberts's and a title card reading: 'Based on the Japanese film *Seven Samurai*'.

McQueen had wanted to play Chico and this caused friction, as Sturges spent more time with Buchholz; meanwhile Brynner thought he had Mifune's role, but discovered he was recreating Shimura's. McQueen was constantly trying to upstage Brynner – attracting attention to himself in scenes by fiddling with his hat, flapping his hat, fanning himself with his hat, checking his gun – anything to make the audience look at him. In addition to this, the rest of the seven were trying to make their roles count and get noticed on screen. For publicity, however, everyone appeared to get along, with the cast often playing cards after a day's work (as Vin and Britt do in the film) and practising for hours with their pistols.

The introduction of each mercenary is memorable, delineating their style and showcasing the actors. In Los Toritos, Chamlee (Whit Bissell) the local undertaker can't find anyone to take his hearse up to Boot Hill – there is a racist faction in town who don't think that the deceased, Old Sam, an Indian, is fit to rest among civilised folks. 'Oh Hell,' says Chris from the crowd, 'if that's all that's holding things up, I'll drive the rig.' He's joined by Vin, 'Never rode shotgun on a hearse before.' Chris lights a cigar and throws away the match. 'Litterbug,' says Vin, as they head off up the street. The tension mounts, as someone takes a shot at the hearse from a second storey window. Vin kills them: 'You elected?' checks Vin. 'No,' answers Chris, 'I got nominated real good,' as he surveys the end of his cigar, now tattered and two inches shorter. As they approach Boot Hill, five men wait for them: 'A reception committee is forming'. In the confrontation, Chris whips out his pistol and wounds two of the men, before Old Sam's coffin is carried by townsfolk into the graveyard and Chris wheels the hearse triumphantly back down the hill. The sequence is pure style, Brynner and McQueen's macho gestures ushering in the new brand of taciturn, mannered gunslinger that would rise to prominence in the sixties. More importantly, the heroes are liberals, better suited to more socially enlightened times: Chris and Vin make sure an Indian is buried on Boot Hill, in contrast with earlier westerns' 'only good Indian is a dead Indian' stance.

For Bronson's introductory scene, Chris and Vin find O'Reilly chopping wood to pay for his breakfast. They ask if he's broke. O'Reilly replies, 'No, I'm doing this because I'm an eccentric millionaire.' O'Reilly is a professional gun, who has settled disputes in the Travis County War and Salinas, for fees topping $800. Chris offers O'Reilly $20. O'Reilly pauses, '$20? Right now that's a lot.' The Rio Grande Cattle Company depot, beside the railway track and among the cattle pens, is the setting for Britt's entrance. He naps against a hitching rail, hat over his eyes, while braggart Wallace (Robert Wilke, from *High Noon*) tries to provoke him. Wallace wants to know if Britt's knife is faster than Wallace's pistol. Eventually stirred into action, they have a contest and Britt wins. Unsatisfied, Wallace wants to face Britt for real. Filene, Wallace's cohort, tries to stop the contest, but to no avail. In the duel, Britt plants his flick-knife in Wallace's chest, killing him. Ice-cool Coburn utters two words in the whole scene, 'You lost'.

The depiction of gringo gunslingers at work in Mexico was a major shift in subject matter. These weren't Erin and Trane in *Vera Cruz*, fighting in the revolution, and owed more to Roger Corman's trendsetting *Five Guns West* (1954), which saw a group of convicts pardoned by the Confederacy for a special mission: the recovery of a gold shipment. Chris's gunslingers are moving towards Peckinpah territory – where the gringos are often hiding out from the US authorities, or else searching for redemption south of the border. Chris says of their life, 'It's only a matter of being able to shoot a gun – nothing big about that.' They have no home, no family, no ties. 'No enemies,' adds Lee. 'No enemies?' questions Chris. 'Alive,' says Lee, whose tough talk is a façade. He later suffers tormenting nightmares, admitting, 'I have lost count of my enemies' and calling himself, 'a deserter hiding out in the middle of a battlefield' (in Bernstein's original screenplay, the seven are much older Civil War veterans). In *The Magnificent Seven* sequels the depiction of squalor south of the border becomes more explicit: a Mexico of bullfights and cockfights, of filthy bars and bad tequila. In Sturges's film, the censor ensured the Mexican peons wore immaculately clean white costumes and giant straw sombreros; unfortunately their characterisations, particularly in the opening scenes, are strictly of the *Speedy Gonzales* variety. But the gringos are not exploitative characters – only one expects a reward for his services, the gold-seeking Harry Luck. The rest are desperate for money, but equally in need of self-esteem, of belonging and a sense of worth. Chris is from Dodge City, Vin a drifter from Tombstone – both are blowing south, catching flies, until their lives are given purpose.

The Ixcatlan peasants are so desperate for help that they sacrifice all they have. A moment that equals Kurosawa's acuity occurs when Chris says, 'I've been offered a lot for my work...but never everything.' When the seven first arrive in Ixcatlan, the peons hide from them, though Chris notes, 'We didn't expect flowers and speeches.' But they quickly settle into the slow pace of village life. Gunman Bernardo O'Reilly is even 'adopted' by three Mexican boys. This sympathetic portrayal was apparently much closer to the real Bronson than his tough-guy screen roles. Harry jokes that he fell in with a fast crowd that hangs around the fountain, 'We got to predicting the weather for today and didn't break up till twilight.' Vin notes that he's been in towns where the girls weren't very pretty, and some where they were 'downright ugly', 'But this is the first town I've been in where there's no girls at all – except little ones.' The wary peasants have hidden away all the women, for fear of the mercenaries raping them. When Chris discovers this he's disgusted, 'Well we might – In my opinion though, you might have given us the benefit of the doubt.' But soon it dawns on everyone that Calvera isn't going to give up so easily – his men are starving ('The price of corn is going up,' says Chico). The gunmen thought Calvera would go and 'play somewhere else': 'We didn't figure on being the only game in town.' But the fearful peasants eventually sell out the seven, allowing Calvera's men to sneak into town and surprise the gunmen, capturing them.

Calvera is a vicious, red-shirted Mexican bandido warlord, who observes of the farmers, 'If God didn't want them sheared, he would not have made them sheep.' He is a true archetype for the genre – the laughing, larger-than-life Mexican badman. In the opening scene, Calvera pleads sympathy from the people of Ixcatlan, 'The days of good hunting are over...now I must hunt with a price on my head.' He recounts how last month the San Juan poor box was almost empty, but he took it anyway. He cleans out Ixcatlan spokesman Sotero's cigars and callously shoots Rafael, a sickle-wielding peon, before riding out, promising, 'I'll be back…I love this village.' He leaves them just enough food not to starve, so they can go harvesting, for him to come back and steal more. When he read the script, Wallach thought Calvera was a nothing role, but then realised that his threat overshadowed an hour of the film, until his reappearance. As the trailer put it: 'He had a town at his mercy, the Magnificent Seven at his throat'.

When Calvera returns, looking for food, he is told by the seven to ride on. Eyeing the newly built defences, Calvera notes that they won't keep the bandits out. Chris corrects him: 'They were built to keep you in.'; 'Some-how,' says Calvera, 'I don't think you solved my problem.'; 'Solving your problems isn't our line,' Chris answers. 'We deal in lead, friend,' adds Vin. 'So do I,' says Calvera, 'We're in the same business, huh?' 'Only as competitors,' replies Vin. Later, when he has the

upper hand, Calvera makes the mistake of letting the seven live, as a gesture, 'Only a crazy man makes the same mistake twice.' Following the final shootout, he dies incredulous that the mercenaries returned, saying to his killer, Chris, 'You came back – for a place like this…why? A man like you…why?'

For all the talk about 'the price of corn', the team of professional gunslingers for hire and their working methods are what really interested Sturges, especially in the pyrotechnic dust and bullets finale. As posters stated: 'They Were Seven…They Fought Like Seven Hundred'. In one scene, Britt fells an escaping bandit riding

'They Fought Like Seven Hundred': US poster for John Sturges's *The Magnificent Seven* (1960).

into the distance – a seemingly impossible shot with a pistol. 'That was the greatest shot I've ever seen,' marvels Chico. 'The worst,' snaps Britt, 'I was aiming at his horse.' In the finale, the seven go back to Ixcatlan at sunrise to face Calvera in a gun battle. Harry Luck is killed in the plaza (still thinking they were really there for a fortune in Aztec gold); Lee overcomes his cowardice, but is shot down; Britt catches a bullet (his last action throwing his knife into an adobe wall, as he falls) and O'Reilly dies in the graveyard, protecting the three Mexican children. 'What's my name?' asks slumped O'Reilly. 'Bernardo! Bernardo!' the children cry. 'You're damn right,' says O'Reilly, as he dies. After the fight, as the remaining mercenaries prepare to leave, the old village head man (Vladimir Solokov) tells them that gunfighters are like the wind: 'Blowing over the land and passing on.' Only Chico stays, to change his life – taking on responsibilities with Petra and putting down roots.

The memorable score, composed and conducted by Elmer Bernstein, is one of the most famous western themes ever recorded. The title music begins with a punchy five-note fanfare, before syncopated strings jump-start the piece with gusto. The strong melody is taken by violins, with the horn accompaniment driving the pace, for the majestic riding theme used throughout the film. In the title sequence, this optimistic refrain segues into the more ominous, percussion-driven discord of 'Bandidos' (Calvera's theme), as the bandits ride through the cornfields towards Ixcatlan. The edgy hearse ride is backed by the slow, tension-filled requiem of 'Strange Funeral'. Folk themes predominate in Ixcatlan: the carnivalesque 'Fiesta', with its clattering drums and flute, the lively 'Mariachis De Mexico' for the scenes where the seven train the peons in marksmanship, and themes incorporating Spanish guitars, harps and flutes, as in 'Defeat', when the three Mexican children put flowers on O'Reilly's grave. For Chico's bullfighting scene with a stray steer, Bernstein deploys a swirling matador-style Mariachi trumpet. Bernstein's score is still a popular staple of film compilations and film concerts (it often appears on the programme for outdoor live music events) alongside another great western theme: Jerome Moss's 'Another Day, Another Sunset' from *The Big Country*. Bernstein's variations of these themes were used in all the official *Magnificent Seven* follow-ups and later became the theme of the Marlboro cigarette adverts. He also wrote an equally memorable score for Sturges's Second World War movie, *The Great Escape* (1963 – also starring McQueen, Bronson and Coburn).

The Magnificent Seven was unleashed on US cinemas in October 1960. Posters described the film as 'The Magnificent One!' The specially filmed trailer featured the seven in Ixcatlan (standing in the shape of a '7') and an awful title song entitled 'Seven' voiced by a male chorus, which doesn't feature in the movie ('Seven, seven, seven – they fought for the future to wipe away their past'). 'Once you've seen them, you'll never forget them,' said the voiceover; Calvera is 'The Evil One', Vin 'The Dangerous One' and Chico 'The Violent One'. Reviews were a mixed bag: *Time* loved it, noting that 'color, camera work, acting and directing are competent' but the script was even better than Kurosawa's: 'expert but sensitive'. *Variety* said 'Until the women and children arrive...about two-thirds of the way through (it's actually exactly halfway through), *The Magnificent Seven* is a rip-roaring, rootin'-tootin' western with lots of bite and tang and old-fashioned abandon. The last third is downhill…in which *The Magnificent Seven* grows slightly too magnificent for comfort.' It was passed in the UK as a certificate 'U'. It is one of only two westerns in the 100 most successful films of all time in the UK, in 100th place, having taken £7.7 million (the other was *The Big Country* in 71st place, with £9 million). Penelope Gilliatt in the *London Observer* said the film demonstrated what makes the western hero tick, but further noted that 'it is part of the essence of the epic hero that he should not be able to hear himself ticking'.

Though it was reasonably popular in the US, *The Magnificent Seven* was a smash in France (as *Les Sept Mercenaires*), Spain, and especially Italy, where it was the most influential western of the sixties. The working title for Sergio Leone's *A Fistful of Dollars* (1964) was *Il Magnifico Straniero* ('The Magnificent Stranger'). Wallach, Brynner, Coburn and Bronson all went on to appear in Italian westerns, while many other spaghetti westerns exploited the title, including *The Magnificent Three* (1963), *Seven Guns from Texas* (1964), *Seven Guns for the MacGregors* (1965), *Seven Magnificent Guns* (1966) and *The Magnificent Texan* (1968). The movie's success outside the US led to United Artists re-releasing the film, where it became an enormous hit. A new trailer said: 'Seven Magnificent Men in One Magnificent Motion Picture' with the rising stars' names, especially Bronson, Coburn and Vaughn, enough to garner attention. Many sixties westerns replayed *The Magnificent Seven*'s spectacular finale, with superior examples including the Spanish-shot Lee Van Cleef vehicle *Death Rides a Horse* (1967) and *Guns for San Sebastian* (1968), filmed in Durango, Mexico, starring Anthony Quinn as a bandit who poses as a priest and saves a village from Yaqui villain Teclo, played by Charles Bronson.

Three sequels rode in *The Magnificent Seven*'s wake, none of which were directed by Sturges, though they were all produced by Mirisch. The moody *Return of the Seven* (1966), directed by Burt Kennedy, was a familiar sixties action package. Chris (Brynner again) and Vin (Robert Fuller – McQueen refused) save Chico (Julian Matteos), who has married Petra (Elisa Montes). Bandit Lorca (Emilio Fernandez) has taken the male Ixcatlan villagers as slaves to rebuild a church in the sierras to honour his dead sons. Chris recruits new members Frank (Claude Akins) and Luis Delgado (Virgilio Teixeira) from a local prison, and picks up a young peon Manuel (Jordon Christopher) and philanderer Colbee (toothily played by Warren Oates). This time the odds are higher with the seven taking on 200 bandits in the final shootout.

Filmed in Spain, around Alicante, Colmenar De Oreja and Nuevo Baztan (with interiors at Samuel Bronston's Madrid studio), *Return* is much more violent than *The Magnificent Seven*; the film has since been edited for DVD, with most of a cockfight and Lorca's horse fall now missing. There are lulls in the action where the gunmen dredge their past via cliché-ridden soul-searching. At one point even Chris has second thoughts about their mission. There are good performances from Brynner, Matteos and Oates, plus Fernando Rey as the priest at the ruined church. Brynner is never photographed without his hat and this time he packs two guns for extra firepower. As expected, lower billing bodes ill, with Akins, Teixeira and 'Introducing Jordon Christopher' stopping lead.

Directed by Paul Wendkos, *Guns of the Magnificent Seven* (1969) saw Chris recruiting a variety of dodgy characters to break politico Quintero (Fernando Rey) out of jail, where he is being held by vicious Federale commandant, Colonel Diego (Michael Ansara). As the ads put it: 'Seven men to free a nation of peasants, from an army of madmen'. By now you'd think that anyone who saw Chris approaching, with an idea for a new adventure, would steer well clear – perhaps they didn't recognise him, as Chris was now played by George Kennedy. The fresh 'seven' are Mexican peon Max (Reni Santoni), dynamiter Cassie (Bernie Casey – 'a walking charge of TNT with a very short fuse'), PJ, a Doc Holliday-esque rope expert with a bad cough (Scott Thomas), psychotic, ex-Confederate Slater (Joe Don Baker – 'half man, half gun'), knife thrower Levi Morgan (James Whitmore) and non-specialist Keno (Monte Markham), though the trailer tries to make him sound special ('Good with a gun, just as good without one'). 'Separately they were seven deadly weapons,' said publicity, 'together they were magnificent.'

Again filmed in Spain (around La Pedriza, Manzanares El Real and at Hojo De Manzanares, north of Madrid), the seven are less sketchily drawn, with Slater, one arm hanging uselessly by his side, the most interesting. He is eking out a living in a carnival as sharpshooter 'Buffalo Ben – half-brother of Buffalo Bill', before Chris saves him. Frank Silvera tries to do an Eli Wallach impersonation as bandit rebel Lobero, while the action is well staged, with a Spanish fortress used as the prison dynamited in the finale. The film's biggest failing is some awful dialogue. Chris's proficiency is described as being, 'As cool as the other side of the pillow', while Max recounts the old Mexican proverb, 'A cat with mittens doesn't catch the rat'. Kennedy is announced in the publicity as 'Academy Award Winner George Kennedy'; rest assured it wasn't for *Guns of the Magnificent Seven*.

For the last instalment, *The Magnificent Seven Ride!* (1972 – 'A reunion of vengeance and violence south of the border'), Lee Van Cleef played Chris Adams, now a marshal. When his wife is murdered, Chris goes after the killers and during his journey becomes involved in saving a village of women from bandit Juan Totoro. Chris recruits five convicts to help him: bandido Pepe, Walt the giant ('With the strength of ten men and the mind of a child'), ex-soldier Hayes, engineer Elliot and killer Skinner ('They put him away for life and let him out for death'). The seventh member was writer Noah (Michael Callan) who is penning Chris's biography. Taglines included: 'A Brand New Seven – Doing Their Number!' and 'They Put Their Lives on the Line and Let it Ride!', but the film was a pale imitation of its originator. *¡Three Amigos!* (1986) parodied Sturges's film – 'Can I have your watch when you are dead?' a Mexican boy asks one of the 'amigos' on his arrival in the beleaguered village – while Roger Corman's *Battle Beyond the Stars* (1980) relocated the plot to outer space and recast Robert Vaughn. There was also a 22-episode *Magnificent Seven* series made for US TV (1998–2000), with Michael Biehn (as Chris Larrabee) and Eric Close (as Vin Tanner). But the enduring popularity of the original *The Magnificent Seven*, one of the most well-liked westerns of all time, makes it unlikely that the seven will ride away into the sunset forever.

16

'I Seen the Other Side of Your Face'

— One-Eyed Jacks (1961)

One-Eyed Jacks (1961)
Credits
DIRECTOR – Marlon Brando
PRODUCER – Frank P. Rosenberg
STORY – Charles Neider
SCREENPLAY – Guy Trosper and Calder Willingham
DIRECTOR OF PHOTOGRAPHY – Charles Lang Jnr
EDITOR – Archie Marshek
ART DIRECTORS – Hal Pereira and Joseph MacMillan Johnson
MUSIC – Hugo W. Friedhofer
VistaVision/Technicolor
A Pennebaker Production
Released by Paramount Pictures
141 minutes
Cast
Marlon Brando (Rio); Karl Malden (Sheriff Dad
Longworth); Katy Jurado (Maria Longworth); Pina Pellicer
(Louisa Longworth); Ben Johnson (Bob Amory); Slim
Pickens (Deputy Lon Dedrick); Larry Duran (Modesto);
Sam Gilman (Harvey Johnson); Timothy Carey (Howard
Tetley, the drunk); Miriam Colon (Red); Elisha Cook Jnr
(Carvey, the bank teller); Rodolfo Acosta (Rurale captain);
Joan Petrone (Flower girl at fiesta); Joe Dominguez (Mexican
farmer at San Filipe corral); Tom Web (Mexican farmer's
son); Ray Teal (Barney); John Dierkes (Chet); Philip Ahn
(Uncle); Margarita Cordove (Flamenco dancer at fiesta);
Hank Worden (Doc); Clem Harvey (Tim); William Forrest
(Banker); Mina Martinez (Margarita); Mickey Finn
(Blacksmith); Fenton Jones (Square-dance caller);

Shichizo Takeda (Cantina owner at Punto Del Diablo); Felipe
Turich (Cardsharp)

*   *   *

In 1957, Sam Peckinpah spent six months adapting a screenplay from Charles
Neider's novel *The Authentic Death of Hendry Jones*, the story of 'The Kid', a Billy
the Kid-style outlaw, and his paternal relationship with lawman Dad Longworth, a
Pat Garrett figure. Garrett's own dime novel rendering of the legend had been called
An Authentic Life of Billy the Kid. Actor Marlon Brando, who had long planned to
make a western from the screenplay called *A Burst of Vermilion*, became interested
in Peckinpah's script, with Brando bringing in director Stanley Kubrick. Kubrick
fired Peckinpah, but then fell out with Brando and departed after 26 weeks'
development work, to make *Spartacus*. Other prospective directors were Elia Kazan
and Sydney Lumet, while several writers (including Niven Busch) worked on the
project. Only two of Peckinpah's scenes remained in the final draft and the authors
credited on screen are Guy Trosper and Calder Willingham (who was also
eventually fired by Brando after eight months rewriting). So it was that Brando
finally decided to direct his first film, an epic western, now entitled *One-Eyed Jacks*.

Mexico, 1880: Dad Longworth, Rio and Doc relieve the bank of Sonora of two
sacks of gold and go on the run. Hiding out in a brothel, they are ambushed by
Rurales who kill Doc and chase the other two into the sierras. Trapped, they agree
that Dad should go for help, but Dad never returns and Rio is thrown into the
Sonora lead mines, escaping with Modesto, a Mexican convict, after five years'
hard labour. They join up with Bob Amory and Harvey Johnson, who plan to rob
the bank in the coastal town of Monterey, where Dad, having shed his lawless past,
is now sheriff. Rio integrates himself into Dad's world, pretending there is nothing
to settle between them ('A man can't stay angry for five years, can he?'). But he
seduces Dad's stepdaughter, Louisa, and following a celebratory fiesta, they make
love. During an argument in a saloon, Rio shoots a local drunk and is punished
publicly by Dad, who bullwhips him and smashes his gun hand. Rio licks his
wounds down the coast at the beach settlement of Punto Del Diablo, until the day
comes when he can return to town. But Rio is arrested on a trumped-up robbery
charge and thrown into prison. 'You'll get a fair trial,' says Dad, 'and then I'm
gonna hang you ... personally.'

In the original scenario, Dad was to have shot Rio as he tried to escape, but
Brando took a vote on set among the crew, who decided Rio should live. Thus in
the final shootout in the town plaza, Dad and Rio shoot it out on either side of a
fountain, and Rio guns Dad down. Initially Louisa, who is expecting Rio's child,
was to have been hit by Dad's dying shot. The new scenario saw the lovers parting
on a beach, agreeing to meet up in the spring when their child would be born
('We'll find someplace'), giving the film an upbeat ending.

Brando was a massive star worldwide in 1958, following the success of mumbling,
kinetic 'Method' performances in *A Streetcar Named Desire* (1951), *The Wild One*

and *On the Waterfront* (both 1954). With Brando casting himself as Rio, the original choice for Dad was Spencer Tracy, but Brando decided to use another Method actor, Karl Malden, from *Streetcar* and *Waterfront*. Katy Jurado and Pina Pellicer were both Mexican actresses, cast respectively as Dad's wife and stepdaughter. It was Pellicer's first US film, while Jurado had appeared in several westerns, including *High Noon*. Bearded Ben Johnson (as unsavoury gunman Bob Amory) was unrecognisable from his wholesome days in John Ford movies, as was Hank Worden, as Rio's cohort Doc, while croaky-voiced, ex-rodeo performer Slim Pickens (real name Louis Bert Lindley) viciously played lumbering deputy Lon; Pickens finally worked for Kubrick as the cowboy B-52 pilot in *Dr Strangelove* (1964).

The making of *One-Eyed Jacks* is almost as famous as the film itself. It had a provisional budget from Paramount of $1.8 million, but Brando had spent $350,000 on development before the film began shooting, while his own company, Pennebaker, produced. Principal photography commenced on 2 December 1958, with a two-month shooting schedule. Brando, having laboured so long over the screenplay, discarded it, saying, 'Forget the script...that's what they did in silent movies.' Malden remembered that he improvised with everyone, 'even the extras'. Shooting on the spectacularly rugged Monterey Peninsula in California, Brando waited for days for the right cloud formation, the ideal light or the perfect wave to crash onto the beach as a backdrop to the love scenes. Pfeiffer Beach, Big Sur was used for Rio's recovery at Punto Del Diablo ('Devil's Point'), his convalescent target practice and his revelatory moments with Louisa. Rio's flight and capture in the sierras outside Sonora were filmed in the scorching Death Valley National Park. 'Monterey' was the western street set on the Warner Ranch property. The Mexican plaza, arches and Sonora 'banco' were Mexico City sets at Calabasas, leftovers from the 34 sets built for the Warners' biopic *Juarez* (1939).

Sticking to the 'Method' style of acting, Brando and Malden got drunk when the scene required it, causing further delays. Location shooting ran for six months. On set, a Paramount executive was less than amused when he saw Brando looking into the wrong end of viewfinder. 'Holy shit! Maybe that's why the picture's so late,' laughed the director. To make matters worse, Brando dislocated his shoulder demonstrating to Malden how to crack a bullwhip. His working methods proved costly, with the eventual budget topping $6 million. Back at Paramount Studios, there were multiple re-shoots on studio interiors as late as October 1960. For many dialogue scenes, they used back-projections of the landscape, with the actors in front of them, which looked awful next to the impressive VistaVision location footage. Several scenes in the finished film were shot this way and conspicuously stand out, but master cinematographer Charles Lang Jnr still received an Oscar nomination.

Though *One-Eyed Jacks* is physically sadistic, it is the violent use of western dialect that increases its impact. It is impossible to ascribe this to any single writer, as so many were involved. Bob Amory and Harvey Johnson are described as 'crow-bait'; Rio tells a drunken reveller who has molested a Mexican woman, 'Get up, you big tub 'o guts.' When Rio and his gang are holed up in a shack on the beach (a 'pukehole'), Amory is bored out of his mind, 'I'm through with the fish...that and them damn waves flopping in all day long.' To entertain himself Amory riles Rio, calling him 'Romeo' and irritating him over his courtship of Louisa. Finally, one night over poker Rio snaps in explosive fashion when Amory continues to refer to 'that little jumpin' bean'. 'Get up, you scum-suckin' pig!' roars Rio, tearing the poker table up and throwing it across the room. 'You got right on the edge,' he continues, calmer and, if Amory mentions Louisa again, 'I'm gonna tear your arms out.' When Amory and his partner Harvey first spot Rio in a bar, they think they recognise the gunman, but figure that they 'wouldn't want to lose me a handful of brains trying to find out'. Elsewhere, Rio goads Deputy Lon into manhandling him, even with his imminent hanging. 'You ain't getting any older than tomorrow,' crows Lon. 'You gob of spit,' Rio retaliates.

Brando is a coiled spring, spectacularly released at various points in the film. Most of the time he broods, for dramatic effect. The camera lingers on Brando: he is at his physical peak with his sun-tanned, sculptured face and deep, glowering eyes riveting the audience, his noble air enhanced by dandyish outfits. The brooding seems to take up half the film and when he isn't in contemplation, he is mumbling to Pellicer. When Dad says apparently without malice that Rio's return is a weight off his conscience, Brando answers, 'Ah baid' (translation: 'I'll bet'). The deliberate pace is also dictated by the symbolism and nuance Brando deploys – *One-Eyed Jacks* has been described as a 'psychological western'. Brando uses images,

'He didn't give me no selection': Brando broods as killer Kid in *One-Eyed Jacks* (1961), his flawed but fascinating psychological western.

particularly of landscapes, as metaphors for feelings. For instance, in the coastal scenes, as Rio silently contemplates his fate, waves crash and roar, and gulls circle, representing his raging inner turmoil.

'Jack' isn't the name of a hero sporting an eye patch, as might be expected – the film's title is actually a reference to Dad's two-facedness. As Rio tells him when locked in prison, 'You're the one-eyed jack around here, Dad ... I seen the other side of your face.' He's referring to the two jacks pictured in profile in every pack of cards. His parental relationship with Dad, who refers to him throughout as 'Kid', is accentuated, making the final shootout even more powerful.

Rio's other key relationship is with Dad's stepdaughter. He initially lies to Louisa, telling her he works for the government (he's already told an earlier paramour, 'I transport money for the banks'). It is when Louisa under the misapprehension that Rio is not an outlaw that she spends the night with him. Rio also makes a habit of claiming his gifts of stolen jewellery to her were given to him by his mother, 'just before she died'. These lies drew condemnation when the film was released, but Rio does eventually do what's right, 'I shamed you – and I wish to God I hadn't.' The scenes between Brando and Pellicer are effective, but decelerate the pace, with everyone embroiled in the soap opera subplot guilty of talking too much, resulting in 'Horse Oprah'.

The psychology is offset by some explosive, imaginatively staged action scenes. The opening Sonora bank robbery begins with an elaborate tracking shot, depicting Rio balancing out the scales of justice with two banana skins, as petrified customers lie on the floor. In 'La Playa' ('The Beach'), a bar in Monterey, Rio guns down a drunkard who pulls a shotgun on him, in front of a painting of the Mona Lisa. 'He didn't give me no selection,' proffers Rio, but Dad wants to make an example of him. Rio is tied to a hitching rail and is savagely lashed a dozen times, then has his gun hand mashed. 'Your gun days are over,' sneers Dad. Unarmed, Modesto is shot down by Amory, while Amory's attempt to rob the Monterey bank ends in bullet-riddled disaster. Rio's breakout from the Monterey jail owes much to Billy the Kid's true-life flight from the Lincoln County pen on 28 April 1881 – a scene that is restaged in Peckinpah's *Pat Garrett & Billy the Kid* (1973).

Brando had exposed a million feet of footage while making *One-Eyed Jacks*, which is a record for a single feature. He was still editing the film when he began his next acting assignment, in Tennessee Williams's *The Fugitive Kind*. *One-Eyed Jacks* was initially five hours long, then four, with Paramount finally settling on two hours and 21 minutes. Brando said, 'By then I was bored with the whole project and walked away from it.' Paramount had already demanded that Brando cut two key explanatory scenes during filming, which according to Malden, 'Took the guts out of the story'. In the UK, the movie was released uncut, but was granted an 'A' certificate for its language and violence. Posters used the taglines: 'The Motion Picture that Starts its own Tradition of Greatness!' and 'The One Man ... The One Story ... The One Motion Picture to See', and imposing images of Brando dominated advertising copy.

The hype surrounding the extended shooting schedule ensured publicity, and the film grossed $4.3 million in the US on its initial release, but internationally it fared better. In France it was released as *Vengeance Aux Deux Visage* ('Revenge Has Two Faces'), cut down to 137 minutes. In Italy it was *I Due Volta Della Vendetta* ('The Two Faces of the Vendetta'); in Germany it was *Der Besessene* ('The Possessed'). In Spain and Mexico it was *El Rostro Impenetrable* ('The Impenetrable Face') and featured Mexican star Pina Pellicer prominently on the posters. It remains her only US film; she sadly committed suicide aged 30, in 1964. *One-Eyed Jacks* eventually went into profit worldwide, but it was still classed as a failure. As Malden noted, 'If we'd made it the way Marlon wanted it to be made, like a Greek tragedy, it could have been a breakthrough western...a classic.' Peckinpah thought, 'Marlon screwed it up. He's a hell of an actor, but in those days he had to end up as the hero and that's not the point of the story.'

One-Eyed Jacks' style was very influential on sixties westerns, in particular Brando's riveting silences and the credible action. Scenes in the film, including the Sonora and manhunt sequences, with their deserts, Rurales, Mariachi trumpets, filthy brothel gambling dens and grungy extras, look like spaghetti western out-takes, while Lon (Pickens) and Bob Amory (Johnson) could have walked straight out of a Peckinpah movie – both actors later worked for the director, in similar roles.

During the making of *One-Eyed Jacks*, Brando began to binge-eat in five-star Monterey restaurants. His developing paunch is evident on screen throughout the film and he struggled to find film roles to fit his talent throughout the sixties, until *The Godfather* resurrected his career in 1972. He also made two more westerns: the painfully slow *The Appaloosa* (1966 – renamed *Southwest to Sonora* in the UK, after the bank robbery in *One-Eyed Jacks*) and *The Missouri Breaks* (1976). The former saw Brando trying to retrieve his prized Appaloosa horse from Mexican bandit John Saxon. Stylised to the point of irritation, the film only hit the mark in a couple of scenes: a macho arm-wrestling contest over deadly Durango scorpions and Brando's final revenge on Saxon and his mean, tough hombres. Brando again slowed down the production with his attention to detail, taking ten days to perfect a simple scene that should have taken a few hours.

The Missouri Breaks (1976 – actually filmed in Montana) was one of the most bizarre westerns ever made, with Brando's Robert E. Lee Clayton, a professional killer, hired to break up a rustling ring led by Tom Logan (Jack Nicholson). Clayton is a 'regulator', known for killing at distance with his long-range Creedmore rifle. Their cat and mouse relationship is treated as a game. When asked about his binoculars, Clayton answers, 'I've taken to looking at funny-looking birds,' while 'rancher' Logan explains his large collection of guns, 'I'm a sportsman.' Envisioned as a revisionist western, *Missouri Breaks* veers off the rails whenever Brando, in one of his most eccentric roles, appears: he offers a variety of different accents (including Scottish and Irish) and wears a bonnet and dress to unnerve his opponents. As Brando informed director Arthur Penn, 'The character has no psychological spine, so I can do anything I want...move like an eel dipped in Vaseline. I'm here, I'm there, I'm all over the place.' And so was the film. Like *The Missouri Breaks*, *One-Eyed Jacks* is a folly, and an expensive one, but it is also a unique slice of western history, Brando-style.

17

'All I Want is to Enter My House Justified'

— Ride the High Country (1962)

Ride the High Country (1962)
Credits
DIRECTOR – Sam Peckinpah
PRODUCER – Richard E. Lyons
WRITTEN BY – N.B. Stone Jnr
DIRECTOR OF PHOTOGRAPHY – Lucien Ballard
EDITOR – Frank Santillo
ART DIRECTORS – George W. Davis and Leroy Coleman
MUSIC – George Bassman
CinemaScope/Metrocolor
An MGM Production
Released by Metro-Goldwyn-Mayer
94 minutes
Cast
  Randolph Scott (Gil Westrum); Joel McCrea (Steve
  Judd); Mariette Hartley (Elsa Knudsen); Ron Starr
  (Heck Longtree); Edgar Buchanan (Judge Tolliver);
  R.G. Armstrong (Joshua Knudsen); Jenie Jackson (Kate,
  the madam); James Drury (Billy Hammond); L.Q. Jones
  (Sylvus Hammond); John Anderson (Elder Hammond);
  John Davis Chandler (Jimmy Hammond); Warren Oates
  (Henry Hammond); Percy Helton (Luther Sampson,
  bank president); Byron Foulger (Abner Sampson, bank
  vice-president)

* * *

Though often blamed for the western's demise in the early sixties, TV also produced
some exciting new talent, who benefited screen westerns. While working on TV

western scripts, including *Gunsmoke*, David Samuel Peckinpah created the TV series *The Rifleman* (1958–1963 with Chuck Connors as the sharpshooting, rapid-firing Lucas McCain), and *The Westerner* (1959–1960), starring Brian Keith as Dave Blessingame. Peckinpah left the former in 1959 after disagreeing on the show's direction, while *The Westerner*, notable for its realism and pithy dialogue, garnered some excellent notices, but was cancelled by NBC after one season in the winter of 1960. Peckinpah also directed five of the 13 episodes of the series, which have since been hailed as classics of the TV genre.

Peckinpah's opportunity to make a feature film came when Keith asked him to direct *The Deadly Companions* (1961 – also released as *Trigger Happy*). It was a low-budget production: the shooting schedule was 21 days at a cost of $530,000. Keith was cast as the cashiered Yankee soldier 'Yellowleg', with Maureen O'Hara as the heroine, Kit Tilden (she also sings the title song). Yellowleg has spent the last five years searching for the Confederate who attempted to scalp him with a Bowie knife during the Civil War. He teams up with two rebs, Turkey (Chill Wills) and Billy (Steve Cochran) with an eye to knocking off the bank in Gila City. But before they can, an outlaw gang hits the bank and in the ensuing confusion Yellowleg kills Mead, the teenage son of Kit who is a local saloon dancer. Kit transports Mead's coffin to Siringo, the village where her husband, Mead Snr, is interred, to bury the boy next to his father. Yellowleg rides shotgun on the journey through Apache territory, and makes sure Turkey and Billy tag along for the ride – Yellowleg knows that Turkey is the man who tried to scalp him.

Though often criticised as a poor debut, *The Deadly Companions* is still unmistakably the west, Peckinpah-style. It resembles a stretched TV episode, but the great locations (including the cactus-strewn landscape of Arizona and the town set at Old Tucson, as both Gila City and ghost town Siringo), the Panavision photography and the violence set it apart from westerns of the time. Keith's hero is a particularly tragic figure: he has an old wound in his shoulder that paralyses his gun arm and he never removes his hat, which conceals the hideous scar across his forehead. Wills's performance as sweaty killer Turkey, dressed in a bearskin coat and bowler hat under the scorching Arizona sun, menacingly provides the most recognisable Peckinpah moments. Turkey is rescued from a lynching by Yellowleg (he is balanced precariously on a rolling barrel, with his head in a noose) and Yellowleg recognises Turkey from his own teeth marks in Turkey's scalping hand. In an unsettling scene, Yellowleg and Kit spot what appears to be a raiding party of Apaches chasing a coach. As they watch, it becomes apparent that the coach passengers are Apaches too, dressed in the remnants of clothes stolen from the former passengers, with the warriors drunkenly re-enacting the robbery.

The Deadly Companions was re-edited without Peckinpah and released with little success, promoted by the tagline: 'Trapped by her past and the sins of the men who pursued her through a savage land'. But in late 1961, Peckinpah was asked by MGM to direct another western, entitled *Guns in the Afternoon*, for $15,000. Peckinpah reworked the existing screenplay, drafted by N. B. Stone Jnr and an uncredited William Roberts, and retitled it *Ride the High Country*, recalling where he grew up in Fresno, California, and the locale of his deer hunting in the Sierra Nevada. In the story, ageing ex-marshal Steve Judd is hired to transport a shipment of $11,486 in gold from the mining settlement of Coarse Gold in the sierras to the town of Hornitos in the valley. For help, he employs his ex-partner, down-on-his-luck Gil Westrum and his green sidekick Heck. On the way to Coarse Gold, they are joined by runaway Elsa Knudsen who is engaged to Billy Hammond, one of the miners. When they arrive, Elsa marries Billy, but discovers that she will have to live with his brothers too. In a drunken wedding celebration she is abused and when the gold guards head back down the mountain with their shipment, they take Elsa with them – with the Hammonds in pursuit. Westrum's plan all along has been to steal the gold for himself, but Judd catches him and vows he will face justice. In an ambush at Knudsen's farm, the escort face the Hammonds; the brothers are killed, and Judd is mortally wounded. 'I'll take care of it,' assures Westrum of the gold, 'Just like you would have.' 'Hell, I know that,' answers Judd, 'I always did. You just forgot it for a while, that's all.'

Peckinpah cast two western stalwarts as his protagonists. Joel McCrea was the grandson of a stagecoach driver. An experienced rider, as a youngster he worked as a horse-holder on Tom Mix and William S. Hart westerns and later as a wrangler and stuntman, eventually becoming a popular cowboy star himself in such films as *Buffalo Bill* (1944) and *Colorado Territory* (1949). Randolph Scott was fresh from his latter-day success with Budd Boetticher on *Ride Lonesome* and *Comanche Station*. *Variety* saw *Ride the High Country* as stuck halfway between an expensive B-western and an 'A' production and doubted if Scott or McCrea 'teamed for the first time, can draw the mainstream crowds'. Peckinpah had no such misgivings, although both stars made it plain during the filming that it was the last film of their respective careers. Initially McCrea was cast as Westrum, with Scott as Judd, but by the time filming began, their roles had reversed. Their billing was decided on the flip of a coin in the Brown Derby restaurant. Peckinpah had already altered the ending to the original story: in the draft, it was Westrum who was killed in the shootout and Judd survived, the outlaw paying the price for his transgression.

Mariette Hartley (real name Mary Loretta Hartley) made her film debut as Elsa, the lonely daughter of widowed zealot Joshua, played by Robert Golden Armstrong. Armstrong who had played the wicked patriarch of the Boyd clan, in pursuit of Don Murray in *From Hell to Texas* (1958). Mole-ish Percy Helton played the Hornitos bank president; Ron Starr was cast as hotheaded Heck. Edgar Buchanan, as Coarse Gold's drunken Judge Tolliver, had appeared in countless westerns, including *Shane* (1953).

Peckinpah exhibits a great eye for character in the casting of the Hammond clan: handsome ruffian Billy (James Drury), bug-eyed Jimmy (John Davis Chandler), wild-eyed Sylvus (played to the hilt by L.Q. Jones) and gaunt Elder (John Anderson). Warren Oates as Henry (who smells 'bad enough to gag a dog off a gutwagon'), with his forage cap and a crow perched on shoulder, looks more Poe than prairie. An excellent character actor, Oates had guest-starred on TV in *The Rifleman*, *Wanted: Dead or Alive*, *Rawhide* and *The Westerner*. Jones had altered his real name (Justus McQueen) to 'L.Q. Jones' after the name of the character he played in *Battle Cry* (1955). Drury went on to play *The Virginian* on TV for its entire run (1962–1971), Anderson also stayed mainly in TV, while Chandler appeared in *Barquero* (1970 – as a member of Oates's outlaw gang) and *The Outlaw Josey Wales* (1976 – as a memorable bounty hunter on Wales's trail). Oates, Chandler and Jones all worked on subsequent Peckinpah projects.

Ride the High Country was budgeted at $800,000, on a 24 day shooting schedule. Filming began in mid-October, in the Californian mountains, wood and lakes of Inyo National Forest, around Mammoth Lakes. But only four days footage was shot there, including the group riding to and from Coarse Gold, and a windy mountain shootout between the gold escort and the Hammonds. Snow fell, the worst Mammoth had seen for years, and forced the production to move elsewhere. They shot the rest of the mountain footage north of Los Angeles, in the Eastern Sierra of the Santa Monica Mountains, Frenchman's Flat (on the Santa Clara River) and in the Hollywood Hills, including the Knudsen farm sequences in the Conejo Valley. The final shootout was the last scene to be shot. Few scenes, notably a campfire conversation and some cutaways, were shot on studio-bound sets. The town of Hornitos was constructed on an MGM backlot.

The mining camp of Coarse Gold was filmed in Bronson Canyon, Griffith Park, near LA, a familiar location from dozens of low-budget westerns and sci-fi films. There, Peckinpah created his rough miners' camp and Kate's saloon-brothel. The tent canvas was stolen from MGM's storeroom and had originally been sails in *Mutiny on the Bounty*, while the on-set snow was created with soapsuds (a close look at L.Q. Jones's jacket following a fight scene reveals a patch of soapsud bubbles). The CinemaScope cinematographer was Lucien Ballard, a part-Cherokee Indian, who had made a name for himself in the thirties, though it is his western work over the next decade for Peckinpah that is most remembered. The eventual cost of *High County* was $852,000 spent over 28 days; filming was completed in mid-November.

The setting for Peckinpah's film is a turn of the century west. Judd rides into Hornitos and a travelling carnival is in town, black-uniformed cops patrol the streets and Judd is

French poster artwork for Sam Peckinpah's second western *Ride the High Country* (1962), with Randolph Scott and Joel McCrea. (Picture courtesy of Ian Caunce Collection).

almost run over by a newfangled automobile. In 'The Phantom of the Desert Race', a camel outdistancing horses for money (Heck is the camel's jockey) and belly dancers entertain the crowd, while Westrum is reduced to working as a sideshow turn, 'The Oregon Kid', complete with Buffalo Bill buckskins, moustache, goatee and long wig. Judd and Westrum want to escape from this world into the high country, away from progress, where the land is unspoilt and life resembles the good old days, with all its associated danger. As Westrum says of himself, when he accepts the escort job, 'I know a fella who's got an overwhelming hankering for a little old-time activity.'

The modern world of the opening scenes is contrasted with Coarse Gold, the tented village, a transient boomtown that may only exist for a few weeks until the gold plays out. The banker in Hornitos refers to Coarse Gold's Judge Tolliver saying, 'The only law up there's too drunk to hit the ground with his hat.' The single wooden building is the saloon-brothel, 'Kate's Place', with its bawdy sign: 'MEN TAKEN IN AND DONE FOR'. The saloon interior is similarly authentic and suitably seedy, with its honky-tonk piano playing 'Here Comes the Bride' and buxom redheaded madam, Kate, taking a fortune in gold from the miners for her employees' services.

Old-timers like Judd and Westrum hate Coarse Gold. Westrum calls it, 'A Garden of Eden...for the short on cash.' Their relationship sparkles with such typically brusque Peckinpah prose and Scott's dry asides add much to the film. Following a brief mêlée during which Judd has felled Heck with a single punch, Westrum observes, 'Good fight. I enjoyed it.' While listening to Elsa and Billy's wild wedding from the safety of his tent, he notes, 'Glad they didn't invite me. I always cry at weddings.' Judd used to be a lawman, Westrum his deputy, but both have fallen on hard times. Westrum sarcastically marvels at Judd's lot, 'A bluegrass thoroughbred, silver mounted saddle, magnificent wardrobe...I'm envious,' while Judd looks at his nag, worn saddle and threadbare clothes. But Judd still believes in the law, while Westrum's faith in it has lapsed.

During the journey, Judd and Westrum reminisce about their rowdy past, memories that bring a smile to their craggy faces, and the passing of time is their biggest enemy: creaky rheumatism, the aches and pains of old age and old war wounds are taking their toll. The most poignant line in the film comes with Westrum asking to have his wrist bindings removed to bed down. Judd asks why. ''Cos I don't sleep so good anymore,' replies Westrum honestly. When Judd arrives in Hornitos, the banker was expecting someone younger, 'Well I used to be,' the hired gun answers. In their most famous exchange, Westrum can't comprehend why Judd will honour his contract. 'Partner', says Westrum, 'you know what's on the back of a poor man when he dies? The clothes of pride, and they're not a bit warmer to him dead than when he was alive. Is that all you want Steve?' 'All I want,' says Judd, 'is to enter my house justified.' Peckinpah reputedly based Judd's character on his own father, David, just as the name Coarse Gold was an actual place from Peckinpah's younger days.

Peckinpah seems less interested in the youthful characters in the film. Heck and Elsa's love story is sketchy and the director is more concerned with Elsa's overbearing father, for whom every suitor is 'The wrong kind of man'. The wedding scene still packs a punch and was one of the sequences trimmed by the censor for its initial release. Elsa, proudly dressed in her mother's wedding gown and flower head-dress, discovers her honeymoon suite is a tent and during the boisterous wedding ceremony seems to be in shock. When Billy's brothers try to assault her, Heck saves her ('The marriage didn't work out') and manages to dupe the miners' court into annulling the nuptials.

Zealot Knudsen calls Coarse Gold a 'sinkhole of depravity', an apt name for the home of the wretched man who will marry his daughter, and his four depraved brothers. The lyricism of the mountain journey – scored by George Bassman's theme, majestically rising and falling, like the landscape – is a world away from the Hammonds' rowdy antics: forcing Henry to take a bath, bickering over who will dance with Elsa next, or singing 'Oh, the Hammond boys are comin'!', as they ride in their Sunday best suits behind the bride for the wedding procession into Coarse Gold. The Hammond gang anticipate demonic Preacher Quint (Donald Pleasance) and his vengeful clan of raw-hiders in the Charlton Heston western *Will Penny* (1968). This unromantic film, directed by Tom Gries and also starring Ben Johnson and Bruce Dern, strongly resembles Peckinpah's west. It was even shot by Lucien Ballard in the Inyo National Forest and was based on the 'Line Camp' episode of Peckinpah's *The Westerner*. While making *High Country*, Peckinpah wound up the five Hammond actors on set and off, making them share a room together and created a rift between them and the rest of the crew ('You are the Hammonds, you hate everybody here'), to ensure he got the right venom in their performances. Yet as L.Q. Jones noted, 'Us Hammond brothers, Warren, John and I, kept looking at each other and grinning, because we knew what we were making was something really special.'

High Country's final confrontation, with Judd and Westrum facing the 'dry-gulching Southern trash' Hammond clan in the farmyard, is a precursor of *The Wild Bunch* (1969). The escort arrives at Knudsen's farm and finds Knudsen who appears to be praying, but in a rapid zoom, Peckinpah reveals a bloody bullet wound to his face. It's an ambush and the Hammonds' presence is revealed by Henry's pet crow which is seen squabbling among Knudsen's chickens. Pinned down in a ditch, Judd suggests, 'Let's meet 'em head on, halfway, just like always.'; 'My sentiments exactly,' Westrum concurs. The two old-timers face the three remaining Hammonds in a face to face shootout, blasting at each other at point-blank range, following Billy's call to, 'Start the ball rolling, old man.' As the smoke clears the Hammonds are dead and Judd is gut-shot. 'I'll go it alone...so long partner,' says Judd. 'I'll see you later,' Westrum answers, as he leaves. The final shot shows Judd looking back at the mountains, his cherished high country, before he slumps out of the frame and dies. It is very moving finale, among the most resonant in the genre, and both McCrea and Scott were reduced to tears on set.

Though Peckinpah wasn't allowed to assemble the final cut and MGM's president Joseph Vogel hated the film so much he almost didn't release it, *Ride the High Country* was exhibited in the US in May 1962. In the UK it was passed by the BBFC as a certificate 'A', with minor cuts. The UK version reverted to its original title, *Guns in the Afternoon*, alluding to the waning autumnal sun, the end of the west and the ageing gunfighters, in the 'afternoon' of their lives. The fact that Judd and the group arrive at Knudsen's farm in the afternoon provides the clue to the ambush: father Joshua always prays at his wife's grave in the morning and Elsa senses something is amiss. Posters played up the two stars: 'Two Western Stars in One Great Movie' – or touted a 'Showdown in the High Sierra', with poster imagery that implied the 'showdown' was between Scott and McCrea: 'They each had a gun and a last chance to make good…on one side of the law or the other'. Publicity claimed that combined, the two stars had 'starred in 230 films, fired 150,000 bullets, ridden 200 horses and killed 130 outlaws'.

Ride the High Country was initially unsuccessful when released as the second stringer on a double bill with the epic *The Tartars*. Then it began to attract attention with some good reviews. In the US, *Time* said the film: 'has a rare honesty of script, performance and theme – that goodness is not a gift but a quest', while *Newsweek* thought 'everything about the picture has the ring of truth' and voted it film of the year. In Europe it was also a critical and commercial success. In Brussels it won the International Film Award (beating Federico Fellini's *8 1/2*), in Paris, where it was released as *Coups de Feu dans La Sierra* ('Gunshots in the Sierra'), it won the critics' award, and first prize at the Venice Film Festival. In Italy it was *Sfida nell'alta Sierra* ('Challenge in the High Sierra'), in Spain, *Duelo en la Alta Sierra* ('Duel in the High Sierra') and in West Germany, *Sacramento*.

Following his success with *High Country*, Peckinpah was hired to direct *Major Dundee*, detailing the pursuit of renegade Apaches into Mexico over Christmas 1864–1865: 'Until the Apache is taken or destroyed'. Following a massacre at Rostes ranch, Unionist Major Dundee (Charlton Heston) leads a strike force out of Fort Benlin to apprehend the perpetrator, chief Sierra Chariba (Michael Pate from *Hondo*) and to recover white children taken hostage in the raid. His command consists of a ragtag bunch of Confederate prisoners of war, horse thieves, renegades and deserters, augmented with black regulars, civilian volunteers, a mule train and a baby Howitzer. As they ride deeper into Mexico, coming into conflict with French lancers fighting the Juaristas, the command teeters on the brink of implosion.

Major Dundee's making was similarly a trial for all concerned, running over budget, over schedule and out of ideas. Powered along by the rousing 'Major Dundee March' sung by Mitch Miller's Sing Along Gang, but narrated in monotonous fashion by young bugler Ryan (Michael Anderson Jnr), it is a flawed movie. It was, however, memorable for its opening scene (the aftermath of the ranch massacre), some tremendous action (staged by Cliff Lyons, notably the lancers' charge across the Rio Grande) and one of the strongest casts ever assembled for a western: Richard Harris, Warren Oates, James Coburn, Senta Berger, L.Q. Jones, R.G. Armstrong, Ben Johnson, Slim Pickens and Dub Taylor. Peckinpah's name was poison after this fiasco, which was edited without him and which died at the box office when released by Columbia in 1965. It has since been restored and re-scored in a special release for DVD, in an attempt to better illustrate Peckinpah's intent.

Ride the High Country was Randolph Scott's last film and Joel McCrea also retired, only returning in *Cry Blood Apache* (1970), which starred his son Jody, and *Mustang Country* (1976). *High Country* is a moving tribute to these two great actors and to the passing of the golden age of westerns. In the next few years there would be a major revision of the western myth on film, and Peckinpah would be at the forefront of this shift. But after *Major Dundee* it was to be four years before Peckinpah was allowed to direct another cinema feature. The bitterness of the intervening years showed in his next western, which featured a 'wild bunch' that made the Hammonds look like *The Waltons*.

18

'Ain't You Got No Respect For Your Elders?'

— *The Sons of Katie Elder* (1965)

The Sons of Katie Elder (1965)
Credits
DIRECTOR – Henry Hathaway
PRODUCER – Hal B. Wallis
ASSOCIATE PRODUCER – Paul Nathan
STORY – Talbot Jennings
SCREENPLAY – William H. Wright, Allan Weiss and Harry Essex
DIRECTOR OF PHOTOGRAPHY – Lucien Ballard
EDITOR – Warren Low
ART DIRECTOR – Hal Pereira and Walter Tyler
MUSIC – Elmer Bernstein
Panavision/Technicolor
A Paramount Production
Released by Paramount Pictures
122 minutes
Cast
    John Wayne (John Elder); Dean Martin (Tom Elder);
Michael Anderson Jnr (Bud Elder); Earl Holliman (Matt
Elder); Jeremy Slate (Deputy Ben Latta); Martha Hyer
(Mary Gordon); James Gregory (Morgan Hastings); Dennis
Hopper (Dave Hastings); George Kennedy (Curley, the hired
gun); Paul Fix (Sheriff Billy Wilson); Sheldon Allman
(Deputy Harry Evers); John Litel (Minister); John Doucette
(Henry Hyselman, undertaker); Rhys Williams (Charlie
Striker); James Westerfield (Mr Vanner, banker); John Qualen
(Deputy Charlie Biller); Rodolfo Acosta (Bondie Adams);
Strother Martin (Jeb Ross); Karl Swenson (Doc Isdell);
Percy Helton (Mr Peevey, storekeeper); Harvey Grant (Jeb,
blacksmith's son); Chuck Roberson (Burr Sandeman); Jerry

Gatlin (Amboy); Loren Janes (Ned Reese); Jack Williams
(Andy Sharp); Henry Wills (Gus Dolly); Joe Yrigoyen
(Buck Mason); Boyd 'Red' Morgan and Chuck Heywood
(members of Hastings' gang); Ralph Volkie, Glen Anderson
and Paul Whitson

*   *   *

Since appearing in *She Wore a Yellow Ribbon* in 1949, John 'Duke' Wayne had
appeared in the *Motion Picture Herald*'s top ten list of the biggest stars for 23 of the
24 years (he didn't feature in the 1958 list), until 1973, where he was positioned ninth.
In 1950, 1951, 1954 and 1971 he topped it. The massive success of *The Searchers* and
Rio Bravo gave Wayne the funds to direct and star in his version of *The Alamo* (1960).
Its subsequent failure ensured that the actor returned to his familiar 'Big John Wayne'
persona for almost all of his subsequent westerns. Of the 32 films Wayne made
after *Rio Bravo* until his death in 1979, 20 were westerns, including such classics
as *The Comancheros*, *The Sons of Katie Elder*, *The War Wagon* and *True Grit*.

Importantly, by the sixties Wayne's heroes had stopped killing Indians; from now
on he starred mainly in gunslinging westerns, fighting villains who were gringo,
Mexican or Comanchero. The Native Americans were, if anything, his allies.
Wayne made *The Alamo* on his specially built Brackettville set in Texas, from
September to December 1959; it was premiered in October 1960. John Ford
optimistically called it, 'the greatest picture I've ever seen' and George Stevens
claimed it was 'a modern classic', but it cost so much money ($12 million) it was
doomed to failure (it took almost $8 million in the US). *Newsweek* called it: 'The
most lavish B-picture ever made'. This was despite some great action scenes of the
assault on the mission by the Mexican army, with the Alamo battery blasting at
Santa Anna's massed ranks – and good performances by Richard Widmark,
Lawrence Harvey and Wayne himself, as outnumbered Alamo defenders Jim
Bowie, William Travis and Davy Crockett.

Wayne followed *The Alamo* with *North to Alaska* (1960 – a knockabout gold mining
saga), Michael Curtiz's *The Comancheros* (1961), the classic *The Man Who Shot
Liberty Valance* (1962), a cameo as General Sherman in *How the West Was Won* (1962)
and *McLintock!* (1963), a less-than-serious fistfest, made at Old Tucson Studios by
Wayne's own company Batjac and directed by Andrew V. McLaglen, the son of
Ford's actor, Victor McLaglen. It was in this film that Wayne uttered his gravelly,
much-imitated catchphrase, 'The Hell I will'.

The Comancheros was the first of Wayne's post-Ford, all-action westerns where
he appeared in the same costume as *Rio Bravo*'s John T. Chance: tan slacks, waistcoat,
bib shirt and 'Red River D' buckle – his trouser turn-ups and tall hat increased his
stature. The story was based on Paul I. Wellman's novel of the same name. Wayne
starred as Texas Ranger Jake Cutter, who poses as gunrunner Ed McBain to contact
Tully Crow (a raucous, half-scalped performance by Lee Marvin). Crow is in cahoots
with Comancheros, renegades who deal illegal guns to the Comanche. With the help

of Paul Regret (Stuart Whitman), a gambler from Louisiana, he infiltrates the Comanchero headquarters in the Upper Brazos with a wagonload of repeating rifles, but the duo are exposed as impostors and tortured in the sun. The arrival of Comanche chief Iron Shirt (so-called because of his conquistador breastplate) to trade liquor and guns, heightens their predicament. Cutter and Regret manage to escape as the rangers arrive, and proceed to raze the Comancheros' canyon hideout.

Wayne and second unit director Cliff Lyons directed much of the film (lensed in Moab, Utah from June to August 1961) after Curtiz fell ill, with the accent on explosions and pugilism. The most famous scene in the film depicts Cutter and Regret driving their gunrunning wagon at full speed, with howling Comanches galloping alongside and Elmer Bernstein's heroic riding theme on the soundtrack. Cutter's credo is typical screen Wayne rhetoric, 'Words are what men live by – words they say and mean'. Wayne's love interest, widow Melinda Marshall (Joan O'Brien), adds some shading to his action hero (recounting how he lost his wife two years ago), while Wayne's own daughter, five-year-old Aissa, played Melinda's daughter Bessy. Wayne's 22-year-old son Patrick appeared as Tobe, their ranger contact. Bruce Cabot played ranger Major Henry, Ina Balin was Regret's lover, Pilar, while the Comanchero villainy was represented by Michael Ansara's Amelung and Jack Elam's sadistic 'Horseface'. The film was so successful it was remade as *Rio Conchos* three years later, again with Whitman.

Wayne was diagnosed with lung cancer in 1964, but underwent successful surgery. By January 1965 he was making *The Sons of Katie Elder*, one of his finest films, directed by Henry Hathaway, an actor who turned to directing in 1932 with Zane Grey westerns like *Wild Horse Mesa*. He made *Garden of Evil* (1954 – with Gary Cooper, Richard Widmark and Cameron Mitchell) and the manhunt western *From Hell to Texas* (1958 – with Don Murray as the hunted). Hathaway had also directed *North to Alaska* and filmed three of the five episodes of *How the West Was Won*: 'The Rivers', 'The Plains' and 'The Outlaws'.

Although *Katie Elder* had come to Paramount years before via John Sturges, producer Hal Wallis had developed it for Wayne; in 1965 Sturges was too busy to direct it, so Hathaway took the helm. Based on a Talbot Jennings story, with a screenplay by William H. Wright, Allan Weiss and Harry Essex, *The Sons of Katie Elder* saw the four Elder brothers, John, Tom, Matt and Bud, returning to the town of Clearwater to attend the funeral of their mother Katie. Having been absent for a long time, the brothers discover that their father Bass was murdered by greedy landowner and gunsmith Morgan Hastings, following a Blackjack game in which Bass had lost the ranch to Hastings. Katie had been forced to give up the property and had scraped a living, doing sewing and giving guitar lessons. Expecting trouble, especially from gunslinger John and gambler Tom who have bad reputations, Hastings and his cowardly son Dave hire professional gun Curley to protect them. Discovering that Tom is wanted for murder, Hastings kills Clearwater sheriff, Billy Wilson and frames the brothers for it. While they are being escorted to Laredo for trial, they are ambushed at a river crossing by Hastings' gang. Curley tries to blow them up –

Matt is killed and Bud is wounded, but John kills Curley. Back in Clearwater, John and Tom face the Hastings clan.

Katie Elder teamed Wayne (as John) with Dean Martin (as Tom), reunited six years after *Rio Bravo*. Michael Anderson Jnr (from *Major Dundee*) and Earl Holliman (from many westerns, including *Gunfight at the O.K. Corral* and *Last Train from Gun Hill*) played the other two Elder brothers, Bud and Matt. Considering Katie's childbearing years, there's a rather unlikely age span between the brothers: Bud is described as being 18, though Anderson Jnr was 21 at the time. Holliman was 36, Martin 47 and Wayne 57. Soon-to-be genial western stalwart George Kennedy played lumbering thug Curley, the killer who arrives by train. Dennis Hopper, a regular in Hathaway's westerns, often as a cowering, psychotic juvenile, appeared as Dave Hastings. James Gregory as Morgan (the gunsmith villain who packs a rifle with a telescopic sight), later played Dean Martin's boss MacDonald at I.C.E (Intelligence Counter Espionage), in the 'Matt Helm' spy series. An indication of the story's macho stance is Martha Hyer as Katie's confidante Mary, the lone female presence in the film (Hyer married producer Wallis the following year). Paul Fix had been appearing with Wayne since Lone Star days (*The Desert Trail* [1935]) and was the marshal in TV's *The Rifleman*. Western regulars John Doucette, Rodolfo Acosta and John Qualen filled out the cast, as did several stuntmen, including Chuck Roberson, Boyd Morgan and Henry Wills. Strother Martin had a cameo as duped cowboy Jeb Ross in a saloon bar. Tom Elder apparently raffles his glass eye and Jeb is the 'lucky' winner, crowing, 'I always wanted a third eye.'

Katie Elder was the first of Wayne's movies filmed in what would become his favourite western setting, a series of sets and locations in Durango, Mexico. 'Clearwater' was a town street set at Chupaderos; the riverside ambush was filmed near the El Saltito waterfalls, with its shady overhanging trees and gnarly roots. The opening train scenes were filmed on the Denver & Rio Grande Railroad, in Durango, Colorado, while filming was completed with the town and ranch interiors at Churubusco Studios, Mexico City.

With a rousing Elmer Bernstein score, plenty of action and hints of pathos, *The Sons of Katie Elder* is the archetypal Wayne vehicle. Since *The Magnificent Seven* Bernstein had been renowned for his punchy western scores – he was known as 'Bernstein West', to differentiate him from composer Leonard Bernstein ('Bernstein East'), of New York's *West Side Story* fame. *The Sons of Katie Elder* shares *The Magnificent Seven*'s brassy exuberance and driving, syncopated backing, and is one of Bernstein's best scores – adding equally to the action and the moments of sadness.

The action scenes, as to be expected from a Wayne movie, are frequent and lively. The four siblings are always quarrelling, 'I don't want to be rich and respectable,' pipes up youngster Bud, 'I wanna be just like the rest of you.' In a memorable scene, Big John smashes Curley in the nose with a pickaxe handle. The violent finale, more brutal than most Wayne movies, is well handled. First, the ambush on the way to Laredo is an explosion of bullet-shredded splintered wood, with Matt skewered by a shard of timber. Its second act, in Clearwater, ends with Morgan shooting his own son, who is about to implicate Morgan in the murders of Sheriff Wilson and

Bass, and then John Elder faces Morgan in Hastings's gunsmith shop. John shoots a keg of black powder, blowing Morgan and the gunsmith's shop to smithereens.

Katie Elder has more human drama than many of Wayne's straightforward action vehicles and a good mystery element, with the solving of Bass's murder – no matter how obvious the culprit's identity is. John's first appearance at the funeral, framed between two rocks up on the hillside, looking at Katie's grave from afar and unable to attend his own mother's burial, is very effective. Subsequent scenes at her graveside, his reminiscences throughout the film and Katie's empty rocking chair beside the fire, moving back and forth (a Fordian image of homeliness) are equally so. We learn that Katie even traded her prized grey horse for advance payment of her funeral and claimed 'her boys' looked after her, sending her money, when in fact none had visited for years. The name 'Katie Elder' may have been inspired by Doc Holliday's mistress, Kate Fisher (real name Catherine Elder), known as 'Big Nosed Kate'.

As in *Rio Bravo*, Wayne's screen relationship with Dean Martin is easygoing; there is even a reference to Hawks's film at the end, with the pair of them under siege in the Clearwater stable. Like almost all Wayne's post-*Alamo* westerns, it is contrived that he is single – his wife has either deserted him (as in *The Undefeated*) or died (*The Comancheros*), or he is too individualistic to have got married, as in *Katie Elder*. This contrivance was a shortcut to providing Wayne's characters with depth, and enhanced his 'don't need nobody' self-sufficient screen persona. In real life Wayne was married three times, to Josephine Saenz, Esperanza Diaz Ceballos (called 'Chata') and Pilar Palette Weldy. But on screen, with the exception of the slapstick western courtship of *McLintock* (essentially *The Quiet Man* out west, complete with Maureen O'Hara), Wayne never ends his latter-day westerns in a relationship.

The film was released in the US on 1 July 1965; posters ran with the tagline: '*The Sons of Katie Elder*…their eyes smoking and their fingers itching'. Johnny Cash released a tie-in single, which didn't feature in the film, entitled 'The Sons of Katie Elder' ('From the four winds we have come, four brothers on the run'). The Mexican sets had been swarming with press throughout the shoot, following Wayne's health scare, which ensured that the film received publicity. The *New York Times* said *Katie Elder* was 'not a rare film – but lean, gory and well served…with a professional stamp and a laconic bite'. It took $6 million, putting it just inside the top ten most successful westerns of the sixties, behind Sergio Leone's *The Good, the Bad and the Ugly* (1966).

Wayne followed *Katie Elder* with *El Dorado* (1967), a *Rio Bravo* companion piece with Robert Mitchum, filmed in Arizona, and *The War Wagon*. Made in September 1966 and released in 1967, *War Wagon* is one of Wayne's best-plotted westerns, directed in knowing style by Burt Kennedy as an action comedy (with more of the former than the latter). Again filmed around Durango in Mexico, much of *War Wagon* was lensed in the Sierra De Organos ('The Organ Mountains'), Zacatecas, a spectacular landscape, where the jutting rock formations resemble towering church organ pipes. Interiors were shot at Churubusco Studios, Mexico City; 'Churubusco' is also the name of one of the towns in the film. Wayne headlined as paroled Taw Jackson, who has been framed and swindled out of his ranch by Frank Pierce (Bruce Cabot), a mining magnate in Emmett, New Mexico. Pierce has since struck gold on

Duke's first appearance, framed in the rocks during his mother's funeral; John Wayne as John, the eldest of *The Sons of Katie Elder* (1965).

Jackson's land and transports it to the railhead at El Paso in an armour-plated coach, dubbed the 'War Wagon' (a horse-drawn armoured car, with a turret and Gatling gun), escorted by 33 heavily armed guards. Jackson decides to steal Pierce's $500,000 mining shipment and assembles a crack team: alcoholic explosives ace Billy Hyatt, grumpy haulier Wes Fletcher and his wife Kate, Kiowa Levi Walking Bear (their 'Indian expert') and acrobatic safecracking gunslinger Lomax (Kirk Douglas). Lomax has actually been hired by Pierce to kill Jackson, but realises it's more profitable to steal Pierce's gold – which they do, in a deftly executed raid staged on Stony Flats, involving a blown trestle ('Sawtooth Bridge'), nitro-glycerine and a big log. For the raid to succeed, they have to employ Wild Horse and his band of renegade Kiowas, who cause trouble. The wagon carrying the gold dust, now concealed in barrels of flour, careers off without a driver and scatters the fortune far and wide. 'What am I supposed to do?' fumes Lomax, 'Live with the Indians for the next year and open up a bakery?'

The screenplay was based on Clair Huffaker's 1957 novel 'Badman', which was a longer version of Huffaker's *Ranch Romances* short story 'Holdup at Stony Flat'. The hero of the novel was Jack Tawlin, who teams up with his double-crossing brother Jess and a gang including Sioux warrior Iron Eyes, to take 'Old Ironsides, a fortress on wheels'. The film version plays on the *Rio Bravo* formula, by having Wayne recruit a bunch of oddballs for his revenge on Pierce. Keenan Wynn is good as Wes (the complaining old coot), Robert Walker plays drunken kid Billy (handling nitro with the shakes) and Howard Keel is especially well cast, against type, as comic relief Kiowa Levi (Iron Eyes is considerably more brutal in the book). Douglas and Wayne are fine, uneasy partners – one memorable scene sees Jackson and Lomax competitively gunning down two of Pierce's henchmen, Dink Hammond and Brown (Bruce Dern and Chuck Roberson). 'Mine hit the ground first,' says Lomax, 'Mine was taller,' tops Jackson. Douglas clearly enjoys playing quick-witted Lomax, vaulting into his saddle and swinging from saloon chandeliers. The catchy title song 'Ballad of the War Wagon', yet another from the Tiomkin-Washington team, begins the film in style ('Three years in prison made me dream a lot of dreams; sometimes the dream is not as easy as it seems') and the Batjac production was a success, taking over $6 million in the US.

Henry Hathaway followed *Katie Elder* with the $5.5 million grossing *Nevada Smith* (1966), which saw vengeful Max Sand (Steve McQueen) on a vendetta to track down his parents' three killers (Karl Malden, Arthur Kennedy and Martin Landau). The trail leads him from the Nevada desert, to a prison camp in an alligator-infested Louisiana swamp and the California gold fields. Tortoise-paced and with an unsatisfactory conclusion, *Nevada Smith* is undeserving of its huge success, which was a result of McQueen's colossal box-office appeal.

Following the mediocre murder mystery *5 Card Stud* (1968 – starring Dean Martin and Robert Mitchum), Hathaway was reunited with Wayne for *True Grit*, based on Charles Portis's 1968 novel. Wayne played one-eyed US deputy marshal, 'Rooster' Cogburn, who along with Texas Ranger Sergeant LaBoeuf ('Rhinestone Cowboy' Glen Campbell, also hired to croon the title song), reluctantly accompanies

14-year-old Mattie Ross (Kim Darby) into the Indian Nations in pursuit of Tom Chaney (Jeff Corey), the man who killed her father in Fort Smith. Portis's novel is told through Mattie's first-person narration. Chaney is also wanted in Texas for the murder of Senator Bibbs and has teamed up with Lucky Ned Pepper's outlaw gang. On the trail, Mattie and Rooster grow to respect one another's grit (as Rooster says, 'By God, she reminds me of me'). In a spectacular finale, with Mattie trapped in a rattlesnake pit, Rooster rides at Pepper and his three cohorts, reins between his teeth, Winchester in one hand, Colt in the other. Pepper doesn't like Cogburn's cockiness, 'I call that bold talk for a one-eyed fat man.' 'Fill your hands you son of a bitch!' counters Rooster. A typical supporting gallery of Hathaway badmen include Lucky Ned Pepper (Robert Duvall, with a bullet-scarred lip) and Moon (Dennis Hopper), who at one point has his fingers chopped off.

In *True Grit*, Wayne plays an old man who has lost much in his life: his eye in the Civil War, his wife, intolerant of his boozing. Wayne may wear a copper wrist bracelet for rheumatism, but he still twirls his customised Winchester to reload, just like the Ringo Kid. Scored by Elmer Bernstein and photographed by Peckinpah's regular cinematographer Lucien Ballard in the wooded mountains of Mammoth Lakes, California and in Montrose, Colorado, *True Grit* is a solid western. Perhaps it is because Wayne wasn't playing 'John Wayne', but a 'one-eyed sonofabitch', who 'loves to pull a cork' that he won his only Best Actor Oscar for the role at the 1970 Academy Awards (he was up against Richard Burton, Peter O'Toole, Dustin Hoffman and Jon Voight). 'If I'd known that,' said Wayne during his acceptance speech, 'I'd have put that patch on 35 years earlier.' Rooster was originally to have had a moustache too, but the star refused. *True Grit* took $14.5 million in the US, making it the fourth biggest western of the sixties and Wayne's most successful starring vehicle. 'As True as John Wayne's gun,' said the trailer, 'As Gritty as the trail to High Adventure!'

Off screen, Wayne always stood up for his ultra right-wing principles and had been a fervent anti-Communist in the fifties. In the same year as *High Noon*, he had starred as the eponymous hero of *Big Jim McLain* (1952), an agent for the HUAC, who with hulking sidekick James Arness embarked on Operation Pineapple, rooting out Reds in Honolulu. Wayne recorded a patriotic spoken-word album in 1973 for RCA called 'America, Why I Love Her' and made Hollywood's only pro-Vietnam War movie, the widely criticised *The Green Berets* (1969). But the popularity of his westerns remained undiminished into the seventies. For *The Undefeated* (1969) Wayne was back in familiar character and surroundings – as Union Colonel John Henry Thomas (filmed in Durango, with Civil War scenes shot in Baton Rouge, Louisiana). Directed by Andrew V. McLaglen, the sprawling, overlong film looked at comradeship and loyalty through two groups travelling south to Durango, Mexico, in the aftermath of the Civil War. A Confederate wagon train of 'pilgrims' is led by Colonel James Langdon (Rock Hudson); the Unionists (led by Wayne) are driving 3,000 horses to sell during the Mexican Revolution – as a Juarista general notes, 'Our forces need horses'. Predictably, both groups find themselves 'mixed-up in somebody else's war'. The old Ford bunch – Ben Johnson, Harry Carey Jnr and John Agar – ride along. The music was by Hugo Montenegro, who had just had a huge hit on both sides of the Atlantic with his cover version of *The Good, the Bad and the Ugly.* Wayne is his usual stalwart, rough-hewn, charming self. When explaining why he shot a Mexican bandit, he notes to a bystander, 'The conversation kinda dried up, ma'am.'

The Undefeated grossed $4 million in the US and Wayne followed it with another rip-snorting McLaglen western, *Chisum* (1970), one of his most patriotic, again filmed

John Wayne under fire in Andrew V. McLaglen's *The Undefeated* (1969), a typical, late-period Duke actioner.

in Durango. A deluxe Batjac production, and probably the best McLaglan-Wayne western, *Chisum* took $6 million, promoted by a trailer that blurred the lines between the real person and the screen icon: 'John Wayne, the Legend,' intoned the voiceover, 'the Hero, the Winner, the Man', intercut with action scenes from the film and Wayne's Oscar-night triumph. *Chisum* cast him as New Mexico cattleman John Chisum and depicts his role in the Lincoln County War, the Murphy-Tunstall range feud of 1878. By this point Wayne often appeared to be a guest-starring passenger in his own vehicle; the historical backdrop to *Chisum*, with most of the events depicted as they actually happened, accentuates this. The consortium formed by Chisum, English cattleman John Tunstall and Jeremy McSween, the murder of Tunstall, and the presence of Billy the Kid are all based on fact, though the siege finale, with Chisum driving a herd of cattle into Lincoln, is entirely fictitious. Ford regulars Ben Johnson, John Agar and Hank Worden lope past in supporting roles.

McLaglen also directed the Civil War soap opera *Shenandoah* (1965 – with James Stewart, Katherine Ross and Patrick Wayne), the plodding wagon train marathon *The Way West* (1967) starring Kirk Douglas, Robert Mitchum and Richard Widmark (which Pauline Kael scathingly described as 'a jerk's idea of an epic'), *Bandolero!* (1967 – with Stewart and Dean Martin cast as brothers) and Ford parody *Something Big* (1971), which mocks *She Wore a Yellow Ribbon*, *Stagecoach* and Ford's cinema in broadly comic terms. *Something Big* starred Dean Martin as outlaw Joe Baker, riding a horse fitted with gold-plated teeth and planning 'something big' with a Gatling gun, which he plans to acquire in a trade for Honor Blackman. Ben Johnson (as grizzled scout Bookbinder), Denver Pyle (trapper Junior Frisbee) and Harry Carey Jnr (as a peg-legged cook) supported, while Brian Keith, as Colonel Morgan, sent up Wayne's retiring Nathan Brittles from Ford's cavalry trilogy. *Variety* slated it, noting that it was destined for, 'okay (box office) responses in general redneck situations'.

Wayne's own career at this point was summed up in the December 1970 *Variety* review of *Rio Lobo*, another *Rio Bravo* clone, shot in Arizona earlier in the year: 'A Wayne western still creates a certain predictable conditioned response at the box office, which should give *Lobo* a modest success'. Its 'conditioned response' garnered $4.25 million. *Big Jake*, made in October 1970 around Durango (including the El Saltito waterfall and Sierra De Organos) took $7.5 million. Here, Jacob 'Big Jake' McCandles (Wayne) pursues John Fain (Richard Boone) and his gang of cut-throats, who have kidnapped McCandles's eight-year-old grandson (played by Wayne's own son John Ethan) following a massacre at the 'Bar MC' ranch. McCandles has been hired by his estranged wife Martha (Maureen O'Hara) to deliver the $1 million ransom. With uncharacteristically bloody action and a trademark score by Elmer Bernstein, Wayne is excellent as Jake, steamrollering his way through the best of his late period Batjac action westerns.

Big Jake is set in 1909; the title sequence contrasts technological wonders of 'The Edwardian Golden Age', with life out west (lynchings, gunfights and Geronimo). Big Jake sets off on his mission on horseback, while a squad of rangers are packed into newfangled automobile 'velocipedes'. An ambush by the Fain gang, where they shoot the car tyres, radiators and drivers, soon renders the rangers immobile, while Big Jake moseys on after the kidnappers. He's accompanied by a black German Shepherd (named 'Dog'), Apache tracker Sam Sharpnose (Bruce Cabot in unconvincing make-up) and McCandles's sons James (Wayne's son Patrick) and Michael (Christopher Mitchum, Robert's son). Michael is an interesting addition to the story. Dressed in flat cap and goggles, Michael rides an incongruous, high-performance motorcycle through the well-staged action scenes (like Steve McQueen in *The Great Escape*) and is armed with a telescopic sighted sniper's rifle and a 1911 prototype Bergmann automatic pistol. In a running gag, everyone who crosses Jake's path comments, 'I thought you were dead' ('That'll be the day,' answers Wayne at one point, an echo from *The Searchers*), while villain Boone wears a poncho (like Clint Eastwood) and genial Ford actor Harry Carey Jnr plays a sneering killer with a baccy-stained beard.

Mark Rydell's *The Cowboys*, made in April 1971 at the San Cristobal ranch near Santa Fe, and Pagosa Springs, Colorado, grossed $7.5 million. Burt Kennedy's *The Train Robbers* and Andrew V. McLaglan's *Cahill United States Marshal* (both Durango-shot Batjac productions released in 1973), had Wayne on auto pilot, with a resultant drop in the takings. *Cahill* saw the sons of lawman Wayne turn bad through neglect; *Train Robbers* was a treasure hunt for half a million dollars in gold, starring Ann-Margret, Rod Taylor and Ben Johnson, its eerie climax featuring the discovery of a locomotive half-buried in a sand dune.

Even as his health deteriorated, Wayne diversified into *Dirty Harry* cop thrillers (*McQ* and *Brannigan*) and made a *True Grit* sequel, *Rooster Cogburn* (1975), co-starring Katherine Hepburn, which took $8 million. But it was fitting that his western hero would have one last hurrah. In an interview in 1967 for *Western Stars of Television and Film Annual*, Wayne noted, 'I don't act – I react. I try to give each character I play a code of ethics. He may be brutal, but he's a real man, and I like playing *real* men, wearing buckskins instead of striped pants. I shall continue to do so even when they have to lift me into the saddle.'

In his last film, *The Shootist* (1976), Wayne played John Bernard Books. Realising that he's dying of cancer (as Wayne now was in reality), gunfighter Books arrives in Carson City, Nevada on 22 January 1901 and spends the last week of his life staying at a boarding house run by widow Bond Rogers (Lauren Bacall) and her son Gillom (Ron Howard, from TV's *Happy Days*). Books passes the time, enjoying a buggy ride with Bond and talking to Gillom about gunfighting and his code of honour ('I won't be wronged, I won't be insulted and I won't be laid a hand on'), while buffering his agony with the opium painkiller, laudanum. No longer a big tough gunman, Books is now 'a dying man, scared of the dark'. Wishing to avoid a long, painful death, Books makes his funeral arrangements and orders a headstone. On the morning of 29 January, his birthday, he arranges to meet three of his old enemies in the Metropole bar: Mike Sweeney (Richard Boone, from *Big Jake*), Jack Pulford (Hugh O'Brian) and J. Cobb (Bill McKinney) to settle old scores. In the shootout, Books kills all three, but is shot-gunned in the back by the barman. Gillom picks up Books's pistol and avenges his hero, who got his wish and died with his boots on.

Prospective actors for the lead role of Books included George C. Scott, Charles Bronson, Paul Newman, Gene Hackman and even Clint Eastwood, until Wayne took the role. *The Shootist* is the summation of Wayne's screen life; in France the film was released as *Le Dernier des Géants* ('The Last of the Giants'). The title sequence uses sepia-tinted shootout footage from Wayne's westerns (*Red River*, *Hondo*, *Rio Bravo* and *El Dorado*) as J.B. Books's 'greatest hits' from his career between 1871 and 1895. James Stewart appears as Doctor Hostatler, who diagnoses Books's cancer, and John Carradine (from *Stagecoach*) is undertaker Beckum. Produced by Paramount and Dino De Laurentiis, *The Shootist* was filmed in Carson City and at Burbank Studios' western street, with its horse-drawn trams ('Carson City Traction'), automobiles and telegraph poles. Books is lost in this modern world. Old friends from the past surface to try to make a buck out of his legend (a biography, 'The Shootist – The Life and Bloody Times of J.B. Books'), but the gunman has too much integrity (though he jokingly introduces himself to Bond as 'William Hickok'). The added resonance of Wayne's own illness makes the drama very moving and, for John Wayne fans, very difficult to watch. Posters declared: 'He's got to face a gunfight once more...To live up to his legend once more...to win just one more time'. *The Shootist* took almost $6 million when it was released in August 1976.

After years of deafening shoot 'em ups, it seemed appropriate that in the autumn of 1976, Wayne made his last return to Monument Valley, for a series of commercials advertising Datril 500, a headache remedy. But the 'Big C', as Wayne called it, eventually caught up with him; he died on 11 June 1979 and was interred in Pacific View Memorial Park, Newport Beach, in an unmarked grave. For a man who for many epitomised everything that was great about America, the embodiment of the American dream and its values and ideals, Wayne has taken his place in history as one of the biggest stars of all time. You may disagree with his politics, but you'd be a fool to argue with the screen icon. He's liable to punch you.

19

'The End of the Line'

— *Once Upon a Time in the West* (1968)

Once Upon a Time in the West (1968)
Credits
DIRECTOR – Sergio Leone
EXECUTIVE PRODUCER – Fulvio Morsella
PRODUCER – Bino Cicogna
STORY – Sergio Leone, Bernardo Bertolucci and Dario Argento
SCREENPLAY – Sergio Donati and Sergio Leone
DIRECTOR OF PHOTOGRAPHY – Tonino Delli Colli
EDITOR – Nino Baragli
ART DIRECTOR – Carlo Simi
MUSIC – Ennio Morricone
Technicolor/Techniscope
A Rafran–San Marco Production
Released by Paramount Pictures
171 minutes (Restored Italian version)
Cast
    Claudia Cardinale (Jill McBain); Henry Fonda (Frank); Jason
    Robards (Manuel 'Cheyenne' Gutierrez); Charles Bronson
    (Harmonica); Gabriele Ferzetti (Mr Morton); Paolo Stoppa
    (Sam); Marco Zuanelli (Wobbles); Keenan Wynn (Marshal of
    Flagstone City); Frank Wolff (Brett McBain); Lionel Stander
    (Way station barman); Claudio Mancini (Harmonica's
    brother); Dino Mele (Young Harmonica); Enzo Santaniello
    (Timmy McBain); Marilu Carteny (Maureen McBain);
    Raffaella and Francesca Leone (Little girls looking out of
    train window); Giorgio Trestini and Luigi Ciavarro
    (Flagstone deputies); Luana Strode (Indian woman);
    Conrado Sanmartin (Leader of posse); Tullio Palmieri
    (Timber merchant); Renato Pinciroli (Elderly bidder at

auction); Frank's gang: Jack Elam (Snaky); Al Mulock
(Knuckles); Woody Strode (Stony); John Fredrick
(Lewton); Sergio Mendizabal (Jim); Michael Harvey
(Frank's lieutenant); Spartaco Conversi (Gunman with
white beard); Benito Stefanelli (Chequered jacket); Aldo
Berti (Dark-haired card player); Fabio Testi (Pink shirt);
Frank Braña (Pipe-smoker); Antonio Molino Rojo (Cigar-
smoker); Ivan Scratuglia (Nose-pusher); Cheyenne's Gang:
Aldo Sambrell (Cheyenne's lieutenant); Lorenzo Robledo
and Bruno Corazzari (gang members at way station)

*   *   *

Once Upon a Time in the West is an unusual international mix. Directed by Italian
Sergio Leone, it was financed by US Paramount Pictures, filmed in Utah, Almeria
and Rome, with US actors Henry Fonda, Jason Robards and Charles Bronson co-
starring with Italians Claudia Cardinale and Gabriele Ferzetti. If imitation is the
sincerest form of flattery, then Leone was the most esteemed film director of the
sixties. The popularity of his debut Western, *A Fistful of Dollars* (1964), turned Clint
Eastwood into a worldwide star and founded the 'spaghetti western' style. US
publicists called Eastwood's hero 'The Man With No Name', which became his
name. *Fistful*'s success ensured two sequels: *For a Few Dollars More* (1965) and *The
Good, the Bad and the Ugly* (1966). These films became very popular, resulting in
dozens of imitative European westerns. As Leone noted, 'They call me the father of
the Italian western. If so, how many sons-of-bitches have I spawned?' Conservative
estimates exceed 500.

In *Fistful* Eastwood faced gunrunners and liquor smugglers in the Mexican border
town of San Miguel. In *For a Few* he joined up with Colonel Mortimer, a Wyatt
Earp-style bounty hunter (Lee Van Cleef – armed with a Buntline Special), to track
down a reefer-smoking killer, El Indio (Gian Maria Volonte) and his cadre of wanted
bandidos. In *The Good*, Leone's most successful film, Eastwood was pitted against
Mexican bandit Tuco (Eli Wallach) and hired gun Angel Eyes (Van Cleef again), as he
tried to locate a Confederate army payroll buried in Sad Hill Cemetery during the
American Civil War. After staging epic-scale Civil War battles to the north of Madrid,
Leone's next project was even more ambitious. There were rumours in the press
that Leone was to remake *Gone With the Wind*. Instead he embarked on *C'era Una
Volta il West* ('Once Upon a Time There was the West'). The original story was
written early in 1967 by Leone with Bernardo Bertolucci and Dario Argento, two
budding film directors. Sergio Donati, working with Leone, turned it into a
screenplay, with Mickey Knox providing an English translation before filming began.

In Arizona, during the hectic railroad boom of the 1880s, newlywed easterner
Jill McBain, an ex-prostitute, arrives in Flagstone City. She finds that her husband
Brett and his family have been murdered by hired killer Frank, who guns down
'obstacles' for railroad magnate Mr Morton. Morton wants McBain's Sweetwater

ranch and its precious wells. During Jill's stay at the ranch, she tries to unmask her husband's murderer and comes into contact with Cheyenne (an outlaw on the run, who has been falsely blamed for the McBain killings) and Harmonica (who has a score to settle with Frank). Morton buys off Frank's gang and turns them against their boss, but Frank survives the ambush in Flagstone. Cheyenne is captured and while he's being transported to Yuma prison on Morton's train, his renegades attack, freeing the outlaw and killing Morton. At Sweetwater, Frank discovers that he lynched Harmonica's older brother and Harmonica kills Frank in a duel. As the first locomotive pulls into the newly built station, Harmonica rides away with Cheyenne, who dies from wounds suffered in the Morton raid, while Jill stays on at Sweetwater.

Leone had wanted to cast Henry Fonda as 'The Man With No Name' in *Fistful*, but Fonda was too big a star for Leone's $200,000, shot-in-Spain production. By *Once Upon a Time*, Leone had an international reputation and a $3 million budget. Fonda screened the 'Dollars' trilogy before agreeing to star, against type, as Frank, the railroad's killer for hire. 'I once shot poor Jimmy Stewart in the leg deliberately (in *Firecreek* [1968]), and that was bad enough, heaven knows,' remembered Fonda, 'But now I kill a little boy in cold blood ... what am I coming to?' Actually, Fonda's big-screen appeal had dropped during the sixties. He'd been guest-starring in big-budget, 'all-star' movies (*The Longest Day*, *How the West Was Won*, *The Dirty Game*), had his own western TV series (*The Deputy*, 1959–1961) and appeared in the David Frost anchor role in the 1965 US pilot for *That Was the Week That Was*.

Charles Bronson was cast as his adversary, avenger Harmonica; Fonda and Bronson had appeared together as allies in *The Battle of the Bulge* (1965). Tunisia-born actress Claudia Cardinale had starred in Luchino Visconti's *The Leopard* (1961) and Fellini's *8 1/2* (1963), as well as commercial hits like *The Pink Panther* (1963); she had also starred in some western-themed movies: *The Magnificent Showman* (1964 – depicting a wild-west show touring Spain) and *The Professionals* (1966). Jason Robards was a Broadway actor, who moved into films in 1959; he'd appeared with Fonda in the cardsharp comedy *Big Deal at Dodge City* (1966) and played Doc Holliday in *Hour of the Gun* (1967). Leone cast him as Manuel 'Cheyenne' Gutierrez, the haggard, nostalgic Mexican bandit – something of a departure for Robards. Gabriele Ferzetti, a popular Italian actor who had appeared in *L'Avventura* (1960), was cast as Morton; Robert Hussein passed on the role, due to a theatre engagement. Ferzetti had to wear a heavy leather corset, restricting his movements, to replicate Morton's tubercular condition. Paolo Stoppa appeared as buggy driver, Sam. US 'guest stars' Frank Wolff, Lionel Stander and Keenan Wynn played farmer Brett McBain, a barman and the Flagstone City marshal respectively (the original choice for the marshal was Robert Ryan). Woody Strode, Jack Elam and Al Mulock were Stony, Snaky and Knuckles, the trio of gunmen waiting to murder Harmonica at Cattle Corner station; Strode's wife, Luana, played the Indian woman in the same scene. Leone's daughters Raffaella and Francesca can be seen looking out of a train carriage window at Flagstone City station.

Leone filmed from April to July 1968, first at Cinecitta Studios in Rome for interiors, then on location. The crew travelled to the ochre deserts of Almeria, where

Flagstone City was designed and built by Carlo Simi, for $250,000, beside the Guadix-Almeria railroad at Estacion La Calahorra. In the original script, the town was called Abilene. A banner on a half-built theatre advertises: 'Metropolitan Life Unveiled by the Cosmopolitan Theatre: Fantastic Foods from Paris – Opening Soon'. Flagstone's population was played by local expatriate Americans and northern Europeans, who were paid $14 a day. Cattle Corner station, with its squeaky windmill, leaky water tower, sea of platform sleepers and empty cattle pens, was filmed further down the track. McBain's alpine-style Sweetwater farm was constructed near Tabernas. The Gold Coin Saloon bar, the auction room and Jill's Palace Hotel accommodation were on set in Almeria, as was the interior of Sweetwater. All the railway sequences were filmed in Spain, with two existing Spanish locomotives disguised as 'A. & P.H. Morton' trains. Locomotive No. 71 drops Harmonica off at Cattle Corner and also brings Jill to Flagstone. Train tickets featured in the film note that the line travels between 'Flag Stone' and 'Santa Fe', with stops including Aubrey City, Prescott and Albuquerque.

In July, Leone travelled to Monument Valley for some key sequences. Jill's buggy ride to Sweetwater was filmed in Monument Valley itself. In the first shot she passes Sentinel Mesa (with Big Chief and Castle Rock in the distance), then heads towards East and West Mitten, and Merrick Butte. Morton's rail gangs work near the Totem Pole and Yei Bi Chei monuments, in the shadow of Thunderbird Mesa (with Rain God Mesa to their backs). Jill then passes an array of Fordian icons: Three Sisters, Mitchell Mesa and the 'Ford Point' promontory, Merrick Butte, the two Mittens and Elephant Butte (with Big Chief and Castle Rock in the background). The way station exterior was built in the valley, between Merrick Butte and East Mitten (with Sentinel Mesa, King-on-his-Throne, Castle Rock and Stagecoach on the north-eastern horizon). The station's interior was filmed at Cinecitta, including such details as the sign on the bar 'Kitchen – Keep the Hell Out – This Means You' and authentic red dust actually brought over from Utah. Frank's hideout at Navajo Cliff, a mountainous pueblo Indian cave dwelling, was filmed at Kayenta, Arizona; the interior, with its suspended bed, was at Cinecitta. The most famous scene shot in Monument Valley was the flashback depicting a lynching from a huge, specially constructed sandstone brick archway, with a panorama of the northern valley looming in the far distance. Harmonica's brother has his head in a noose, suspended from the archway bell; young Harmonica bears the weight of his brother, who is standing on his shoulders, while Frank and his four men enjoy the endurance test. Frank pushes a harmonica into the boy's mouth and tells him, 'Keep your loving brother happy,' until Harmonica can't support his brother any longer. He crumples into the dust and the bell tolls (this grotesque torture had previously appeared in Tinto Brass's western *Yankee* [1966]). John Wayne once said that it would be sacrilege for anyone but John Ford to use Monument Valley, so associated with him was the location, but Leone, much as he admired Ford, did use it.

Composer Ennio Morricone wrote much of the music for *Once Upon a Time* before Leone shot the film, so the director was able to play it on set to establish mood. Two of the pieces are among Morricone's most popular of all time: the main orchestral theme (still a standard of Morricone's live concerts) and the scything 'Man With a Harmonica'. The former is used when Jill arrives at Flagstone City station and during the end titles as the train arrives in Sweetwater. Initially a tinkling melody, it develops into a lush orchestration, with soaring violins and soprano soloist Edda Dell'Orso's floating vocal. 'Jill's America', reorchestrated for cor anglais and French horn, scores Jill's buggy ride in Monument Valley. For Jill's arrival in town, Leone used a Chapman crane; the camera rises from the station platform, over the shingle roof, revealing bustling Flagstone City beyond, with the music swelling as the camera reaches its apex. 'Man With a Harmonica' is used in its entirety at the McBain massacre, as Frank and his gang stride towards the ranch, with their long duster coats flapping in the wind, to finish the job, murdering little Timmy. Beginning with a sawing, discordant harmonica (played by Franco De Gemini), the tune has layers that uncoil like a snake, rising in intensity, until the electric guitar and syncopated strings burst through, as the piece becomes a macabre march, with chorus, strings and drums. The root guitar melody of this becomes Frank's theme, 'As a Judgement', played on electric guitar or horn and can be heard when Frank rides across the plain towards Morton's devastated train and arrives at Sweetwater for the settling of accounts. These reorchestrations resemble Alessandro Marcello's adagio 'Oboe Concerto in D Minor', with its descending strings and ascending oboe. 'Man With a Harmonica' is also used for the final duel between Frank and Harmonica, their two themes linked within the piece. In the film, Harmonica plays a Hohner Marine Band diatonic harmonica; in a continuity error during the lynching flashback, the instrument has various dents in the cover, which are repaired in the next shot. 'The Transgression', all eerie piano and death-rattle percussion, scores Frank's gunfight with his own traitorous men in Flagstone City, while the honky-tonk 'Bad Orchestra', with oompah brass, piano and swanny whistle, plays as new arrivals disembark at Flagstone station. 'Adios Cheyenne' is a clippety-clop theme with electric piano, banjo and whistler, while the ebbing piano and strings of 'Morton', echoing his dream of reaching the Pacific, is one of Morricone's most understated, moving compositions.

Leone, Bertolucci and Argento watched the cream of classic Hollywood westerns as they wrote the story outline and many references crept into the film. The opening scene resembles *High Noon* and Leone's photography of desert railroad tracks recalls *Bad Day at Black Rock*. There are references (names, places or whole scenes) from *Shane*, *Warlock*, *Texas Lady*, 'The Railroad' section of *How the West Was Won*, *Man With the Gun*, *My Darling Clementine*, *Ride Lonesome*, *The Searchers*, *The Comancheros*, *Ride the High County*, *The Big Country* and *The Violent Men*. Leone's most obvious influences are *The Iron Horse* (though there are no Cheyenne attacks, cattle drives, buffalo hunts or track laying races here) and *Johnny Guitar*, with the railway land-grabbing plot and a determined female protagonist teamed with a musical gunman; Johnny's guitar is replaced by Harmonica's mouth organ. There is even a model town at McBain's, and Morton has a model train, while snatches of dialogue from *Johnny Guitar* ('Can you play?', 'Can you dance?') are recycled by Leone and Donati.

Costumes and props also reappeared from Hollywood westerns – Leone imported outfits from Western Costume in the US. Cheyenne's men wear ankle-length duster coats, which were worn in Ford's *My Darling Clementine*, *The Man Who Shot Liberty Valance* and *Straight Shooting*, in the latter, by an outlaw called Cheyenne Harry. Frank's gang disguise themselves in these distinctive coats in an attempt to blame Cheyenne for Harmonica's ambush and the McBain massacre – a duster's collar is found on a nail by the door of the ranch. Woody Strode uses a sawn-off Winchester, like the one used on TV by Steve McQueen in *Wanted: Dead or Alive*. Some critics have dismissed Leone's film as nothing more than a roll-call of fragments of other westerns, in the way Quentin Tarantino plays 'spot the movie reference' throughout his oeuvre.

Jill is the only female protagonist in Leone's westerns and Cardinale's performance is the finest of her career. Jill is defending her dead husband's dream of building the town of Sweetwater, but when she first arrives, having been a prostitute in the most 'elegant whorehouse on Bourbon Street', New Orleans, she can't even light a fire in the grate at Sweetwater – she concludes that 'a quiet simple country life' isn't for her. Cheyenne recognises his own mother in Jill's strength and with Harmonica, protects her from Frank's men. As Jill becomes used to the west, she is finally ready to run Sweetwater station, which according to the small print in her husband's land deal, must be built by the time the railroad arrives. When the first train comes in, she

Monument Valley, the setting for seven of John Ford's celebrations of American history, was used by Sergio Leone as the backdrop to his cynical demolition of wild-west myths. Seen here are the iconic West Mitten and Merrick Butte as they appear today. (Photograph courtesy of Victoria Millington and Mark Chester.)

is the railroad workers' first contact with civilisation. Jill shares Brett's 'dream of a lifetime' and Sweetwater will grow around her. Harmonica and Cheyenne must move on. Civilisation doesn't suit them – they must stay ahead of the railroad's tendrils. In Leone's west, life is cheap, land expensive.

Parallel to Jill's stand against the railroad barons, Leone tells the story of Harmonica's revenge. Harmonica has arranged to meet Frank at Cattle Corner station, but three of his henchmen lurk instead. When Frank comes face to face with Harmonica, the avenger notes, 'Your friends have a high mortality rate... first three, then two.'; 'So you're the one who makes appointments,' says Frank. 'And you're the one who doesn't keep them.' The hired gun asks Harmonica's name; he replies with a list of men killed by Frank, 'They were all alive until they met you.' This 'man with no name' appropriates the names of the dead. The US trailer calls Harmonica: 'The Man in Search of a Name', pressbook cast-lists bill him simply as: 'The Man', while the *New York Times* noted he was: 'en route from nowhere to nowhere, a kind of Flying Dutchman of the plains'. At three moments in the film, Harmonica experiences blurred flashbacks of a figure slowly emerging from a desert landscape; in the final reckoning we discover it's Frank. Since the death of his brother, Harmonica has been emotionally dead. As Cheyenne says, 'People like that have something inside, something to do with death,' which became the title of Christopher Frayling's 2001 biography of Leone. Much of Bronson's dialogue was cut during the making of the film, which makes his character even more mysterious, while his sawing harmonica becomes a requiem for those who hear it.

Frank was hired 'to remove small obstacles from the track', so that snail 'Mr Choo Choo' can leave behind his slime: 'Two beautiful shiny rails.' Morton had instructed Frank to frighten McBain, but Frank reasons, 'People scare better when they're dying.' Frank plays 'businessman', sitting behind Morton's desk in the opulent railway carriage, 'It's almost like holding a gun, only much more powerful.' Later, Morton gestures to Frank's Peacemaker, 'There are many kinds of weapons and the only one that can stop that is this' – as he holds up a wad of $100 bills. 'My weapons might look simple to you Mr Morton, but they can still shoot holes big enough for our little problems.' Eventually their partnership sours. Frank becomes preoccupied with Jill and Sweetwater, while Morton has vowed, 'Before my eyes rot I want to see the blue of the Pacific.' As Frank usurps Morton's position, Morton decides to buy off Frank's men to kill their boss. By the time Frank realises he's not a businessman after all ('Just a man'), he finds Morton mortally wounded in the desert. Stranded outside his carriage, Morton is helpless, beached, as he crawls pitifully towards a puddle of spring water beside the railroad tracks. Leone overdubs crashing waves – the Pacific of Morton's imagination.

If Leone and Donati's script is taciturn – there were only 14 pages of dialogue in the 420-page treatment – Tonino Delli Colli's cinematography speaks volumes. The opening scene, with three men waiting at Cattle Corner station, lasts 12 and a half minutes and incorporates the lengthiest title sequence in film history. Having locked up the station agent, the trio idly passes time. Snaky pulls out the wires of the chattering telegraph and catches a bothersome fly in his pistol barrel (Elam's beard was smeared with honey to attract flies for the scene). Knuckles leans against a trough and loudly cracks his knuckle bones, while Stony stands beneath the leaking water tower and catches dripping water in his hat, then drinks the water that has collected in his hat brim. When the train arrives, no one disembarks, but as the engine pulls out a wailing harmonica announces Bronson, standing on the other side of the track. 'And Frank?' Harmonica enquires, 'Frank sent us,' answers Snaky. 'Did you bring a horse for me?' asks Harmonica. 'Well,' smiles Snaky, 'Looks like we're shy one horse.' Harmonica shakes his head, 'You brought two too many,' before gunning down the trio.

This languorous narrative continues throughout the film, stretching time, then disorientatingly telescoping it. The massacre at Sweetwater has a long build-up, as Brett McBain and his three children from a previous marriage prepare a wedding celebration for Jill's arrival. Frank and his four killers strike from the undergrowth, shooting Brett and his children, Maureen and Patrick. Timmy, the youngest, emerges from the farmhouse, clutching a bottle of blue liquid, to be greeted with the sight of his family's corpses, as Frank's men, in long dusters, stride towards the house. 'What are we going to do with this one Frank?' asks one of his henchmen (Michael Harvey); 'Now that you've called me by name,' says Frank, drawing his pistol and ensuring there'll be no witnesses. When Jill disembarks at Flagstone, Leone fills the screen with detail (well-to-do passengers, black porters, a prospector, a child in a wheelchair, Indians trying to steal feed sacks), then time passes in an instant. Leone films the station clock (reading 7.55) and cuts to Cardinale; in the next shot, she looks at her watch, which indicates 11.20. The platform is now empty and no one has met her. When Frank faces his men in Flagstone, the cagey showdown is protracted, as the hired gun picks his way through the streets to his horse. Harmonica, his guardian angel, helps Frank survive. Jill berates

Artwork from the original Italian poster for *C'era Un Volta il West* depicting Jill (Claudia Cardinale), Frank (Henry Fonda), Harmonica (Charles Bronson), Morton (Gabriele Ferzetti) and Cheyenne (Jason Robards), as three of Frank's men bite the dust at Cattle Corner Station.

Harmonica for saving Frank's life. 'I didn't let them kill him,' Harmonica tells her, 'And that's not the same thing.' The final confrontation between Harmonica and Frank is a familiar Leone duel, with music and image achieving synergy. 'Future don't matter to us,' says Frank to Harmonica, 'Nothing matters now: not the land, not the money, not the woman. I came here to see you, 'cause I know that now you'll tell me what you're after.' Leone films the duo, with huge close-ups of Harmonica's eyes as the two protagonists circle each other. The face-off is intercut with a flashback to the fateful lynching, identifying the mysterious avenger to Frank, but as Harmonica says, 'Only at the point of dying,' from a bullet to the heart.

In Almeria, Sergio Donati pruned the script to remove its longueurs, with dialogue explaining missing plot points shifted elsewhere. Several scenes were removed: Jill hiring Sam to drive her out to the farm; Harmonica being beaten up by three deputies in Wobbles's Chinese laundry and then questioned by the sheriff in a stable about his involvement in the McBain massacre; a meeting between Jill and banker O'Leary, where she reads the deeds to Sweetwater; and Frank having a shave before the bogus auction of Sweetwater. In the release version of the film, Harmonica has facial scars from his beating, while Frank suddenly looks washed and shaved during the showdown in Flagstone. In *My Darling Clementine* Fonda has a haircut and shave before the Tombstone church dance; as Frank, he was to have a cut and shave before a Flagstone gunfight.

C'era Una Volta il West was released in Italy on 21 December 1968. This version, now restored in Italy on DVD, runs at 171 minutes and features numerous additions that don't appear in any other release, including extra or alternate shots, lengthened scenes, added dialogue (Harmonica offers to scrub Jill's back at one point) and different musical cues. For example, the opening scene at Cattle Corner station, Jill's discovery of the wooden Sweetwater models, Frank facing his men in Flagstone and the final duel, are all longer and the pace is slower, the camera lingering on frozen groups of figures and portraits. The most noticeable difference is the end titles. The spiralling 'ONCE UPON A TIME IN THE WEST' appears in the English language print when the train arrives at Sweetwater; 'C'ERA UNA VOLTA IL WEST' appears after Bronson has ridden away into the Almerian landscape.

The film was dubbed into Italian, German, French, Spanish and English. For the English release Fonda, Bronson, Robards, Elam, Wynn, Wolff and Stander used their own voices, Bernard Grant dubbed Ferzetti, while his wife Joyce Gordon re-voiced Cardinale. Though not as successful as the 'Dollars' trilogy in Italy, the film was still very popular, especially in France, where the dusters became the height of fashion and the film became a long-running blockbuster in 1969, mainly due to Bronson's popularity. In Spain it was released in 1970 as *Hasta Que Llego Su Hora* ('Until the Hour Arrives'), while in Germany it was *Spiel mir das Lied vom Tod* ('Play Me the Song of Death'). In the German-language release, Frank tells young Harmonica, 'Spiel me das lied vom tod' as he puts the harmonica in the boy's mouth. When Harmonica later pushes the instrument into Frank's mouth, Harmonica repeats these words and for German record releases, Harmonica's theme was called 'Das Lied vom Tod'. Harald Greve of *Filmkritik* gave *Once Upon a Time* two-and-a-half stars in September 1969, while Wim Wenders, writing in November for *Filmkritik*, titled his review 'Vom Traum zum Trauma – Der fürchterliche western' ('From Dream to Trauma – the awful western'). Famously, he complained that he 'felt like a tourist in a western' and was irate that it featured 'Monument Valley, the real Monument Valley, not a pasteboard replica propped up from behind, no, the genuine article, in America'.

For its US release in May 1969, Paramount shortened the film by 22 minutes. Five scenes were cut, including Harmonica getting to his feet, proving he survived Stony's bullet at Cattle Corner; the entire way station scene where Jill, Cheyenne and Harmonica first meet (thus removing barman Lionel Stander from the film); the scene with Morton at Frank's cliffside hideout; and Cheyenne's death (as he and Harmonica ride away from Sweetwater). These scenes have since been reinstated, with UK/US DVD releases 158 minutes long (this restored version was finally released into US cinemas in 1984). In the US the film was rated 'M' (for Mature Audiences), then re-rated 'PG' when cut; in the UK it was rated 'AA'. The English-language trailer outlined its epic scope: 'The railroad, the boomtowns, a new life and the promised land – a manhunt, a vendetta, in a new land, in a new kind of western'. Poster art featured the dubious tagline, referring to Jill: 'There were three men in her life. One to take her...one to love her and one to kill her'. *Time* called the film: 'Tedium in the Tumbleweed' and said that 'the intent is operatic, but the effect is soporific'. The *Washington Post* said: 'We have the best of the two worlds with Leone – he loves his tradition, but can't pretend to believe in it', while film director Alex Cox has called it, 'The longest art western of all time'. Vincent Canby in the *New York Times* wrote that the film was 'quite bad' but 'almost always interesting, wobbling as it does between being an epic lampoon and a serious homage'. *Hang 'Em High*, Eastwood's first western without Leone, released stateside in July 1968, took $6.8 million; *Once Upon a Time in the West*, Leone's first western without Eastwood, took $1 million.

Unlike the 'Dollars' films, *Once Upon a Time in the West* wasn't influential on mainstream Italian cinema, though *C'era una Volta questo Pazzo Pazzo West* (1973) parodies its title. Literally 'Once Upon a Time this Mad Mad West', though more often referred to as *Once Upon a Time in the Wild, Wild West*, this 'comedy' is rated by most aficionados as the bottom of the Euro-barrel. In France, Leone's *Duck You Sucker* (1971 – also released as *A Fistful of Dynamite*) was retitled *Il était une Fois...la Révolution* ('Once Upon a Time...the Revolution'). Tonino Valerii, who had worked with Leone on the 'Dollars' films, recycled Leone's Flagstone City set as Dallas in *The Price of Power* (1969), his JFK-inspired tale of presidential assassination and corruption set in 1880s Texas. *Once Upon a Time in the West* proved to be the beginning of Leone's second trilogy, following the 'old west' of the 'Dollars' films. It was completed by *Duck You Sucker*, which depicts the Mexican Revolution, and *Once Upon a Time in America* (1984), charting the rise of New York gangsters, bringing the story of America into the modern era; *America* ends in 1968, the same year Leone directed his epic western fairytale.

It has been many years since the arrival of Morton's train, but Sweetwater still stands – the set was built from hefty timber left over from Orson Welles's *Chimes at Midnight* (1966) and it's now a Spanish tourist attraction called 'Rancho Leone'. Unfortunately Flagstone City has fallen into ruinous disrepair. Many critics now see *Once Upon a Time in the West* as the last truly classical western and Leone as the last master craftsman of the genre. Fonda once told James Coburn that Leone was the finest director he had ever worked with. At the end of Leone's railway tracks, where the wild west no longer exists, the archway bell tolls the death knell of the western. For many, *Once Upon a Time in the West* is the end of the line.

20

'The Fastest Finger in the West'

— *Support Your Local Sheriff!* (1969)

Support Your Local Sheriff! (1969)
Credits
DIRECTOR – Burt Kennedy
PRODUCERS – William Bowers and William Finnegan
STORY AND SCREENPLAY – William Bowers
DIRECTOR OF PHOTOGRAPHY – Harry Stradling Jnr
EDITOR – George W. Brooks
ART DIRECTOR – Leroy A. Coleman
MUSIC – Jeff Alexander
Technicolor
A Cherokee Production
Released by United Artists
93 minutes
Cast
>   James Garner (Sheriff Jason McCullough); Joan Hackett
>   (Prudy Perkins); Walter Brennan (Pa Danby); Harry Morgan
>   (Mayor Olly Perkins), Jack Elam (Deputy Jake); Henry Jones
>   (Councillor Henry Jackson); Bruce Dern (Joe Danby); Willis
>   Bouchey (Thomas Devery, mine owner); Gene Evans (Tom
>   Danby); Dick Peabody (Luke Danby); Walter Burke (Councillor
>   Fred Johnson); Chubby Johnson (Brady); Kathleen Freeman
>   (Mrs Danvers); Dick Haynes (Bartender in Mint Saloon); Paul
>   Sorenson (Bricklayer); Richard Hoyt (First hired gun); Tom
>   Reese (Second hired gun); John Milford (Third hired gun)

*   *   *

The clichéd ingredients of a good western are instantly recognisable, which also
makes them easy targets for ridicule and parody. Comedy westerns populated by

bumbling heroes, crooked sheriffs, hopeless outlaws and damsels in distress, are a sub-genre of their own and have presented the western with some of its biggest box-office successes. Among the funniest comedy westerns was Laurel and Hardy's *Way Out West* (1937), with Stan and Ollie delivering an inheritance to the wild-west town of Brushwood Gulch. *Destry Rides Again* (1939) too, featuring James Stewart as milk-drinking deputy Tom Destry and Marlene Dietrich as Frenchy, Bottleneck's resident hellcat, was a comedy western highlight. Other lesser examples include the Marx Brothers' *Go West* (1940) and Abbott and Costello's *Ride 'Em Cowboy* (1942).

Comedian Bob Hope made four popular westerns, including *The Paleface* (1948) and *Son of Paleface* (1952). In *Paleface*, Calamity Jane (Jane Russell) is released from prison for an undercover mission to unmask the gunrunners selling rifles and dynamite to the Indians. A federal agent, she poses as the wife of 'Painless' Peter Potter (Hope), an inept eastern dentist, so she can travel incognito with a wagon train. Potter inadvertently saves the wagon train from Indian attack, Calamity actually does the shooting, but the pair are eventually captured by the hostiles; Potter is about to be torn in half between two trees ('Maybe in the next world you'll meet two nice fellas,' he tells Calamity, 'Look close – they'll both be me'), before escaping and foiling the gunrunners' scheme.

Predominately shot on Paramount Studios interior sound stages, *Paleface* was directed by Norman Zenos McLeod (who had directed the Marx Brothers) and co-scripted by Frank Tashlin (a cartoonist, who had worked for Disney). In one scene, Potter is having a shave near a cabin in a pine wood, when he catches sight of an Indian disguised as a bush stealthily moving through the undergrowth ('Must be a Virginia Creeper,' cracks Hope). His dental practice provides further humour (including an extraction involving a hammer and chisel, and laughing gas), while the film features the Oscar-winning song, 'Buttons and Bows' ('A western ranch is just a branch of nowhere junction to me; give me the city, where living is pretty and the girls wear finery') and Hope's garbling of western slang ('He plumb riled me'). In the best scene, Potter has been challenged to face gunslinger Joe (Jeff York) in a gundown at sundown. Three patrons of the Dirty Shame saloon tip off Potter about Joe's gunfighting tricks, 'He draws from the left, so lean to the right.'; 'There's a wind from the east, so you better aim to the west.'; 'He crouches when he shoots, so stand on your toes.' Potter struggles to remember the advice as he walks down the street to face Joe, reciting his own jumbled version, 'He draws from the left, so stand on your toes…there's a wind from the east, better lean to the right…he stands on his crouch with his toes in the wind.'

Hope followed *Paleface*, which took $4.5 million in the US, with *Fancy Pants* (1950), appearing as wild cowgirl Lucille Ball's butler, then *Son of Paleface*. Junior Potter (Hope), an idiot Harvard grad, arrives in the western town of Sawbuck Pass to claim his inheritance. His father was 'Paleface' Potter, the great Indian fighter. A statue bears the inscription 'He Won the West'; 'He was using loaded dice,' Junior observes. Federal agent Roy (singing cowboy Roy Rogers, with a rifle hidden in his guitar) is also in town investigating 'The Torch', an outlaw who has been knocking off gold shipments in the locality – wealthy saloon owner Mike (Jane Russell) is revealed to be the Torch's alter ego. *Son of Paleface* was directed and co-written by Tashlin in cartoonish style, with speeded-up sight gags. It featured several songs, including a revamp of 'Buttons and Bows', Russell's rendition of 'Wing-Ding Tonight', and Rogers's 'Four-Legged Friend', sung to his smart steed, Trigger. Hope again mangles western dialect ('I was sashaying my maverick') as a dude in a land where 'men are men.' 'That's what she likes about me,' says Junior of Mike, 'I'm a novelty.' Not as funny as the original and less successful at the box office (there are too many musical interludes and Harvard in-jokes), the film revs up for a desert finale featuring an Indian attack, Junior's speeding jalopy (in a *Stagecoach* chase parody), two buzzards named 'Martin and Lewis', two penguins, Sterling City ghost town, a barber's chair, banana skins and a moose-head full of gold. 'Let's see 'em top this on television,' says Hope at 'The End'.

Alias Jesse James (1959), directed by McLeod, saw Hope as a life insurance salesman who has sold Jesse James a policy. The film is notable for cameo appearances by TV western regulars, including Ward Bond (*Wagon Train*), Hugh O'Brian (*The Life and Legend of Wyatt Earp*), James Arness (*Gunsmoke*) and James Garner (*Maverick*), plus Gene Autry, Gary Cooper, Bing Crosby and Roy Rogers. Crosby's own *Rhythm on the Range* (1936) was remade by Jerry Lewis and Dean Martin as *Pardners* (1956). Other western comedies of the period include *Once Upon a Horse* (1958) starring soon-to-be *Laugh In* stars Dan Rowan and Dick Martin, Phil Silvers's *The Slowest Gun in the West* (1960), Duccio Tessari's underrated *Seven Guns for the MacGregors* (1965), *Carry on Cowboy* (1966), where Johnny Finger alias 'The Rumpo Kid' (Sid James) terrorised Stodge City, and *The Outlaws is Coming* (1965), with Larry, Curly Joe and Moe in their last screen appearance – the film is also known by the tell-all title *The Three Stooges Meet the Gunslinger*.

But it was Elliot Silverstein's *Cat Ballou* (1965) that reinvigorated comedy westerns. Jane Fonda starred as Catherine Ballou, a schoolteacher who becomes 'Queen of the Outlaws'. She returns from finishing school to Wolf City, Wyoming, to find her father Frankie (John Marley) threatened by ruthless developers who want his water rights; they hire killer Tim Strawn, who shoots Frankie dead. Cat writes to dime novel hero Kid Sheleen for help, but when he arrives, Sheleen is a washed-up drunkard. With aid from two rogues, Clay Boone and his Uncle Jed (a bogus priest with a Derringer hidden in his Bible), and Sioux Jackson Two-Bears, Cat's gang strike back at Wolf City. She aims to make 'Sherman's march to the sea look like a bird walk' and robs a payroll train. Kid Sheleen dries out long enough to kill Strawn, who is actually his brother, and Cat poses as prostitute 'Trixie' to shoot Sir Harry Percival, the head of the developers, for which she is sentenced to be hanged.

What makes the film memorable is Lee Marvin's terrific turn as Kid Sheleen, the buckskinned, unshaven bum (he can't even hit a barn when sober), who transforms into a wisecracking, cracker-barrel gunslinger after a slug of liquor. Often too drunk to ride, he travels sprawled on a travois. Marvin also played mercenary Tim Strawn, in Jack Palance's wardrobe and fitted with a silver artificial nose. Cat's incompetent bandit gang use Sheleen's dime novel 'Massacre of Whiskey Slide' as an instruction manual, lifting his method of train robbery for their own heist. 'You did escape in that book, didn't you?' they check. The gang hides out at 'Hole-in-the-wall', where the outlaw heroes hiding there, including Butch Cassidy (played by Arthur Hunnicutt) are now too old to trouble the law, while Sheleen recalls that the O.K. Corral has been turned into a roller-skating rink. *Cat Ballou* is narrated by a series of ballads, sung by two on-screen troubadours (Nat King Cole and Stubby Kaye) and the climax has Cat rescued from hanging by her gang and escaping in a hearse. Sheleen has since fallen off the wagon – both he and his horse appear, slumped napping against a wall, the horse cross-legged, in the scene that will forever define the film. Marvin won the Best Actor Oscar for 1965 – in his speech he noted, 'Half of this probably belongs to a horse out there somewhere' – and the film took $9.3 million.

It was another four years before a comedy western scored such a hit, as John Wayne and Clint Eastwood's westerns dominated the US box office. Burt Kennedy's *Support Your Local Sheriff!* was a send-up of *Rio Bravo*, *High Noon* and *My Darling Clementine*. The story was written by William Bowers, who had co-written *The Gunfighter* (1950), plus screenplays for *The Law and Jake Wade* (1958), the Civil War comedy *Advance to the Rear* (1964) and Hope's *Alias Jesse James*. *Sheriff!* follows the adventures of Jason McCullough, who arrives in the boomtown of Calendar and takes the job of lawman, even though he stresses he is just on his way to Australia, where the real wild frontier is. Calendar is a rowdy mining town, ruled by the Danby family – Pa and his three sons Joe, Luke and Tom. Following a murder in the Mint Saloon, Jason throws guilty Joe in jail and uses brains rather than guns to keep the peace in his own inimitable way. This is no mean feat considering the newly built jail is still waiting for its iron bars and Jason's only help against the Danby clan is incompetent deputy Jake, formerly the 'town character'.

James Garner, cast as Jason, became a star via the comedy western TV series *Maverick* (1957–1962), where he played gambler Brett Maverick. The series is among the best TV westerns, but despite its great success, he left in 1960 to pursue a film career. Garner (real name James Scott Baumgarner) also started his own company, called 'Maverick', which became Cherokee Productions (the financiers of *Sheriff!*). Walter Brennan played Pa Danby, trying to release his son Joe (Bruce Dern) from jail. Brennan sent up his Old Man Clanton from *My Darling Clementine*, while Dern is the thickest jailbird ever put behind bars, or rather behind where the bars should be. In one scene, Brennan references his 'eatin' teeth' in a pouch from *Red River*, handing them over to his son for safekeeping prior to a shootout. Dern appeared in counterculture movies (like *The Wild Angels* [1966] and *Psych-Out* [1967]) and moved into westerns with *Waterhole #3*, *Hang 'Em High* (both 1967), *Will Penny* (1968) and Kennedy's *The War Wagon*. He later secured western infamy by shooting John Wayne dead in *The Cowboys* (1972). The other two Danby boys were played by Gene Evans (also from *The War Wagon*) and Dick Peabody, looking like Warren Oates, who was asked to appear in the film, but made *The Wild Bunch* instead.

The quartet of town dignitaries who hire Jason were played by Harry Morgan, Henry Jones, Willis Bouchey and Walter Burke. Morgan was a western regular from

The Ox-Bow Incident, *Yellow Sky*, *High Noon* and *Bend of the River*, who later went on to great success as Colonel Potter in TV's *M*A*S*H*. Henry Jones was the bicycle salesman in *Butch Cassidy and the Sundance Kid* and had appeared in *The Girl Can't Help It* (1956), *3:10 to Yuma* (1957) and *Vertigo* (1958); Bouchey and Burke had worked extensively on TV westerns. The mayor's accident-prone daughter Prudy Perkins, who falls for the new sheriff and at one point serves dinner with her dress on fire, was played by Joan Hackett. A former Broadway actress, she had appeared in the revisionist western *Will Penny*, as the nervous squatter Catherine Allen, who nurses the eponymous hero back to health. Jack Elam, a walk-on ruffian, hoodlum or gunslinger, was cast as stable hand Jake, a dimwit who finds himself in the firing line when he is appointed McCullough's deputy, 'Take it easy boys – me and the sheriff takes a dim view of show-offs with guns,' Jake warns a saloon rabble, unconvincingly.

Like *Cat Ballou*, *Support Your Local Sheriff!*'s exteriors were filmed at the Columbia-Warner Bros western backlot in Burbank. It was photographed in Technicolor in the screen ratio 1.85:1 and often looks like a TV western, but a very

Support Your Local Sherriff!: Jason McCullough (James Garner) supports Prudy Perkins (Joan Hackett) in the finale of Burt Kennedy's 1969 comedy hit, while the Calendar townsfolk (including Jack Elam, Willis Bouchey, Walter Burke, Henry Jones and Harry Morgan) look on.

well-produced one. The film begins on a note of grave seriousness: it's the funeral of Millard Frymore in the tiny mining camp of Calendar, accompanied by 'Rock of Ages' on the accordion. 'Origin unknown,' says the pastor, 'Cause of death unknown … and of considerable concern to those of us who were thrown into contact with him.' Then Prudy spots gold in the open grave and stakes her claim, triggering a Cherokee Land Rush parody straight out of *Cimarron*, behind the film's titles. Calendar is soon a boomtown, awash with mud and riffraff, and with upward spiralling inflation. Into this den of iniquity, where fortunes are made overnight and menu prices rise between mouthfuls, rides Jason, a notable departure from previous two-fisted, town tamers.

Jason is a drifter with a fast gun, but instead of being a noble 'righter-of-wrongs', he's on his way to Australia, to a life of pioneering in frontier country; 'I thought this was frontier country,' says Councillor Johnson, 'and we was pioneers.' Jason demonstrates his crack marksmanship to the dignitaries by shooting at a washer flicked into the air, claiming that the bullet passed right through the hole – only takes the job he receives a bullet-dented badge and is informed that the jail is equipped with all mod cons: 'Our last sheriff was a good organiser – yellow clean through, but a good organiser. The only thing it hasn't got is iron bars for the cells.' Jason draws a chalk line across the gaping hole in the wall and dribbles a messy blob of red paint just beyond the line, telling inmate Joe that the puddle is from the last prisoner who stepped over the line.

The Danbys are the most hopeless of outlaw clans – 'Out of the father and three brothers, [Joe's] about the second toughest,' but he's no match for Jason, who outwits him at every turn. Jason even convinces him that his pistol is empty. Joe whines to his pa, 'He lies to me about whether or not my gun is loaded.' 'He does what?' shouts exasperated Pa. When Pa confronts Jason in the Sheriff's Office, Jason calmly sticks his finger in the end of Pa's pistol, rendering it useless. Bested, Pa and his two sons discuss their next move in the saloon. 'What can he do against three of us?' asks Tom. 'He can kill two of us,' snaps Pa, who decides to hire three gunfighters to get rid of Jason. 'You always said the Danbys fight their own battles,' says Luke. 'Well maybe I was talking about another branch of the family,' Pa concedes. On his way to face the third of the hired killers, Jason is asked by Prudy, 'You gonna kill another man?' 'Well I'm sure we all hope it turns out that way.' In keeping with Danby tradition, the trio of hired guns fails and the clan members end up having to take care of the matter personally.

In the finale, the entire Danby clan, including Uncles Milt and Ira and their sons, head for town to storm the jail. Abandoned by the townsfolk (as in *High Noon*), with the help of dead-shot Prudy and Deputy Jake, Jason takes on the Danbys in a main street shootout. He outfoxes the outlaws, tying Joe across the barrel of a cannon and threatening to light the fuse unless the troublemakers disarm. In the familiar western fadeout, with the Danbys safely in jail (now fitted with bars), Deputy Jake fills in the story's end. Jason married Prudy, the wealthy, sole owner of the 'Millard Frymore Memorial Mining Company', and became state governor (never reaching Australia). 'Then I go on to become one of the most beloved characters in western folklore.'

Released in March 1969, *Support Your Local Sheriff!* was a big hit, taking $5.1 million in the US. 'Bad men…Bad Women…Bad Horses', smirked the posters, adding, 'Our Trouble-shooting Sheriff Always Puts his finger on it (or in it)'. The *New York Times* said the film: 'serves up dollop of three-line jokes' and scathingly noted that Burt Kennedy's westerns resembled Andrew V. McLaglen's: 'They are imitations of imitations'. Ad material christened Garner's hero: 'The Fastest Finger in the West'; in Italy, the film was known by that title, as *Il Dito più veloce del West*.

Kennedy and Garner followed *Sheriff!* with a sequel, *Support Your Local Gunfighter* (1971 – also called *Latigo*), again for Cherokee. Many of the *Sheriff!* cast returned, though in different roles. Garner was Latigo Smith, a gambling con man from New York. He arrives in Purgatory, where two gold mining companies are drilling towards the mother lode. Rumour has it that Colonel Ames, the leader of one faction, has sent for hired gunfighter Swifty Morgan. Taylor Barton, Ames's rival, mistakes Latigo for Swifty and tries to buy him off. Instead, Latigo somehow convinces the townsfolk that shambling layabout Jug May is Swifty and 'more than the stupid cowhand he looks like'. Their charade works well, until they discover that the real Morgan is as bald as an egg (Jug has a full head of hair) and is on his way to town to deal with the impostor. 'There are some things a man can't ride around,' says Latigo, quoting from Kennedy's own script to *Ride Lonesome*, 'Then again, maybe he can.'

This in-name-only sequel wasn't up to the original and was less successful at the box office. Harry Morgan played Taylor Barton, Henry Jones returned (as the Purgatory telegrapher) and Willis Bouchey and Walter Burke reappeared as town dignitaries. Latigo's love interest is tomboy Patience Barton (Suzanne Pleshette). A subplot sees Latigo attempting to have a gaudy tattoo ('I Love Goldie') removed from his chest. The 'real, genuine, one hundred percent, dyed-in-the-wool Swifty Morgan' was played by western hardman Chuck Connors, from *The Rifleman* and *Branded* TV series. The film's meandering narrative comes alive the moment Latigo puts his scheme into action. Jack Elam slopes off with the film as Jug, with his slouching walk, mean expression and growly delivery of lines like, 'Don't crowd my gun side.' Jug is a hopeless gunfighter, 'I'm slow, Jug,' says Latigo, 'But you're the slowest.' Latigo, his 'business manager', is always out to make a buck; he receives $5,000 from Barton as payment, but tells Jug they only received $1,000, which they'll split fifty-fifty: 'That means 400 for you.' As in *Sheriff!* Garner relies on his wits and wit to survive, knocking out a thug who challenges him to a gunfight, then breaking the man's right trigger finger with a flat iron, until Jug points out that the man is left-handed, so Latigo breaks the other one too. On Latigo's arrival in Purgatory by rail, Taylor Barton asks if he came on the train. 'D'you ever hear of an eagle picking up a grown man and carrying him across country?' 'No, I can't say that I have,' replies Barton. 'Well now you have: I come by eagle.' On its release in spring 1971, posters imitated *Sheriff!*'s marketing campaign, saying: 'The Fastest Finger in the West Returns with Dynamite!' in 'The Story of a Man Who Took the Law Into His Own Finger!' In the film's curtain line, Elam addresses the audience directly, 'And me, I go on to become a big star in Italian Westerns.'

Garner's next film was another Cherokee western, the social tragicomedy *Skin Game* (released in September 1971). Here Garner played Quincy Drew, teamed with

Lou Gossett as Jason O'Rourke, two con men roaming Missouri and Kansas in 1857. Jason poses as a slave; he's actually from 'the garden state of New Jersey'. Quincy sells him at auction, then returns later and frees his partner, pocketing the proceeds. The scam works until Jason is emancipated by John Brown (wild-haired Royal Dano), then captured by real slave dealer Plunkett (Edward Asner) and sold to a Texan plantation owner. The first half of the film is their 'Skin Game', with Jason as a fake slave; the second half depicts Quincy's search for his partner, now a real slave. Quincy is joined by pickpocketing con woman Ginger (Susan Clark) and the pair impersonate 'Captain Nathaniel Mountjoy' and 'Nurse Blodget', who disguise their search by claiming to be isolating slave victims with the 'Spasmodic Lung Pest' and leprosy.

Garner and Gossett are a great team, sparking real chemistry, and Gossett's 'act' as a slave at their bogus auctions elicits both laughs and sympathy, 'Please mas' Quincy, I don't need no *three* meals a day.' The film opens as a straight western, with Quincy leading Jason into Dirty Shame on a rope (accompanied by David Shire's haunting main theme, with wailing harmonica, bluegrass guitar, high-pitched strings and piano) and sells his friend in an impromptu auction for $400. Later Quincy recounts how they first met in jail: Quincy dressed in a turban as a fake fortune-teller, Jason as a pirate selling bogus treasure maps – a con match made in heaven. But the film is at its best when it concentrates on their humorous yet touching relationship, which dictates that Quincy will always be the seller and Jason the lot.

With the massive success on TV of series such as *Alias Smith and Jones*, the early seventies were something of a golden age for western comedy. Among the most successful films were *The Apple Dumpling Gang* (1974 – which took $16.5 million) and its sequel *The Apple Dumpling Gang Ride Again* (1979), family westerns from the Walt Disney studios. With *They Call Me Trinity*, Christmas 1970 saw the beginning of a fad for jokey Italian westerns, called 'fangioli' westerns in Italy, after the slovenly heroes' penchant for baked beans.

Garner followed *Skin Game* with *Nichols* (1971–1972, again produced by Cherokee), another western comedy series, before great success with his private eye *Rockford Files* teleseries (1974–1980). He also appeared as Wyatt Earp in the murder mystery western *Sunset* (1988), set in the world of twenties oaters (Bruce Willis played Tom Mix) and had a cameo as a marshal in the film version of *Maverick* (1994), which cast Mel Gibson in the title role. Director Kennedy remade *Skin Game* as TV movie, *Sidekicks* (1974). Larry Hagman played Quince Drew, Gossett Jnr reprised his role as Jason and the cast included Jack Elam, Harry Morgan and Noah Beery Jnr (later 'Rocky' Rockford, Garner's father, in *The Rockford Files*). Kennedy also made another TV movie western, *Shootout in a One-Dog Town* (1974) starring Richard Crenna, Stephanie Powers and Jack Elam. Striking a rich vein of comedy, Elam also played Kid Sheleen in a US TV pilot for the never-commissioned series *Cat Ballou* (1971).

One of the best and certainly the daftest TV comedy westerns of the period was Jerry Paris's little seen *Evil Roy Slade* (1972), played by John Astin (who'll 'never be as popular as Billy the Kid'). With its silly campfire ballads like 'Stubby Index Finger' ('lookin' like a toe'), pintsized railroad baron Nelson L. Stool (Mickey

Rooney) and relentless sight-gags, *Evil Roy Slade* equals Garner's movies for laughs. Slade falls for blonde Betty Potter (Pamela Austin), a former 'Miss Frontier', now a schoolteacher, who tries to cure him of evil. She takes him to a psychiatrist and finds him employment in the Boston shoe shop owned by her cousin, who moans, 'My in-laws are outlaws.' When Slade reverts to bank robbery, camp singing cowboy Bing Bell (Dick Shawn – with a shotgun concealed in his guitar) comes out of retirement and takes his spangly suit out of mothballs, to catch him.

In recent years there have been more laughs at the genre's expense than straight westerns. Lee Marvin teamed with Oliver Reed in the broad *The Great Scout and Cathouse Thursday* (1976), George Segal and Goldie Hawn were *The Duchess and the Dirtwater Fox* (1976), Jack Nicholson shambled through *Goin' South* (1978) and Robert Aldrich's *The Frisco Kid* (1979) headlined the bizarre team of Gene Wilder and Harrison Ford. Paul Bartel's randy *Lust in the Dust* (1985) starred Tab Hunter (as 'Man With No Name' parody Abel) and also featured Henry Silva, Geoffrey Lewis, Cesar Romero and Woody Strode. The story centred on a gold hunt in the fleapit town of Chilli Verde, with the location map tattooed on two saloon girl sisters' bottoms (played by Lainie Kazan and extrovert transvestite Divine); the treasure chest was appropriately buried on 'Bute Hill'. *Rustler's Rhapsody* (1985) was a Roy Rogers parody filmed in Almeria. *¡Three Amigos!* (1986) starred comedy favourites Steve Martin, Chevy Chase and Martin Short as Lucky Day, Dusty Bottoms and Ned Nederlander, harmonising series western stars who are hired for what they think is a public appearance in the Mexican village of Santo Poco; but the village needs the fictional heroes to save them from a bandit gang, led by El Guapo (Alfonso Arau, from *The Wild Bunch*). 'Wherever there is suffering,' says singing cowboy Ned, 'We'll be there.' *Wagons East* (1994) and *Almost Heroes* (1998) depicted pioneer trailblazers, while *Wild Wild West* (1999) saw James West (Will Smith) and inventor Artemus Gordon (Kevin Kline) floundering in a glib, special effects-laden sci-fi western. *Shanghai Noon* (2000), with Jackie Chan as Chon Wang (pronounced John Wayne) and Owen Wilson as outlaw Roy O'Bannon, was better – trading heavily on Chan's acrobatics and Wilson's Sundance Kid impersonation.

Probably the most infamous of all comedy westerns is Mel Brooks's *Blazing Saddles* (1974), which is also one of the most financially successful westerns of all time, grossing $47.8 million. It was written in irreverent style by Brooks, Norman Steinberg, Andrew Bergman, Alan Uger and Richard Pryor (who came up with the central premise). The town of Rock Ridge is menaced by land-snatcher Hedley ('That's Hedley') Lamarr and the oppressed townsfolk decide to wire Governor Le Petomane (Brooks himself) for help. They are sent black sheriff Bart (Cleavon Little), who on his arrival is offered a laurel, and a hardy handshake, before being ostracised by the racist townsfolk. Bart teams up with washed-up alcoholic, the Waco Kid (who introduces himself, 'My name is Jim, but most people call me…Jim'), to clean up the town. 'Look at that,' says Waco (Gene Wilder), holding out his right hand. 'Steady as a rock,' marvels Bart. 'Yea,' answers the Kid, holding up his left, quivering with the shakes, 'But I shoot with this hand.' Waco is a parody of every clichéd gunslinger with 'a rep', 'I must have killed more men than Cecil B.

De Mille.' *Blazing Saddles* is unrelentingly paced bad taste and patchy. Cowboys polish off plates of beans, then fart breezily around the campfire, beefy villain Mongo is blown up by a 'candy-o-gram', and Madeline Kahn, as Lili Von Shtupp ('The Teutonic Titwillow'), sends up Marlene Dietrich's torch songs and accent ('Hewo Shewiff'). Redneck gunslingers harmonise on 'De Camptown Races' and Lamarr, foiled at every turn, ends up recruiting Bedouins, bikers, Nazi stormtroopers and klansmen for a final attack on the town. But it is just such scattershot parody and ridicule that eventually succeeded in burying the genre. If fifties westerns had elevated their heroes to mythical status, and the sixties created their anti-heroic antitheses, then by the seventies the comedy western took its revenge, the genre's respect diminished with mockery and its heroes laughed out of town.

21

'This Time We Do it Right'

— *The Wild Bunch* (1969)

The Wild Bunch (1969)
Credits
DIRECTOR – Sam Peckinpah
PRODUCER – Phil Feldman
ASSOCIATE PRODUCER – Roy N. Sickner
STORY – Walon Green and Roy N. Sickner
SCREENPLAY – Walon Green and Sam Peckinpah
DIRECTOR OF PHOTOGRAPHY – Lucien Ballard
EDITOR – Louis Lombardo
ART DIRECTOR – Edward Carrere
MUSIC – Jerry Fielding
Panavision 70/Technicolor
A Warner Bros-Seven Arts Production
Released by Warner Bros
145 minutes
Cast
  William Holden (Pike Bishop); Ernest Borgnine (Dutch
  Engstrom); Robert Ryan (Deke Thornton); Edmond O'Brien
  (Freddy Sykes); Ben Johnson and Warren Oats (Lyle and
  Tector Gorch); Jaime Sanchez (Angel); Emilio Fernandez
  (General Mapache); Albert Decker (Pat Harrigan); Strother
  Martin (Coffer); L.Q. Jones (T.C. Nash); Bo Hopkins
  (Clarence 'Crazy' Lee Stringfellow); Dub Taylor (Reverend
  Wainscoat); Jorge Russek (Major Zamorra); Alfonso Arau
  (Lieutenant Herrera); Chano Urueta (Don José in village);
  Sonia Amelio (Teresa, Angel's girl); Aurora Clavel (Aurora,
  Pike's lover); Fernando Wagner (Commander Frederick
  Mohr); Jorge Rado (Ernst, Mohr's aide); Paul Harper and
  Bill Hart (Ross and Jess, bounty hunters); Elsa Cardenas

(Elsa); Rayford Barnes (Buck, outlaw); Stephen Ferry
(Sergeant McHale); Enrique Lucero (Ignacio, Villista);
Elizabeth Dupeyron (Rocio); Yolanda Ponce (Yolis); Jose
Chavez (Juan Jose); Rene Dupeyron (Juan, boy soldier);
Pedro Galvan (Mr Benson in Starbuck); Graciela Doring
(Emma); Major Perez (Perez); Ivan Scott (Paymaster in
Starbuck); Sra Madero (Margaret); Margherito Luna (Luna),
Chalo Gonzalez (Gonzalez); Lilia Castillo (Lilia); Elizabeth
Unda (Carmen); Julio Corona (Julio) with Constance White
and Lilia Richards

*   *   *

Since the debacle over *Major Dundee*, Sam Peckinpah had found directorial
assignments hard to come by. He'd been fired from *The Cincinnati Kid* (1965),
directed an adaptation of Katherine Anne Porter's *Noon Wine* (1967) for TV's *Stage
67* and written the script for *Villa Rides* (1968), an adventure set in the Mexican
Revolution. Star Yul Brynner had fired Peckinpah from the latter because he didn't
like Peckinpah's too-realistic depiction of the revolutionary, and Peckinpah suspected
he would never direct again. Then he read a script written by Roy N. Sickner and
Walon Green, which had interested Lee Marvin. It was also set in the Mexican
Revolution, like Marvin's recent *The Professionals* (1966). Peckinpah's background
research for *Villa Rides* was useful on this next project – an anti-western depicting
The Wild Bunch, a hell-on-wheels outlaw gang down Mexico way.

Peckinpah worked on the script, rewriting the dialogue to explore themes he'd
broached in *Ride the High Country*. *The Wild Bunch* are a gang of train robbers, led
by Pike Bishop, who target railroad property owned by Harrigan. Harrigan forces
Bishop's ex-partner Deke Thornton to turn traitor and track down his former
friend. The Bunch try to rob the 'Pecos and South Texas Railroad Administration
Offices' in the border town of Starbuck, but are ambushed and decimated by
Thornton and his bounty hunters, who want the $4,500 reward. The remains of the
Bunch – Bishop, Dutch Engstrom, Lyle and Tector Gorch, Sykes and the Mexican
'Angel' – flee across the border into Mexico. Thornton is given 30 days to capture
Bishop, or he'll be back in Yuma Penitentiary. The Bunch pause for breath in Angel's
home village, before hiding out at Agua Verde (Green Water in Spanish), the
stronghold of cut-throat General Mapache, who is fighting Villista revolutionaries in
Northern Mexico. The outlaws agree to work for Mapache – stealing armaments from
one of General Pershing's army trains across the frontier, in return for $10,000 in
gold. The raid is a success, but Thornton's posse are also on the train and give chase
into Mexico. Angel is a Villista, a sworn enemy of Mapache, and the Bunch have
allowed Angel to keep a box of weapons in lieu of his share of the gold. But when
Mapache finds out, he captures Angel and tortures him. The Bunch decide that,
even though they have their gold, they must rescue Angel. Returning to Agua
Verde, they confront Mapache's army. The Bunch are wiped out, but Mapache

and his militia are destroyed – all Thornton's vultures find is a charnel house of rotting corpses.

The actual Wild Bunch was the gang headed by Butch Cassidy in Wyoming. It included such notorious gunmen as Harry Longbaugh (the 'Sundance Kid'), Ben Kilpatrick (the 'Tall Texan'), Frank Elliot ('Peg Leg') and Tom Horn. This gang was also the source material for William Goldman's script for *Butch Cassidy and the Sundance Kid* (1969 – made after *The Wild Bunch*, but scripted before). The two films even share set pieces and plotting – a train robbery, a railroad 'super posse', a daring escape involving a river and a shootout against massive odds.

Peckinpah's fictitious Wild Bunch was portrayed by a grizzled cast. William Holden played Pike Bishop, when Marvin pulled out; other prospective Pikes had been Burt Lancaster (from *The Professionals*), Robert Mitchum (*Villa Rides*), Gregory Peck and Charlton Heston. Once a big star, Holden had been number one at the US box office in 1956. Ernest Borgnine, as Dutch, appeared as a mercenary in *Vera Cruz*, as the limping, bullying hotellier in *The Bounty Hunter* (1954) and most memorably as Coley Trimble, the goading heavy who pushes one-armed Spencer Tracy too far in *Bad Day at Black Rock* (1955). Robert Ryan, as traitorous Deke, had also appeared in *Bad Day* and had recently made two tough westerns: *The*

'We want Angel': In Agua Verde the bunch confront General Mapache – Tector and Lyle Gorch (Ben Johnson and Warren Oates), Pike Bishop (William Holden) and Dutch Engstrom (Ernest Borgnine) in Sam Peckinpah's *The Wild Bunch*. (Picture courtesy of Kevin Wilkinson Collection.)

Professionals and *Hour of the Gun* (1967). Jaime Sanchez was cast as Angel, though Robert Blake had been the original choice. Ben Johnson, now older, heavier and bearded, fitted into Peckinpah's west. Warren Oates had worked on *Ride the High Country* and *Major Dundee*. Both Johnson and Oates were ideally cast as the quarrelling brothers Tector and Lyle Gorch. According to their reward posters, Bishop, Engstrom and Tector are murderers and train robbers, while Lyle is a rapist. Edmond O'Brien, as tobacco-chawin' old-timer Sykes, had made several noirs (*White Heat* [1949] and *DOA* [1950]) and westerns: he was a deranged Confederate colonel in *Rio Conchos* (1964) and newspaper editor Dutton Peabody in *The Man Who Shot Liberty Valance* (1962).

Emilio Fernandez, known as 'El Indio', played monstrous General Mapache, who is chauffeured around in a red Model T Ford. He had previously been bandit Lorca, who died messily with a squibbed blood splatter to the guts in *Return of the Seven* (1966) and drunken renegade Calito in *The War Wagon* (1967). Fernandez, a Mexican director who lived in a castle and once shot a film critic during an argument, went on to appear in more Peckinpah adventures. Strother Martin, as whining leather-jacketed bounty hunter Coffer, with a crucifix hung around his neck, had appeared as a villain in *Liberty Valance* and as the Gila City preacher in *The Deadly Companions*. L.Q. Jones had also worked with Peckinpah before and was cast as pony-tailed bounty killer T.C. Nash. Albert Decker, who played railroad baron Harrigan, suffocated shortly after the completion of *Wild Bunch* in 1968 – though this was deemed an accident, some suggested that it was suicide. The cast was filled out with Bo Hopkins as Bunch member Crazy Lee, Dub Taylor as South Texas Temperance Union leader Wainscoat, and Jorge Russek and Alfonso Arau as Mapache's sidekicks: crafty Zamorra and dopey Herrera.

With Phil Feldman producing for Warner Bros-Seven Arts (soon to be bought by the Kinney National conglomerate) and a budget of almost $3.5 million, Peckinpah shot the film on location in Mexico, receiving $72,000 for rewriting the script and $100,000 for directing. Scheduled for 70 days, *Wild Bunch* was shot around the Mexican towns of Parras and Torreon, with interiors completed at Estudios Churubusco, Mexico City. It was photographed by Lucien Ballard, from *Ride the High Country*. The opening raid at Starbuck was filmed first on the streets of Parras, followed by the final shootout at Agua Verde and the train robbery. Warners asked Parras to delay the installation of electric power lines until filming was completed. The location used for Mapache's headquarters was the Hacienda Cienga Del Carmen. Working nine-hour days in extreme heat, it took 12 days to film the shootout and the crew were at the hacienda for a month. The scene where the Bunch blow a bridge from beneath Thornton's posse was filmed with six cameras on the Rio Nazas, near Torreon, at 1.55 pm on Sunday 30 June 1968. The bridge had a special hinged section, plunging the five stuntmen and their steeds into the river (the stuntmen received $2,000 each). Peckinpah finished shooting in Mexico City in the last week of June 1968 at a final cost of $6 million.

In *Ride the High Country*, Steve Judd was based on Peckinpah's father. Pike Bishop is Peckinpah himself – clean-shaven Holden even wore a Peckinpah-style moustache and adopted the director's posture and mannerisms. In an interview, Peckinpah said, 'I suppose I'm something of an outlaw myself... I identify with them.' His outsider status in Hollywood has always placed him as a maverick, with his own way of making films. As Pike notes of railroad boss Harrigan, with satisfaction, 'He used to have a way of doing things – I made him change his ways.'

The strongest theme in *The Wild Bunch* is the aged outlaws' place in a rapidly modernising world during the terror reign of General Huerta, between February 1913 and July 1914. Posters stated: 'Unchanging men in a changing land. Out of step, out of place and desperately out of time'. Sykes notes of the Bunch, 'You boys ain't getting any younger,' and Tector goads the older men in the party, 'Running with Brother Pike and old man Sykes makes a man wonder if it ain't time to pick up his chips and find another game.' Following the disaster of the Starbuck set-up, what's left of the Bunch limp south. Pike says, 'I'd like to make one good score and back off,' to which Dutch incredulously replies, 'Back off to what?' In the course of their journey, Pike and Dutch talk about the past, how Thornton once rode with them as a comrade and how Pike was wounded when the husband of his lover Aurora came home unexpectedly. Of their dealings with Mapache, Pike says, 'This is our last go around, Dutch... this time we do it right.' The armaments train robbery may hark back to the good old days – but their 'days are closing fast'.

While Bishop is still living the life of an outlaw, Deke Thornton is forced to betray his friends and become a 'Judas goat' for the law. His gang are officially 'railroad deputies', but they're bounty killers by any other name – 'egg-suckin', chicken-stealin' gutter-trash', as Thornton terms them. 'How does it feel' asks Thornton of Harrigan, 'Getting paid to sit back and hire your killings with the law's arms around you? How does it feel to be so God damn right?' 'Good,' sneers Harrigan. It becomes apparent during his pursuit of Bishop that Thornton would rather be with his old Bunch. Composer Jerry Fielding touchingly scored the film according to the 'love affair' he saw between Bishop and Thornton. When Thornton finds his friend's corpse at Mapache's, he carefully retrieves Bishop's pistol from its holster and takes it. Contradicting Thornton's turncoat behaviour, Pike tells his Bunch, 'When you side with a man you stay with him and if you can't do that you're like some animal; you're finished... we're finished... all of us.' In the dénouement, Sykes, the only member of the Bunch not present at the massacre, arrives with Angel's Villista friends and tells Thornton that his bounty hunters returning with the Bunch's corpses to claim the reward have been killed. Sykes is staying in Mexico and invites Thornton to join him, 'It ain't like it used to be, but it'll do.' Thornton, for the first time in the film, smiles.

As elsewhere in Peckinpah's cinema, children's behaviour is used as a metaphor for adults' cruelty. *The Wild Bunch* begins with a desaturated still image of the Bunch, riding along the railroad tracks into Starbuck, past a group of 12 children. The kids are watching two scorpions being overrun by a swarm of ants, in a tiny, makeshift twig 'arena' (a similar scene had appeared in Tinto Brass's western *Yankee* [1966]). The children's cruelty, which includes placing dried straw on the insects and setting it alight, has its counterpoint later, when Don Jose (the village elder in Angel's home) watches the Gorchs' behaviour, playing cat's cradle with Rocio, Angel's teenage sister. Jose notes, 'We all dream of being a child again – even the worst of us…perhaps the worst most of all.' But not the children in the title sequence. Peckinpah freeze-frames on the kids' demonic faces, their black eyes and hollow grins. Later, we see children at Agua Verde cruelly riding on Angel's back, when he is being dragged behind Mapache's car. Mapache, Harrigan and bounty vultures, T.C. and Coffer, are such children, grown up and still poking scorpions and tormenting ants with glee.

When the Bunch arrive at despot Mapache's headquarters, it's soon obvious he's the maddest hombre south of the Rio Grande. The fortified stronghold of Agua Verde is a dangerous place – teeming with his ragged community of camp followers, pigs, market stalls, Mariachi players, militia, chickens and squalor. The grand opulence of their surroundings, built by Spanish dons 300 years ago, has fallen into disrepair – the decaying arches of the aqueduct, the crumbling palisade walls and the weathered wooden gateway. In the middle of this slum is a central walled yard, the hub of Mapache's stronghold, where the general and his staff sit on a raised dais at their long table slugging wine, and messily wolfing food, like pigs at a trough. Major Zamorra leers over a slobbered glass of red wine and Mapache, half drunk, woozily paws at the gaudy prostitutes that hang around the camp. Are these really the kind of people the Wild Bunch wants to do business with? The volatile, unpleasant mix of alcohol, sex and guns defines Mapache's scorpion's nest: no one here gets out alive.

The Wild Bunch is most famous for the two explosive shootout scenes that raised the stakes in sixties screen violence. Arthur Penn's blood-splattered finale to *Bonnie and Clyde* (1967) was a major influence on Peckinpah, who took Penn's bloody showstopper and extended it, deploying slow motion and squibs (blood-filled bags attached to the actors and then exploded with a charge). Slow motion accentuates this violence, stretching death throes and coagulating the fountains of blood in mid-air. This is intercut with footage cranked at normal speed, creating surreal imagery. For the Starbuck ambush, there were 230 people and 56 horses on set. Peckinpah's orchestration of the pandemonium is inspired, with the bounty hunters picking off the outlaws as they try to reach their horses. The Bunch use members of a Temperance parade as human shields and blast their way out of town, while bystanders are trampled under horses' hooves and mown down in the ferocious crossfire.

The second shootout, at Mapache's, is more pyrotechnic, with grenades exploding and machine-guns dispensing death eight times a second. The horrible irony of this confrontation is that the Bunch are taking on the 200-strong army they have just equipped. This wholesale slaughter, called 'The Battle of Bloody Porch', is triggered when the Bunch return to Agua Verde and see Angel, his skin in ribbons, being dragged behind Mapache's car. His mistreatment touches a nerve in the Bunch. They spend the night in a filthy bordello, and the next morning Pike is galvanised – he knows what he must do and the Bunch are with him. 'Let's go,' he tells the Gorch brothers. 'Why not?' answers Lyle. In the street they are joined by Dutch, load up with hardware, including their shotguns and automatic pistols, and form up.

Their famous striding walk to face Mapache was largely improvised on set by Peckinpah – it was only three lines in the script. They pass though the army camp, past Mariachi singers and peasants, until they arrive in Mapache's lair. The general and his staff are still half-stoned after the previous night's revelry. 'We want Angel,' states Pike. In answer to Pike's request, Mapache slashes Angel's throat. Pike and Dutch shoot Mapache and then, after a moment's silence that seems to last an eternity, mayhem erupts – the Bunch spray the courtyard with shots and Mapache's army stumble into action. This final battle was originally going to be staged at night, but is all the more effective in unflinching sunshine. A regiment of real Mexican soldiers was deployed as Mapache's army. The Bunch clear Mapache's table of diners with a volley and commandeer the 1917 A1 Browning water-cooled machine-gun, as the Mexicans launch an assault from all sides. Lyle, his finger locked on the trigger of the machine-gun, screams wordlessly as bullets slam into him. Tector blasts all-comers with his pump-action shotgun. Pike's men blow lumps out of their attackers, but eventually superior numbers count and the four men are overwhelmed. Tector and Lyle are pirouetted and slammed in a slow-motion ballet of blood; Pike slumps, riddled, still holding onto the machine-gun trigger, while Dutch shouts Pike's name,

Pulp Fiction: Reprints of source materials and novelisation tie-ins have always proved popular with western fans; pictured here are adaptations of *The Wild Bunch*, *Chato's Land*, *The Hunting Party* and *Hannie Caulder*, spaghetti westerns *A Fistful of Dollars* and *The Good, the Bad and the Ugly*, Charles Portis's *True Grit* and a reprint of Marvin Albert's *Apache Rising*, under its movie title *Duel at Diablo*.

staggering to die beside his friend, himself blood-sodden and wasted. With the sacrificial end of *The Wild Bunch* comes the end of the west. But this time they did 'do it right'.

Peckinpah had had problems in the past with his work being taken away from him and re-cut against his wishes, as in *Major Dundee*. *The Wild Bunch* was no exception; post-production took a year. Peckinpah and his editor Lou Lombardo stayed in Torreon to prepare the rough-cut. By September they had a three hours and 45 minutes version, which was then edited down to a 170-minute movie. Warners wanted a film no longer than 150 minutes. Peckinpah previewed the film to audiences in May 1969, in Kansas City, Fresno and Long Beach, California. Stories abound of people running out of the theatre, of cheering or vomiting at these legendary screenings. Peckinpah cut six more minutes out of the film, mainly blood (including, according to some sources, a disembowelling), lewdness and profanity (though if you can lip-read, some dialogue is merely redubbed) to get an 'R' rating. Peckinpah also removed a flashback depicting Aurora's death and Pike's wounding.

The Wild Bunch was premiered on 28 June 1969, in the Bahamas, almost a year to the day after it wrapped. Posters, with the hunched Bunch casting ominous long shadows, had the taglines: 'The men who came too late and stayed too long' and 'Born too Late for their Own Times…Uncommonly Significant for Ours'. After the first preview, *Variety* said that the 150-minute version needed tightening up 'particularly in the first half'. The *Manhattan Tribune* noted that it 'brings us back to death' with violence as 'cinematic masturbation'. The *Kansas City Star* talked of the film's 'underlying tone of sententious preachiness, its heavy laying-on of moral points bracketed by savage action' and the 'savagery carried beyond the level of horror to the level of numbing surfeit'. It was included on the *New York Times*' Ten Best of 1969 and was nominated for Oscars for Best Original Story and Screenplay (Green, Sickner and Peckinpah) and Fielding for Best Score, but didn't win. In the UK, where the film was rated 'X' on its release in January 1970, *Sight and Sound* said that the film was 'Violent, thoughtful and authoritative, it keeps Peckinpah out on his own among the western directors of his generation'. A novelisation by Brian Fox was published by Universal-Tandem in 1969 (publicised as 'Makes *Bonnie and Clyde* look like a church picnic'), which closely follows the full-length print of the film. John Wayne hated this new style of western, complaining about the escalating violence in the genre, which he described as, 'Bodies opening up and liver flying out at you.' Some loved it, some hated it – none, it seemed, 'quite liked it'.

In New York and Los Angeles *Wild Bunch* was released in 70mm widescreen, with stereo sound (as it was in Sweden, France, Italy, Spain and the UK, in Japan and Australia) and was very popular. This was a so-called 'Roadshow Release' – with an intermission between the planning and execution of the train robbery. It was simultaneously released on the drive-in circuit in Texas and the southwest, in a standard format with much less success and closed quickly. *Wild Bunch* grossed only $5.3 million in the US, but $6.3 million from foreign markets. Warner Bros decided to cut the film by another eight minutes. This new version lost several scenes and saw others shortened, including the festivities in Angel's village. Cut were the flashback to

Thornton's capture in a bordello; the death of wounded Bunch member Buck in the desert; the scene of Thornton's flogging in Yuma; and the confession by Sykes that outlaw Crazy Lee was his grandson. A huge battle scene was also axed, depicting Mapache waiting for a telegram at a railway station, under attack from Villa's vast División del Norte forces; its aftermath, as the wounded are tended in Agua Verde, was also lost. Because these cuts were made once the film had been distributed, Warners didn't re-call the reels, but did the cuts to each individual print. Many editors carried out the wrong cuts, which resulted in many different versions – TV prints have included some of the additions (the flashbacks, or the Villista–Mapache depot battle), but then have others missing.

The longest version is the 'Director's Cut', the first version of the film Peckinpah assembled in 1968. A fully restored print of this was released in cinemas in 1995; it runs 144 minutes and 38 seconds and includes all the footage mentioned above, plus the Aurora flashback. Re-release posters use the tagline: '*The Wild Bunch* is loose again'. There is a 123-minute print, shortened for nudity and violence for US Network TV showings in 1972. *Wild Bunch* was reissued in the US in 1981 at 142 minutes, with deleted scenes restored (this version included everything except the Aurora flashback). For years the most widely screened print ran 134 minutes and was the accepted version of the film. In the UK, according to the BBFC, the 1970 release ran 138 minutes, 31 seconds. By the eighties, *Wild Bunch* had such a reputation that it was one of the first 20 Warner Bros' titles released worldwide on video, though one such release was the faded pan-and-scan, 127-minute version. The 1988 video release ran 135 minutes 27 seconds, re-rated '18'; a 1996 video release ran 138 minutes, 28 seconds (the 'Director's Cut' at the faster frames-per-minute PAL format), which is now also available on DVD.

So recognisable is 'Bloody Sam's' violent style that his editing, dialogue and bloodletting have been widely copied and parodied. 'Sam Peckinpah's Salad Days' in *Monty Python's Flying Circus* featured a Wodehouse garden party's descent into a bloodbath, while UK TV's *Big Train* saw the Bee Gees literal attempt at 'Stayin' Alive' during a Peckinpah slow-mo shootout with Chaka Khan. In the pop culture referencing *Buffy the Vampire Slayer*, Buffy finds herself up against two villainous demons in dusters called Lyle and Tector Gorch in the 'Bad Eggs' episode; Lyle survives their encounter and reappears in 'Homecoming'.

Gore westerns, especially the UK-produced *The Hunting Party* (1971), starring Oliver Reed and Gene Hackman, had graphic, visceral cruelty, hearts of stone and gallons of blood, but no plot. Quibbed explosions and splattering impact wounds were similarly plentiful in *Machismo – 40 Graves for 40 Guns* (1970), *Lawman* (1971), *A Town Called Bastard* (1971), *The Deadly Trackers* (1973) and *The Fighting Fist of Shanghai Joe* (1973), though avoid trimmed prints or you may end up wondering where these films' ferocious reputations came from. Holden himself made the awful *The Revengers* (1972), a blunt, vengeance-driven cross between *The Wild Bunch* and *The Magnificent Seven*. Alexandro Jodorowsky's Mexistential western *El Topo* (1971) took tips from Peckinpah's special-effects team with even more bloody and repulsive results (Alfonso Arau also appeared as a bandit). Exploitation king Al

Adamson made *The Female Bunch* in 1969, a modern western partly shot on the western sets at the infamous Spahn Ranch in Chatsworth, the HQ of Charles Manson's cult. Adamson also made the unpleasant, low-budget *Five Bloody Graves* (1969 – retitled *The Gun Riders*) and *Jessie's Girls* (1975 – or *Wanted Women*), the former with voiceover narration by 'Death' himself.

Shot-in-Spain Mexican Revolution westerns like *The Five Man Army* (1969) and *Cannon for Cordoba* (1970) were *Wild Bunch*-style adventures, while others featured cataclysmic, one-sided shootouts. In *Vengeance is Mine* (1969 – also called *A Bullet for Sandoval*), George Hilton's outlaw quartet are trapped in a bullring by Ernest Borgnine's bitter land baron Sandoval, facing tier upon tier of Regulares. In *Compañeros* (1970), Franco Nero's Swedish professional gun rides into San Bernardino alone and takes on General Mongo's bandit army, while in *My Name is Nobody* (1973), Henry Fonda faces 'The Wild Bunch' ('a hundred and fifty pure-bred sons of bitches on horseback') to ensure his place in the history books. The latter film also features Nobody (Terence Hill) reading an inscription on a grave in Acoma cemetery, 'Sam Peckinpah...that's a beautiful name in Navajo'. It may be a beautiful name, but it became synonymous with increasingly violent, censor-baiting fare, especially the non-western *Straw Dogs* (1971).

Peckinpah followed *The Wild Bunch* with one of his tenderest films, *The Ballad of Cable Hogue* (1970), detailing hermit loner Hogue (Jason Robards) opening a profitable watering hole way station when his partners (Strother Martin and L.Q. Jones) leave him to die in the desert. 'Cable Hogue says, "Do Unto Others as you would have Others Do Unto You"' ran the tagline, a sentiment *The Wild Bunch* would agree with. Peckinpah also made neo-westerns, like *Junior Bonner*, *The Getaway* (both 1972) and *Bring me the Head of Alfredo Garcia* (1974 – with Warren Oates and Emilio Fernandez). Of *Garcia*, Gene Shalit in the *Ladies' Home Journal* punned: 'Bring me the head of the studio that released this one', though some aficionados rate it as Peckinpah's finest, most autobiographical work.

Peckinpah also directed *Pat Garrett & Billy the Kid* (1973), with James Coburn starring as a jaded Garrett. Singer Kris Kristofferson plays Billy (but more closely resembles Jim Morrison) and Bob Dylan was cast as knife-throwing Alias. Dylan also contributed the acoustic soundtrack, including 'Knockin' on Heaven's Door'. 'Best Of Enemies...Deadliest of Friends', said posters of the title duo. The film was severely cut by MGM, from 124 to 106 minutes, though the flashback structure bookends to the film – depicting Garrett's murder in 1909 – have since been restored, confirming it as a major western, if only for its incredible 'who's who' cast: Katy Jurado, Richard Jaeckel, Jason Robards, Slim Pickens, Chill Wills, R.G. Armstrong, Matt Clark, Jack Elam, Dub Taylor, Emilio Fernandez, L.Q. Jones, Harry Dean Stanton and Elisha Cook Jnr. In his introduction to this full version in *The Film Club* on BBC2 in 1989, Philip French called the film 'a succession of scenes that erupt into violence'. Peckinpah himself cameoed in *Garrett* as coffin-maker Will, and fittingly played dime novelist Wilbur Olsen in Monte Hellman's Italian-Spanish *China 9, Liberty 37* (1978), who just wants 'To buy a little legend. The lies they need – we all need.' Peckinpah was once quoted as saying, 'Hollywood no longer exists. Look at MGM – it's now in the hotel business and maybe their old directors can get jobs as bellhops.' He died in 1984, though his legacy of only six westerns, depicting uncompromising violence and the passing of the west, have made him a legend of the genre. He was a maverick, a true member of the Wild Bunch, who just wouldn't change.

22

'Who Are Those Guys?'

— *Butch Cassidy and the Sundance Kid* (1969)

Butch Cassidy and the Sundance Kid (1969)
Credits
DIRECTOR – George Roy Hill
PRODUCER – John Foreman
STORY AND SCREENPLAY – William Goldman
DIRECTOR OF PHOTOGRAPHY – Conrad Hall
EDITOR – Elmo Williams
ART DIRECTORS – Walter M. Scott and Chester L. Bayhi
MUSIC COMPOSER AND CONDUCTOR – Burt Bacharach
Panavision/De Luxe
Campanile Productions/20th Century-Fox
Released by 20th Century-Fox
110 minutes
Cast

Paul Newman (Robert LeRoy Parker alias 'Butch Cassidy');
Robert Redford (Harry Longbaugh alias 'the Sundance
Kid'); Katharine Ross (Etta Place); Strother Martin (Percy
Garris, tin mine payroll clerk); Henry Jones (Bicycle
salesman); Jeff Corey (Sheriff Bledsoe); George Furth
(Woodcock, bank guard on Union Pacific Flier); Cloris
Leechman (Agnes, prostitute); Ted Cassidy (Harvey Logan
alias 'Kid Curry'); Kenneth Mars (Marshal raising posse in
Fort Worth); Donnelly Rhodes (Macon); Jody Gilbert (Fat
lady on train); Timothy Scott (William Carver alias 'News
Carver'); Don Keefer (Fireman on train); Charles Dierkop
(George L. Curry alias 'Flat Nose Curry'); Francisco Cordova
(Bank manager); Nelson Olmstead (Photographer in New
York); Paul Bryer (First poker player); Sam Elliott (Second
poker player); Charles Akins (Bank employee); Eric Sinclair

(Tiffany salesman in New York); David Dunlap (Member of
the Wild Bunch); Percy Helton (Sweetface); Francisco
Reiguera (Innkeeper in San Vicente); Jose Chavez (Bolivian
cavalry captain)

*   *   *

Butch Cassidy and the Sundance Kid is one of the most popular westerns of all time.
Its contemporary verve transcends the genre – with its blend of comedy-drama, a
catchy soundtrack and tragic ending, it is the quintessential example of sixties
counterculture chic, a West Coast western in every sense, reflecting the politics
and values of the era. The heroes, played with easy charm by Paul Newman and
Robert Redford, are the ultimate wisecracking buddy pairing who, unlike lonesome
cowboys such as Clint Eastwood and Charles Bronson, rather enjoyed each other's
bad company.

In 1968, 20th Century-Fox bought a script called 'The Sundance Kid and Butch
Cassidy' for $400,000. The screenplay was written by William Goldman, a renowned
playwright, author and screenwriter, who had spent several years researching his
subject. Goldman even published some of his writing under the pseudonym
'Harry Longbaugh', Sundance's real name. Goldman detailed the escapades of the
historical 'Wild Bunch', an outlaw gang led by Butch Cassidy and his fast-shooting
sidekick, the Sundance Kid. Following two robberies on the Union Pacific Flyer,
rail boss E. H. Harriman hires a crack posse of scouts, trackers and professional
manhunters to break up the Bunch, but after an arduous chase, Butch and
Sundance elude their pursuers. Deciding that the US is getting too dangerous,
the duo, together with Sundance's schoolteacher lover Etta Place, relocate to Bolivia
(via a visit to New York City). Finding easy pickings, they embark on a crime spree
in the still-wild west of Bolivia, becoming famous as the 'Bandidos Yanquis'. Etta
senses that even here their days are numbered and returns to the States. Butch and
Sundance attempt to go straight, adopting the pseudonyms 'Smith and Jones', and
ride escort on tin mine wage shipments, but the law catches up with them when they
steal one of their own payrolls. In a shootout with the army in San Vicente, Butch
and the Kid die in the village plaza in a hail of Bolivian bullets.

It is ironic that for a film that begins with the caption: 'Most of what follows is
True', most of what follows isn't. Goldman's historical sources were the Pinkerton's
Detective Agency files and the *Pictorial History of the Wild West* by James D. Horan
and Paul Sann, first published in 1954. In 1950 Horan had interviewed 90-year-old
Pinkerton Agent Frank Dimaio and heard a first-hand account of Butch and
Sundance's exploits and demise in Bolivia. The historical Wild Bunch operated out
of Wyoming's Hole-in-the-Wall country, so-called because the entrance was a steep,
shaley bank that appeared to vanish into a sheer rock face. Riddled with caves and
cabins, including the famous Robbers' Roost, this lush landscape beyond was an
ideal hiding place for a man with a price on his head. Butch fell in with rustlers and
bank robbers at the Hole and spent two years in prison, being released in January

1896. By 1898 he was leader of the Wild Bunch. In Goldman's script, three regular Bunch members appear as incidental characters: Harvey Logan (alias 'Kid Curry'), George L. Curry ('Flat Nose Curry') and William Carver ('News Carver').

Hollywood had depicted the Wild Bunch before, though in a very different light – and always as the villains. In *The Maverick Queen* (1956), shot in 'Naturama' amid the Colorado mountains, Barry Sullivan starred as a Pinkerton agent assigned to infiltrate the Hole-in-the-Wall badlands, where, according to the title ballad, 'the air smelled of trouble'. Barbara Stanwyck portrayed Kit Bannion (based on Cattle Kate), who is in cahoots with the bunch. Butch is depicted as a red-bearded Irishman, with Sundance a thuggish, womanising half-breed (the real Sundance looked like 'a quarter-breed Indian'). The truth of their demise was not yet widely known and the film opts for the dime novel rendering of the legend: the Wild Bunch and the Maverick Queen are killed in a log cabin shootout. In *Wyoming Renegades* (1955), Butch Cassidy (Gene Evans) and Sundance (William Bishop) rob the train to Wilcox, in an otherwise fictitious narrative. Their Hole-in-the-Wall hideout was filmed in Bronson Canyon, while the finale has the Wild Bunch cut down in Broken Bow (when they attempt to rob the Cattlemen's bank) by the townswomen whose husbands are out on posse duty. Other Hollywood references to the Bunch include the Dancing Kid's 'hole-in-the-waterfall' hideout in *Johnny Guitar* (1954), the outlaw haven of 'Chuck-A-Luck' in *Rancho Notorious* (1952) and Tim Holt tracking refugee outlaws hiding *Under the Tonto Rim* (1947).

In 1967, Goldman approached Paul Newman on set at Old Tucson during the making of *Hombre* and the actor was immediately interested in the script. With a $6.3 million budget, Goldman wanted to cast Newman as Sundance and Jack Lemmon as Butch. Steve McQueen soon replaced Lemmon, but lost interest in the project. Warren Beatty was also a possibility for Sundance. Eventually, relatively unknown Robert Redford convinced the producers that he could play Sundance and despite his misgivings, Newman agreed to play the lighter role of Butch – Newman had previously portrayed outlaw Billy the Kid in *The Left Handed Gun* (1958). The title was then switched to *Butch Cassidy and the Sundance Kid*, with the accent on Newman's character; he received $750,000 for the role and acted as co-executive producer.

Katharine Ross, Oscar-nominated two years before for *The Graduate*, was cast as Etta Place – in the film a schoolteacher, but rumoured to have been a prostitute. Tall outlaw Harvey Logan was played by Ted Cassidy (better known as Lurch in TV's *The Addams Family*), while almost all the other roles in the film were sketchy background characters to the central trio. Only the reliable western character actor Strother Martin made an impact, with some good lines, as Percy Garris, a gringo mine superintendent at the Concordia Tin Mine. The duo see Garris for a job as payroll guards; he takes one look at Sundance's marksmanship and says, 'Considering that I'm desperate and you are just what I'm looking for, we start tomorrow morning.' He later explains his eccentricity, 'That's what happens when you live ten years alone in Bolivia – you get colourful.'

Following two weeks' rehearsal, the film commenced shooting on 16 September 1968 and was completed in 84 days. Most of the shoot was on location, with interiors at Fox Studios. The schedule was chronological, with the exception of the train robbery scenes, shot first to avoid the winter snow. The scenes were shot on a period railroad that ran between Durango and Silvertown, Colorado, with some sequences shot at Snow Canyon. The Hole-in-the-Wall hideout was in St George, Utah. A wooden house was constructed at Grafton, Utah (near the Zion National Park) for a scene where Butch rides a bicycle to impress Etta. The famous cliff jump, where Butch and Sundance elude the posse, was shot on the Animas River, near Durango; the jump into the water was filmed as a matte shot, with Redford and Newman's stuntmen jumping off a 70-foot crane into a lagoon at the Fox Ranch in Malibu. The sepia stills for the New York sequence, where Butch, Sundance and Etta book passage on the *SS Soldier Prince* were shot on Fox's *Hello Dolly!* set and then inserted into actual period photographs of New York's crowded tramway streets. All the Bolivian scenes were shot in Mexico, in and around the town of Tlayacapan, south of Cuernavaca, Morelos. Five hundred Mexican soldiers were deployed across the roofs and palisades of the town for the shootout in the plaza of 'San Vicente'. The tin mine was an actual mine near La Paz, while the scene where Butch and Sundance mow down a gang of Bolivian bandidos was shot in the mountain country at Tepoztlàn.

Though Redford and Newman had never met, they liked one another and their chemistry helped with the 'buddy movie' interplay between Butch and Sundance. Newman says that he 'kept Butch loose...there was a good deal of myself in the part', while Redford played Sundance as 'aloof, a loner, a bit schizoid'. Ross didn't get on with director Hill and preferred to work with second unit director Michael Moore. Legend has it that Newman wore a beer bottle-opener around his neck throughout filming under his shirt, while Ross remembers, 'Newman was always telling jokes, Redford was always on the phone and I was always waiting for them.'

Sundance opens with a sepia-tinted silent film depicting the Wild Bunch's exploits entitled *The Hole in the Wall Gang*. In the early twentieth century, the myth and the history of the west synchronised, as the last of the outlaws saw their exploits become movies. *Sundance* develops this theme in three sections: the early carefree train robbing sequences, the edgy chase scenes and the lively Bolivian 'Bandidos Yanqui' sequences.

At the Hole-in-the-Wall hideout, the gang embark on two train robberies. Both are based on fact, though the impression is that the Bunch rob a train every other day, for recreation, whereas in reality the raids were over a year apart. In their first Union Pacific Flyer robbery, Sundance leaps onto the roof of the moving train and Woodcock, the bank vault guard, barely manages to get away with his life when the gang blow up the Adams Express car. In the second robbery, they again hit the Flyer, and Woodcock is conned into opening the door when Butch mimics the voice of a terrified woman passenger. Here the gang accidentally demolish the safe and have to collect the thousands of dollar bills fluttering in the wind. 'Think you used enough dynamite there, Butch?' asks Sundance. As they collect their booty, a mysterious express train pulls up and the heavily armed super-posse disembarks. 'Whatever they're selling,' says Butch, 'I don't want it.'

This chronology is wrong, however. The Bunch robbed the Flyer near Wilcox, Wyoming in June 1899 by blowing up a bridge; here the outlaws used too much explosive and escaped with singed bills. In August 1900 the outlaws held up the Flyer again (Train No. 3), two and a half miles west of Tipton, Sweetwater County, Wyoming. Woodcock was on duty, but the gang managed to open the door peaceably. The gang stole $5,000 in cash and several hundred dollars worth of watch movements. It was only then that the Union Pacific management hired Special Agent T. T. Kelliher to organise a super-posse, out for the $8,000 reward. The Bunch pulled one more job (not depicted in the film) in July 1903 between Malta and Wagner, Montana, taking $40,000 in banknotes which were minus their authenticity signatures, which the gang scribbled in themselves.

The extended chase sequence, which lasts almost half an hour, is the best section of the film. The sustained tension of the inexorable pursuit was the responsibility of cinematographer Conrad Hall, who designed and filmed the entire sequence. The chase is silent, except for the clatter of Butch and Sundance's horses' hooves, and the ominous thunder of the relentless posse. The duo begin to worry when they recognise one of the riders as specialist manhunter Joe Lefors. The railroad

Los Bandidos Yanquis: Frozen in time and propelled into the history books, buddies Butch and Sundance make a break for it in San Vicente – Paul Newman and Robert Redford in George Roy Hill's classic *Butch Cassidy and the Sundance Kid* (1969).

super-posse was led by Lefors, his five men kitted out with specially made high-powered Winchesters and field glasses. In *Sundance* they are teamed with an expert Indian tracker, Lord Baltimore, a mysterious figure about whom little is known. One thing that is known is that he wasn't in Lefors's super-posse. Butch's increasingly exasperated, 'Who are those guys?' is one of the most memorable lines in the film, with the posse even trailing the outlaws by torchlight and over rocks. Even when the tension mounts, Butch's quips lighten the mood. 'I think we lost 'em,' he says, squinting across a vast empty plain from a mountainous vantage point, 'Do you think we lost 'em?' 'No,' deadpans Sundance. Butch reflects, 'Neither do I.'

With the law on their trail, Butch, Sundance and Etta decide to head for Bolivia – they actually went via Uruguay and Argentina, where they worked as cattle drovers. To link the American west sequences with exotic Bolivia, Hill used a bridging sequence, which depicts Butch and Sundance's brush with 'back east'. Here Hill used hundreds of stills of turn-of-the-century New York, in a rapidly cut montage, accompanied by a lively Charleston, called 'Old Fun City'.

The heroes finally arrive in the land of the llama, at the deserted, ruined Santa Ines railway station. Sundance complains that this could be the 'Atlantic City, New Jersey of all Bolivia', Butch says that the exchange rate in Bolivia is favourable and Sundance answers, 'What could they have here that you could possibly want to buy?' Their first robbery is a complete failure, with the language problem putting paid to their heist, so schoolteacher Etta tutors them with some useful Spanish phrases (*Esto es un robo* – 'this is a robbery'; *las manos arriba* – 'raise your hands'). But their carefree life of crime gives way to Etta's departure and the outlaws' attempt to go straight.

Their time in Bolivia takes a turn for the worse, as the authorities catch on to their activities. In a lyrical scene, Etta says that she's going back to the US. It recalls her pledge before they left for Bolivia, 'I'll do anything you ask of me, except one thing: I won't watch you die. I'll miss that scene, if you don't mind.' She senses that the law is closing in on the duo, though in actuality Etta left to have an operation for appendicitis. The effectiveness of her goodbye is reduced by the abridgement of the scenes where she packs her bags and leaves, while Butch and Sundance watch a silent movie called *The Hole in the Wall Gang* in a Bolivian cinema, depicting their demise on the silver screen. Earlier their friend, Sheriff Bledsoe has told the duo, 'Your times is over and you're gonna die bloody. And all you can do is choose where.'

Butch and the Kid are eventually taken by surprise in a marketplace, their stolen mules spotted by a vigilant local. Low on ammunition and badly wounded the duo find themselves slumped bleeding in a pueblo. Butch has a new idea: they'll head for Australia – 'They speak English in Australia, so we wouldn't be foreigners.' Sundance loads Butch's Colt and pushes it into his friend's hand, as they struggle to their feet. Commenting that at least they haven't seen Lefors outside, Butch adds, 'For a moment there I thought we were in trouble,' as they run outside, headlong into a hail of lead. Three volleys ring out, a firing squad execution. But like Etta we 'miss that scene' and Hill spares us the bloodletting of *The Wild Bunch*, freezing the heroes as a sepia image in a history book.

The music for *Butch Cassidy and the Sundance Kid* was composed by songwriter Burt Bacharach. Hal David contributed the lyric to the featured song: 'Raindrops Keep Fallin' on My Head', sung by B.J. Thomas (a Texan country singer), while Butch, in Derby and waistcoat, rides his bike, with Etta perched on the handlebars. The bicycle phenomenon did sweep the west in the early 1900s, but it was no matter that the real Butch used to ride his bike through the red-light district of Fort Worth, and outside Porter's brothel, with his gang cheering him on. Bacharach's bouncy refrain ('I'm never going to stop the rain by complaining, because I'm free, nothing's worrying me') gives way to a circus tune called 'On a Bicycle Built for Joy', as Butch performs daredevil stunts for Etta, before crashing through a fence and being chased by an irate bull (a stunt-bull named Bill). Elsewhere, Bacharach used a simple guitar theme, 'Not Goin' Home Anymore', for the silent-film title sequence, and a piano and harpsichord reprise accompanies the final freeze-frame. During the 'Bandidos Yanqui' robbery and chase sequences, Bacharach deployed the frantic 'South American Getaway' for the pursuit scenes, sobered by a mournful a cappella bridge, as Lefors and his posse appear in Bolivia.

Sundance premiered in Durango on 2 September 1969 at 110 minutes. The posters announced: 'You never met a pair like Butch and the Kid' and Fox prepared three trailers: one 'buddy' trailer (focusing on Newman and Redford, accompanied by the Charleston), one romantic trailer (concentrating more on Ross and featuring 'Raindrops', like a western *Bonnie and Clyde*, or even *Jules et Jim*) and one action-packed combination of the two. Reviews were generally disappointing. Vincent Canby in the *New York Times* said the film had a 'gnawing emptiness' and took 'shortcuts to lyricism'. Pauline Kael in the *New Yorker* saw the film as 'the bottom of the pit', in reference to Etta telling the outlaws the reasons why she wants to go with them to South America, 'I'm 26 and I'm single and a schoolteacher and that's the bottom of the pit.' But the public loved the film. On its initial release, *Sundance* grossed almost $46 million in the US. Re-release posters announced: 'Butch and the Kid are Back…Just for the Fun of It' and called the film: 'Probably the most entertaining western ever made'. In the UK it was passed uncut as a Certificate 'A' in September 1969 (it was rated 'M' in the US). In Italy, where Redford was less known, it was released simply as *Butch Cassidy*, in France it was called *Butch Cassidy et Le Kid* and in Germany *Zwei Banditen* ('Two Bandits'). 'Raindrops Keep Fallin'' went to number one in the US charts in January 1970 and stayed there for four weeks; in the UK it reached number 38 – it also won the Oscar for Best Song. The film won awards for Best Original Score, Best Cinematography for Conrad Hall and Best Story and Screenplay for Goldman, though it failed in its nominations for Best Director and Best Picture.

Sundance was highly influential on westerns, though perhaps its closest descendant in style and tone was Hill's own *The Sting* (1973), again teaming Newman and Redford, this time operating a betting scam in Depression-era Chicago. On TV, the comedy western pilot *Alias Smith and Jones* (1970) used Butch and Sundance's pseudonyms from their time in Bolivia. Pete Duel played Hannibal Hayes (aka 'Joshua Smith') and Ben Murphy was Jed 'Kid' Curry (aka 'Thaddeus Jones'), while Susan

Saint James played a whitewashed Fanny Porter (as 'Miss Porter', a prim local banker). The pilot began: 'This is the story of two pretty good badmen, who robbed the rich…and kept the money for themselves.' The subsequent series (1971–1973) was filled with jokey references to Butch and Sundance's escapades. Tom Berenger was cast as Butch and William Katt as Sundance in *Butch and Sundance, the Early Days* (1978), a prequel to Hill's movie. Katherine Ross made the TV movie *Wanted: The Sundance Woman* (1976), a fictionalised account of Etta Place's further adventures and Elizabeth Montgomery (from TV's *Bewitched*) played Etta in *Mrs Sundance* (1973).

Newman was the number one box-office star in the US from 1969 to 1970, and was third only to Wayne and Eastwood in 1971, while Redford also became hugely popular, topping the list in 1974, 1975 and 1976. Both made more westerns, with very different fortunes. Newman's projects, including John Huston's *The Life and Times of Judge Roy Bean* (1972) and Robert Altman's *Buffalo Bill and the Indians…or Sitting Bull's History Lesson* (1976), were less successful than Redford's. *Judge Roy Bean* was envisaged and marketed as a knockabout comedy in the *Sundance* mould – 'If This Story Ain't True, it Shoulda Been!' Audiences weren't as receptive to grizzled Newman in a witty, understated black comedy, though it still took $8 million in the US. It features Huston's take on the fashion for a song montage in the middle of the film; here Andy Williams croons 'Marmalade, Molasses & Honey', while Newman pushes a six-foot black bear on a swing and fools around on a seesaw. Often with a liberal, ecological theme, Redford's westerns included *Tell Them Willie Boy is Here* (1969 – with Katherine Ross) and the blockbusters *Jeremiah Johnson* (1972 – which took $21 million in the US) and *The Electric Horseman* (1979 – $31 million). Redford also wrote *The Outlaw Trail: A Journey Through Time*, published in 1978, in which western enthusiast Redford and a group of expert cowboys and historians visited many of the locations depicted in *Sundance*, including Hole-in-the-Wall and Robbers' Roost. Redford's odyssey ended with the actor meeting Cassidy's 94-year-old sister, Lula Parker Betenson, at Cassidy's childhood home in Circleville, Utah. Redford had first met her while working on *Sundance* – Newman famously greeted her on set with, 'Hi, I'm Butch,' to be answered with, 'Hi, I'm your sister.' Both Newman and Redford are still deeply associated with *Sundance* and it remains the most popular film of their respective careers. Redford founded the Sundance Institute in Park City, Utah, in 1980 (a training facility for young filmmakers) and the annual Sundance indie film festival, while Newman is patron of the 'Hole in the Wall' charity summer camp scheme throughout the US.

The myth of Hole-in-the-Wall, the Wild Bunch and Butch and Sundance still fascinates today. Rumours abound of what actually happened in the plaza of San Vicente. Most plausible is that Sundance was killed in the square and Butch, when he realised the odds, shot himself – the Bolivian soldiers reported that they found his body behind a barricade of furniture. Others believe that the two were bushwhacked and Sundance was so badly wounded that Butch had to shoot him – then Butch stole a dead soldier's uniform and slipped away during the night. Butch's family maintain that he returned to the US and lived under the name William Thadeus Phillips, set up a business making adding machines, served in the Mexican Revolution and later tried to sell a manuscript of his life story as Butch Cassidy entitled 'The Bandit Invincible', before his death in 1937. But the blaze of glory demise is how Butch and Sundance will always be remembered. The frozen sepia image of the duo, guns smoking, on the run, has passed into cinematic folklore, as much as their western exploits illuminate the history books. Most importantly, with *Butch Cassidy and the Sundance Kid*, Hill, Newman and Redford succeeded in creating a western that is loved by filmgoers who don't even like westerns.

23

'I Got Poetry in Me'

— *McCabe & Mrs Miller* (1971)

McCabe & Mrs Miller (1971)
Credits
DIRECTOR – Robert Altman
PRODUCERS – David Foster and Mitchell Brower
ASSOCIATE PRODUCER – Robert Eggenweiler
STORY – Edmund Naughton
SCREENPLAY – Robert Altman and Brian McKay
DIRECTOR OF PHOTOGRAPHY – Vilmos Zsigmond
EDITOR – Louis Lombardo
ART DIRECTORS – Philip Thomas and Al Locatelli
MUSIC – Leonard Cohen
Panavision/Technicolor
A Robert Altman-David Foster Production
Released by Warner Bros (A Kinney Leisure Service)
121 minutes
Cast
Warren Beatty (John Q. 'Pudgy' McCabe); Julie Christie
(Constance Miller); Rene Auberjonois (Patrick 'Paddy'
Sheehan); John Schuck (Freddy Smalley); Bert Remsen
(Bartley Coyle); Keith Carradine (Cowboy); Hugh Millais
(Jake 'Dog' Butler); Shelley Duvall (Ida Coyle); Tom Hill
(Archer, Bearpaw brothel owner); Michael Murphy (Eugene
Sears); Antony Holland (Ernie Hollander); Manfred Schulz
(Kid); Jace Vander Veen (Breed); Corey Fischer (Reverend
Mr Elliott); William Devane (Clement Samuels, the lawyer);
Jackie Crossland ('Two-for-One Lily') Elizabeth Murphy
('Pinto Kate'); Carey Lee McKenzie ('Almighty Alma'); Janet
Wright (Eunice); Linda Sorensen (Blanche); Elisabeth
Knight (Birdie); Maysie Hoy (Maisie); Linda Kupecek

(Ruth); Wayne Grace (Sheehan's bartender); Jack Riley
(Riley Quinn); Jeremy Newson (Jeremy Berg); Robert Fortier
(Town Drunk); Wayne Robson (McCabe's bartender); Wesley
Taylor (Shorty Dunn); Anne Cameron (Mrs Dunn); Graeme
Campbell (Bill Cubbs); J.S. Johnson (J.J.); Joe Clarke (Joe
Shortreed); Harry Frazier (Andy Anderson); Edwin Collier
(Gilchrist); Terence Kelly (Quigley); Brantley F. Kearns
(Fiddle player); Don Francks (Buffalo); Rodney Gage
(Sumner Washington, the barber); Lili Francks (Mrs
Washington); Joan Maguire, Harvey Lowe, Eric Schneider,
Milos Zatovic, Caludine Melgrave, Derek Deurvorst,
Alexander Diakun and Gordon Robertson (Townspeople)

*   *   *

In the early seventies, Robert Altman rose to prominence with a series of unique, quirky films with an unmistakable style – not genre films, but dramas made within well-known genres. His first big success was *M*A*S*H* (1970), a Korean War black comedy, which won the Palm D'Or at Cannes. He later made the Raymond Chandler private-eye movie *The Long Goodbye* (1973), a country and western musical called *Nashville* (1975) and the Hollywood satire *The Player* (1992). *McCabe & Mrs Miller*, released in 1971, is the first of Altman's two westerns.

Made under the working title 'The Presbyterian Church Wager', but released as *McCabe & Mrs Miller*, it was based on the novel *McCabe* by Edmund Naughton. The screenplay adaptation was written by Brian McKay, with further work by Altman. In 1902, gambler John Q. McCabe drifts into the zinc mining town of Presbyterian Church, on the Washington–Canadian border, where he is mistaken for notorious gunman 'Pudgy' McCabe, the killer of Bill Roundtree. Together with local saloon owner Patrick Sheehan, McCabe establishes himself as a businessman, taking a stake in the gambling house and saloon. In a town with a male population of over 100, he notices a gap in the market and buys three prostitutes from Archer, a brothel owner in the valley town of Bearpaw, to start his own business. As Presbyterian Church flourishes, Constance Miller arrives from Bearpaw with a proposition for McCabe. He can provide finance for a high-class bordello, which she will manage and she promptly imports five prostitutes from Seattle. McCabe falls for Constance, though she is more interested in finding comfort from smoking opium. The town grows and business booms, but the Harrison Shaunassey Mining Company in Bearpaw begins to take an interest in McCabe's success. They make him substantial offers for his holdings; Sheehan takes them up on their deal, but cocky McCabe turns them down, claiming he's 'as smart as a possum'. When he realises the mining company won't increase their deal and plan to kill him, McCabe panics, but it's too late. Three hired gunmen, Butler, Breed and Kid, are dispatched to Presbyterian Church to murder him.

According to producer Mitchell Brower, John Wayne and Raquel Welch were suggested for the title roles. Altman wanted Elliot Gould for John McCabe, but

Warren Beatty – who was impressed with *M*A*S*H* – became involved and it was he who was cast as the bearded braggart with no head for big business. Beatty was a superstar, who had made a fortune from his success with *Bonnie and Clyde* (1967), where he had starred as robber Clyde Barrow. English actress Julie Christie was cast as cockney Constance Miller. Christie had appeared in *Billy Liar* (1963), as Lara in *Doctor Zhivago* (1965), in *Darling* (1966) and as Bathsheba Everdene in *Far from the Madding Crowd* (1967). One of the top actresses of her generation, Christie had just made the eerie Norfolk-set period romance *The Go-Between* (1971) and would follow *McCabe* with the supernatural thriller, *Don't Look Now* (1973). She was also Beatty's lover at the time.

Altman filled the supporting roles with a cast that appeared to have sprung straight from the grimy pages of western history books. Whiskers were de rigueur for the men, with the women pasty and without make-up. The actors' costumes look lived-in and so do their faces, aptly so for such a harsh mountainous climate: a perpetual autumn-winter of rain, misty mornings, frost forms, ice and snow. Many of these roles were taken by Altman's stock actors. Shelley Duvall played mail-order bride Ida, whose husband Bartley Coyle is killed in a fracas, so she has had to turn to prostitution. French-Canadian New Yorker Rene Auberjonois was excellent as 'Paddy' Sheehan; Keith Carradine appeared in his film debut as drifter 'Cowboy' who is murdered by the Harrison Shaunassey gunmen. Michael Murphy and Antony Holland played Sears and Hollander, the mining company's polite business representatives. Imposing British actor Hugh Millais was suitably threatening as the mining company's less subtle hired gun, Butler, backed by his henchmen: caped Breed (Jace Vander Veen) and blond Kid (Manfred Schultz). Millais was formerly a singer and was Edmund Naughton's suggestion for the role. Corey Fischer and John Schuck played local reverend Mr Elliot and well-dressed businessman Smalley. Jeremy Newson had an excellent supporting role as McCabe's dense, bumbling foreman Jeremy Berg, with bottletop glasses, lank blond hair and beard, who is given to misquoting McCabe's witticisms.

Budgeted at $2.4 million, *McCabe & Mrs Miller* was filmed chronologically in Vancouver, British Columbia, Canada. The town grew during production, with the rough canvas and timber hovels becoming Presbyterian Church (the valley settlement of 'Bearpaw' was a more robust construction and boasted a vintage traction engine). The buildings are huddled around the creek and a wobbly planked rope bridge. In the historical west, professional gamblers arrived in the first wave with the cattle drives or prospectors in boomtowns like this one, to fleece the miners and drovers of their earnings. McCabe's saloon-brothel begins life as timber shell (and sheet banners daubed: 'Good Liquor and Fair Games of Chance – Opening Soon') and evolves into sturdy 'McCabe's House of Fortune'. Other structures included a bathhouse, mercantile shops, a waterwheel, saloons, the shacks of Chinatown and the church on a hill with its tall spire, which gives the town its name; historically, there were many saloons in these boomtowns, but few churches.

Shooting took place in the winter of 1970–1971. Interiors were filmed on the grimy sets, with sound recorded live, which proved problematic in post-production.

Altman dictated that his actors lived their roles and the result is one of the most authentic depictions of the frontier on film. Altman lensed the interior group scenes with two cameras, so that he could zoom in on unsuspecting actors and pick out their performances from the saloon's general hubbub; tiny details and bit parts were thus brought into the foreground and highlighted. Even Constance's first appearance is filmed this way, with brief glimpses of her in a doorway in Bearpaw. Altman's style was unconventional and Beatty wasn't keen; he improved over numerous takes, while Christie and Altman preferred only one or two. The eventual cost of Altman's working methods added $600,000 to the budget but was well worth it.

At Altman's suggestion, the music in the film was provided by Canadian Leonard Cohen, the poet, novelist and singer-songwriter, who had published four books of poetry between 1956 and 1966, and a novel *The Favourite Game* (1963). The songs used in the film, 'The Stranger Song', 'Winter Lady' and 'Sisters of Mercy' were among the writer's most beautiful, from his 1968 debut album 'Songs of Leonard Cohen'. These mournful acoustic folk tunes, with Cohen's lyrics, deft and lovely in their simplicity, offer an ideal evocation of lonely life in Presbyterian Church and the temporal nature of love. Roving gambler ballad 'Stranger Song' becomes McCabe's theme ('He was just some Joseph looking for a manger…his golden arm dispatching cards …watching for the card that is so high and wild he'll never need to deal another'), the love song of separation 'Winter Lady' is Constance's ('Travelling lady, stay awhile, until the night is over…I lived with a child of snow'), while 'Sisters of Mercy' is used for the prostitutes ('They brought me their comfort and later they brought me their song'). Fiddler Brantley F. Kearns, who also plays on the soundtrack (often

'Name Your Poison': Original UK pressbook depicting Constance (Julie Christie) and John (Warren Beatty) – business partners, then lovers, in Robert Altman's *McCabe & Mrs Miller* (1971).

as punctuation to jokey dialogue in the film), appears on screen in the saloon and during the funeral of Bartley Coyle, when the prostitutes sing the hymn, 'Asleep in Jesus'.

The murky Panavision photography was by Vilmos Zsigmond, who had started out on very low-budget horror-thrillers, including cult favourite *The Incredibly Strange Creatures who gave up Living and became Mixed Up Zombies* (1964), and westerns like *Five Bloody Graves* (1969). Following *McCabe* he lensed Altman's *Images* and *The Long Goodbye*, plus Peter Fonda's dreamlike acid western *The Hired Hand* (1971), *Deliverance* (1972) and *The Deer Hunter* (1978). Lens-flair, that refracted, technicolor rainbow effect seen in *Easy Rider* and *The Hired Hand*, was used by Zsigmond for some of *McCabe*'s early morning autumn sunrise exteriors. For the finale, extra falling snowflakes were added with an optical effect, to create the blizzard; the actual snowfall was melting, so fake snow was also spread on the ground. Zsigmond contrasts the burnished warmth of the interior of the brothel, a wombly glow, with the freezing exteriors. The cinematographer was instructed by Altman to 'flash' the film stock (pre-exposing the film to light, before it is used) to attain a strange, blurry hue to the fuzzy-edged images – flashed stock is best used in underlit conditions.

Though Altman had directed western TV episodes of *Sugarfoot*, *Maverick* and *Bonanza*, *McCabe & Mrs Miller* was a major stylistic departure for the genre on the cinema screen. In *M*A*S*H* Altman had overlapped dialogue on the soundtrack, so the audience hear a blur of voices, which don't seem to make sense, but interweave into a unique aural presentation, as the audience catch fragments of character exposition and plot nuance through these half-heard conversations. Unfortunately, the sound is especially muddy early in *McCabe*, which makes the initial expository scenes confusing – Beatty was livid about this and ended up looping some of his lines to make them audible above the mumble. Many euphemisms, colloquialisms, profanities and slang are used throughout (for instance, a brothel is a 'gooseberry ranch', prostitutes are 'chippies'), which adds to the quirky atmosphere, as miners discuss such offbeat subjects as tonsorial elegance and the price of a bath.

Altman's films are laced with black humour. McCabe acts tough, but squirms before the miners' gunmen, during a meeting at Sheehan's. Butler, the company's ursine, moustached killer, tells McCabe, 'I don't make deals...I came up here to hunt bear,' a comment that is lost on McCabe, as the gambler dons his bearskin coat. In the finale, McCabe takes shelter in the church on the hill – a safe haven in his hour of need, but also it is the first time in the entire film we have seen inside the building, which has no pews or pulpit, just piles of junk. In the town named Presbyterian Church, the most important buildings are pleasure-palaces: brothels, bathhouses and saloons.

The verbal sparring between Constance and McCabe is well played by Christie and Beatty. On her arrival, Constance says, 'I could eat a bloody horse.' 'At Sheehan's place you probably will,' answers McCabe. 'Another frontier wit, I see,' Constance notes sarcastically, as she ridicules McCabe, 'If you want to make out you're such a fancy dude, you ought to wear something besides that cheap Jockey Club cologne.'

She wants to give the town 'a proper sporting house', while he's trying to run an unhygienic brothel from a row of tents. 'I'm a whore,' she says, 'And I know an awful lot about whorehouses.' It's clear throughout their relationship that she is in the driving seat – she has the business head, the ambition to think big. McCabe tells his employees, 'You got the Goddamn saddle on the wrong horse' (meaning that he is running the show), but even he has to pay Constance in order to spend the night with her. They are both drifters, temporarily in each other's orbit: as Cohen's 'Winter Lady' puts it, 'I'm just a station on your way, I know I'm not your lover.' For its chilly setting, *McCabe* is infused with warmth, with moments of perceptive tenderness.

McCabe's persona is all bluff and bravado. The locals suspect he's notorious gunman 'Pudgy' McCabe. McCabe's usual is an egg-nog (a double whisky and a raw egg) while he enjoys quoting his favourite, meaningless saying, 'If a frog had wings, he wouldn't bump his ass so much'. But following his early success, McCabe quickly finds himself out of his depth. The locals don't help him face the mining gunmen, presuming a gunman of 'Pudgy's' reputation can easily handle them; only Constance tries to talk him out of the confrontation, one that foolish McCabe has brought upon himself. The ruthless mining companies are only interested in the zinc deposits. Butler recounts that Chinese workers carrying a charge of dynamite are dispatched down the zinc mine; the fine for 'Johnny Chinaman's' accidental death is only $50 and the discovery of a rich vein will more than bear the cost. Cold gunman Butler recognises the kind of men able to kill and notes of phoney McCabe, 'That man never killed anybody.'

Constance Miller, with her cockney accent, frizzy hair and straw hat, evokes an opium-fuelled Eliza Doolittle. Forthright in her opinions and driven in her business strategy, she has the maths and the know-how to make their venture work. The bathhouse is a subsidiary of the sporting house – patrons can't visit the latter if they haven't visited the former. McCabe complains that his saloon is empty, then changes his tune when Constance delivers her profits. Constance looks after her employees – they receive bed and board, and earn a bit of money for themselves. Constance herself uses opium as a buffer, smoked from a pipe held over a lantern, in her cosy boudoir. After an evening puff, she's smiling and glittery-eyed, a different person from the snappy, sarcastic madame of daytime. McCabe notices this change, 'You're a funny little thing – sometimes you're just as sweet and then other times…' without recognising her addiction.

McCabe is related to the ultra-realistic 'mud and rags' style of westerns that became popular in the early seventies. Examples of this grungy, often excessively violent, sub-trend include *Macho Callahan* (1970), *The Great Northfield Minnesota Raid* (1971) and *Bad Company* (1972). Stan Dragoti's *Dirty Little Billy* (1972) had the sloppiest mud and tattiest rags, in its anti-western tale of Billy McCarty's early years in the puddled town of Coffeyville, before he shot people and became Billy the Kid. Altman's sudden violence jars the audience, as in the director's *The Long Goodbye*, where hoodlum Mark Rydell wantonly smashes a Coke bottle into his girlfriend's face, disfiguring her, to prove a point. In *McCabe*, prostitute Almighty Alma emerges screaming from her tent struggling with a patron and proceeds to stab him maniacally several times. Hired gun Kid traps amiable 'Cowboy' on a rope bridge across the icy creek and instead of provoking him into action, Kid tricks the naïve drifter by asking to see his pistol. When the cowboy goes to draw his gun, Kid blasts him off the rope bridge in slow motion, leaving Cowboy's corpse bobbing in an icy creek – a horrible scene that illustrates the worthlessness of life in Altman's cynical, wild north-west.

The finale begins as a straightforward shootout, with McCabe being stalked though the snow-blanketed, early morning streets – an encounter he can only win by cheating, he's no marksman. McCabe shoots Kid in the back (in the bathhouse), shoots Breed in the back (through a window) and kills Butler with a typical gambler's trick – a Remington Derringer concealed up his sleeve. But this stock western showdown is twisted by Altman into something unexpected, with the church catching fire and the appearance of a traction engine puffing to the rescue. Ironically, having been ignored throughout the film, the church is the focal point of the finale, with its near-destruction unifying the community into action. Their euphoria at having saved the church distracts them; Constance is lost in opium, while McCabe cashes in his chips, unnoticed, in a snowdrift nearby. This was one gamble that didn't pay off.

The film was premiered in the US in June 1971. The apt poster, an image of a wooden saloon sign with portraits of Beatty and Christie, featured the tagline: 'Name Your Poison'. UK variations substituted the line: 'The Story of a Gambling Man and a Hustling Lady'. Lacklustre trailers, scored with Cohen's 'Stranger Song' and 'Winter Lady' failed to show the film at its best. Critics were mixed in their reviews. Judith Crist in *New York* called it 'a sad and haunting frontier ballad' and Pauline Kael saw, 'a beautiful pipe dream', but many didn't like the muffled soundtrack and murky visuals. *Variety* said the 'moody photography backfired into pretentiousness', while Rex Reed in the *New York Daily News* called Altman 'once talented', who had now released 'an incoherent, amateurish, simple-minded, boring and totally worthless piece of garbage'. Such press did not help the film's commercial fortunes and it was outgrossed by Warners' 1971–1972 hits: *Summer of '42*, *Dirty Harry*, *Klute*, *A Clockwork Orange* and Tom Laughlin's hugely popular *Billy Jack*, a neo-western featuring a karate-kicking, half-breed Vietnam War veteran protecting wild mustangs against redneck lawmen, which earned $32.5 million in the US. Beatty lobbied Warners to re-release the film, saying they hadn't put their weight behind its first release; new posters featured some positive press reviews ('Beautiful', 'Superb', 'Remarkable') and it eventually took $4 million. Leonard Cohen's contribution was released as a three-song EP to tie-in with the film. Christie was nominated for a Best Actress Oscar for her performance, but lost out to another Warners film: *Klute* with Jane Fonda. Christie went on to star with Beatty in the sex comedy *Shampoo* (1975), which was much more commercially successful than *McCabe*, to the tune of $60 million. In Spain *McCabe* was *Los Vividores* ('The Scroungers'), in France *John McCabe* and in Italy *I Compari* ('The Friends'). In 1976 Altman returned to the genre with *Buffalo Bill and the Indians, or Sitting Bull's History Lesson*, a bicentennial, myth-busting anti-western, which despite the presence of Paul Newman and Burt Lancaster, died at the box office.

McCabe & Mrs Miller is now hailed as one of the jewels of seventies cinema and one of Altman's best films. HBO's hit TV series *Deadwood* (2004–2006) certainly owes something of its atmosphere to *McCabe*. From its title sequence, with a galloping black steed and disorientating folksy bluegrass theme music (by David Schwartz), *Deadwood* was a departure for TV westerns. Created by David Milch and set in Deadwood City, Indian Territory *circa* 1876, the series told the story of the growing town and its unsavoury inhabitants. In this filthy place, everybody is out to make a buck, while murdered copses are fed to pigs and wolves run off with the severed limbs of settlers, the hacked remains of a Sioux massacre. Unlike *McCabe* the dialogue comes over loud and clear, with some of the worst language ever heard on TV screens; the concept was to substitute authentic frontier cussing with its contemporary equivalents, resulting in such epigrams as, 'I may have fucked my life up flatter than hammered shit'. One of the foulest is Calamity Jane (Robin Weigert). Keith Carradine (from *McCabe*) turned up at the beginning of the series as Wild Bill Hickok (or 'Wild Bill Fucking Hickok' as he's referred to). Timothy Olyphant was excellent as marshal turned Deadwood storekeeper Seth Bullock, while Ian McShane buried his *Lovejoy* persona in the Dakota Hills, as Al Swearengen, the cussing, Gem saloon-owner, con man and thief. *Deadwood* is a satisfyingly disgusting town, which wallows in the mud of *McCabe & Mrs Miller*'s demythologised, profane west.

24

'Here in This Land, Man Must Have Power'

— *Ulzana's Raid* (1972)

Ulzana's Raid (1972)
Credits
DIRECTOR – Robert Aldrich
PRODUCER – Carter DeHaven
ASSOCIATE PRODUCER – Alan Sharp
STORY AND SCREENPLAY – Alan Sharp
DIRECTOR OF PHOTOGRAPHY – Joseph Biroc
EDITOR – Michael Luciano
ART DIRECTOR – James D. Vance
MUSIC – Frank DeVol
Technicolor
A Universal Production
Released by Universal Pictures
103 minutes
Cast

Burt Lancaster (Archie McIntosh, chief-of-scouts); Bruce
Davison (Lieutenant Garnett DeBuin); Jorge Luke (Ke-Ni-
Tay); Richard Jaeckel (Sergeant Burns); Joaquin Martinez
(Ulzana); Lloyd Bochner (Captain Charles Gates); Douglas
Watson (Major Cartwright); Karl Swenson (Willy Rukeyser);
Gladys Holland (Mrs Rukeyser); Dran Hamilton (Mrs
Riordan); John Pearce (Corporal); Margaret Fairchild (Mrs
Abbie Ginsford); Aimee Eccles (McIntosh's wife); Richard
Bull (Ginsford); Otto Reichow ('Dutch' Steegmeyer, Indian
Agent); Dean Smith (Trooper Horowitz); Larry Randles
(Trooper Mulkearn); Hal Maguire, Bill Burton, Ted
Markland, R.L. Armstrong, John McKee, Nick Cravat,
Tony Epper, Fred Brookfield, Walter Scott, Richard
Farnsworth, Jerry Gatlin (Cavalry troopers); Larry Colelay,

Henry Camargo, Marvin Fragua, Gil Escandon, Benny
Thomson, George Aguilar, Frank Gonzales, Wallace Sinyella
(Ulzana's raiders)

*   *   *

Conceived as an allegory of Vietnam, Robert Aldrich's *Ulzana's Raid* is the most gruesome, hard-hitting western of all concerning the southwestern guerrilla warfare of the Apache Wars, its tactics, tortures and mutilations. It is not for the faint-hearted, nor those with fond memories of John Ford's patriotic 7th Cavalry movies.

For decades filmmakers used Native American 'savages' on screen as cinematic cannon fodder and it was 1950 until the cycle was broken with Delmer Daves's *Broken Arrow*. Scout Tom Jeffords (James Stewart, who also narrates) settles with Chief Cochise's Apache band and eventually takes an Apache wife, Morning Star (Debra Paget). Peace is brokered with the army, but renegade Apaches under Geronimo, as well as troublemaking whites, shatter the calm and Morning Star is killed. Made before Stewart's *Winchester '73*, but released afterwards, *Broken Arrow* was filmed in Technicolor in the red buttes of Sedona, Arizona. Jeffords was a real historical figure, actually a New Yorker, who became a stagecoach superintendent in the west. Daves's presentation of Apache culture is detailed, with rituals and ceremonies recreated; it was the first time Indian dances on screen hadn't been 'War' or 'Rain' dances. Jeff Chandler scored particularly well as Cochise, a role he repeated in *The Battle at Apache Pass* (1951) and *Taza, Son of Cochise* (1954 – Rock Hudson was Taza). The Apache roles are real characterisations, fleshed-out and believable, not one-dimensional clichés: Cochise tells Jeffords that his affair with Morning Star isn't news to anyone ('Your secret was as quiet as the thunder'), while the peace is broken by Geronimo, the archetypal 'warlike Apache'. But most importantly, instead of saying 'How', the Native Americans were now asking 'Why?'

'Cavalry and Indian' action movies petered out during the fifties. A film like *Arrowhead* (1953 – filmed on location at Fort Clark, Bracketville, Texas), featuring a racist vendetta between chief-of-scouts Ed Bannon (a rigid Charlton Heston, based on scout Al Sieber) and Apache chief Toriano (Jack Palance), was an exception. Indian Wars scenarios were also used as vehicles for exploring contemporary issues, with Ralph Nelson's *Duel at Diablo* (1966) probably the best example. Based on Marvin H. Albert's 1957 novel 'Apache Rising', the story follows a special mission to escort two wagons of ammunition from Fort Creel, through Apache country, to beleaguered Fort Concho (Fort Duell in the book). Led by Lieutenant McAllister (Scottish-accented Bill Travers), the 30-strong escort of raw recruits are guided by scout Jess Remsberg (James Garner), who plots revenge on the murderer of his Comanche wife Singing Sky. Add to this bronco-buster Toller (Sidney Poitier), racist trader Willard Grange (Willard Graff in the book), his estranged wife Ellen, her mixed-race baby with an Apache father, and Chief Chata on the warpath, and tensions run high. The racial conflicts within the group, especially between intolerant Grange, and Ellen and Toller, are intensified en route to Concho. Ambushed and decimated, the command end up trapped at a waterhole in Diablo Canyon. Remsberg rides for help, arriving with the cavalry led by Colonel Foster (director Nelson).

Filmed in Kanab, southern Utah and the surrounding rugged deserts and mountains, *Duel at Diablo* is one of the most violent westerns of the sixties. From the opening shot, when a knife slashes through the United Artists logo, there are several instances of white cadavers discovered strung up, spread eagled, burned or tortured: 'Two days dying, Apache-style'. These moments are actually quite restrained compared to Albert's savage novel. Grange, who is revealed as Singing Sky's killer, is captured by the Apache and roasted on a revolving wagon wheel and Remsberg hands him a pistol with which to commit suicide (in the book, the scout shoots him). Dennis Weaver was excellent as Grange, while Ingmar Bergman's thoughtful Swedish blonde icon Bibi Andersson (as Ellen) makes an unusual addition to the western cast. Neal Hefti's terrific score, with its groovy, syncopated title track, and Nelson's offbeat style, make *Diablo* a breath of fresh air compared to most Hollywood 'Cavalry and Indian' shoot-'em-ups. The slow-motion scenes of Remsberg, struggling through the blistering heat haze, holding on to his horse's tail, on his mission of mercy to Concho, and the frequent, tightly edited action scenes stand out. Posters introduced the protagonists: 'The Outrider…the Loner…the Lieutenant…the Outcast Bride…her Husband' and declared: 'Yesterday they fought each other – Today they fought together in a dead end canyon called Diablo'.

Another popular, action-packed 'Cavalry and Indians' western was Gordon Douglas's actioner *Rio Conchos* (1964). A box-office hit for 20th Century-Fox, it starred Richard Boone as Apache-killing James Lassiter, who teams up with Captain Haven (Stuart Whitman), Sergeant Franklin (Jim Brown) and Mexican murderer Rodriguez (Tony Franciosa) on an assignment to discover who stole 2,000 repeating rifles. It was based on Clair Huffaker's 'Guns of Rio Conchos' and *The Comancheros*. The culprit is Confederate renegade Colonel Theron Pardee (Edmond O'Brien), who has armed Apache Chief Bloodshirt for a war against the 'white-eyes'. Captured at Pardee's half-constructed mansion headquarters in the desert (filmed in spectacular Moab, Utah), Lassiter, Haven and Franklin are dragged behind Apache horses around the camp, in a scene noticeably violent for its time.

By the time Aldrich was preparing *Ulzana's Raid* in 1971, American troops in Vietnam were dying every night on the 6 o'clock news. Finally a true depiction of the southwest seeped onto cinema screens. A true story from the mining town of Mogollon, New Mexico, illustrates the desperate times of the 1870s and 1880s. As a raiding party of Apaches approached, the miners concealed themselves in a thicket, but their dog growled, so the miners throttled it, rather than be given away. It is impossible to imagine John Wayne, or even Clint Eastwood, doing this on screen, but several westerns in the early seventies began to show this dark side of the genre. For barbarism, the Apache Wars had no equal: the long, slow death of a campfire (lit between tethered legs, or smouldering on a spread eagled victim's chest), being eaten by ants, skinned alive, or strangled by dampened rawhide in the midday sun.

Written by Alan Sharp, *Ulzana's Raid* was based on actual events, when reservation Chiricahua Apache Ulzana (sometimes called Jolsanny or Josanie) went on the rampage with ten warriors in November, 1885, causing mayhem across New Mexico. Sharp's script details the pursuit of renegade Ulzana and his eight-strong band, who break out of the San Carlos Reservation. A party of troopers from Fort Lowell are dispatched to apprehend or kill the fugitives. They are led by inexperienced Lieutenant DeBuin, with seasoned scout McIntosh along as his adviser and Apache Ke-Ni-Tay as their tracker. The raiders loot, burn, torture and kill their way across Arizona, and Ulzana tries to outmanoeuvre the cavalry, by dismounting his warriors, leaving a phony pony trail and then doubling back, his horses fresh, to catch the troops off-guard. But McIntosh outwits Ulzana and beats him to his own horses, leaving the raiders on foot. Eventually the soldiers decide to call Ulzana's bluff, splitting their force and coaxing Ulzana into an ambush in Dog Cañon. The plan works, but many of the soldiers' decoy party and most of the Apaches are killed. Admitting defeat, Ulzana allows Ke-Ni-Tay to execute him. McIntosh is also one of the casualties and stays behind to die as DeBuin and the survivors depart for Fort Lowell.

The raid resembles warrior Geronimo's numerous forays from the San Carlos Reservation, between 1876 and his surrender in 1886. Geronimo and other Apaches loathed the reservation, where the US government tried to turn hunters into farmers. For its appalling conditions, overcrowding, corruption and intertribal disputes, it was known as 'Hell's Forty Acres'; in the film, McIntosh accuses Indian Agent, 'Dutch' Steegmeyer of watering the Apaches' beef, increasing its weight. Photos of Geronimo's band on the run, wearing blue cavalry jackets and brandishing Winchesters and telescopes, closely resemble Ulzana's raiding party.

Scout Archie McIntosh hunkers down behind his felled mount, one of many, in Robert Aldrich's *Ulzana's Raid* (1972).

Burt Lancaster, cast as McIntosh, was reunited with Aldrich on *Ulzana*, with whom he had made *Apache* and *Vera Cruz*. Lancaster had just made *Valdez is Coming* (1971) in Almeria, and *Lawman* (1971) in Durango, Mexico. Lancaster's character, McIntosh, was based on General Crook's chief of scouts, tough half-Indian, half-Scottish Archie McIntosh, who served with ace scout Al Sieber in Arizona and New Mexico; Lancaster deploys the hint of a Scottish accent in some scenes.

Cast opposite Lancaster was a young actor: fresh-faced, 26-year-old Bruce Davison as DeBuin. *Ulzana* shares the central 'rough westerner versus clean-shaven soldier boy' dynamic of *Rio Conchos* (1964) and *A Thunder of Drums* (1961). Davison had previously been successful as *Willard* (1971), the rat-training cult horror movie hero. The supporting cast included Richard Jaeckel as leathery Sergeant Burns, hardened and full of hatred for the Apache. Jaeckel had appeared in some of the great action movies of the fifties and sixties, often as a tough NCO, including Aldrich's *Attack!* (1956) and *The Dirty Dozen* (1967). He'd also put in good performances in westerns, notably *3:10 to Yuma*, *Cowboy* and *Chisum*. Aimee Eccles, as McIntosh's Indian wife, had played *Little Big Man*'s wife Sunshine; Dran Hamilton as tortured Mrs Riordan, appeared as Billy the Kid's mum Catherine, in *Dirty Little Billy* (1972). Jorge Luke gave one of the film's best performances, as monosyllabic tracker Ke-Ni-Tay. He also appeared as one of William Holden's wild bunch, in *The Revengers* (1972), in pursuit of a murderous Comanchero. Joaquin Martinez's powerful silent portrayal of Ulzana recalls his role as Paints His Shirt Red, the Crow chief whose sudden appearances unnerve Robert Redford's mountain man *Jeremiah Johnson* (1972).

Ulzana's Raid was shot near Nogales, Arizona, in the Coronado National Forest and the Valley of Fire in Overton, Nevada in 48 days, from 18 January to 11 March 1972. Universal Pictures provided the modest $2.4 million budget and the cast was small for a western – primarily a squad of troopers and nine Apaches. As in *Chato's Land* (1971), the Apaches are a harsh reflection of their inhospitable, barren land. Major Cartwright, Fort Lowell's commander, notes that General Sheridan once said if he owned Hell and Arizona, 'He'd live in Hell and rent out Arizona.' DeBuin corrects him, saying that Sheridan was speaking of Texas. 'Maybe,' says Cartwright, 'But he meant Arizona.' *Ulzana's Raid* was photographed by Joseph Biroc in 1.85:1 ratio Technicolor. There is no finesse or poetry to the images, which often make the film look like a TV movie: it's the script that counts here – and the gallons of blood. Alan Sharp recalled that Lancaster was interested in the film's Vietnam parallels, the 'art' of the piece, while Aldrich cared more for the action. *Ulzana's Raid* was a tough film to make in the heat of the desert, when filming the ambush in Dog Cañon or the chase between an Apache lookout and Ke-Ni-Tay on the Mountain of Fire, but is an even tougher one to watch.

Until *Duel at Diablo*, tortures and atrocities perpetrated by Native American warriors were thoughtfully off screen, the audience's eyes averted by considerate filmmakers. In Ford's 'Cavalry Trilogy', troopers are found tied to wagon wheels 'roasted' and a gunrunning sutler is thrown alive on a fire, but these are exceptions. *Ulzana's Raid* exhibits no such consideration. In the first horrific action spot, Trooper Horowitz is escorting a buckboard carrying homesteader Mrs Ginsford and her son, Billy. They are bushwhacked by Ulzana, and Horowitz shoots Mrs Ginsford through the forehead, then makes a dash for it with the boy. When their horse is felled, Horowitz sticks a revolver in his mouth and pulls the trigger. An Apache spits at the smoking-mouthed corpse in disgust, before he and his comrades cut out Horowitz's liver and play catch with it. Later, settler Rukeyser is captured and tortured. McIntosh and company then discover him tied to a tree, disembowelled – his legs spread, a fire set at his groin and his pet dog's tail stuffed in his mouth, an example of the Apaches' sense of humour: 'Nothing you'd recognise,' says McIntosh, 'They just find some things funny.' In *Duel at Diablo*, scout Remsberg knifes his exhausted horse, Lobo, to put it out of its misery; in *Ulzana's Raid* the Apaches gut one of their lame animals, to poison a waterhole. At Riordan's farm, Mr Riordan is tied to a fence upside-down, over a smouldering fire, while Mrs Riordan is found, assaulted and battered, in a flatbed wagon; she has only been spared death because the Apache know she will slow the troop down. The censors had a field day with such gruesome fare. After all the bloodletting, Ulzana himself is dispatched by Ke-Ni-Tay off screen and buried respectfully.

The tension within the group, especially the mistrust between Christian soldier DeBuin and Apache scout Ke-Ni-Tay, echoes the racial conflicts of *Duel at Diablo*. Ke-Ni-Tay explains why Apaches kill in such an inhumane way; they gain 'power'

Apache scout Ke-Ni-Tay, Ulzana's brother-in-law, tracker and eventually executioner; Jorge Luke, impassive in *Ulzana's Raid*.

from watching men suffer. Since his time on the reservation, Ulzana's power is 'thin' – 'Here in this land, man must have power' – otherwise the raid will be a failure. Ulzana plans to take power from wiping out the patrol. Ke-Ni-Tay is Ulzana's brother-in-law; in reality, Ulzana was the brother of famed raider Chihuahua and it was McIntosh who was married to an Apache woman related to Chihuahua. At one point, four soldiers disfigure an Apache corpse in the same way that Trooper Horowitz was hacked up. DeBuin has trouble rationalising this behaviour. 'Kind of confuses the issue, don't it,' notes McIntosh. In the seventies, in the middle of the Vietnam War, this relevant 'who is right?' moral issue had added resonance.

Although they are outnumbered, Ulzana's nine-man group are the superior force in this finely balanced power play; as McIntosh says, 'Apache war parties come in all sizes – there's the kind with a hundred braves, the kind with one.' The violence in *Ulzana's Raid* was effective because it made audiences think. The well-drilled Apache raiding party are equipped with a bugle and binocular field glasses ('the long glass' as Ke-Ni-Tay calls them). They surround Rukeyser's creek-side homestead and observe his movements from afar. The raiders put three arrows into Rukeyser's dog and try to burn him out, but at the moment he's about to be overrun, a bugle sounds. Rukeyser thinks the cavalry have arrived to save him and walks outside, giving thanks ('God, you have all the praise and all the glory'), not realising he's been tricked – it isn't a trooper playing the bugle.

Ulzana's tactical plot is also influenced by *Duel at Diablo*, as the two groups try to outfox each other. 'He don't mean to fight you no place,' McIntosh tells DeBuin, 'He only means to kill you.' The key to this battle of wits is steeds. McIntosh notes that Ulzana wants the troopers to push hard, to wear out their mounts, but, 'I sure as Hell don't want to be on foot around no horse-backing Apaches.' Once Ulzana loses his horses, he has lost his edge. In the harsh deserts and sierras, mobility is all-important and the horse the essential commodity; in the endgame at Dog Cañon, McIntosh instructs the troopers to shoot their own mounts, rather than let them fall into Ulzana's hands.

The central relationship in *Ulzana's Raid* is between McIntosh, the experienced, buckskinned old Indian fighter and the son of a preacher, young Lieutenant DeBuin, six months out of the eastern military academy, who believes it's possible to be both a Christian and a soldier. McIntosh, the realist, has a strong stomach and is unmoved by the carnage that confronts him, while DeBuin, the idealist with scant frontier knowledge, turns pale when he catches sight of Rukeyser's bloody, charred remains. At Fort Lowell, the officers speculate as to what the raiders' intentions are, 'Their probable intention,' says McIntosh, 'is to burn, maim, torture, rape and murder.' The major asks the scout how many have escaped and whether they're hostile. 'Well the first is open to question, the second you can bet money on.' But at the centre of the film are the lieutenant's failings and inexperience; his indecision at the crucial moment at Dog Cañon delays his relief of McIntosh, costing the scout and several troopers their lives. Just as McIntosh has said, 'Remember the rules lieutenant – first one to make a mistake gets to burying some people.' Mortally wounded McIntosh is left behind, beneath a bedroll tarpaulin shelter. 'I don't suppose making cigarettes is one of your accomplishments?' he asks the lieutenant, who answers no. 'Never mind, you'll learn.' Leaving McIntosh to the buzzards, DeBuin says, is 'not Christian'. 'That's right lieutenant,' answers the scout, 'it's not.'

Two versions of *Ulzana's Raid* were prepared. Lancaster assembled the European version (removing Ulzana's pre-title escape from the San Carlos agency) Aldrich the US cut. Both have since been available on video or DVD. In the US the film was rated 'R'; it was premiered on 18 October 1972 in Chicago and 22 November 1972 in Los Angeles. Posters depicting McIntosh had the wordy tagline: 'One man alone understood the savagery of the early American west from both sides'. The film wasn't a commercial success, though it received favourable reviews and contains one of Lancaster's finest performances. Andrew Sarris called it the 'aptest movie yet on the senseless agony of the Vietnam War'. It is also one of best action westerns of the seventies. *Ulzana* was distributed by the Rank Organisation in the UK at

the beginning of 1973, with an 'X' rating, even after it was trimmed for violence. European prints, especially Italian (*Nessuna Pietà per Ulzana* – 'No Mercy for Ulzana') and Spanish (*La Venganza De Ulzana* – 'The Vengeance of Ulzana'), didn't cut the blood. In East Germany, Gojko Mitic starred as Ulzana in two further adventures: *Apachen: Teil 1* (1973 – Apaches: Part 1) and *Ulzana* (1974 – or *Apachen: Teil 2*) directed by Gottfried Kolditz.

Ulzana's Raid is one of those rare films. Like its contemporary *Chato's Land*, it is so violent and controversial it will never be shown in its entirety on television. In the seventies it was edited for its bloodletting; now it's abridged for horse falls. Stunts involving falling horses are the most sensitive issue regarding old westerns on TV (for this

Beautiful Spanish poster artwork for *Ulzana's Raid*, depicting Burt Lancaster as scout McIntosh and Ulzana himself, played by Joaquin Martinez. (Picture courtesy of Ian Caunce Collection).

reason it's worth hanging on to original VHS versions of the films). All the horse falls in *Ulzana's Raid* have been removed, in accordance with the Cinematograph Film [Animals] Act 1937. Riders are now galloping along in one shot and rolling on the floor in the next. Some of these falls were achieved with practices that are now illegal – often in westerns these involved tripwires, pits, hobbles or stakes. In 1985, the film was released on UK home video, rated '18', with 45 seconds of violence cut by the BBFC. In 2003 it was released on DVD, with the violence restored, but with 17 seconds of horse falls removed. UK TV showings have been edited for violence and further edited for falls: BBC2's *Moviedrome* TV presentation of the film in 1990, included all the horse stunts, but cut much of the graphic violence (the horse knifing, the liver, the dog tail). Subsequent shoddily edited TV showings have reinstated some of the violence (the dog's tail has reappeared in some versions), while further cutting the more extreme brutality and torture (the shooting of Mrs Ginsford, Trooper Horowitz's suicide), plus removing outlawed horse falls – the climax of all TV versions are now confusingly disjointed. Frank DeVol's evocative score, with subdued flute themes contrasted with 'Boots and Saddles'-style military marches, is also ruined, as the cues snap off abruptly where cuts have been made. The German DVD, *Keine Gnade für Ulzana* ('No Mercy for Ulzana'), which includes all the violence and horse stunts, runs two seconds less than 99 minutes (103 minutes at theatrical frames-per-minute timing) and has an English-language track. It is the most complete version of the film and fully depicts the powerful events of Ulzana's bloodthirsty raid.

In the early seventies, Native American issues, especially their poor treatment on and off screen, was a hot topic. Marlon Brando sent Princess Sacheen Littlefeather (actually Mexican actress Maria Cruz) to receive his Best Actor Oscar for *The Godfather* at the 1972 Oscars, where she read a critical speech protesting the treatment of Native Americans in the US, as the audience booed. 'Maybe we should give an Oscar to all the cowboys shot in John Ford movies,' said stand-in host Clint Eastwood. In 1971, Dee Brown published *Bury My Heart at Wounded Knee*, American western history told from the Native Americans' point of view, which became a bestseller. Adapted from the novel *Arrow in the Sun* by Theodore Victor Olsen, Ralph Nelson's *Soldier Blue* (1970), his companion piece to *Duel at Diablo*, featured some brutal Indian Wars footage and a scathing, accusatory depiction of the US Cavalry, trampling the US flag and Indian villages, while slaughtering innocent Cheyenne women and children. The hopeful hippy title song 'Soldier Blue', sung by Buffy Sainte-Marie ('Yes this is my country, I sprang from her and I'm learning how to count upon her') is more an indication of where Nelson's concerns lie. The film's leaden midsection concerns the relationship between an odd pair of travelling companions: Cresta Mary-Belle Lee, a white woman who once lived with the Cheyenne (played by Candice Bergen) and rookie cavalryman Honus Gant (Peter Strauss). But the shocking action that bookends the film eclipses this mushy romance. In the opening scene, an army paymaster's wagon and escort are ambushed by circling, whooping Cheyenne. Trapped in a burning thicket, the troops are subsequently massacred and dismembered. The finale is a horrible depiction of the US Cavalry's darkest hour: the attack on a Cheyenne village by the 700-strong, artillery-packing 3rd Colorado Volunteers – the 'Sand Creek Massacre'. Nelson leaves little to the imagination in the ensuing carnage.

A Man Called Horse (1970), based on a novel by Dorothy M. Johnson, cast Richard Harris as John Morgan, an English lord captured by the Sioux (Crows in the book). He learns their customs, endures their Sun Vow initiation ceremony – he is suspended from his pectorals by awls and buckskin thongs – and becomes a member of the tribe. In a brave move, almost all the dialogue is in Sioux, with no subtitles or narration. Ecologically-minded trapper *Jeremiah Johnson* may save the environment, but he still kills Blackfeet and Crow Indians (the character was based on a 'Crow Killer' named Liver-eating Johnson), while liberal *Little Big Man* (1970) was a preposterous, rollercoaster history lesson and biography of tall-tale-telling Jack Crabb, the 121-year-old survivor of the Battle of the Little Big Horn. Played with endearing charm by Dustin Hoffman, Crabb had been captured as a child by the Cheyenne (the 'Human Beings') and spent his life drifting between variant career highs and lows: storekeeper, gunfighter, religious zealot, medicine-show huckster, drunkard, hermit and scout to General Custer, while being a friend of Wild Bill Hickok and witnessing the Washita River massacre of Cheyenne by the 7th Cavalry. Custer himself has been depicted many times on screen, from Errol Flynn's heroic portrayal in *They Died With Their Boots On* (1941) and the big-budget, shot-in-Spain *Custer of the West* (1968 – starring Robert Shaw), to TV treatments such as NBC's *The Court-Martial of General George Armstrong Custer* (1977), the superior *Son of the Morning Star* (1991) and *Stolen Women, Captured Hearts* (1998).

After a long absence from cinema screens during the eighties, Native American issues came back into focus with *Dances with Wolves* (1990), directed by and starring Kevin Costner, who had previously starred in the 1985 western *Silverado*. *Dances* was a sensation – it took $81.5 million and won seven Oscars, including Best Picture, Best Director, Best Adapted Screenplay (Michael Blake, from his own story), Best Original Score (John Barry), plus cinematography, editing and sound. *Dances* tells the story of Unionist John Dunbar (Costner), who during the Civil War requests a posting out west to see the frontier 'before it's gone'. He arrives at tumbledown Fort Sedgewick to find the post deserted, save for a wolf, which he befriends. Dunbar comes into contact with the local Lakota Sioux, especially their holy man, Kicking Bird, and eventually joins the tribe, marrying Stands With a Fist, a white woman raised a Sioux, and receiving the name 'Dances with Wolves'. But when troops are posted to Fort Sedgewick, Dunbar is branded a renegade and traitor, and the army resolve to hunt him down, which begins the end of the Sioux way of life.

Breathtakingly filmed by Dean Selmer in Panavision on the rolling plains of South Dakota, *Dances with Wolves* depicts this majestic wide-open space, while Barry's score recalls his own expansive compositions for *Born Free*, *Out of Africa* and *Zulu*. The casting of several Native American actors, including Graham Greene as Kicking Bird and Rodney A. Grant as Wind in His Hair, repays the drama. Mary McDonnell as Christine is good in a moving role – a white woman who has forgotten how to speak English, desperately trying to evade her traumatic past, but forced to reawaken long-suppressed memories. *Dances* is clichéd in its depiction of whites as the baddies. An insane major posts Dunbar to a deserted fort, then commits suicide. The troopers shoot Dunbar's faithful horse, Cisco, and his wolf friend 'Two Socks', and use the pages of Dunbar's cherished journal as toilet paper, while buffalo hunters leave the plains littered with the bloody bodies of bison, their hides stripped. *Dances* has two great western set pieces: the buffalo hunt (which deployed 'Animatronic' radio-controlled bison) and a Pawnee raid on the Sioux camp, the Pawnee being the resident 'Bad Injuns'. The trailer trumpeted: 'In 1864, a man went looking for America…and found himself'. Costner has since assembled an augmented 227-minute 'Director's Cut', though the numerous explanatory scenes dispel much of the film's mystery. This version does become rather self-indulgent and the images too beautiful, resembling a National Geographic postcard from South Dakota. The Oscar-winner is the 173-minute version.

If *Dances with Wolves* treats its Native Americans with too much nostalgia and sentiment, *Ulzana's Raid* impartially depicts brutality from both sides. Both films elicit sympathy for Native Americans, but in vastly different ways. In the Arizona desert, on the trail of Ulzana, there are lessons of survival and tolerance to be learned – if they're not heeded, it is requiescant Apache.

25

'Whooped 'Em Again, Josey'

— *The Outlaw Josey Wales* (1976)

The Outlaw Josey Wales (1976)
Credits
DIRECTOR – Clint Eastwood
PRODUCER – Robert Daley
ASSOCIATE PRODUCERS – James Fargo and John G. Wilson
STORY – Forrest Carter
SCREENPLAY – Philip Kaufman and Sonia Chernus
DIRECTOR OF PHOTOGRAPHY – Bruce Surtees
EDITOR – Ferris Webster
PRODUCTION DESIGN – Tambi Larsen
MUSIC – Jerry Fielding
Panavision/DeLuxe Color
A Malpaso Production
Released by Warner Bros Pictures
135 minutes
Cast
Clint Eastwood (Josey Wales); Chief Dan George (Lone
Watie); Sondra Locke (Laura Lee Turner); Paula Trueman
(Grandma Sarah Turner); Geraldine Keams (Little
Moonlight); John Vernon (Fletcher), Bill McKinney (Captain
'Redlegs' Terrill); Sam Bottoms (Jamie); Woodrow Parfrey
(Major Best, carpetbagger on ferry); Will Sampson (Ten
Bears); John Quade (Comanchero leader); John Russell
(William 'Bloody Bill' Anderson); Joyce James (Rose); Sheb
Wooley (Travis Cobb); William O'Connell (Sim Carstairs);
Royal Dano (Ten Spot); John Mitchum (Al); John Davis
Chandler (Blond bounty hunter); Tim Roy Lowe (Second
bounty hunter); Charles Tyner (Zukie Limmer, trading post
owner); Matt Clark (Kelly); Cissy Wellman (Josey's wife);

Kyle Eastwood (Little Josey); Clay Tanner (First Texas
Ranger); Bob Hoy (Second Texas Ranger); Erik Holland
(Union army sergeant); Madeline T. Holmes (Grannie
Hawkins); Faye Hamblin (Grandpa); Buck Kartalian
(Shopkeeper); John Verros (Chato); Frank Schofield (Senator
Lane); Len Lasser (Abe); Doug McGrath (Lige); Bruce M.
Fischer (Yoke); Danny Green (Lemuel, the ferryman)

*   *   *

In the mid-sixties Clint Eastwood became one of the most bankable western stars
and a worthy successor to John Wayne. Eastwood grew up watching and enjoying
westerns, then became involved making them regularly. He started appearing in
westerns in the fifties – a walk-on in *Star in the Dust* (1956 – six lines of dialogue as
cowboy Tom, chatting to Gunlock Marshal Bill Jordan [John Agar]); Carol Channing's
cavalryman love interest Jack Rice in the musical comedy *The First Travelling
Saleslady* (1956); and second lead Keith Williams in the taut but little-seen, nine-day,
no-budget *Ambush at Cimarron Pass* (1958). Eastwood played Rowdy Yates in TV's
Rawhide (1959–1966) and then Italian Sergio Leone cast him in a trio of European-
shot spaghetti westerns: *A Fistful of Dollars* (1964), *For a Few Dollars More* (1965)
and *The Good, the Bad and the Ugly* (1966). Eastwood's unshaven spaghetti-
western hero, 'The Man With No Name', was an instant success in Europe.

The actor came back to the US and followed his 'Dollars' trilogy with American
adaptations in the ultraviolet 'spaghetti western' tradition. *Hang 'Em High* (1967)
saw Eastwood as Jed Cooper, a man wrongly lynched for cattle rustling, who survives
to become a US marshal in order to track down the perpetrators – a spaghetti-style
spin on one of Eastwood's favourite films: *The Ox-Bow Incident* (1943). *Two Mules
for Sister Sara* (1970) teamed Eastwood's taciturn stranger with a nun (Shirley
MacLaine) in the Maximilian-era Mexican Revolution. *Joe Kidd* (1972) was
Eastwood's laziest western, with Kidd (Eastwood) caught betwixt poor Mexican
farmers fighting for their land and baronial US capitalists armed with high-powered
hunting rifles.

More interesting than these was *High Plains Drifter* (1972), Eastwood's first
western as director. A spectral stranger arrives in Lago (built for the film on the
shores of Mono Lake, California), which is expecting reprisals from a trio of recently
released killers whom the locals jailed following the whipping to death of their
marshal. The stranger says he'll protect the cowardly townsfolk who didn't help the
murdered lawman. He tells them to set out picnic tables, raise a banner reading
'Welcome Home Boys' and paint the town bright red (renaming it 'Hell'), before
riding out as the killers approach. Eastwood mockingly reworked *High Noon*, as the
stranger abandons the settlement to its fate, having installed a dwarf as sheriff and
robbed the town of its dignity. Obviously influenced in part by Leone's films (the
film was released in Italy as *Il Straniero Senza Nome* – 'The Stranger with No Name'),
director Eastwood revealed a surreal style of his own.

Eastwood was a massive star by this point. In 1973 he topped the top ten box office stars list. He was second in 1974, sixth in 1975, fourth in 1976 and third in 1977. In comparison with Wayne's westerns, Eastwood's films were violent, usually gaining 'AA' or 'X' certificates from the BBFC in the UK; Wayne's were almost always 'U' or 'A'. Wayne once said, 'Of all the actors of the new generation, it is Clint Eastwood who gives me the most hope. He is the best cowboy of modern cinema.' But Eastwood has a hard, cynical edge, especially in his early films, which contradicts Wayne's fairer, more homespun, patriotic values.

In 1975, for the first film in a new deal between Malpaso (Eastwood's own production company) and Warner Bros, the star commissioned a screenplay based on the 1972 hardback novel *Gone to Texas*, written by Forrest Carter and published in Arkansas by Whippoorwill Publishing. Only 75 copies of Carter's book were issued, though it was later reprinted as *The Rebel Outlaw: Josey Wales*. Sonia Chernus worked on the adaptation of the book into a screenplay, then Philip Kaufman prepared a final draft. He was also going to direct and had previously made *The Great Northfield Minnesota Raid* (1971).

The Outlaw Josey Wales, as the film was titled, is set during the Civil War. The wife and son of Missouri farmer Wales, have been killed and their house burned by Unionist Kansas 'Redlegs' (so-called due to their crimson gaiters) led by Captain Terrill. Wales learns to shoot and joins a band of Confederate border raiders, under Bloody Bill Anderson, to exact retribution. At the close of hostilities in 1865, Wales refuses to surrender and becomes a wanted renegade, with Terrill and Wales's ex-comrade Fletcher assigned to: 'Hound this Wales to Kingdom Come'. Initially Wales rides with young Confederate Jamie, but the

'They'll never forget the day he drifted into town': Clint Eastwood's stranger outstays his welcome in *High Plains Drifter* (1972).

boy is badly wounded in a Redleg ambush and dies shortly afterwards. Wales travels through the Indian Nations, meeting civilised Cherokee Chief Lone Watie, who tags along with him towards Mexico. Wales and Watie are joined by Little Moonlight, a Navajo, whom Wales liberates from a crooked Indian trader. Arriving in Texas, the outlaw also saves the lives of Grandma Sarah and her granddaughter Laura Lee from Comancheros. Grandma's son has been killed in the war and they are travelling to set up home in his ranch on Crooked River, near the town of Santo Rio. The party arrives there safely, even though it is deep in Comanche territory. Wales negotiates peace with Comanche chief Ten Bears, but the arrival of Terrill, Fletcher and the Redlegs forces Wales to fight his old nemeses. In a shootout, with his travelling companions backing him up, Wales survives, returning to his previous life, now as a farmer on Crooked Creek.

Eastwood took the role of Wales, 'a hard-put and desperate man', while Sam Bottoms (younger brother of actors Timothy and Joseph) played Jamie. Native American actors Chief Dan George and Will Sampson were cast in the film in prominent roles. Eastwood had seen British Colombian Sioux chief George as Cheyenne Old Lodge Skins in *Little Big Man* (1970), which had earned him an Oscar nomination for Best Supporting Actor. He was 76-years-old when he was cast as Lone Watie. Sampson, cast as Comanche Chief Ten Bears, had played 'The Chief' in *One Flew Over the Cuckoo's Nest* (1975), while Geraldine Keams played chatterbox Navajo, Little Moonlight. Paula Trueman appeared as Grandma Sarah and Sondra Locke (later Eastwood's lover) was cast as her waif-like hippy daughter-in-law Laura Lee. Woodrow Parfrey (as a carpetbagger), John Vernon (turncoat Fletcher), Bill McKinney (Terrill), Charles Tyner (vicious trader Zukie Limmer) and John Mitchum (grizzled hunter Al) all appeared in other Eastwood projects. McKinney compared the cast to John Ford's stock company. William O'Connell, who played nervous ferryman Sim Carstairs, also played the nervous Lago barber in *High Plains Drifter*; John Quade, the leader of the Comancheros, went on to play Cholla, head honcho of inept biker gang, the Black Widows, in Eastwood's comedies with Orangutan Clyde. The 'Lost Lady' saloon regulars, ghosts from the 'old west', include Sheb Wooley (from *Rawhide*), Joyce James (as Rose), Matt Clark (barman Kelly) and Royal Dano (gambler Ten Spot). Kyle, Eastwood's own son, played Wales's son (also called Josey) in the film's opening sequence.

Budgeted at just under $4 million, filming began in late September 1975, in South Arizona and Utah. By the end of the month, after 12 days of shooting, Kaufman was fired as director after disagreements with the star and Eastwood took the reins. Ten Bears' Kiowa camp was filmed in Utah and the scenes in the grey-coloured desert were filmed in a disused mine, still covered with coal dust. Kanab Canyon, Utah was the site of grandma's Crooked River Ranch, near Blood Butte. The crew spent several days there, rehearsing and filming. Eastwood did many of his own stunts in the action scenes, while also directing from the thick of the shootout with Terrill's men. This final confrontation with the Redlegs was filmed beside the creek, in early November. During a night-time campfire scene between Josey and Laura, Locke recalled that due to the lighting needed, the fire was so big that she singed her eyebrows. The played-out silver town of Santo Rio was filmed in the ghost town of Paria, Utah. The Texas town teeming with Confederate veterans, traders, carpetbaggers, bluecoats and Redlegs was filmed on Old Tucson's sister western set, at Mescal, near Benson, Arizona. The crew then shot the Civil War and other autumn scenes in Northern California. Eastwood liked the light and colours of autumn, which suited the bittersweet story – the early morning mist, watery sunlight and fallen leaves. Carstairs Ferry was on the banks of the Feather River, standing in for the Missouri, while other locations were filmed around Oroville. Chief Dan George wasn't a professionally trained actor and Eastwood coaxed a great performance out of him, dispensing with distracting cue cards and instead telling George, 'Okay Chief, forget about the dialogue, just tell me the story.' The film was shot over eight and a half weeks, finishing in November, eight days early and $200,000 over budget.

The script required Wales to 'chaw' and spit tobacco throughout the film – hitting everything between the eyes, be it a mangy hound or a dead bounty hunter. In one scene, having grown tired of a carpetbagger's spiel promoting his multi-purpose 'Secret Elixir', Eastwood spits tobacco juice down the salesman's white suit, asking 'How's it with stains?' Eastwood noted chawing put him in a 'very bad mood' for the role. For tough scenes, with only one take, he chewed a tobacco called 'Day's Work', for multiple takes 'Red Man', while for scenes with many takes and many angles Eastwood recommended, 'Stick with Beechnut'.

There had been many depictions of historical outlaws in westerns: Frank and Jesse James, Billy the Kid, the Daltons and Youngers. Rock Hudson had played John Wesley Hardin in *The Lawless Breed* (1952). *Kansas Raiders* (1950), with Audie Murphy as Jesse James, Brian Donlevy as Quantrill and Scott Brady as Bill Anderson, notably featured northern Redlegs as the villains. But outlaws' reputations were often inflated. A sharp marksman, Hardin killed 11 people in his gunfighting career; Billy the Kid killed four (with five further possible killings). Lesser-known gunslingers like Jim Miller, Bill Longley, John Hughes and King Fisher were equally prolific. Jesse James only killed one man in his entire career, while the Sundance Kid didn't kill anyone.

Fictitious southerner Josey Wales shares certain biographical details with Confederate gunmen like Hardin, the James's and Youngers; for example, as a child, Texan Hardin used to practice by shooting at effigies of Abraham Lincoln. After his farm is razed, Wales joins the border raiders, riding out of Missouri into Kansas, led by William 'Bloody Bill' Anderson. 'We're going up there and set things aright,' says Anderson. William Clarke Quantrill formed this band of 'secesh' (secessionist) supporters in 1861 and infamously raided Lawrence, Kansas on 21 August 1863, murdering 150 men and boys. Union reprisals scattered Quantrill's band and by the time the James boys joined in 1864, they were led by Anderson. In September 1864, Anderson attacked Centralia, Missouri, where he personally executed 25 unarmed Union soldiers. The border conflict was a dirty war, with towns burned, farms torched and the Unionist Kansas 'Jayhawkers' Anderson's foes. In *The Outlaw Josey Wales*, Josey becomes toughened by the guerrilla war, while the Jayhawkers are represented in the film by Terrill's 'Redlegs'.

Wales is ideal material for an Eastwood western hero. His wife and son are killed and Wales rises from the ashes, becoming an outlaw with a vendetta. Eastwood noted, with considerable understatement, 'Because of his war experiences [he's] not necessarily in a chipper mood'. Wales packs a brace of heavy-duty Walker .44 calibre Colts (the four-and-a-half pound Walkers were so weighty that they were more usually carried in pommel holsters on the saddle) and is so fast that he's known as 'Mr Chain Blue-lightning'. Wales despises all northern aspects of post-Civil War society, including carpetbaggers, Kansas settlers and bluecoats. In the early scenes he resembles an autumnal version of Eastwood's 'Man With No Name' and faces a variety of bushwhackers smelling blood money. With each escape, Jamie crows, 'Whooped 'em again, Josey' in triumph. Wales's reputation grows and he becomes a folk hero to Confederates who still believe in 'the cause'. But with Jamie's death, the film's mood changes, as Josey's redemption begins.

In interviews, Eastwood talked about the 'basic illness of war'. His depiction of the Civil War and the post-war Reconstruction Era is highly convincing, with scenes of the human cost of war, for example injured Confederate soldiers on crutches. There is even a shot of a group of Unionists having their photograph taken, in a repeat of a moment from Leone's *The Good, the Bad and the Ugly*. Wales initially plans to stay in Missouri, but Lone Watie tells him that General Joe Shelby is reorganising the Confederacy in Texas, so they head south. The big difference between Eastwood and Leone is that the bounty hunters are now the villains. In the dénouement, Fletcher recognises Wales, even though he is identified by the Santo Rio locals as 'Mr Wilson', who claim that Wales has been killed in Monterey. Fletcher says that he doesn't believe Wales is dead and plans to find him 'And tell him the war is over.' He asks Wilson's opinion, 'I reckon so … I guess we all died a little in that damn war.'

Wales is redeemed through his relationships with a growing band of travelling companions. As he rides through the southwest, he attracts strays, who latch onto him, undermining his 'loner' persona (a similar fate befalls Robert Redford's trapper Jeremiah Johnson). Wales tries to distance himself from emotional involvement with anyone, saying, 'Whenever I get to liking someone, they aren't around long.' 'I noticed when you get to disliking someone,' adds Watie, 'they aren't around for long neither.' 'I don't want nobody belonging to me,' observes Wales, but his disparate companions are the mistreated, the lonely and the lost. When a 'mangy red-boned hound' is hanging around the camp, Wales says, 'Well he might as well ride along with us,' through gritted teeth. 'Hell, everybody else is.' At the end of the film, a community has formed around him, shielded under his protection. Wales questions his vendetta and begins to fall for introspective Laura Lee, who is given to comments like, 'Clouds are like dreams floating across the sky blue mind' and 'Kansas was all golden and smelled like sunshine.' In the book Wales even marries her. Like Chris and Vin in *The Magnificent Seven*, early Eastwood heroes, particularly in the Italian films, never became assimilated into society, but by *Josey Wales* Eastwood was displaying an interest in seeing his characters settle down.

Josey Wales is notable for its authentic, sympathetic depiction of Native Americans. Actress Geraldine Keams noted that the Native American characters were 'sensitively written', while Carter's book was dedicated 'for Ten Bears'. Cherokee Lone Watie saw his wife and two sons die on the 'Trail of Tears' from their homeland to the Indian Nations, a glorified reservation. He is initially dressed like Abraham Lincoln and tells Wales that when he travelled to Washington to meet the Secretary of the Interior, they were told 'Endeavour to Persevere' at continuing to be 'civilised'. Watie says they thought about what the phrase meant and then declared war on the Union. 'I didn't surrender either,' Watie tells Wales, 'but they took my horse and made him surrender.' Initially Watie lies in wait to shoot Josey for the reward money, but Wales outwits him. 'They call us civilised,' moans Watie, 'because we're easy to sneak up on.' Later, Wales makes peace with the Comanche he encounters near Crooked Creek ranch – Chief Ten Bears knows Wales as the 'Grey Rider', a kindred spirit, also at war with the 'blue-bellies'. Wales's speech to Ten Bears, an uncharacteristically lengthy monologue from monosyllabic Eastwood, advocates peace, 'I came here to die with you, or live with you. Dying ain't so hard for men like you and me … it's living that's hard. The bear lives here, the wolf, the antelope, the Comanche … and so will we. That is my word of life.' 'There is iron in your words,' replies Ten Bears, 'It shall be life.'

'Mr Chain Blue-lightning': *The Outlaw Josey Wales* (1976), a renegade on the run towards post-Civil War Texas; director-star Clint Eastwood and his matching pair of .44 Calibre Walker Colts.

The final confrontation is a traditional western pitched battle, with the homesteaders holding their ground and the Redlegs subbing for the Indians; it ends with Wales chasing Terrill into Santo Rio and skewering the Redleg on his own sabre. But Wales's other duels are more like those of Eastwood's spaghetti-western alter ego. Wales outguns four Union soldiers on the sidewalk in a Texan town ('Well are you gonna pull those pistols or whistle Dixie?' goads Wales) and takes on a whole gang of tanked-up Comancheros who look as though they have just walked out of the Italian west. 'Get ready, little lady,' Watie tells Grandma at Wales's approach, 'Hell is coming to breakfast.' Later, a bounty hunter (John Davis Chandler) shows up in the Santo Rio saloon. 'I'm looking for Josey Wales.' 'That'd be me,' says Wales from the shadows. 'You're wanted Wales.' 'Reckon I'm right popular ... you a bounty hunter?'; 'Man's gotta do something for a living these days.' 'Dying ain't much of a living, boy,' answers Wales, before blasting him back through the swinging saloon doors.

The Outlaw Josey Wales received its US premiere on 26 July 1976 at 6.30 pm at the Sun Valley Centre for the Arts and Humanities conference on western movies. The trailer voiceover filled in Wales's background ('Suddenly his wife and child were dead ... a feud was about to begin') and outlined his character ('He lives by his gun, he lives by his word and he lives for revenge'). Released in the US in August 1976, bicentennial year, the same month as Wayne's *The Shootist*, the film was rated 'R' in its uncut 135-minute version, 'PG' when trimmed. Even so *Variety* noted that *Josey Wales* was a 'Formula Eastwood slaughter film for [the] regular market', adding that 'it stretched to the breaking point of credulity ... the PG rating' and missed the film's subtlety, terming it 'a prairie *Death Wish*'. On the *Merve Griffin Show* Orson Welles called it one of the best-directed films of all time. Posters christened Wales 'An Army of One', with snarling, wild-maned Eastwood brandishing his pair of Walkers. Richard Schickel in *Time* noted the film had, 'a fair amount of dull slogging along the way', the *New York Times* called it 'a soggy ... post-Civil War epic' and the *New York Daily News* thought it 'seems to last two days': 'Eastwood manages a grunt, a mumble and an occasional "I reckon so".' The mixed reviews didn't hurt and the film grossed $13.5 million on its initial release, placing it in the top twenty most successful westerns of all time. It was one of Warners's biggest hits of the year, with *All the President's Men* and *Ode to Billy Joe*. Jerry Fielding's score, with its rousing tin-whistle march theme ('The War is Over') and Civil War ballad references (including 'Rose of Alabama' and 'Dixie') was nominated for an Academy Award, while *Time* named the film on their ten best list of 1976.

The film was slightly cut in the UK (for Laura Lee's nudity, during an assault on her by the Comancheros) to gain a 'AA' certificate, rather than an 'X'; it is now available uncut on DVD, rated '18', though the treatment of this assault is unpleasantly voyeuristic and the film is better for its abridgement. In Germany the film was *Der Texaner* (even though Wales is from Missouri); in Italy it was *Il Texano dagli Occhi di Ghiaccio* ('The Texan with Icy Eyes'). *Eastwood in Action*, a seven-minute documentary shot on location, depicted the director-star's thorough working methods, while a 1999 documentary called *Hell Hath No Fury* offered insights into the film's making, including interviews with Eastwood, Vernon, Bottoms, McKinney and Keams.

Forrest Carter published a sequel, *The Vengeance Trail of Josey Wales*, which was adapted for the screen as *The Return of Josey Wales* (1986), with director-star Michael Parks in the lead. In the film, set in 1868, Santo Rio (spelt 'Santa Rio') is attacked by Rurales, led by Captain Jesus Escobedo (who looks like Dom De Luise); Rose and Kelly are killed and Ten Spot is taken prisoner. Josey packs up his gun and his tobacco and chews his way down to Mexico in pursuit. It's amateur night in the old corral and the acting is uniformly dreadful, while the murky photography and jumpy editing render some scenes incomprehensible. It was filmed in John Wayne's 'Alamo Village' at Bracketville and includes more shots of birds, snakes, gophers, scorpions and tarantulas than a Disney wildlife film – a credit thanks 'Snake Farm Reptiles'. The score consists of country and western ballads of the 'Ronco Western Collection' variety, while the incidental cues include such tension-inducing effects as someone interminably tuning a one-stringed guitar and what sounds like a mouse running along a harpsichord. Inspired by Eastwood's handling of Philip Kaufman on *Josey Wales*, Parks the actor should have fired Parks the director.

Eastwood says nostalgically that *The Outlaw Josey Wales* is 'very close to me' and 'certainly one of the high-points of my career – it's meant a lot'. He also notes that it is the film that most fans want to talk about when they meet him and is his most popular with them. Eastwood is a great American filmmaker and *Josey Wales* has been dissected by film scholars as his comment on Vietnam, on politics and the plight of the Native American, but perhaps Eastwood's co-star Bill McKinney put it best, 'It's a very straight-up film.' Certainly, it seems the legend of mythical outlaw Josey Wales will endure – as Wales himself would have it, 'I reckon so.'

26

'I've Always Been Lucky When it Comes to Killing Folks'

— *Unforgiven* (1992)

Unforgiven (1992)

Credits

DIRECTOR AND PRODUCER – Clint Eastwood
EXECUTIVE PRODUCER – David Valdes
ASSOCIATE PRODUCER – Julian Ludwig
SCREENPLAY – David Webb Peoples
DIRECTOR OF PHOTOGRAPHY – Jack N. Green
EDITOR – Joel Cox
PRODUCTION DESIGNER – Henry Bumstead
MUSIC – Lennie Niehaus
Panavision/Technicolor
A Malpaso Production
Released by Warner Bros
130 minutes

Cast

Clint Eastwood (William Munny, alias 'William Hendershot'); Gene Hackman (Sheriff William 'Little Bill' Daggett); Morgan Freeman (Ned Logan); Richard Harris (English Bob); Jaimz Woolvett (The Schofield Kid); Saul Rubinek (W. W. Beauchamp); Frances Fisher (Strawberry Alice); Anna Thomson (Delilah Fitzgerald); Tara Dawn Frederick (Little Sue); Beverley Elliott (Silky); Liisa Repo-Martell (Faith); Josie Smith (Crow Creek Kate); Anthony James (Skinny Dubois); Rob Campbell (Davey Bunting); David Mucci (Quick Mike); Shane Meier and Aline Levasseur (Will and Penny Munny); Cherrilene Cardinal (Sally Two Trees, Ned's wife); Ron White (Deputy Clyde Ledbetter); Jeremy Ratchford (Deputy Andy Russell); John Pyper-Ferguson (Deputy Charley Hecker); Jefferson Mappin

(Deputy Fatty Rossiter); Walter Marsh (I. B. Bell, barber);
Mina E. Mina (Muddy Chandler, coach driver); Henry Kope
(German Joe Schultz, storekeeper); Robert Koons (Crocker);
Garner Butler (Eggs Anderson); Larry Reese (Tom
Luckinbill); Lochlyn Munro (Texas Slim); Blair Haynes
(Paddy McGee); Sam Karas (Thirsty Thurston); Frank
C. Turner (Fuzzy); Ben Cardinal (Johnny Foley); Philip
Haynes (Lippy MacGregor); Michael Charrois (Wiggens);
Bill Davidson (Buck Barthol); Larry Joshua (Bucky);
George Orrison (The Shadow); Greg Goossen (Fighter);
Paul McLean, James Herman and Michael Maurer
(train passengers)

*   *   *

By the mid-seventies, westerns were a rare breed and a success like *The Outlaw Josey Wales* (1976) did little to renew the genre's fortunes. Robert Redford's contemporary *The Electric Horseman* (1979) rapidly became the fourth most popular western of all time, after *Butch Cassidy and the Sundance Kid*, *Blazing Saddles* and *Billy Jack*. The *Roadrunner*-inspired comedy *Cactus Jack* (1979 – or *The Villain*), starring Kirk Douglas as Jack, Ann-Margret as heroine-in-peril Charming Jones and Arnold Schwarzenegger as 'Handsome Stranger', was also a massive hit. Walter Hill's superior *The Long Riders* (1980) was an accurate depiction of the James gang's Northfield, Minnesota bank raid, starring Stacy Keach as Frank, and his brother James (looking like William S. Hart) playing Jesse. It's told in gory, post-Peckinpah fashion, complete with slow-motion gunplay, whizzing bullet sound effects and a twanging Ry Cooder score.

But any hope in an early-eighties resurgence of the genre was scuppered by Michael Cimino's *Heaven's Gate* (1980). Its cost escalated from $7.5 to $44 million and almost bankrupted United Artists when it took $1.5 million at the US box office. UA were bought shortly afterwards by MGM, becoming MGM/UA and *Heaven's Gate* ensured westerns were again box-office poison, though the film is not entirely deserving of its pariah status. Apart from a prologue set in 1870 at Harvard University (actually filmed in Oxford), and an epilogue in 1903 aboard a yacht off Rhode Island, *Heaven's Gate* takes place over three days during Wyoming's Johnson County War (here set in 1890, though it actually took place in April 1892) between the cattlemen's hired 'regulators' and immigrant 'nesters'. The plot concerns a love triangle between sheriff Kris Kristofferson, madam Isabelle Huppert (who plays many of her scenes naked) and regulator Christopher Walken. Unfortunately with its arty pacing, the three days feel like they unfold in real time, but the finale – a blistering, nihilistic pitched battle – redeems the film. 'Heaven's Gate' is the name of a frontier roller-skating rink, which promises 'A Moral and Exhilarating Experience', which the film definitely is not. It remains most notable for Vilmos Zsigmond's lyrical cinematography (by turns dusty, smoky and steamy, all but obscuring the action of some scenes), the very violent murders by the regulators and Cimino's penchant for hoedowns – it features almost as much dancing as a musical.

Mod-ish westerns like *Young Guns* (1988) and *Young Guns II: Blaze of Glory* (1990) were popular, to the tune of almost $20 million each, through their combination of 'Brat Pack' actors (Emilio Estevez, Charlie Sheen, Lou Diamond Phillips and Kiefer Sutherland), cowboy stalwarts (Jack Palance, Brian Keith, Patrick Wayne and James Coburn) and rock ballads provided by Jon Bon Jovi. They were set against the backdrop of the famous Lincoln County War. The third part of the *Back to the Future* trilogy (1985–1990) was set in 1885, with Marty McFly (Michael J. Fox) adopting a poncho and the pseudonym 'Clint Eastwood' in another massive hit for the franchise. On television, in the 'Inca Mummy Girl' episode of *Buffy the Vampire Slayer* (6 October 1997), Xander Harris (Nicholas Brendon) attended the World Culture fancy dress dance in cowboy hat, poncho and smoking a cigar, claiming to be from the country of Leone – 'It's in Italy, pretending to be Montana'.

Eastwood himself continued to dabble periodically in the genre, against fashion. In *Bronco Billy* (1980) he was cast as a wild-west show performer named after the first silent western hero, a dreamer who still lives by the gentlemanly codes of Gene Autry and adrift in the modern world, where his dwindling circus audience echoes the eighties' lack of interest in westerns. *Pale Rider* (1985) was a snowbound remake of *Shane* with director-star Eastwood appearing as the Preacher, a reformed gunfighter, who arrives as if beckoned by the miraculous hand of God to answer the prayers of a gold mining community in Carbon Canyon. These 'tin-panners' are being run out of the valley by the corporate mining company C.K. LaHood & Son, whose hydraulic water jets wash away the landscape in their hunt for deposits. The Preacher fires up the miners and eventually LaHood hires crooked Marshal Stockburn and his six deputies to dispose of the Preacher – but the Preacher straps on his gunbelt and disposes of them instead.

Pale Rider was filmed in autumn 1984 against the spectacular backdrop of Sun Valley, Idaho and the jagged Sawtooth Mountains (with pines, canyons, mountains and snow), but unfortunately it isn't one of Eastwood's greats. A supernatural subplot recalls *High Plains Drifter* (the Preacher has seven bullet hole scars on his back), while his relationship with 14-year-old Megan (Sydney Penny – the Joey Starrett equivalent) doesn't quite work. What makes the film difficult to watch is the cinematography by Bruce Surtees (from *The Beguiled*, *The Great Northfield Minnesota Raid*, *The Outlaw Josey Wales* and *The Shootist*). Some exteriors, even in bright sunshine, are often underlit and the interiors are impenetrable. *Pale Rider* was the first Eastwood film I saw on its original release and I remember sitting in the cinema, attempting to work out what was happening in the murky depths of dimly lit cabin interiors, while disembodied voices drifted from the black screen.

Like all Eastwood's westerns, *Pale Rider* has its moments, mostly of action: on his arrival in town, the Preacher defeats LaHood's hoods by wielding a pickaxe handle ('There's nothing like a nice piece of hickory'). Later, LaHood henchman Club (played by seven-feet-two-inch tall Richard Kiel, metal-toothed 'Jaws' from the James Bond movies) is dispatched to nobble the Preacher, who calmly smashes the hulk in the groin with a sledgehammer, making Club's eyes water. But the duster-wearing marshal and his deputies are pale *Once Upon a Time in the West* clones, while the *Shane* parallels (a giant rock blocking the creek, instead of the sturdy tree stump; the shooting of Spider Conway outside LaHood's saloon by the deputies; Megan calling after the departing Preacher) are overtly contrived and hollow. Nevertheless, *Pale Rider* took almost $21 million at the US box office.

In 1990, the western epic *Dances with Wolves* waltzed off with Oscars for Best Picture and Best Director for Kevin Costner and proved that there was still mileage in the genre. Buoyed by this, Eastwood set to work on a project that had been in his possession for eight years. The screenplay 'The Cut Whore Killings' was written by David Webb Peoples in 1976 and had arrived in Eastwood's office in 1983, since Francis Ford Coppola had passed on the option. The film's eventual working title was 'The William Munny Killings', until it was changed to *Unforgiven* for release. Eastwood is one of many hyphenates (jargon for any dual-role personnel) in Hollywood. He is director-star and his own production company Malpaso is usually involved, often in tandem with Warner Bros. This was the case on *Unforgiven*.

In 1881, killer William Munny now lives as a Kansas pig farmer with his children, Will and Penny; their mother Claudia Feathers died of smallpox in 1878 and Munny struggles to support them alone. He hears from young gunslinger the Schofield Kid that a $1,000 reward is being offered by a group of prostitutes in the town of Big Whiskey, Wyoming. The previous year, Davey Bunting and Quick Mike, two cowboys from the 'Bar T', facially scarred Delilah, one of the prostitutes, with a knife and were inadequately punished by town sheriff, 'Little Bill' Daggett. Munny decides to revert to his bad old ways. Hooking up with his ex-partner, Ned Logan and the Schofield Kid, Munny sets off. Crooked Sheriff Daggett has implemented 'Ordinance 14', banning firearms in town. Anyone who comes after the 'whores' gold' will be dealt with. Arriving in Big Whiskey, Munny is caught alone in the saloon and severely beaten by Daggett. Sheltering outside town, the trio manage to kill Bunting, but Logan soon loses his nerve and heads for home. Schofield and Munny kill not-so-Quick Mike, but when they receive their money, they learn that Logan has been captured by the Bar T boys and thrashed to death by Daggett. Munny tells Schofield to take the reward to his children, and rides into town to find Logan's body on display in the street, with Little Bill and his deputies waiting.

Eastwood cast himself as William Munny, a broken, guilt-ridden man, scared of dying and of visions of 'the Angel of Death'. Gene Hackman, who played Daggett, had enjoyed box-office success with *The French Connection* (1971 – for which he won a Best Actor Oscar), *The Poseidon Adventure* (1972) and *Superman, the Movie* (1978 – as Lex Luthor), but he hadn't appeared in a western since *The Hunting Party* (1971) and *Bite the Bullet* (1975). Initially reluctant to appear in such a violent film, Hackman explained, '[Eastwood] was very explicit about his desire to demythologise violence. I'm really glad Clint convinced me this was not a Clint Eastwood film!' Morgan Freeman, Oscar-nominated for his role as chauffeur Holk Colburn in *Driving Miss Daisy* (1989), was cast as rehabilitated killer, Logan, an old friend who will do anything for Munny. A strong actor, with immense screen presence and a commanding voice, Freeman was later re-teamed with Eastwood in the Oscar-winning *Million Dollar Baby* (2004). Cinema newcomer Canadian Jaimz Woolvett was cast as boastful show-off the Schofield Kid, so-called because of his Schofield Model No. 3 Smith & Wesson pistol. Logan carries a formidable seven-shot Spencer repeater, while Munny favours a sawn-off shotgun.

Limerick-born actor Richard Harris appeared in a subplot cameo as aristocratic English Bob, a Doc Holliday-style gunman with a rather inflated opinion of his deeds. Harris, a tough actor renowned for his hellraising exploits off-screen, had appeared in many westerns, including *Major Dundee*, *A Man Called Horse*, *Man in the Wilderness* (1971), *The Deadly Trackers* (1973) and *The Return of a Man Called Horse* (1976). *Unforgiven*'s supporting cast included Frances Fisher, Eastwood's lover of the time (as madame Strawberry Alice), Anna Thomson (in a difficult role, as facially scarred Delilah) and Saul Rubinek, as English Bob's sycophantic dime novel biographer, W.W. Beauchamp. Anthony James, as stringy Skinny Dubois, the morally bankrupt saloonkeeper, had previously played a vengeful killer in *High Plains Drifter*. Daggett is backed by a memorable crew of gristly deputies – in contrast to their faceless equivalents in *Pale Rider* – tall Andy Russell (played by Jeremy Ratchford), nervous Charley Hecker (John Pyper-Ferguson), rotund 'Fatty' Rossiter (Jefferson Mappin) and one-armed Clyde Ledbetter (Ron White). Preparing to face English Bob, Fatty moans to Clyde, 'You got three pistols and you only got one arm.' Clyde responds, 'I just don't want to get killed for lack of shooting back.'

Budgeted at $14.4 million, *Unforgiven* was filmed on location in 11 weeks. The town of Big Whiskey was built in 32 days at Longview, Alberta, Canada in August 1991, before filming commenced in September. The town set has a typical 'mud and rags' revisionist look in its cobbled-together, haphazard construction. For Munny's arrival and his final revenge, the street is lashed with pelting rain. Eastwood wouldn't allow any vehicles on set to leave tell-tale tyre tracks in the mud and the crew travelled in period wagons. The street is filled with authentic detail and is one of the most convincing western movie sets, resembling photographs of Tombstone, Dodge City and Deadwood, with their muddy thoroughfares and plethora of shop signs and advertising filling every available space. Interiors were suitably grimy and Jack N. Green's vividly lit cinematography ensured they were visible on screen. Green's Panavision landscapes of sun-drenched cornfields, mountains and snowy whiteouts make this one of Eastwood's best-looking films as director. The hellish final saloon firefight sees Munny brandishing his shotgun, lit by flaming torches outside the window, where Logan's corpse is on display in front of 'Greely's Beer Garden and Billiard Parlour'. Other locations include Drumheller, Brooks and High River, all in Alberta. The 'Northwest Railroad' scenes were filmed in two weeks with a narrow-gauge period locomotive in Sonora, California. Incidental details include the train passengers reading the *Cheyenne Gazette* with its headline 'President Garfield in Critical Condition' placing the main action of the film in the days after Charles Guiteau assassinated him on 2 July 1881. *Unforgiven* wrapped by the end of October, just beating a blizzard, which would have wreaked havoc with the end of the schedule.

Eastwood's hero has an interesting relationship with his earlier cowboy incarnations. His stylish, superheroic 'Man With No Name' remains Eastwood's most popular western icon, while Jed Cooper in *Hang 'Em High* and the hero of *Joe Kidd* were rather more Hollywood than Italian, and Hogan in *Two Mules for Sister Sara* was the Man With No Name with a name. The *High Plains Drifter* was Eastwood's last word on his 'stranger in town', while Josey Wales was an older, more introspective hero. Like Wales, Munny is 'out of Missouri'.

William Munny is an ageing 'Man With No Name' from the 'Dollars' trilogy – he even references the younger man's mercenary greed for monetary gain in his name. But even 'No Name' didn't kill women and children, as Munny is reputed to have done, when he 'dynamited the Rock Island and Pacific in '69'. Munny was a ruthless killer, 'a known thief and murderer, a man of notoriously vicious and intemperate disposition', who now downplays his exploits. Later, when Delilah tends his wounds, Munny notes, 'We both got scars' – though Munny's are inside. His wife has reformed him ('cured me of drink and wickedness') and he hasn't fired a gun or drunk whisky for 11 years. As Schofield notes of the pig farmer, 'You don't look like no rootin', tootin', son of a bitchin', cold-blooded assassin,' but an outbreak of swine

'We all have it coming, kid': William Munny makes sure Little Bill gets his; Clint Eastwood dispenses doubled-barrelled revenge at Greely's in the climax of *Unforgiven* (1992).

fever looks set to decimate his stock. In a running joke, Munny has trouble staying on his horse – 'Ain't hardly been in the saddle myself in a while' – a comment too on the few westerns Eastwood had made in the past few years. When Munny dusts off his Colt Walker revolver for target practice, he misses a tea caddy with all six shots – a most un-Eastwood-like moment that prompts Munny's little daughter Penny to ask of her brother, 'Did pa used to kill folks?' Munny remedies this by fetching a scattergun and blasting the tin with buckshot.

Little Bill Daggett is one of the genre's most despicable, wretched sheriffs. Hackman claimed that, 'Though (Daggett) feels he's doing the right thing, he's a fascist, a control freak. But he's not the villain of the piece. The villain is the violence – he just gets dragged into it.' Daggett's treatment of the prostitutes triggers the confrontation in Big Whiskey. Daggett sees them as inferior citizens, while 'respectable' cowboys from the Bar T get away with their crimes. The prostitutes' house is situated on the edge of town, on the fringes of polite society, while their services are euphemistically billed as 'Billiards'. Daggett fails to punish the perpetrators of the terrible violence against Delilah. He doesn't even flog them, instead fining them ponies, to be brought by springtime as compensation for Skinny's 'loss of earnings'. This outrages the prostitutes, who resolve to see justice done. As Frances Fisher said, 'Part of the film's irony is that it's the women who drive the story forward.'

Unforgiven uses the framework of a western to look at the romance of western fiction and killing, and the unforgiving reality. English Bob, the dandyish gunfighter, known by the dime novel epithet 'The Duke of Death' (which Little Bill disparagingly mispronounces as 'The Duck') has Beauchamp, his own dime novelist, in tow to record his exploits. Currently making an ignoble living 'shooting Chinamen for the railroad', Bob arrives in town to kill the two cowboys, but Daggett disarms and captures him, administering a rigorous beating. In jail, Daggett reads aloud Bob's pulp-fiction adventures in the Bluebottle Saloon, Wichita, when Bob killed Two-gun Corcoran, 'But the Duck was faster and hot lead blazed from his smoking guns'. Daggett then reveals that he was present in the Bluebottle that night: it was a drunken gunfight, not the heroism depicted. Corcoran shot himself in the foot, then his pistol backfired and exploded, blowing the gunman's hand off and Bob calmly put a bullet through the unarmed man's liver. The cocky Schofield Kid claims to have killed five men, even though he's myopic and hasn't killed anyone. When he finally does commit murder at point-blank range, while Quick Mike is sitting on the toilet in an outhouse, he is distraught. 'First one I ever killed,' says the Kid, supping whisky to settle his nerves, 'It don't seem real.' 'It's a hell of a thing, killing a man,' answers Munny, 'You take away all he's got and all he's ever gonna have.' 'Well, I guess they had it coming,' says the Kid, trying to rationalise. 'We all have it coming, Kid,' adds Munny.

From the opening scene, when Quick Mike slashes Delilah's face with a Bowie knife, to the point-blank finale, *Unforgiven* depicts violence uncompromisingly, as a condemnation of violence. On their first meeting, Daggett disarms Munny and kicks him around the saloon, leaving Munny to crawl out on his belly into the main-street mud, humiliated; he's injured so badly that Ned has to sew his cheek back together. Wanting to avoid trouble, Munny had even moved a whisky glass out of temptation's reach. But when Little Sue pays Munny and Schofield the reward on the outskirts of town, and tells them Ned has been killed, Munny's mood changes. He begins to drink Schofield's whisky, getting meaner by the minute. Seeing this sudden transformation, Schofield acknowledges, 'I ain't like you, Will.'

Munny's furious temper and violence, previously curbed by his abstinence from liquor, resurfaces in the finale, when he becomes a 'crazy, killing fool'. A storm breaks as Munny rides into town alone, tossing an empty whisky bottle into the mud; he wants revenge and he's had a drink. Munny sees Ned propped up in a coffin outside Greely's bar, with the warning notice: 'This is what happens to assassins around here'. While Sheriff Daggett, Skinny, the Bar T boys and the deputies enjoy a drink, Munny enters the shadowy bar brandishing a sawn-off double-barrelled shotgun and asks who the owner is, before blasting proprietor Skinny. Little Bill says that Munny has just killed an unarmed man, 'Well he should have armed himself, if he's gonna decorate his saloon with my friend.' With one barrel left, Munny admits, 'I've killed women and children...killed just about everything that walked or crawled at one time or another. And I'm here to kill you Little Bill, for what you did to Ned.' But the second barrel clicks hollowly on a misfire and all hell breaks loose. The deputies panic, blasting away, while bystanders hit the floor. Munny, cool-headed, takes his time, carefully aiming the Kid's Schofield pistol and shooting Bill and three deputies – Clyde, Fatty and Andy. As the smoke clears, with the firefight over, Munny pours himself a big whisky at the bar. Taking notes, Beauchamp asks Munny in what order he killed the quartet, 'I was lucky in the order,' says Munny, 'But I've always been lucky when it comes to killing folks' (a reference to Eastwood's 'Do I feel lucky?' cop *Dirty Harry*). As a final act of vengeance, Munny commandeers Logan's Spencer and aims the heavy bore at still-living Daggett's head. 'I'll see you in Hell, William Munny,' Little Bill spits. 'Yea,' says Munny, pulling the trigger.

Unforgiven boasts a majestic score by Lennie Niehaus. 'Claudia's Theme', the fragile acoustic guitar melody, was actually composed uncredited by Eastwood himself (the star is an accomplished jazz pianist and had also composed 'Megan's Theme' for *Pale Rider*). The opening shot, accompanied by guitar and gentle strings, shows Munny digging Claudia's grave against a golden sunset. This guitar cue is reorchestrated for full orchestra in lush style throughout the film. At the close, Eastwood repeats the simple opening imagery, again underscored with the acoustic guitar theme: the farm shack, now deserted, with a single shivering windblown tree and Claudia's gravestone, silhouetted against a magnificent setting sun. We learn that Munny has gone to San Francisco with his blood money, 'where it was rumoured he prospered in dry goods' – Eastwood himself was born in San Francisco. As the darkness gathers, a caption: 'Dedicated to Sergio and Don' appears, in a nod to Eastwood's two directorial mentors, both of whom had now died (in 1989 and 1991 respectively).

A rough cut of *Unforgiven* was assembled by Joel Cox in January 1992, with the film released in the US in August, rated 'R'. The poster depicted a dimly lit portrait gallery of leads (Harris, Hackman, Freeman, Eastwood) and a shadowy profile of

Munny, in his long coat, with a pistol concealed behind his back. The trailer's voiceover warned, 'It was a matter of honour in a time when lawmen were killers, outlaws were heroes and a bad reputation was as good as gold,' continuing, 'Some legends will never be forgotten, some wrongs can never be forgiven... *Unforgiven.*' *Variety* thought it was 'a classic western for the ages'. *Time* called *Unforgiven* 'Eastwood's meditation on age, repute, courage and heroism – all those burdens he has been carrying with such grace for decades'. To *Newhouse News Services* it was 'Eastwood's finest hour as a moviemaker... it towers over every other film in current release'. The *New York Times*' Vincent Canby headed his positive review 'A Western Without Good Guys', while Rex Reed in the *New York Observer* saw 'A profound work of art'. It made many top ten lists for the year. Critical acclaim was emulated at the box office: at over $101 million, *Unforgiven* was the 11th largest US box-office take in 1992, making it the most successful western of all time and one of Eastwood's best, a thoughtful summation of his work in the genre and a fine adios.

Oscar nominations followed – at the ceremony on 19 March 1993, *Unforgiven* won Best Picture and Eastwood Best Director, Hackman won Best Supporting Actor and Joel Cox Best Editing, among unsuccessful nominations for Cinematography, Original Screenplay, Sound, Set Decoration and Eastwood as Best Actor. Eastwood proudly accepted the awards in front of his mother, Ruth. Among many other accolades, it won Golden Globes for Hackman and director Eastwood. In Europe the film was also successful, critically and commercially. In France it was *Impitoyable* ('Pitiless'), in Spain *Sin Perdon* ('Without Pardon') and in Italy *Gli Spietati* ('The Pitiless Ones'). It was granted a '15' certificate in the UK (though TV prints have subsequently been edited for language and violence) where it was released in September 1992 and took £4.6 million. In *Sight and Sound*, Christopher Frayling hailed the film as 'Eastwood's best western – the most distinguished film he has appeared in and directed – since *The Outlaw Josey Wales*', while Hackman picked up a BAFTA for his performance.

While Eastwood has yet to get back in the saddle, Hackman made three more westerns on the trot. He played General Crook in Walter Hill's *Geronimo: An American Legend* (1993), Wyatt's father Nicholas in *Wyatt Earp* (1994) and town tyrant John Herod in *The Quick and the Dead* (1995), a brisk western directed by Sam Raimi (of *Evil Dead* fame). It delivered a shootout every few minutes by being set in the town of Redemption (the Mescal, Arizona town set) during a quick-draw competition for a $123,000 prize. Sharon Stone starred as mysterious, sexy gunslinger Ellen, who seeks revenge on Herod (she was tricked into shooting her own father dead when she was a child) and enters the contest. Russell Crowe was Cort, a repenting gunman dubbed 'Preacher'. Woody Strode, to whom the film is dedicated, had a cameo as an undertaker, while teen star Leonardo DiCaprio was cast as Herod's son, 'The Kid', a cocky, irritating little brat. Stuntmen hurtle across the screen and pirouette in slow motion in Raimi's pop-video western, a splatter-western comic book come to life, while his camerawork is a gun fetishist's dream, lovingly caressing the protagonists' gleaming pistols. The ultra-stylised events in Redemption are backed by Alan Silvestri's spaghetti-western pastiche score, while Herod is a cardboard cut-out compared to Little Bill Daggett: no Oscars for Hackman here.

Eastwood proved with *Unforgiven* that the genre could still be commercially viable, albeit as a one-off. It could still surprise and entertain audiences, and comment on social ills, in particular the gun culture and violence of contemporary America. It is his *The Shootist*, or *Ride the High Country*, his last hurrah in a genre that he has been involved with for five decades. Redemption is something that all gunfighters yearn for; they are 'never forgiven' for their past sins. William Munny may look like a pig farmer, but he'll always be a killer and remain 'unforgiven' for his intemperate, wicked ways.

27

'I'm Your Huckleberry'

— *Tombstone* (1993)

Tombstone (1993)
Credits
DIRECTOR – George P. Cosmatos
EXECUTIVE PRODUCERS – Buzz Feitshans and Andrew G. Vajna
PRODUCERS – James Jacks, Sean Daniel and Bob Misiorowski
SCREENPLAY – Kevin Jarre
DIRECTOR OF PHOTOGRAPHY – William A. Fraker
EDITORS – Harvey Rosenstock, Robert Silvi and Frank J. Urioste
PRODUCTION DESIGN – Catherine Hardwick
MUSIC – Bruce Broughton
Panavision/Technicolor
A Cinergi Pictures-Hollywood Pictures Production
Released by Buena Vista Pictures
130 minutes
Cast
    Kurt Russell (Deputy Wyatt Earp); Val Kilmer (John Henry
'Doc' Holliday); Sam Elliott (Marshal Virgil Earp); Bill
Paxton (Deputy Morgan Earp); Powers Boothe (Curly Bill
Brocious); Michael Biehn (Johnny Ringo); Charlton Heston
(Henry Hooker); Jason Priestly (Deputy Billy Breckinridge);
Jon Tenney (John Behan, Cochise County Sheriff); Stephen
Lang (Ike Clanton); Thomas Haden Church (Billy Clanton);
Dana Delany (Josephine Marcus); Paula Malcomson (Allie
Earp, Virgil's wife); Lisa Collins (Louisa Earp, Morgan's
wife); Dana Wheeler-Nicholson (Mattie Earp, Wyatt's wife);
Joanna Pacula (Kate Fisher, Doc's lover); Michael Rooker
(Sherman McMasters); Harry Carey Jnr (Fred White,
Tombstone Marshal); Billy Bob Thornton (Johnny Tyler);
Pat Brady (Milt Joyce, barman and owner of Oriental

Saloon); Tomas Arana (Frank Stillwell); Billy Zane (Mr
Romulus Fabian); Paul Ben-Victor (Florentino); John Philbin
and Robert John Burke (Tom and Frank McLaury); Wyatt
Earp (Billy Claiborne); Peter Sherayko (Texas Jack
Vermillion); Buck Taylor (Turkey Creek Jack Johnson); Frank
Stallone (Ed Bailey); Gary Clark (Marshal Crawley Dake);
Sandy Gibbons (Father Feeney)

*   *   *

In the partial renaissance of westerns in the wake of *Unforgiven*, American
filmmakers revisited one of the west's most famous moments, not once but twice.
Guns spoke again at the O.K. Corral, the centrepiece of both *Tombstone* (1993) and
Wyatt Earp (1994). These films strove to re-evaluate the Earp legend and put
something like his true story on screen. *Wyatt Earp* starred Kevin Costner as the
lawman and despite its epic three-hour length ends up a muddled, meandering saga.
But *Tombstone*, an hour shorter, has a great cast, excellent locations, a true spirit of
classic westerns and superior moustaches.

Scripted by Kevin Jarre, *Tombstone* begins with Wyatt and wife Mattie joining his
brothers Virgil and Morgan (and their wives Allie and Louisa) in the powder keg of
Tombstone, where they take a stake in the rough Oriental Saloon ('a regular
slaughterhouse'). But the territory's self-appointed law, the Cowboys, led by Curly
Bill Brocious and Johnny Ringo, in collusion with the Clanton-McLaury gang, are
causing trouble. Curly Bill murders Marshal Fred White and Virgil becomes the
town's lawman, with Morgan as his deputy. Though initially reluctant to be drawn
into the feud, Wyatt eventually sides with his brothers, while beginning an adulterous
affair with actress Josephine Marcus. Tubercular gambler Doc Holliday pitches in
with the lawmen for a confrontation with the Clantons at the O.K. Corral, which the
Earps win. Soon afterwards Morgan is murdered, Virgil is badly wounded and the
Earp family leaves Tombstone – except Wyatt, who takes the US marshal's star and
resolves to defeat the Cowboys once and for all.

In *Tombstone* the two lead actors – Kurt Russell and Val Kilmer – were better known
for their screen portrayals of rock legends. Hardman Russell was cast as Wyatt. As a
12-year-old, he'd appeared in the ABC western TV series *The Travels of Jaime
McPheeters* (1963–1964, opposite Charles Bronson), and subsequently several Disney
adventures, before his breakthrough role as the King in the 1979 TV movie *Elvis*,
which gained massive viewing figures. His roles in *Escape from New York* (1981)
and *The Thing* (1982) for John Carpenter established him as a tough action hero,
though he has had a varied screen career, including comedies like *Overboard* (1987),
opposite his wife Goldie Hawn. Kilmer had appeared in the smash hit *Top Gun*
(1986), but had most famously played the Lizard King, Jim Morrison, in *The Doors*
(1991). He had also appeared in the mysterious *Thunderheart* (1992), as a Sioux
FBI agent investigating a murder case on an Oglala Sioux reservation, based on a
true incident. Despite his robust good looks, Kilmer was an excellent choice for

'skinny lunger' Doc, and gave one of the most watchable screen portrayals of the doomed hero.

Patrician westerner Sam Elliott was cast as Virgil Earp. He'd previously appeared as a poker player in *Butch Cassidy and the Sundance Kid* and an outlaw in *Molly and Lawless John* (1971); he had also starred in a series of TV adaptations of Louis L'Amour novels, including *The Sacketts* (1979), *The Shadow Riders* (1982) and *The Quick and the Dead* (1986 – no relation to Sam Raimi's cinema version). Reliable Bill Paxton was convincing as Morgan Earp and subsequently appeared as Frank James, to Rob Lowe's Jesse, in *Jesse and Frank* (1994), which also featured Dana Wheeler-Nicholson as Annie – she is Wyatt's laudanum-addicted wife, Mattie, in *Tombstone*. Dana Delany played Wyatt's temptress Josephine Marcus ('a dusky-hued lady Satan' in Doc's summation), while Joanna Pacula was equally effective as Doc's libertine mistress, Kate.

Powerhouse Powers Boothe leads the Cowboys' line as psychopath Curly Bill Brocious, looking like a Remington cowboy, in his red shirt and boots, with 'Aces' playing cards emblazoned on the front. Boothe later appeared as Cy Tolliver in the TV series *Deadwood*. Charismatic Michael Biehn, cast as Johnny Ringo, went on to play Chris in the TV series *The Magnificent Seven*, while Stephen Lang, as cowardly maniac Ike Clanton, is as convincing a westerner as the genre has seen. The Cowboys, decked out in their uniform red sashes, are introduced viciously shooting up a Rurale captain's marriage ceremony, then enjoying their victims' wedding feast.

Good support was provided by Billy Zane, as thespian Mr Romulus Fabian (billed as 'Tragedian in Excelsis', who offers 'Selections from the Bard') and Billy Bob Thornton, as Johnny Tyler, a tough card dealer slapped around by Wyatt. 'Skin that smoke wagon and see what happens,' Wyatt goads, 'Jerk that pistol and go to work – I said: throw down boy, you gonna do something or just stand there and bleed?' Western stalwart Harry Carey Jnr was cast as Tombstone Marshal Fred White, Charlton Heston cameoed as rancher Henry Hooker, Chris Mitchum was a ranch hand, while his father Robert, who was originally to have appeared in the film, narrated the action. In a bizarre piece of casting, Billy Claiborne, shot by the Earps at the corral, was played by Wyatt Earp – the real lawman's fifth cousin.

Tombstone was to have been directed by screenwriter Jarre, but the project was helmed by George Pan Cosmatos, the Greek-born director of such all-star productions as the germ thriller *The Cassandra Crossing* (1977) and war movie *Escape to Athena* (1979). Cosmatos had enjoyed great success with Sylvester Stallone's noisy *Rambo: First Blood Part II* (1985). *Tombstone* was shot in Panavision at Old Tucson Studios, with the Mescal town set as Tombstone itself and the Babocomari Ranch as Henry Hooker's spread. The interior of the 'Oriental Saloon' and the 'Bird Cage' theatre were reproduced with an eye on authentic features; the theatre's curtain is decorated with replicas of the famous portrait of 'Fatima' (a belly dancer who performed at the venue – though she didn't dance there until 1882) and Tombstone's town banner: 'Pure Water, Wonderful Climate, Good Schools'. Cinematographer William A. Fraker, who shot *Rosemary's Baby*

(1968) and *Paint your Wagon* (1969), had directed the low-key, elegiac western *Monte Walsh* (1970), with Lee Marvin and Jack Palance as struggling cowboys in a changing west.

Russell's tough portrayal of Wyatt owes little to the lawman's previous screen appearances. If Fonda's forties Wyatt in *My Darling Clementine* is a decent man, tongue-tied in love and impeccable in his morality, and Lancaster in the fifties *Gunfight at the O.K. Corral* is a larger-than-life superhero, Russell is a tough man who just wants to forget his days as a peace officer and get on with his life as a faro dealer. He doesn't even 'go heeled' (armed) any more. When Wyatt arrives in Tombstone, the locals want him to be their marshal, saying that if he becomes a rich businessman he'll end up with a guilty conscience. 'I already got a guilty conscience,' Wyatt answers, 'I might as well have the money too.' Wyatt manages to dodge the town's feud with the Cowboys and is incensed when Virgil and Morgan become marshals – they feel like 'vultures', feeding off the town. When it comes to the showdown, blood's thicker than water and Wyatt's sworn in as a deputy. Wyatt's deteriorating marriage to laudanum-sodden Mattie makes him question his happiness, but his relationship with Josephine, who is also seeing Sheriff Behan, puts him in the firing line; crooked Behan is in league with the Cowboys. The film ends in Denver, outside the Palace Theatre, where Josephine is now headlining in *H.M.S. Pinafore*, with her waltzing with Wyatt in the snow. Like the real lawman, Wyatt is portrayed as morally flawed, but his heroism towards the film's conclusion shifts towards dime novel legend – in pursuit of the Cowboys, Wyatt fires a shotgun from the shoulder, at full gallop, one-handed, when in actuality the recoil would have put him in traction.

The Earp faction are depicted here as something approaching the historical 'Fighting Pimps' reality, rather than virtuous do-gooders. In an exchange in the Oriental prior to the O.K. Corral, Ike accuses lawmen Virgil and Morgan, and faro dealer Wyatt, 'You Goddamn pimps, y'all in it together.' Between the Earps' various interests, they've got the town sewn up. Director Cosmatos endeavoured to make, 'A great saga of a family – like *The Godfather*, but about the west'. In interviews, the actors and crew further stressed the parallels between the clannish Cowboys and the Mafia's organised crime. 'It's the beginning of the end of the west,' said Cosmatos. In the

'Justice is coming': promotional artwork for George Cosmatos' epic *Tombstone* (1993). Doc Holliday (Val Kilmer) sides with Virgil (Sam Elliott), Wyatt (Kurt Russell) and Morgan (Bill Paxton).

film Marshal White notes, 'The only real law around here's the Cowboys.' Sheriff Behan proudly notes that the locals dress smartly in the latest fashions and the town does have a whiff of sophistication, while a shootout in the Crystal Palace Saloon spills out into the street – a man staggers clutching his bloody throat, another is shot dead. 'Very cosmopolitan,' sniffs Doc. The Earps plan to make a killing from such 'sophistication'.

The O.K. Corral gunfight is *Tombstone*'s action highlight, with the Earps and Doc striding down the main street, past a burning house, to the corral. So powerful is this heroic image that the walk is replayed under the end titles. The actual shootout is an explosive firefight, with much flying lead and few casualties, just like actual western confrontations. In this scene, Wyatt uses a Buntline Special with a 12-inch barrel, a myth concocted by Earp's biographer Stuart Lake that sneaked into Jarre's screenplay. In reality, the Buntline was far too unwieldy a weapon for a frontier scrap. The historically correct participants for both factions are featured in *Tombstone* and the shootout is one of the most authentic renditions.

Crucially, in *Tombstone* the O.K. Corral is the catalyst for the conflicts that follow: the actual gunfight occurs 70 minutes into the 130-minute film and sets in motion Wyatt's revenge – 'The last charge of Wyatt Earp and his immortals,' says Doc. One stormy night, the Cowboys take retribution for the O.K. Corral. They shoot Mayor Clum's wife, take pot shots at the Earps' wives during a Tarot reading (a surreal moment, when a shrouded shotgunner knocks on their door), kill Morgan in a pool hall and wound Virgil in the street. Virgil was actually injured on 28 December 1881, while Morgan was killed on 18 March 1882. Now marshal, Wyatt tells Ike, 'The law is coming – you tell 'em I'm coming and Hell's coming with me!' Wyatt's posse, including Doc, Sherman McMasters, Turkey Creek Jack Johnson and Texas Jack Vermillion, track down and break up the Cowboys in ruthless fashion, in a series of ambushes and showdowns. Wyatt kills Curly Bill in a riverside bushwhack and then arranges to meet Ringo in Oak Grove, at the mouth of Silver Springs Canyon. But Doc arrives at the rendezvous disguised as Wyatt – he knows Ringo is too fast for the lawman and Doc swiftly dispatches him in a close-range duel.

Kilmer really scores with his pale, sweatily convincing portrayal of Doc. The *New York Times* called him 'a dissolute modern poet, a frontier-era Jim Morrison'. Dressed in cravat, frock coat and cape, carrying a cane, with a dapper moustache, goatee beard and southern-fried drawl, Kilmer's Doc dominates the screen and steals every scene. *Tombstone* includes his brief vendetta with Ed Bailey, though there is no historical precedent for this. Bailey is played in *Tombstone* by Sylvester Stallone's brother, Frank, and is another Stuart Lake adjunct. Doc's chief enemy is Johnny Ringo, a cultured gunman. 'In vino veritas' ('In wine there's truth'), Ringo tells Doc, and he quotes the oft-aired passage from Revelation, 'Behold a pale horse and the man that sat on him was death...and Hell followed with him' (the real Ringo was known to quote Shakespeare). Doc later goads dullard Ike, losing at cards yet again, with, 'Let's have a spelling contest.' The film's final scenes, when Wyatt visits deteriorating Doc in the Glenwood Sanatorium, Colorado, are movingly played by the two actors. Wyatt presents his comrade with a dime novel: 'My Friend Doc Holliday, by Wyatt

Earp' and Doc says, 'You're the only human being in my entire life ever gave me hope.'

As well as superior performances from Kilmer, Russell, Elliott, Paxton, Boothe and Biehn, what makes *Tombstone* so enjoyable is the period script, peppered with frontier twang. After a ruckus in the street, when Curly Bill has shot Marshal White and Wyatt has slugged the Cowboy with his pistol, several of Curly Bill's cohorts arrive at the scene. Wyatt puts a pistol to Ike Clanton's forehead, 'Your friends might get me in a rush, but not before I turn your head into a canoe.' A grave marker in Boot Hill cryptically reads: 'Here lies Lester Moor, Four slugs from a .44 – No Les, No More'. During a heated confrontation in the Oriental, the Cowboys try provocation; Ike calls Wyatt a 'Kansas law dog', Wyatt says he's retired now, though he does keep a shotgun wired under the faro table, in case of trouble. 'You retired too?' Ringo asks Doc. 'Not me,' says pasty, perspiring Doc, 'I'm in my prime.' 'Yea, you look it', scoffs Ringo, who flashily lives up to his name as 'the deadliest pistoleer since Wild Bill', with a demonstration of pistol twirling. Unimpressed, Doc twirls his silver whisky cup, mocking Ringo's bravado. Emphasising Doc's solitary existence, Turkey Creek Johnson asks Doc why he's helping the law to run down the Cowboys. 'Wyatt Earp was my friend,' says Doc; 'Hell, I got lots of friends,' observes Johnson. Doc answers flatly, 'I don't.'

'Justice is Coming!' forewarned posters, when *Tombstone* arrived in US cinemas, rated 'R', in December 1993: 'Every Town Has a Story ... Tombstone Has a Legend'. The trailer called the town: 'a place where a man could start over, where a fortune could be made'. The publicity stressed that the film was the true Earp story: 'Now the time has come for justice and he has to live up to his reputation one last time – in a battle at the O.K. Corral the west would never forget.' The trailer also featured alternative footage not included in the film, notably a shot of Brocious pouring a bottle of whisky on a campfire, additional shots of vengeful Ringo and a close-up of Charlton Heston. The *New York Times* praised the film for its realism and its contemporary characters, but concluded that it was 'a movie that wants to have it both ways. It wants to be at once traditional and morally ambiguous. The two visions don't quite harmonise'. The film took $56.5 million at the US box office. In the UK it garnered a respectable £1.9 million, rated '15'. The *Daily Express* called it 'An all-action gripping epic', the *Daily Star* punned, 'Dead good', while that reliable arbiter of good taste, *Just 17* branded it, 'a rootin' tootin' classic'. It was released in Spain as *Tombstone: La Leyenda de Wyatt Earp* ('The Legend of Wyatt Earp') and in Italy as *Tombstone: La Giustizias sta Venendo* ('Justice is Coming'). A 'Making Of' documentary includes behind the scenes footage of Cosmatos and his actors filming the famous gunfight on the Mescal town set. A 'director's cut' has since been released on DVD, which runs at 134 minutes.

A year after *Tombstone*'s release, Kevin Costner's *Wyatt Earp* appeared. Costner headlined as Wyatt, with Linden Ashby as Morgan and Michael Madsen as Virgil. Isabella Rossellini appeared as sleazy Big Nose Kate, while Dennis Quaid was a suitably emaciated Doc – wheezing, womanising and wobbling along on his cane. It begins with the Earps as children on their father's farm and recounts Wyatt's early life. His first wife, Urilla, dies of typhoid and from out of the gutter Wyatt rises to becomes a famed lawman in Dodge City and Tombstone. Costner's gunfight at the O.K. Corral is probably the most authentic of all Hollywood interpretations. The lawmen's black-clad walk is depicted as the customary 'four pallbearers on an undertaking', but the actual spat takes place up an alley off Fremont Street, near Fly's studio (with no corral in evidence) and is over as quickly as it begins.

But *Wyatt Earp* is an empty film, presenting another of Costner's wholesome American heroes. Backed with edifying music and an impressive landscape (it was filmed in New Mexico and South Dakota), it depicts little more than Costner happy, then sad, then happy again. Directed by Lawrence Kasdan (who guided Costner in *Silverado*) it could easily be called 'Wyatt Earp – the Whole Story', but at 182 minutes it would have improved by being the abridged version. *Wyatt Earp*'s episodic nature recalls *Little Big Man* and beware the 'director's cut' with an extra 20 minutes. With an apparent accent on realism, the film ends with the odd disclaimer: 'This motion picture is in part a fictionalisation of certain events and people in the lives of Wyatt Earp, his family and friends.' In reality, *Wyatt Earp* buys into Stuart Lake's myth, via *Frontier Marshal* and *My Darling Clementine*. Since this brace of 'Earp-ics', many westerns have dwelt on biographical studies of actual western heroes, demonstrating a longing, by filmmakers at least, to return to the 'real west' of their ancestors. For example, Walter Hill made *Wild Bill* (1995), starring Jeff Bridges as a convincing Hickok, and *Geronimo: An American Legend* (1993), with Wes Studi in the title role.

More interesting was a genre departure like Jim Jarmusch's *Dead Man* (1995), with Johnny Depp as 'William Blake', an accountant who arrives in the industrial town of Machine to work for patriarch Dickinson (Robert Mitchum). Discovering his post has already been filled, Blake accidentally shoots Dickinson's son, Charlie (Gabriel Byrne), but is wounded and goes on the run with a bullet lodged in his chest. Dickinson puts up a $500 reward and dispatches three hired killers, Cole Wilson (played by Lance Henriksen), Conway Twill (Michael Wincott) and Johnny 'the Kid' Pickett (Eugene Byrd), to track him down. Blake meets Nobody (Gary Farmer), an Indian who thinks Blake is the reincarnation of the famous poet, and they embark on a mystical, symbolic woodland odyssey. Shot in monochrome stock which resembles Mathew Brady's Civil War plates, or Ansel Adams's landscapes, *Dead Man* benefits from an extraordinarily eerie electric guitar score, composed and performed by Neil Young. At one point Blake is confronted by two marshals, named Lee and Marvin, who ask if he's Blake. 'Yes I am,' answers Depp, 'Do you know my poetry?', before he guns them down. Later the wanted man, now a 'celebrity', is asked to autograph his own reward poster. *Dead Man* is an anomalous film, one unique for the genre, but any western featuring Iggy Pop as a transvestite, Bible-reading trapper named Sally is of interest.

Other post-*Tombstone* westerns have included the cannibalistic horror-western *Ravenous* (1999) and *The Claim* (2000), a westernised version of Thomas Hardy's *The Mayor of Casterbridge*. *The Hi-Lo Country* (1998), *The Three Burials of Melquiades Estrada* (2005 – directed by and starring Tommy Lee Jones) and the much-discussed, multi-award-winning cowboy love story *Brokeback Mountain*

(2005 – 'It was a friendship that became a secret'), are modern stories in western costume. But *Three Burials*, depicting cowboy Pete Perkins's (Jones) attempt to take the murdered corpse of his friend Estrada (preserved in salt and antifreeze) back to his home in Jimenez for interment, owes much to the trek westerns of Anthony Mann and Budd Boetticher, and Peckinpah's depiction of Mexico. Perkins rides a horse, while his pursers, the Border Patrol, follow in 4x4s and helicopters.

The grimy, extremely violent *The Proposition* (2005) is a 'western' set in Benyon, Australia. Irish rogue Charlie Burns (a dishevelled, rotten-toothed Guy Pearce) is given a proposition by Benyon's English lawman, Captain Stanley (Ray Winstone): he must travel into the desert wilds and kill his brother, outlaw Arthur Burns (the perpetrator of the barbaric Hopkins Ranch massacre), to save his younger brother Mikey from hanging on Christmas Day. Written by Bad Seed Nick Cave – who also composed the excellent score with Warren Ellis, all tuneless fiddle, mournful folk shanties and incantations – *The Proposition* is photographed in such acrid, fly-blown, flaky yellowed hues, that the screen feels like it will curl up at the edges.

The most interesting and imaginative of recent westerns actually located historically and geographically in the west, is *The Missing* (2003). Set in 1885 New Mexico, it resembles a mystical, sinister variation on *The Searchers*. Based on the novel 'The Last Ride' by Thomas Eidson, it stars Cate Blanchett as Maggie Gilkeson, a widowed cattle rancher struggling to raise her two daughters, Lilly and little Dot, with the help of her live-in lover, Brake. In an attack by a renegade Apache raiding party, Brake is killed and Lilly kidnapped. The Apaches are slave traders who are heading for Mexico. Maggie's wastrel, long-absent father, Samuel Jones (Tommy Lee Jones), a white man who has lived with the Apache (his Indian name translates as 'Shit for Luck'), suddenly re-enters her life. With mother and daughter, Jones sets off in pursuit of the band, who are led by a witch packing some powerful medicine.

The Missing benefits greatly from two fine central performances by Blanchett and Jones, spectacular New Mexican scenery, authentic costumes and settings, and realistic, bone-crunching action scenes. But the film also has an atmosphere of foreboding and mystery quite unlike most recent westerns. The Apache witch, with his lumbering gait, scar-faced sneer, magic dust capable of blinding and voodoo–like skills, is a memorable villain. He wears the stolen photographs of his victims around his neck and kills settlers with a severed eagle's talon primed with rattlesnake poison. Brake's death is particularly horrible – he is found in a woodland clearing, trussed up in a cowhide cocoon, roasted over a fire. Maggie's determined pursuit of her daughter sustains the tension well, building to an exciting, moving climax that sees the captives freed, but at a price.

There have also been several popular TV westerns, like the highly praised *Deadwood*, Walter Hill's two-part miniseries *Broken Trail* (2006 – which holds the record for the largest US TV audience for a made-for-TV movie) and John Badham's TV movie *The Jack Bull* (made by HBO in 1999), another range-feud melodrama, but a well-executed one. John Cusack starred as Rawlins horse breeder Myrl Redding, whose quarrel with Wyoming rancher Henry C. Ballard (a great performance by L. Q. Jones) escalates until Redding organises a vigilante committee to exact justice, which puts him on trial before Judge Tolliver (John Goodman). The feud is initiated by Ballard erecting a tollgate on his land and severely mistreating two of Redding's ebony stallions. Later Redding's wife is accidentally killed, run over by a wagon in Cheyenne, when she seeks help from the Attorney General. The story has a nihilistic, depressing tone, as any faith in humanity drains from the film – corrupt sheriffs, crooked judges, false witnesses and unforeseen events conspire to seal Redding's fate. The law is found wanting and fails those it should help, as evinced by the film's very downbeat ending. *The Jack Bull* refers to Redding's determination: his bullheadedness and his Jack Russell jaw, which tenaciously won't let go. It is one of the best westerns of the last decade, with a stately, moving score from *Unforgiven*'s Lennie Niehaus.

Executive produced by Steven Spielberg and premiering in the US in 2005, is the ambitious $50 million, six-part miniseries *Into the West*. Spielberg follows *Dances With Wolves*'s lead, with CGI buffalo hunts, mysticism and a sentimental musical score (one US critic scathingly compared it to the 'settling the west' films shown at Disneyland). Structured around the 'Wheel of Life', the series tells the parallel stories of a band of Lakota Sioux and a family of Virginia wheelwrights, the Wheelers, between 1825 and 1890. In the manner of miniseries *Centennial* (1978) and *How the West Was Won* (1977–1979), Dreamworks's production impressively straddles US history, from trapper and pioneer days, the forty-niners' Gold Rush, the transcontinental railroads and the Plains Wars (including in episode five, 'Casualties of War', a puny enactment of Little Big Horn), with a typically wide-eyed 'gee whiz' approach. *Into the West* was beautifully filmed in Canada and New Mexico and deploys a veritable menagerie of Sioux characters, 'Growling Bear', 'Sitting Bull', 'White Bird', 'Running Fox', 'Little Dog' and 'Soaring Eagle', who are more memorable than their white counterparts.

In the US, only Kevin Costner consistently tries to keep the western on cinema screens into the new millennium. Following his three forays west, Costner's most recent and best western is *Open Range* (2003), a character study of two drifting cowpokes trying to make a living as free-grazers, feeding their cattle on the open range. Robert Duvall starred as Boss Spearman, with Costner as his partner Charley Waite. When fellow drover Mose (Abraham Benrubi) is killed and youngster Button (Diego Luna) badly wounded by gunmen employed by Irish rancher Denton Baxter (Michael Gambon), Boss and Charley have to stay in the hostile town of Harmonville while Button recovers. Charley becomes attracted to the doctor's sister, Sue (Annette Bening), but their lives are so different the couple seem destined to remain apart.

Sharing a world-weariness with *Monte Walsh* (1970) and other subtle revisionist westerns, *Open Range* was based on 'The Open Range Men', by Lauren Paine and filmed in Calgary and Stoney Indian Reservation, Canada. It convincingly evokes a hard and lonely life in the great outdoors: 'No Place to Run', said the posters, 'No Reason to Hide'. The climax has Boss and Charley facing Baxter's gun hands in an authentically spasmodic showdown. Costner's deft direction emphasises character over action, though particularly memorable are the haunting, faceless gunmen in Baxter's pay, wearing flour-sack hoods under their cowboy hats (like the ghoulish photograph of outlaw Bill Brazelton's corpse, posed on a chair, still wearing his highwayman's mask). A rainstorm turns the town's main street into a river, navigated by plank duckboards, and Duvall and Costner acquit themselves well, as the tired, free-spirited cowboys increasingly fenced in. There are enough imaginative touches in *Open Range* to prove that there's still mileage in the genre, offering both promise and hope.

Eastwood and Wayne have inspired a whole series of action stars from the late seventies onwards, who relied on their actions speaking louder than their words, which was just as well in some cases. This type of screen hero included Bruce Willis, Arnold Schwarzenegger and Sylvester Stallone, whose *First Blood* (1982) added a post-Vietnam twist on the 'stranger in town' scenario.

But it seems that like Tombstone itself, the western is just too tough to die and is even enjoying something of a revival. Autumn 2007 sees the release of a remake of *3:10 to Yuma* – with Christian Bale recreating Van Heflin's drought-stricken farmer Dan Evans and Russell Crowe as outlaw Ben Wade. *Seraphim Falls* (2007) is a half-decent chase western starring Liam Neeson as the pursuer and Pierce Brosnan as the pursued, while Brad Pitt plays Jesse James in *The Assassination of Jesse James By the Coward Robert Ford*. In May 2007, *Bury My Heart at Wounded Knee*, a well-received 90-minute adaptation of Dee Brown's bestseller, premiered on HBO in the US advertised with the tagline: 'We Will be Known Forever by the Tracks We Leave Behind'. These are period westerns, but western stories and characters have seeped into many different genres – especially action thrillers and sci-fi.

At the extreme, the trendsetting science-fiction movie *Star Wars* (1977) closely resembles a western, in plotting and partly in setting, especially during the early scenes on the desert planet of Tatooine. Director George Lucas acknowledged his debt to Akira Kurosawa (in particular *The Hidden Fortress* [1958]) and John Ford. The hero's name, Luke Skywalker, sounds Native American and the burned out farm in the dunes, following an attack by Imperial Stormtroopers, resembles the aftermath of Ford's farm massacre at the beginning of *The Searchers*. The desert-dwelling sand people, called Tusken Raiders, mounted on giant Banthas, are the equivalents of Native American warriors, forever ready to spring an ambush.

Perhaps the most 'western' moment in *Star Wars* is the famous cantina scene, when Luke (Mark Hamill) and his mentor Ben Obi-wan Kenobi (Alec Guinness) go in search of a pilot to fly them to the planet of Alderaan. The adobe igloos in the settlement of Mos Eisley resemble a Mexican pueblo, while the dimly lit, smoky bar is inhabited by all manner of strange creatures, including the obligatory inhospitable, unhelpful barman (who refuses to serve the androids drinks) and various wanted characters on the run from the law. In the background, a wacky jazz band subs for the usual saloon ragtime trio. Nestled in a corner, freight smuggler Captain Han Solo (Harrison Ford) and his hairy Yeti-like Wookie first mate Chewbacca (Peter Mayhew) resemble gunslingers; Solo wears a shirt, boots and waistcoat and his laser blaster slung gunslinger-style, while 'Chewy' has an ammo-stacked bandoleer. Solo is later confronted by green bug-eyed reptilian bounty hunter Greedo, who has been dispatched by Solo's former employer Jabba the Hut to kill him. 'Jabba's put a price on your head so large,' Greedo tells him, 'every bounty hunter in the galaxy will be looking for you.' During their dialogue, Solo quietly unholsters his laser pistol under the table and blasts Greedo. As Solo leaves the bar, he flicks a coin at the barman, adding, 'Sorry about the mess,' with typical Clint Eastwood aplomb. For all its high-tech gadgetry, *Star Wars* and its progeny are little more than way-out westerns, set in a galaxy far, far away, but with their roots firmly in the American west.

WESTERN FILMOGRAPHY

This is a chronological filmography of important westerns referenced in the text, with brief credits: title, original year of release, directed by (d) and starring (s).

The Great Train Robbery (1903)
d: Edwin S. Porter; s: George Barnes

Hell's Hinges (1916)
d: Charles Swickard; s: William S. Hart

Straight Shooting (1917)
d: John Ford; s: Harry Carey

The Covered Wagon (1923)
d: James Cruze; s: J. Warren Kerrigan

The Iron Horse (1924)
d: John Ford; s: George O'Brien

Tumbleweeds (1925)
d: King Baggott/William S. Hart; s: William S. Hart

3 Bad Men (1926)
d: John Ford; s: George O'Brien

The Big Trail (1930)
d: Raoul Walsh; s: John Wayne

Cimarron (1931)
d: Wesley Ruggles; s: Richard Dix

Destry Rides Again (1939)
d: George Marshall; s: Marlene Dietrich, James Stewart

The Ox-Bow Incident (1943)
d: William A. Wellman; s: Henry Fonda

Duel in the Sun (1946)
d: King Vidor; s: Jennifer Jones, Gregory Peck

Pursued (1947)
d: Raoul Walsh; s: Robert Mitchum

Fort Apache (1948)
d: John Ford; s: John Wayne, Henry Fonda

The Paleface (1948)
d: Norman Z. McLeod; s: Bob Hope

Yellow Sky (1948)
d: William Wellman; s: Gregory Peck, Richard Widmark

Broken Arrow (1950)
d: Delmer Daves; s: James Stewart

The Gunfighter (1950)
d: Henry King; s: Gregory Peck

Rio Grande (1950)
d: John Ford; s: John Wayne

Wagonmaster (1950)
d: John Ford; s: Ben Johnson

Winchester '73 (1950)
d: Anthony Mann; s: James Stewart

Bend of the River (1952)
d: Anthony Mann; s: James Stewart

Rancho Notorious (1952)
d: Fritz Lang; s: Marlene Dietrich

Son of Paleface (1952)
 d: Frank Tashlin; s: Bob Hope

Hondo (1953)
d: John Farrow; s: John Wayne

The Naked Spur (1953)
d: Anthony Mann; s: James Stewart

Apache (1954)
d: Robert Aldrich; s: Burt Lancaster

Bad Day at Black Rock (1955)
 d: John Sturges; s: Spencer Tracy

The Far Country (1955)
d: Anthony Mann; s: James Stewart

The Last Wagon (1956)
d: Delmer Daves; s: Richard Widmark

Seven Men from Now (1956)
d: Budd Boetticher; s: Randolph Scott

Decision at Sundown (1957)
d: Budd Boetticher; s: Randolph Scott

Run of the Arrow (1957)
d: Samuel Fuller; s: Rod Steiger

The Tall T (1957)
d: Budd Boetticher; s: Randolph Scott

3:10 to Yuma (1957)
d: Delmer Daves; s: Van Heflin, Glenn Ford

The Big Country (1958)
d: William Wyler; s: Gregory Peck, Charlton Heston

Man of the West (1958)
d: Anthony Mann; s: Gary Cooper

Warlock (1959)
d: Edward Dmytryk; s: Henry Fonda, Anthony Quinn

The Alamo (1960)
d: John Wayne; s: John Wayne, Richard Widmark

Comanche Station (1960)
d: Budd Boetticher; s: Randolph Scott

The Comancheros (1961)
d: Michael Curtiz; s: John Wayne

The Deadly Companions (1961)
d: Sam Peckinpah; s: Brian Keith, Maureen O'Hara

The Last Sunset (1961)
d: Robert Aldrich; s: Kirk Douglas, Rock Hudson

How the West Was Won (1962) d: Henry Hathaway/John Ford/George Marshall; s: Henry Fonda,
James Stewart, John Wayne, Gregory Peck, Richard Widmark, George Peppard

The Man Who Shot Liberty Valance (1962)
d: John Ford; s: John Wayne, James Stewart

Two Rode Together (1962)
d: John Ford; s: James Stewart, Richard Widmark

Cheyenne Autumn (1964)
d: John Ford; s: Richard Widmark

A Fistful of Dollars (1964)
d: Sergio Leone; s: Clint Eastwood

Rio Conchos (1964)
d: Gordon Douglas; s: Richard Boone

Cat Ballou (1965)
d: Elliot Silverstein; s: Lee Marvin, Jane Fonda

For a Few Dollars More (1965)
d: Sergio Leone; s: Clint Eastwood, Lee Van Cleef

Major Dundee (1965)
d: Sam Peckinpah; s: Charlton Heston, Richard Harris

Duel at Diablo (1966)
d: Ralph Nelson; s: James Garner, Sydney Poitier

The Good, the Bad and the Ugly (1966)
d: Sergio Leone; s: Clint Eastwood, Lee Van Cleef, Eli Wallach

The Professionals (1966)
d: Richard Brooks; s: Lee Marvin, Burt Lancaster

The Shooting (1966)
d: Monte Hellman; s: Warren Oates, Jack Nicholson

El Dorado (1967)
d: Howard Hawks; s: John Wayne, Robert Mitchum

Hang 'Em High (1967)
d: Ted Post; s: Clint Eastwood

Hombre (1967)
d: Martin Ritt; s: Paul Newman

Hour of the Gun (1967)
d: John Sturges; s: James Garner

The War Wagon (1967)
d: Burt Kennedy; s: John Wayne, Kirk Douglas

Will Penny (1968)
d: Tom Gries; s: Charlton Heston

True Grit (1969)
d: Henry Hathaway; s: John Wayne, Kim Darby

The Ballad of Cable Hogue (1970)
d: Sam Peckinpah; s: Jason Robards

Chisum (1970)
d: Andrew V. McLaglen; s: John Wayne

Little Big Man (1970)
d: Arthur Penn; s: Dustin Hoffman

A Man Called Horse (1970)
d: Elliot Silverstein; s: Richard Harris

Rio Lobo (1970)
d: Howard Hawks; s: John Wayne

Soldier Blue (1970)
d: Ralph Nelson; s: Candice Bergen

Two Mules for Sister Sara (1970)
d: Don Siegel; s: Shirley MacLaine, Clint Eastwood

Big Jake (1971)
d: George Sherman; s: John Wayne

The Hired Hand (1971)
d: Peter Fonda; s: Warren Oates, Peter Fonda

Support Your Local Gunfighter (1971)
d: Burt Kennedy; s: James Garner

The Skin Game (1971)
d: Paul Bogart; s: James Garner

High Plains Drifter (1972)
d & s: Clint Eastwood

Jeremiah Johnson (1972)
d: Sydney Pollack; s: Robert Redford

The Life and Times of Judge Roy Bean (1972)
d: John Huston; s: Paul Newman

Pat Garrett & Billy the Kid (1973)
d: Sam Peckinpah; s: James Coburn, Kris Kristofferson

Blazing Saddles (1974)
d: Mel Brooks; s: Gene Wilder, Cleavon Little

The Missouri Breaks (1976)
d: Arthur Penn; s: Marlon Brando, Jack Nicholson

The Shootist (1976)
d: Don Siegel; s: John Wayne

Heaven's Gate (1980)
d: Michael Cimino; s: Kris Kristofferson

The Long Riders (1980)
d: Walter Hill; s: David Carradine, Stacy Keach

Pale Rider (1985)
d & s: Clint Eastwood

Dances with Wolves (1990)
d & s: Kevin Costner

Wyatt Earp (1994)
d: Lawrence Kasdan; s: Kevin Costner

Dead Man (1995)
d: Jim Jarmusch; s: Johnny Depp

The Quick and the Dead (1995)
d: Sam Raimi; s: Sharon Stone

The Jack Bull (1999)
d: John Badham; s: John Cusack

The Missing (2003)
d: Ron Howard; s: Tommy Lee Jones, Cate Blanchett

Open Range (2003)
d & s: Kevin Costner

BIBLIOGRAPHY AND SOURCES

Albert, Marvin H., *Apache Rising* (Hodder Fawcett, 1966)

Bergen, Ronald, *The United Artists Story* (Octopus, 1986)

Betts, Tom (ed.), *Westerns All'Italiana!* (Anaheim, California 1983–present)

Bishop, David, *Starring Michael Caine* (Reynolds & Hearn, 2003)

Biskind, Peter, *Easy Riders, Raging Bulls: How the Sex-Drugs-And-Rock 'n' Roll Generation Saved Hollywood* (Simon & Schuster, 1998)

Blevins, William, *Dictionary of the American West* (Wordsworth, 1995)

Bosworth, Patricia, *Marlon Brando* (Phoenix, 2002)

Botting, Douglas, *Wilderness Europe* (Time-Life, 1976)

Brown, Dee, *Bury My Heart at Wounded Knee* (Barrie & Jenkins, 1971)

Brown, Peter Harry and Pat H. Broeske, *Howard Hughes – The Untold Story* (Warner Books, 1997)

Bruckner, Ulrich P., *Für ein paar Leichen mehr* (Schwarzkopf & Schwarzkopf, 2002)

Buford, Kate, *Burt Lancaster – An American Life* (Aurum, 2001)

Burt, Robert, *Rockerama – 25 Years of Teen Screen Idols* (Blandford, 1983)

Buscombe, Edward, and Roberta E. Pearson (eds), *Back in the Saddle Again: New Essays on the Western* (BFI, 1998)

– *The BFI Companion to the Western* (BFI, 1988)

– *Cinema Today* (Phaidon, 2003)

– *Injuns! Native Americans in the Movies* (Reaktion, 2006)

– *The Searchers* (BFI, 2002)

– *Stagecoach* (BFI, 1992)

– *Unforgiven* (BFI, 2004)

Cannon, Joe, *A Fistful of Euros* (Viva España Magazine, July/August 2005)

Capps, Benjamin, *The Great Chiefs* (Time-Life, 1975)

– *The Indians* (Time-Life, 1973)

Chappell, Connery (ed.), *Picturegoer Film Annual 1955–1956* (Odhams, 1956)

Cole, Gerald and Peter Williams, *Clint Eastwood* (W.H. Allen, 1983)

Connolly, William, *Spaghetti Cinema* (Hollywood, California 1984–present)

Cowie, Peter, *John Ford and the American West* (Harry N. Abrams, 2004)

Cox, Alex and Nick Jones, *Moviedrome – The Guide* (Broadcasting Support Services, 1990)

Crane, Douglas and Harold Myers, *Hollywood-London Film Parade* (Marks & Spencer, 1949)

Crawley, Tom, *Bébé – The Films of Brigitte Bardot* (BCA, 1979)

Cumbow, Robert C., *Once Upon a Time: The Films of Sergio Leone* (Scarecrow Press, 1987)

De Agostini, *The Clint Eastwood Collection, Volume 2* (*Unforgiven*); *Volume 4* (*The Outlaw Josey Wales*); *Volume 9* (*Pale Rider*) (De Agostini, 2004)

Debo, Angie, *Geronimo: The Man, His Time, His Place* (Pimlico, 1993)

De Fornari, Oreste, *Sergio Leone: The Great Italian Dream of Legendary America* (Gremese, 1997)

De Maupassant, Guy, *The Necklace and Other Short Stories* (Dover, 1992) Includes the short story 'Ball-of-Fat' (Boule de Suif)

Dewey, Donald, *James Stewart: A Biography* (Warner Books, 1998)

Douglas, Peter, *Clint Eastwood – Movin' On* (Star, 1975)

Drummond, Phillip, *High Noon* (BFI, 1997)

Eames, John Douglas, *The MGM Story: The Complete History of Over Fifty Roaring Years* (Octopus, 1977)

– *The Paramount Story* (Octopus, 1985)

Earnshaw, Tony, 'It's all a Crapshoot': Interview with producer Mitch Brower (*Cinema Retro*, Volume 3, Issue Number 7, 2007)

Eyman, Scott and Paul Duncan (ed.), *John Ford: The Complete Films* (Taschen, 2004)

Fenin, George N. and William K. Everson, *The Western – From Silents to the Seventies* (Penguin, 1977)

Ferguson, Ken and Sylvia Ferguson (eds), *Western Stars of Television and Film* (Purnell, 1967)

Fitzgerald, Martin, *Orson Welles* (Pocket Essentials, 2000)

Florin, Lambert, *Ghost Towns of the Southwest* (Promontory, 1992)

Forbis, William H., *The Cowboys* (Time-Life, 1973)

Fox, Brian, *The Wild Bunch* (Tandem, 1969)

Fox, Keith and Maitland McDonagh (eds), *The Tenth Virgin Film Guide* (Virgin, 2001)

Franchi, Rudy and Barbara, *Miller's Movie Collectibles* (Octopus, 2002)

Frank, Alan, *The Films of Roger Corman* 'Shooting My Way out of Trouble' (Batsford, 1998)

Frayling, Christopher, *Clint Eastwood* (Virgin, 1992)

– *Sergio Leone: Once Upon a Time in Italy* (Thames and Hudson, 2005)

– *Sergio Leone: Something to Do With Death* (Faber and Faber, 2000)

– *Spaghetti Westerns: Cowboys and Europeans from Karl May to Sergio Leone* (Routledge and Kegan, 1981, reprinted by I.B.Tauris, 1998 and 2004)

French, Philip, *Westerns: Aspects of a Movie Genre* (Carcanet, 2005)

Fuller, Samuel, *A Third Face: My Tale of Writing, Fighting and Filmmaking* (Applause, 2002)

Gallant, Chris (ed.), *Art of Darkness – The Cinema of Dario Argento* (FAB Press, 2000)

Giré, Jean-François, *Il Était une Fois… Le Western Européen* (Dreamland, 2002)

Goldstein, Norm, *Henry Fonda: His Life and Work* (Michael Joseph, 1982)

Guérif, François, *Clint Eastwood: From Rawhide to Pale Rider* (Roger Houghton Ltd, 1986)

Guttmacher, Peter, *Legendary Westerns* (Metrobooks, 1995)

Haining, Peter (compiler), *Classic Westerns* (Pan, 1998) includes short stories 'Stage to Lordsburg' (Ernest Haycox), 'Three-Ten to Yuma' (Elmore Leonard) and 'A Man Called Horse' (Dorothy M. Johnson)

Hardy, Phil (ed.), *The Aurum Film Encyclopedia – Horror* (Aurum Press, 1985)

– *The Aurum Encyclopedia – Science Fiction Movies* (Aurum, 1984)

– *The Aurum Film Encyclopedia – The Western* (Aurum, 1983)

Hart, John Mason, *Revolutionary Mexico* (University of California Press, 1997)

Hicks, Jim (ed.), *The Gamblers* (Time-Life, 1978)

Hillier, Jim, and Peter Wollen (eds), *Howard Hawks, American Artist* (BFI, 1996)

Hirschhorn, Clive, *The Warner Bros. Story* (Octopus, 1983)

Hook, Jason, *American Indian Warrior Chiefs* (Firebird, 1990)

Horan, James D. and Paul Sann, *Pictorial History of the Wild West* (Spring, 1954)

Houston, Penelope, *The Contemporary Cinema* (Penguin, 1963)

Huffaker, Clair, *The War Wagon* (Futura, 1974)

Hughes, Howard, *The American Indian Wars* (Pocket Essentials, 2001)

– *Once Upon a Time in the Italian West* (I.B.Tauris, 2004)

Hurwood, Bernhardt J., *Burt Reynolds* (Quick Fox, 1979)

Jewell, Richard B. and Vernon Harbin, *The RKO Story* (Octopus, 1982)

Johnstone, Iain, *The Man With No Name* (Plexus, 1981)

Kaminsky, Stuart M., *Don Siegel: Director* (Curtis, 1974)

Karney, Robyn (ed.), *Cinema Year By Year – 1894–2003* (Dorling Kindersley, 2003)

Katz, Ephraim, *The Macmillan International Film Encyclopedia* (HarperCollins, 1998)

Kerbel, Michael, *Paul Newman* (Star, 1975)

Kinnard, Roy, *The Blue and the Gray on the Silver Screen* (Birch Lane, 1996)

• Konow, David, *Schlock-O-Rama: The Films of Al Adamson* (Lone Eagle, 1998)

Langellier, John Phillip, *Custer: The Man, the Myth, the Movies* (Stackpole, 2000)

Lewis, Jon E. (ed.), *The Mammoth Book of the Western* (Robinson, 1991) includes 'Arrow in the Sun' (T.V. Olsen), 'Command' (James Warner Bellah) and 'The Captives' (Elmore Leonard)

Lloyd, Ann (ed.), *Good Guys and Bad Guys* (Orbis, 1982)

– *Movies of the Fifties* (Orbis, 1982)

– *Movies of the Seventies* (Orbis, 1984)

– *Movies of the Sixties* (Orbis, 1983)

Lloyd, Ann and Graham Fuller, *The Illustrated Who's Who of the Cinema* (Orbis, 1983)

Luck, Richard, *Sam Peckinpah* (Pocket Essentials, 2000)

– *Steve McQueen* (Pocket Essentials, 2000)

Luck, Steve (ed.), *Philip's Compact Encyclopedia* (Chancellor Press, 1999)

Macnab, Geoffrey, *Key Moments in Cinema* (Hamlyn, 2001)

Madsen, Axel, *John Huston – A Biography* (Robson Books, 1979)

Maltin, Leonard, *2001 Movie and Video Guide* (Penguin, 2001)

Matthews, Tom Dewe, *Censored: The Story of Film Censorship in Britain* (Chatto & Windus, 1994)

May, Robin, *The Story of the West* (Chancellor, 1996)

McBride, Joseph, *Searching for John Ford: A Life* (Faber and Faber, 2003)

McCabe, Bob, *Clint Eastwood 'Quote Unquote'* (Parragon, 1996)

McClure, Arthur F. and Ken D. Jones, *Western Films: Heroes, Heavies and Sagebrush of the 'B' Genre* (Barnes, 1972)

McGilligan, Patrick, *Clint Eastwood – The Life and Legend* (HarperCollins, 1999)

Medved, Harry and Michael, *Son of Golden Turkey Awards: The Best of the Worst from Hollywood* (Angus & Robertson, 1986)

– *The Fifty Worst Films of All Time (And how they got that way)* (Angus & Robertson, 1978)

Meyer, William R., *The Making of the Great Westerns* (Arlington House, 1979)

Müller, Jürgen (ed.), *Best Movies of the 90s* (Taschen, 2005)

– *Movies of the 60s* (Taschen, 2004)

Naughton, John, *Movies* (Simon & Schuster, 1998)

Nevin, David, *The Soldiers* (Time-Life, 1974)

Newman, Kim, *Wild West Movies: How the West was Found, Won, Lost, Lied About, Filmed and Forgotten* (Bloomsbury, 1990)

Nourmand, Tony and Graham Marsh, (eds) *Film Posters of the 60s: The Essential Movies of the Decade* (Aurum, 1997)

Nugent, Frank S., *The Searchers* (Screen Press Publishing/TCM, 2002)

O'Brien, Daniel, *Clint Eastwood – Film-Maker* (Batsford, 1996)

O'Neal, Bill, *The Pimlico Encyclopedia of Western Gunfighters* (Pimlico, 1998)

Parkinson, Michael and Clyde Jeavons, *A Pictorial History of Westerns* (Hamlyn, 1983)

Pointer, Larry, *In Search of Butch Cassidy* (Constable, 1979)

Redford, Robert, *The Outlaw Trail: A Journey Through Time* (Book Club Associates, 1978)

Remington, Frederic, *Paintings and Sculpture* (Leopard Books, 1995)

Richie, Donald, *The Films of Akira Kurosawa* (University of California Press, 1965)

Rogers, Dave, *The Prisoner & Danger Man* (Boxtree, 1989)

Rosa, Joseph G., *Age of the Gunfighter* (Oklahoma Press, 1995)

Rose, Simon, *Classic Films* (HarperCollins, 1999)

Ross, Jonathan, *The Incredibly Strange Film Book: An Alternative History of Cinema* (Simon & Schuster, 1993)

Sarf, Wayne Michael, *God Bless You, Buffalo Bill: A Layman's Guide to History and the Western Film* (Cornwall, 1983)

Schaefer, Jack, *Shane* (Corgi, 1951)

Scheuer, Steven H. (ed.), *Movies on TV* (Bantam Books, 1977)

Shepherd, Donald and Robert Slatzer with Dave Grayson, *Duke: The Life and Times of John Wayne* (Time Warner, 2003)

Shipman, David, *The Movie Makers – Brando* (Macmillan, 1974)

Silver, Alain and James Ursini, *Whatever Happened to Robert Aldrich? His Life & His Films* (Limelight, 1995)

Sinyard, Neil, *Clint Eastwood* (Bison, 1995)

Slide, Anthony (ed.), *De Toth on De Toth – Putting the Drama in Front of the Camera* (Faber and Faber, 1996)

Stacey, Jan and Ryder Syvertsen, *The Great Book of Movie Villains: A Guide to the Screen's Meanies, Tough Guys, and Bullies* (Contemporary, 1984)

Stanfield, Peter, *Hollywood, Westerns and the 1930s: The Lost Trail* (University of Exeter, 2001)

Tchernia, Pierre, *80 Grands Succés Du Western* (Casterman, 1989)

Thomson, Douglas, *Clint Eastwood: Sexual Cowboy* (Warner Books, 1993)

Tonks, Paul, *Film Music* (Pocket Essentials, 2003)

Tosches, Nick, *Dino: Living High in the Dirty Business of Dreams* (Secker & Warburg, 1992)

Trachtman, Paul, *The Gunfighters* (Time-Life, 1974)

Weddle, David, *Sam Peckinpah: 'If They Move ... Kill 'Em'* (Faber and Faber, 1996)

Weisberger, Bernard A., *The Life History of the United States Volume 7 1877–1890: Steel and Steam* (Time-Life, 1964)

Weldon, Michael J., *The Psychotronic Video Guide* (St Martin's Griffin, 1996)

Whitehead, Mark, *Roger Corman* (Pocket Essentials, 2003)

Whitman, Mark, *Clint Eastwood* (LSP, 1982)

Whitney, Steven, *Charles Bronson – Superstar* (Dell, 1975)

Wiegand, Chris, *French New Wave* (Pocket Essentials, 2001)

Wilkinson, Frederick, *Handguns: A Collector's Guide to Pistols and Revolvers from 1950 to the Present* (Apple, 1993)

Williams, T. Harry, *The Life History of the United States – Volume 5 1849–1865: The Union Sundered* (Time-Life, 1963)

– *Volume 6 1861–1876: The Union Restored* (Time-Life, 1964)

Witcombe, Rick Trader, *Savage Cinema* (Lorrimer, 1975)

Zinnemann, Fred, *An Autobiography: A Life in the Movies* (Scribners, 1992)

Zmijewsky, Boris and Lee Pfeiffer, *The Films of Clint Eastwood* (Citadel Press, 1993)

FURTHER SOURCES:

Travel guides and maps of the United States and Spain.

Radio adaptations of *Red River*, *She Wore a Yellow Ribbon* and *Shane*.

DVD audio commentaries for *My Darling Clementine*, *Shane*, *Once Upon a Time in the West*, *The Wild Bunch* and *Butch Cassidy and the Sundance Kid*. All timings mentioned in *Stagecoach to Tombstone* refer to the original theatrical running times of the films. When transferred to DVD and VHS tape their running times are shortened by approximately 4 percent, resulting in a timing discrepancy. This does not mean the films have been cut, though it is worth cross-checking. There have been so many versions available over the years: TV versions with panned-and-scanned images, widescreen versions, remastered versions, director's cuts, cut versions, uncut versions, bootlegs and special editions – it can get very confusing.

Documentaries including *John Wayne: The Unquiet Man*, *The American West of John Ford*, *Sam Peckinpah: Man of Iron*, *The Making of Butch Cassidy and the Sundance Kid*, *The Spaghetti West*, *Sam Peckinpah's West*, *The Wild Bunch: An Album in Montage*, *Once Upon a Time in the West: An Opera of Violence*, *Clint Eastwood: the Man from Malpaso*, *Budd Boetticher: A Man Can Do That*, *Budd Boetticher: An American Original* and *Guns for Hire: The Making of the Magnificent Seven*.

Soundtrack recordings of *Shane*, *The Magnificent Seven*, *Once Upon a Time in the West*, *Butch Cassidy and the Sundance Kid*, *McCabe & Mrs Miller*, *The Outlaw Josey Wales* and *Unforgiven*.

Key Internet sources include the Internet Movie Database (www.imdb.com), the official British Board of Film Classification site (www.bbfc.co.uk) and the Motion Picture Association of America (www.mpaa.org).